Contemporary Sociology

Contemporary SOCIOLOGY

H.K. Rawat

RAWAT PUBLICATIONS

Jaipur • New Delhi • Bangalore • Hyderabad • Guwahati • Kolkata

ISBN 978-81-316-0585-1 (HB)
ISBN 978-81-316-0586-8 (PB)

Published by
Prem Rawat for *Rawat Publications*
Satyam Apts., Sector 3, Jawahar Nagar, Jaipur 302 004 (India)
Phone: 0141 265 1748 / 7006 Fax: 0141 265 1748
E-mail: info@rawatbooks.com
Website: www.rawatbooks.com

Delhi Office
4858/24, Ansari Road, Daryaganj, New Delhi 110 002
Phone: 011-23263290

Also at *Bangalore, Hyderabad, Guwahati* and *Kolkata*

Typeset by Rawat Computers, Jaipur
Printed at Nice Printing Press, New Delhi

Contents

Preface

Sociology has changed a great deal over the past few decades and so as to keep pace with this change, it is necessary to either revise old books or write quite new books incorporating all that has changed in human society. Keeping this fact in mind, I have attempted this book, titled *Contemporary Sociology*.

My previous book *Sociology: Basic Concepts*, published in 2007, was written with a particular aim to introduce the subject to the undergraduate students. The writing of this book grew out of the need of candidates appearing at various state and central government competitive examinations. It is quite a new book in the sense that its format, matter and contents are different from those of my previous book. Not only this, it is fully organized in the light of the needs of the candidates. I have tried to introduce the students as diverse an array of theoretical perspectives, along with latest information, as feasible on different topics.

I am deeply indebted to a host of writers in varied forms and limitless range. I express my heartiest gratitude to them for providing a base to write this book. I apologize for any lapses, omissions or any sorts of distortions that have crept in to this book inadvertently.

I cannot be too lavish in expressing my sincere thanks to my wife Smt Saroj Rawat, who selflessly and unflinchingly provided me with material and moral support so that the book could see the light of the day.

I also thank my younger brother Shri Kailash Rawat and nephews Pranit and Sachin who took all pains to get the lengthy and untidy manuscript of the book published in a record time.

H.K. Rawat

Chapter 1

Why Study Sociology?

KEY FEATURES

- Uses of Sociology
- Careers in Sociology
- Sociology and Commonsense
- Sociology and Social Policy
- Pure and Applied Sociology

> 'Today, we are faced with pre-eminent fact that if civilisation is to survive, we must cultivate the science of human relationships.'
>
> —Franklin Roosevelt

Sociology seeks to deepen our understanding of human relationships by unravelling new truths about them. It helps in removing ignorance about human relationships. It is relevant wherever human relations are at work. Whatever the field the emphasis will be on understanding human behaviour and relationships. 'Sociology enables us to understand the world we live in but also to understand ourselves, for we are the products of that world. This understanding can help us to gain more control over our lives but it can also be put to more practical uses as well' (Fulcher and Scott, 2003). In fact, it can be argued that sociology is indispensable for understanding the present complex world. There are several reasons (listed below under the sub-heading 'uses of sociology') why sociological knowledge is essential in making sense of the contemporary world.

'Sociology is not only an intellectual discipline, it is also a profession … when we speak of a profession, we refer mainly to themes as the uses or applications of a body of knowledge' (Inkeles, 1964). The student may sometimes get confused about sociology and social reform. But sociology is not social reform. The essential principles of sociology are a prerequisite in any study of human relationships and in any proposed solution to a social problem. It is desirable, of course, that 'solutions' be found for the problems of society and that certain universal principles of social life be established.

A student may study sociology for his own sake, just to know more about society and culture. But mere knowledge does not satisfy him. He may probably seek sociological knowledge just to apply it to the social situations in which he finds himself. In general, it may be said that sociological knowledge lends itself to helping an individual and his society achieve results in terms of better social relations. But, a very few students pursue the subject of sociology to either seek knowledge for knowledge sake or applying it in the solution of their own day-to-day life problems. A person can be an expert in sociology but may not be able to solve his own family problems or may behave as a social deviant. Relatively few students become professional sociologists but everybody must all times live in society, associate with people, and enact social roles. It is obvious that sociological knowledge is a basic help in choosing one's own career and vocation. Positions in teaching, salesmanship, business administration or local bodies administration, law, journalism and even in politics and other fields, where an essential occupational activity is 'dealing with people', require more than ordinary knowledge of human relations in society. Reliable knowledge about social phenomena is an essential and basic prerequisite for better human relationships and, in turn, for a better society.

Uses of Sociology

Famous Swedish Noble laureate Gunnar Myrdal (1970) long back said that the social sciences are important in a democracy because they encourage the open discussion of important issues by appealing to the people's rationality rather than to superstition and narrowness. The sociologist can make this contribution. Sociology has its uses. The main uses of sociology may be as listed below:

1. It provides a basic understanding of human society, how social system work, how people's behaviour is modified by their circumstances.
2. It broadens the range of our perspective from which we try to understand the social world.
3. It gives us an insight into our daily life like a tourist guide.
4. It helps in removing ignorance about human relationships.
5. The world we live in is in trouble. It besets with many dilemmas. Sociology guides us in sorting out such dilemmas. The world is shrinking in many ways too—satellite TV, cell phone networks and Internet have created many new conditions and problems. Contact between culturally different groups has increased enormously in the present time. Sociology helps in studying cultures of different societies in various circumstances.

6. It provides us an orientation to the use of research techniques applicable in a wide variety of contexts.
7. It helps us understand ourselves and our positions in society. It is a source of self-enlightenment and increases self-understanding.
8. It is a useful preparation for our careers.
9. It helps us in developing awareness of cultural differences. We adopt the views transmitted to us by our culture, but these views are often limited and superficial and do not constitute any understanding. Quite often, if we properly understand how others live, we also require a better understanding of what their problems are.
10. There is educational value of sociology. It learns us how other people manage their societies and solve their problems. It may lead us to healthy scepticism, a tendency to ask intelligent questions about our own. It has been said that the hallmark of a university trained mind is intelligent and unprejudiced scepticism.
11. Sociological research provides practical help in assessing the results of policy initiatives. A programme of practical reform may simply fail to achieve what its designers sought, or may produce unintended consequences of an unfortunate kind.
12. Knowledge gives humans the power to shake off the past and shape their destiny—and sociology brings this power into the social world.
13. Society and culture change rapidly in our day and age. The stable joint family and even nuclear family is no longer the only common and socially acceptable way of life. It is being replaced slowly by a new type of relationship called 'living together' 'or' 'live-in relationship'. Youth culture and trends in fashion and music change so fast that older people have difficulties in following their twists and turns, food habits are being transformed, leading together diversity within many countries, and so on. These and other changes which impinge upon human behaviour make it necessary to study sociology.

The discipline of sociology can play a valuable role in developing critical thinking. It can help students to better understand the working of their own society and of other cultures. Students will be able to use sociological concepts, approaches and theories in emaciating human interactions and institutions. Sociological imagination can be useful in examining such public policy issues as capital punishment, feminism, reservation (affirmative action) and the AIDS crisis, etc.

All sciences are emancipatory, including sociology. The prime objective of all sciences is to improve the human conditions and liberate the man from all shackles of exploitation and deprivation. Anthony Giddens (1997) aptly remarked: 'Studying sociology should be liberating experience: sociology enlarges our sympathies and imagination, opens up new perspectives on the sources of our own behaviour, and creates an awareness of cultural settings different from our own ... sociological thinking is a vital help to self-understanding, which in turn can be focussed back on an improved understanding of the social world.' Perhaps, the main contribution of sociology is that it makes more sense of our lives. It does so by explaining the relationships between personal experience and 'external events', between self and society. Charles Wright Mills (1956) described the links between self and society in terms of 'personal troubles', such as losing one's job or being wounded in combat and 'public issues', such as rising unemployment or war phobia. It is befitting to conclude this section with the views of founder sociologist Max Weber (1970) who nearly a century ago argued in his lectures on 'Science as a Vocation' and 'Politics as a Vocation' that sociology could not tell members of society what values to hold, but it could demonstrate the possibilities and constraints facing them within their social structure.

Careers in Sociology

Sociology is not only an intellectual discipline, it is also a profession. When we speak of a profession, we refer mainly to such things as the uses or applications of a body of knowledge. Sociologists play a rich and varied role in today's society. They serve in a variety of capacities, such as consultant, teacher, policy maker, researcher, administrator, clinical counsellor, social critic, interviewer, journalist, probation and parole worker, career counsellor, social worker, recreation worker, programme evaluator, urban planner, marketing administration coordinator, personnel manager, etc. They work in areas as broad and diverse as the discipline they have chosen.

Knowledge of sociology can be used in the following areas of social life:

1. Teaching
2. Social research
3. Social work
4. Professions—medicine, law, engineering, business, etc.
5. Industry
6. Rural and urban planning
7. Public administration—civil services
8. Policy making
9. Business consultancy
10. Politics
11. Architecture
12. Child welfare and health care
13. Gerontology (study of old age people)
14. Computer industry

15. Military intelligence and military
16. Entrepreneurship
17. International relations
18. Criminal justice
19. City management
20. New emerging careers: (a) action programme, (b) development, and (c) human resource management.

Sociology and Common Sense

Many a time, it is charged that sociology is nothing but sheer common sense in the garb of jugglery of words or bombastic expression used in the name of science. It is often said that whatever sociologists say, we already have at least a bit of knowledge of it or we may have experienced it at some juncture of our life. Some people opined that it is just our popular wisdom couched in metaphoric language. This notion is not correct. Such knowledge, while sometimes accurate, is not always reliable because it rests on commonly held beliefs rather than systematic analysis of facts. It was once considered 'common sense' to accept that the earth was flat or the sun revolves round the earth. Such notions still remain with us even today. These questions were raised by many early thinkers such as Pythagoras, Aristotle and many others.

For thousands of years people's common sense has made them believe that big objects are faster than small ones, that stone and iron are perfectly solid materials, that the desire for children is instinctive, that the institutions of caste and joint family or the custom of dowry will automatically wither away with the spread of education, that the high caste or white people are more talented than the low caste or black people, etc. But when these statements were investigated scientifically, it was found that they were not true. These common sense statements based on popular wisdom illustrate our point that common sense knowledge is not always true. Many common sense conclusions are based on guesses, ignorance, prejudices, mistaken interpretations and haphazard trial and error learnings. On the other hand, scientific observations are based on verifiable evidence or systematic body of proofs.

Like other scientists, sociologists' perspective of looking at social phenomena is different from the layman or common sense perspective. Sociologist sees the society through the trained eyes of a scientist. Sociologists do not accept something as a fact because 'everyone knows it'. Sociological perspective consists of objectivity, empiricism, precision, ethical neutrality and verifiability. Sociologists gather facts scientifically in order to describe, understand and predict any social phenomenon. Sociologists look at the world critically and do not take things for granted based on traditional beliefs and practices.

Sociology and Social Policy

Sociology at its best is the science of social interactions and social relationships which are the core to the formation of society. While not a precise science that can predict behaviour, it is nonetheless a valuable discipline assisting the search for more rational social arrangements and preparing social policy.

The term 'policy' commonly refers to clearly articulated set of ideas about what should be done in a particular sphere. It differs from a plan. Plans specify in detail the way in which objectives are to be achieved, whereas a policy is typically formulated at a more general level, indicating only objectives and the intended direction of change. A policy is begun in the hope that it will produce a desired effect.

What is social policy? To answer this question in a few words is slightly problematic. Some people chose to answer this question by listing the areas of public (government) policy under this heading. The main areas are social security and social welfare, social services, health service, education, employment services and housing. This simple definition, i.e., listing the areas of welfare fields, is too narrow. It is argued that exclusive concentration on government policies is mistaken and that one should also include the policies of religious and charitable bodies as well as of private corporations also aiming to meet the social needs of the population. Some have gone to the extent of including even economic policies in the gamut of social policy. We shall use the term 'social policy' to mean all policies (carried out by government and private agencies) that are directed towards meeting the social needs (welfare needs) of the population including policies concerning social security, health, education, housing, child, women, sick and disabled and old age welfare. It also includes social division of welfare, or the management of public, fiscal and private allocation of wealth, the organization of employment, the management of wage system and the creation of styles of living. In short, social policy is about the kind of society people want to create and what they do to create it.

There have been a range of approaches to the analysis of social policy. T.H. Marshall (1963), in his classic statement, stated that 'the avowed objective of 20th century social policy is welfare'. Marxists and others argue that the objective of certain social policy measures is to control disaffected groups in the population rather than to act out of concern for their welfare. Similarly, Peter Townsend (1979), Professor of International Social Policy, London School of Economics, argued that the main aim of social policy is the institutional control of services, agencies and organizations, which are engaged in maintaining of changing social structure and values. It is to be noted that much of the work has been done in departments of social administration outside the framework of sociology. 'Social administration' refers to the means by which social policy is implemented.

Pure and Applied Sociology

All sciences contribute to the knowledge base and also to the solution and resolution of practical problems and issues. As such, all sciences have two faces:

1. Pure Science/Pure Sociology
2. Applied Science/Applied Sociology

Logically, the distinction is one between 'pure' research—concerned with advancing fundamental, theoretical knowledge—and 'practical' or 'applied' research—applying already existing scientific knowledge to the solution of practical problems. Both are interdependent, rather than one being dependent on the other. Although technology (applied science) does in fact advance by applying scientific principles to practical problems, its own successes often contribute in anticipated ways to basic science.

Pure Science/Pure Sociology

Pure science is a search for knowledge, without primary concern for its practical use. Knowledge for knowledge sake is the main aim of a pure scientist. Scientists, who seek knowledge for its own sake, no more moved by the question of its utility like the mother and the father who protect and nourish their children without expecting anything in return. Parents commonly love their children without calculating their usefulness. Many students/researchers of science feel much the same thing about their work. Pure sciences (Physics, Chemistry, Biology, Botany, Physiology, Economics, Political Science, Psychology, Anthropology and Sociology, etc.) are concerned with the advancement of knowledge. Their main aim is to investigate the underlying principles of the natural and social world which sustain and change the natural and social order. They are not concerned with the practical application of their results or curing the immediate ills of our natural or social order. The goal of each natural science, including sociology, is the formulation of scientific laws.

Sociology is a pure science, not an applied one. As a scientific endeavour, it is not directly concerned with social welfare or with solving social problems and building a better society. The knowledge gained by sociology can help formulate public policies. Sociologists investigate why people do the things they do and feel and think the way they do. The immediate goal of sociology is the acquisition of knowledge about human society, and not the utilization of that knowledge. According to Lester F. Ward (1841–1913), a pioneer sociologist of America, the main aim of pure sociology is 'to investigate fundamental rules of social structure and social change'. Robert Bierstedt (1974) wrote: 'Sociologists do not determine questions of public policy, do not tell legislators what laws should be passed or repealed and do not dispense relief to the ill, the lame, the blind, or the poor—except, of course, in their capacity as citizens—apply the knowledge that it is their duty and profession to acquire.' This view was held by early sociologists between 1920 and 1940 who believed sociology as a value-free science. But this view is now no more accepted in totality by all sociologists.

Applied Science/Applied Sociology

Applied science is the search for ways of using scientific knowledge to solve practical problems. The sciences, which apply the principles of knowledge or use principles to manipulate something, gained from the basic or pure sciences, are known as applied sciences. All branches of engineering, science of medicine, architecture and social work come under the category of applied sciences. An applied science has quite opposite aim and intent than a pure science. It is not concerned with the theory or formulation of laws or development and systematization of principles. For example, an average doctor is not primarily interested in the theory of disease or the principles that underlie diagnosis but he is primarily concerned with the treatment of the disease of his patient.

The social sciences (e.g., sociology) like all sciences have dual function. They serve to help the people to solve their problems and at the same time explore and understand the world around them. As such, there is an interest in application and also in understanding. When social scientific findings are applied to the solutions of social problems, it is called applied sociology. Sociology, as an applied discipline, uses the knowledge of the pure social scientist to improve social life. Immediately, sociology seeks to understand the fundamental mechanism of social reality, but the desire to understand is always motivated by the wish to control. The main aim of applied sociology is to bring social welfare in society through social scientific investigation. For example, a sociologist making a study of the social structure of a slum is working as a pure scientist but if he studies how to prevent or control delinquency in a slum or how to remove poverty, then he is working as an applied scientist. In the role of applied scientist, a sociologist tries to solve the social problems.

Though sociologists and social workers do share some common tasks, still it is a mistake to regard sociology as equivalent to social work or social welfare.

Types of Applied Sociology

Applied sociology may be divided into five main branches:

1. *Clinical Sociology:* It refers to the use of sociological knowledge in providing assistance to individuals and organizations. This term, analogous to clinical psychology, was introduced in 1931 by Chicago sociologist Louis Wirth for the work of sociologists employed in clinical settings alongside social workers, psychologists and psychiatrists. Clinical

sociology involves the use of sociological knowledge to aid diagnosis, treatment, teaching and research. A clinical sociologist may study the ways of improving employee morale.

2. *Social Engineering:* It attempts to use sociological knowledge to design social policies or institutions with a specific purpose. It refers to planned social change and social development. The planned improvement of society is practically impossible without the scientific knowledge provided by sociology. Social engineering involves the intelligent application of sociological knowledge. It is based on the idea that governments can shape and manage key features of society, in much the same way as the economy is managed. For example, the extent of women's employment is clearly determined in part by government policy to promote to impede women's paid work. For doing such works, applied sociologists use social indicators and social trend reports. Every family, school, club, business and local bodies recognizes and pursues its goal. This is nothing more or less than social engineering.

3. *Social Work:* Though it is a distinct discipline, it is considered as an applied aspect of sociology. Social work is the field in which the principles of the social sciences, especially sociology, are applied to actual social problems in the same way the principles of physiology are applied in medicine or the principles of economics are applied in business management. A social worker might, for example, use information obtained from family research to try to place children in foster homes or to establish centres of spouse abuse.

   The term 'social work' is applied to the various organized methods for promoting human welfare through the prevention and relief of suffering. In the late 19th century, social work was largely voluntary (notably as a charitable activity). Since the Second World War, social work practice has become increasingly professionalized. In India, many institutions of social work training and education were established, notable among them is the renowned Tata Institute of Social Work, Mumbai. Many state governments have also started such institutions on its pattern. These institutions have the aim to train people to step out into society and to assist in the solution of its immediate problems.

4. *Applied Social Research:* It is similar in many respects to the basic/pure research conducted in universities and colleges. At one end of the continuum of social research would be the disciplines involved in research, not to solve a specific problem, but simply to increase our understanding of the social world. Such researches are known as pure/basic research. At the other end of the continuum would be the disciplines that use knowledge to solve actual problems, these researches are called applied social research. Social workers devise their own research methods and techniques to help people solve personal and group

problems, and the resulting applications contribute to our existing body of knowledge. Applied social research may take the form of descriptive research, survey research, analytical or evaluation research such as systematic attempts to estimate the potential effects of a proposed social programme or effects of planned change or a new approach to management in a business firms.

5. *Action Sociology:* Action sociology is also a form of applied sociology in which sociologist is asked to participate in the development process and tackle vital social problems actively. It is directly concerned with the solutions of the social problems. It requires the involvement of the sociologist in all stages of development or the solutions of the problem. This means not only to find out the roots of the social problem and suggest it remedy but to associate ourselves in the diagnosis of the problem, planning, execution, monitoring and evaluation of the programme designed to solve the problem. In India, a fine example of this approach (action sociology) we find in the project of Sulabh International started by a sociologist Bindeshwar Pathak. Intervention is needed to make society better.

   Action sociology/action research places emphasis on the sociologist not only to work as a researcher but to assume the role of a change agent also. Such change agents are often used in local communities, local bodies or in companies as consultants. They work as part of the change process itself. This view was supported by Herbert Gans (in Paul Felix Lazarsfeld et al., 1967). He wrote: 'I believe that the sociologist ought to be more than a detached researcher and he should participate more directly in social action programmes. ... The sociologist can help to develop the means necessary to achieve the goals, i.e., by participating in the development of programmes of action. It is here that he can perhaps make his most useful contribution.'

   Currently, there is a strong trend toward action sociology. Indeed, radical sociologists maintain that action sociology is a sociology of engagement. Recently, French sociologist Alain Touraine (1988) developed a radical new theoretical framework known as *actionalism*. He claimed that the sociologist is an agent of change, not a neutral observer. He has a stake in the conflicts of his or her society. As such he or she should play the role of a 'sociological interventionist' in which he/she should study social change movements by participating in them directly. This actionalist sociology, Touraine believed, will 'replace a sociology of society with a sociology of actors'.

Chapter 2

Culture

KEY FEATURES

- Meaning
- Definitions
- Characteristics or the Nature of Culture
- Universality of Culture
- Culture and Society
- Culture and Civilization
- Culture and Sub-culture
- Counter-culture
- Organization of Culture
- Sociology of Culture
- Cultural Globalization
- Temporocentrism
- Globalization and India

Man has been defined variously. It has been defined as a cultural animal also or an animal which is endowed with the attribute of culture. This attribute we do not find in other animals. This distinguishes man from his closest biological kin—the apes. Culture has enabled man to become the most extraordinary successful animal. This is why, this aspect of man, i.e., culture, is of utmost importance for sociology. How is this concept defined in sociology? What are its attributes? These issues, along with some other related topics, have been examined in the following paragraphs.

Meaning

The word 'culture' like most other sociological concepts has both a popular as well as sociological meaning. In ordinary conversation and even in different branches of knowledge, it is used differently. Often it is used for higher things of mind like art, music, literature and paintings. It is also used in the sense of 'cultured' or 'refinement' or to convey such things as social charm, enlightenment, intellectual excellence, sweetness, etc. All these connotations are loaded with value judgement. Sociologists as scientists do not use the term 'culture' in any sense of evaluation, i.e., good or bad, ethical or unethical, beautiful or ugly, cultured or uncultured or high and popular culture. Sociologists use it in a objective or neutral sense, devoid of any sense of value judgement.

In Hindi, the word *sanskriti* is used as an equivalent for the English term 'culture' which is derived from the Sanskrit term *samskar*. *Samaskar* denotes the process of refinement through some ritual performance. In Hindu culture, it is held that man is born as an asocial being. He becomes social and cultural man by going through the various *samaskars* performed from time to time throughout life from birth to death.

In social sciences, the facts of human life are taken as they are. They are not judged qualitatively. It follows that no culture is good or bad but they may differ from one another, for example, the cultures of Chinese, Japanese or British, Hindus or Todas of Nilgiris are quite different cultures.

Sociologists use the term 'culture' to refer to the 'ways of life' of the people or of groups within a society. This way of life is expressed in group's norms, customs and values and in the shared expression (history) along with language. This is also reflected in the dress pattern, way of cooking and eating, birth, marriage and funeral customs, family life, patterns of work, religious ceremonies, festivals, leisure pursuits and so many other things. It includes: (1) inherited artifacts, goods, technical processes, and (2) social heritages, ideas, habits, values, customs, attitudes, morals, law and art which have some meaning to the group. Therefore, Indian flag is an aspect of culture as much as the national anthem. In Christians to wear a specially made white gown by the bride in the wedding and in Thai tradition that no one be allowed to touch the queen reflects aspects of different cultures. These differences in aspects of culture differentiate one society from another. In brief, culture is the totality of learned socially transmitted behaviour. It encompasses all the human phenomena that are not the products of biological inheritance.

Definitions

The classic definition of culture given by Sir Edward Tylor as early as in 1871 and which has been accepted by almost all sociologists and cultural anthropologists, reads as follows: 'Culture is that complex whole which includes knowledge, belief, art, morals, law, custom and any other capabilities and habits acquired by man as a member of society.'

The above definition clearly states that culture is not something which is genetically determined but it is socially transmitted through the process of communication. In sociological parlance, this process is known as 'socialization'. It is socially learned and shared by the members of a society.

Paraphrasing the above definition of Tylor, noted social anthropologist Bronislaw Malinowski called culture a social heritage which consists of both material (tangible) and non-material (intangible) things. This view has been extended by David Bidney, who defined culture as 'the product of agrofacts (products of cultivation), artifacts (products of industry), sociofacts (social organization) and mentifacts (language, religion, art and so on)'. Early noted sociological writers R.M. MacIver and C.H. Page contended that 'culture is the expression of our nature in our modes of living and thinking, in our everyday intercourse, in art, in literature, in religion, in recreation and enjoyment.'

Summarizing all the above definitions of culture, we may put it in a very simple terms as 'culture' is what we are (our dress pattern, eating patterns, languages, greeting ways, etc.), what we do (our all types of activities and pursuits such as agricultural, industrial, educational, political, informational, etc.) and what we have (tangible and intangible social and cultural heritage).

It is important to note here that culture does not refer to what people actually do, but to the ideas they share about what they do and the material objects that they use. The act of eating with spoon is not culture but the shared expectations (ideas) attached to the act of eating is culture.

Characteristics or the Nature of Culture

The following important characteristics of culture may be discerned from all the above definitions:

1. Culture is a social phenomenon. It is shared by the members of a society. It is a means of dealing with the problems of life, i.e., human needs.
2. Culture is learned as well as acquired from the ancestors. It is not inborn and instinctive like racial characteristics which are genetically transmitted. A human infant is quite helpless at the time of birth. He is taught to eat, drink, speak, walk and to perform all overt actions.
3. Culture is transferable or transmissive. It is transmitted from generation to generation through the process of communication and interaction or historically derived.
4. Culture is material or concrete (objects like building, machinery, tools, implements, ornaments, etc.) and non-material or abstract (things such as ideas, customs, beliefs, values, superstitions, etc.). Saluting a flag, kissing, voting and praying are examples of non-material culture.
5. Culture is both super-individual and super-organic. Super-individual simply means that any culture more than any individual. Its origin, development, continuity and refinement do not depend on individual's existence.

   Super-organic refers to that portion of man's environment which is beyond the organic or the inorganic. But it does not mean that culture is somehow superior to nature. It simply means attaching social meaning to physical and physiological act. Similar or the same physical objects or physiological acts may have different meanings in different cultural settings. For example, a piece of cloth of the same colour, composition and texture may be a national flag in one society while in other society it may be used as headdress or a diaper.

6. Culture is symbolic. A symbol is something that is used to represent something else. These may be physical objects like flags, crosses or may be signs at the road crossings, or acts like shaking hands, kisses or something else such as words, numbers or sequence of sounds, etc. All symbols have some or the other meanings bestowed upon them by those who use them.

   All human behaviour originated in the use of symbols. Thus, all civilizations have been generated and perpetuated only by the use of symbols.
7. Culture is dynamic and adaptive both. It is constantly changing. It is cumulative and progressive. Noted American sociologist Kimball Young wrote that 'culture is expanding and persisting accumulation of ways of doing and thinking which one generation hands down to the next'.
8. Culture is composed of ethos (formal appearance of culture) and eidos (cognitive process of culture) both. Ethos deals with the qualities that pervade the whole culture, while eidos refers to the general principles which gives coherence to a system of belief.

   Describing cultural ethos of Zuni Indians, Ruth Benedict called it *Appollonian* (peace loving and cooperative people), while she characterized plain Indians as *Dionysian* (violent and individualistic).
9. Culture is basically the solution to man's basic needs such as food, shelter, reproduction and hygiene. It also creates needs. It is both rewarding and frustrating. Its origin is grounded in the needs of human beings.

Some Paradoxes and Contradictions of Culture

1. Culture is abstract (non-material culture, such as ideas, beliefs) and concrete (material culture like building, machines) both.
2. Culture is stable, yet it is also dynamic. The form of the family as we see today is not the same as it was found among the primitive people but family still exists in some or the other form.
3. It is learned and acquired both. It is transmissible.
4. It is universal, yet its local and regional manifestation is unique and differs from place to place.
5. Culture differs from time to time. Present and past cultures differ in content and quantity but not in quality.
6. Culture fills and largely determines the course of our lives, yet rarely intrudes into conscious thought.

Universality of Culture

No society is devoid of culture. Even the preliterate (primitive) societies had some or the other form of culture. But it differed in content and form, quality and quantity from societies to societies. As a repository of social heritage (some scholars have even designated culture as a social heritage), it helps in maintaining social order, control the behaviour of people and establish uniformity in the behaviour of people. Despite their differences, all societies have attempted to solve basic human needs by developing aspects of shared, learned behaviour known as 'cultural universals'. These universals are termed as 'psychic unity of mankind'. Well-known field anthropologist Malinowski has grouped these basic needs along with their cultural responses as under:

Basic Needs	*Cultural Responses*
Metabolism	Commissariat
Reproduction	Kinship
Bodily comforts	Shelter
Safety	Protection
Movement and growth	Activities and Training
Health	Hygiene

Clark Wissler has enumerated the following nine cultural universals:

1. *Speech:* Language and writing systems, numerals and gestures.
2. *Material traits:* Food, shelter, clothing, tools, utensils, occupation, industry etc.
3. Mythology and scientific knowledge.
4. *Art:* Carving, paintings, drawings, music, dance, etc.
5. *Religious beliefs and practices:* Ritualistic forms, taboos, habits, treatment of the sick and dead, etc.
6. *Family and social system:* Marriage forms, inheritance, social control, gift giving, sports and games, visiting, etc.
7. *Property:* Real and personal property, trade and exchange.
8. *Government:* Political forms, judicial and legal procedures.
9. War.

While all cultures share certain general practices mentioned above, the expressions of any cultural universals in a society may change from time to time. Each generation and each year, most human cultures change and expand through the processes of innovation, diffusion and cultural borrowings.

Culture and Society

Both terms 'society' and 'culture' are the key concepts of sociology. At many times, in common parlance, both are used synonymously. But sociologists and anthropologists distinguish 'culture' from 'society' though there are very close connections between these terms. 'A society is a system of interrelationships which connects individuals together' (Giddens, 1997). It is also defined to mean 'a group of interacting people living in a specific geographical or political area, organized in a cooperative manner and sharing a common culture (beliefs, customs, values, language and activities)'.

In this sense, India, Britain, China, France and the United States are all societies. Societies may be very small or too big to include millions of people and many groups or communities. In brief, the word 'society' connotes the whole complex of relations of man/woman to his/her fellows.

On the other hand, culture refers to the ways of life or living of the members of a society. How people dress, how and what they eat, how they marry, what are their customs of birth and death, what are their beliefs and values, what are their leisure activities, what is their language and so on. All these elements make a culture.

Thus, drawing a distinction between 'society' and 'culture', it can be stated that a society is a social group while a culture is a society's system of common heritage. Society refers to interrelationships between people that keep them together; on the other hand culture is the totality of learned socially transmitted behaviour. Society connotes a fairly large number of people who are bound by the bond of some kind of social relationships. Culture is a means that gives shape to these relationships. In brief, society refers to the people and culture to the patterns of their behaviour.

Though there is a difference between society and culture but still both are interrelated. No culture could exist without society. But, equally, no society could prolong without culture. We would not be 'human' at all without culture. There cannot be culture apart from society. Describing their relationships, Gillin and Gillin (1948) said, 'Culture is the cement building together into a society, its component individuals … human society is interacting; culture is patterning of their behaviour.'

Culture and Civilization

In our day-to-day talks and discussions, we often use the terms 'culture' and 'civilization' interchangeably. Even in the Anglo-French tradition, the concept of culture was often used synonymously with civilization. But sociologists differentiate culture and civilization as two different levels of phenomena. The concept of civilization was almost equated with highly valued things, such as respect of people for one another, the sanctity of life and high regard for the good, the ethical and the beautiful. In this sense, those who were lacking in these attributes, were regarded as barbaric or uncivilized. Preliterate or primitive people who lived in a state of nature—quite naked, used to eat unbaked animal flesh—were usually termed as barbarians. However, many anthropological studies showed that many preliterate societies had their own values, beliefs, rules, religions and tools, etc. They made certain changes in the natural order of things which are characteristics of culture, in the modern sense of the term. The use of the term 'civilization' as exhibited above is different from its use in sociological or anthropological sense. Defining civilization MacIver and Page (1962) said, 'by civilization we mean the whole mechanism and organization which man has designed in his endeavour to control the conditions of life'. Similarly, S.M. Fairchild (1908) argued that it is the higher stage of cultural development characterized by intellectual, aesthetic, technological and spiritual attainment. On the basis of this meaning, he made reference of 'civilized peoples' in contrast to 'uncivilized or non-civilized peoples'.

A few scholars have equated civilization with technology and progress; e.g., Robert Bierstedt (1974) emphasized on sophistication, self-criticism and other awareness as the chief characteristics of civilization. Sociologists do not use the term 'civilization' in the sense stated above because all above views are value-loaded.

Thus, making a distinction between culture and civilization, the following points may be noted:

1. Culture is an end (values and goals) in itself while civilization is a means (tools and techniques) to an end. Cultural facts like belief, art and literature—prose, poetry or novel, etc., gives direct satisfaction to the reader while equipments of civilization such as cars, computers, refrigerators, etc., do not give direct satisfaction, until and unless they do not satisfy our wants. Thus, civilization is utilitarian. It just helps in achieving the end.
2. Culture has no value in itself but it is a measurement by which we can value other articles of civilization. We cannot determine the value of culture, i.e., beliefs, norms, ideas, etc., but the value of anything can be determined by its measurement standard. Culture is a measuring rod or weighing balance.
3. Civilization is always advancing but not culture. Cultural facts like dramatic plays or poems may not be necessarily better today than the plays or poems of Shakespeare?
4. Civilization is easily passed without much effort to the next generation but not culture. Cultural facts, e.g., any art or a piece of literature, cannot be learned without some intelligence. It requires a few pains to understand it. Contrary to it, the equipments of civilization (building, TV, etc.) can easily be inherited without much or any use of energy and intelligence.
5. Civilization may be borrowed without making any change but not culture. Borrowing any cultural fact like any political, economic or social belief requires some necessary alteration to adjust in the new cultural environment while this is not necessary to make any material change in the civilizational equipments such as TV, computer, etc.

6. Culture relates to the inner qualities of society like religion, customs, conventions, etc., while civilization relates to the outer form of society such as TV, radio, fans, etc.
7. Culture is more stable than civilization—cultural change takes place in years or in centuries but civilization changes very rapidly.
8. Variability of cultures may not be accompanied by variability of civilization at different places. Civilization may be similar in variable cultural areas. For instance, there is a great difference between American and Indian cultures but there are many similarities in their civilizational equipments.
9. Culture is a social fact, i.e., creation of the whole society while civilization, i.e., the invention of any equipment may be by a single individual. Any ordinary person can effect any change in the civilizational equipment but for any modification or alteration in any cultural fact requires the power and imagination of whole society.

There are scholars who have designated culture and civilization as the two sides of the same coin. William F. Ogburn (1964), in his theory of social change, pointed out two aspects of culture, viz., material and non-material. For him, material aspect represents civilization and the non-material aspect is the culture proper. Gillin and Gillin (1948) designated the material or tangible part of culture as civilization or culture equipment which man in his endeavour has modified from environment.

Culture and Sub-culture

Culture, as said above, is a 'total way of life' or 'designs for living'. Thus, each human society has its own way of living, different in its entirety from the culture of any other society. All societies are composed of many groups and communities. The ways of living and behaving peculiar to a large segment or a group of a society are known as sub-culture. This group or the segment shares some of the cultural traits and complexes distinct from the larger society of which it is a part. In a society, thus, there can be many sub-cultures—subculture of young, elderly, workers, elite class, slum people and even of delinquents known as 'delinquent sub-culture'. Sub-culture, though, exists within the confines of a larger culture but also have their own norms, values and lifestyles distinct from the larger culture.

Counter-culture

A counter-culture is a sub-culture that adheres to 'a set of norms and values that sharply contradict the dominant norms and values of the society of which that group is a part' (Yinger, 1982). It rejects societal norms and values of the prevailing culture and seeks alternative lifestyles. This type of culture is typically popular among the young.

Organization of Culture

A culture is not simply an accumulation of isolated elements such as values, norms, behaviour, language, symbols and technology, etc. The elements of culture are interrelated constituting a complex whole. It is an organized system of many interrelated parts or aspects. These parts are known as trait, complex and pattern.

Culture Trait

The smallest particle or unit of a culture is known as culture trait. Culture is woven with so many of its traits just as human or animal body is made of cells. These traits are material and immaterial both. Writing pen, chair, saluting a flag, praying, kissing, handshake, voting are all examples of culture traits.

Culture Complex

When a number of traits cluster together in a meaningful relationship and form an activity, it is known as culture complex. Bats, gloves, stumps, rules, play ground, etc., are the traits to form the complex of cricket game. Similarly, beliefs, ideas of purity and pollution, idols, garlands, flowers, utensils used to perform prayer, bell, conch, etc., are the traits of a Hindu ritual complex.

Culture Pattern

Combination of culture traits and complexes into a sort of generalized picture of the culture as a whole is known as culture pattern. It reflects the total structure of a society. While comparing one society with another, this culture pattern is also used.

Sociology of Culture

Sociology of culture denotes interpretation of social events and elements in cultural contexts. In other words, it is cultural analysis of social issues. Sociologists regard culture as a highly significant concept, since it embraces all learned and shared behaviour. How do members of a society decide which to accept or and what to use? When a society chooses our cultural system, how do its members perceive the systems of other cultures? Answers to such questions can be given through such concepts as ethnocentrism, cultural relativism, culture shock, xenocentrism, xenophobia, culture diversity, universality of culture, popular culture, elite culture, cultural globalization and temporocentrism.

Ethnocentrism

Literally, 'ethno' means people. Hence, sticking or centring of people to certain attitude or thing is called ethnocentrism. This term was coined by an eminent American sociologist W.G. Sumner in 1906, used to describe prejudicial attitudes between in-groups and out-groups. Anthropologists used this term to analyse the bent of mind of the people towards other cultures in term's of their own culture using one's own rating scales. It is 'a tendency to evaluate the culture of others in term's of own culture' (Giddens, 1997). Accordingly, people often evaluate their own culture (beliefs, values, behaviour patterns, ways of living) superior to others. Outsiders or others are thought of as aliens, barbarians or morally and mentally inferior. When we call 'primitives' as barbarians or compare other societies in terms of one's own cultural assumptions or bias, we are in reality governed by this very feeling of ethnocentrism. This feeling gives rise to blindness, narrow and parochial judgements. Many wars were fought or aggression took place because of this feeling of ethnocentrism.

Ethnocentrism can also be looked at as the sociological counterpart to the psychological phenomenon of *egocentrism*. The difference is that in the egocentrism individuals are at the centre of the universe while in ethnocentrism an entire culture is placed in this exalted position.

Sociologists and anthropologists attempt to view all behaviours, lifestyles and ideas in their own context and not from ethnocentrism, though at many times they unknowingly become the culprit of ethnocentric feeling when they believe that their methods are the best to approach problems.

Cultural Relativism

While ethnocentrism evaluates foreign cultures using the familiar culture of the observer as a standard of correct behaviour, cultural relativism views people's behaviour from the perspective of their own culture. The belief that cultures must be judged on their own terms rather than by the standards of another culture is called cultural relativism (Eshleman and Cashion, 1983). Thus, from this perspective, an act, idea, form of dress or other cultural manifestation is not inherently good or bad, right or wrong, correct or incorrect. It does mean that the behaviour appropriate in one place at one time may and may not be appropriate everywhere or every time. Several examples can be given from our day-to-day behaviours; for example, nudity in the bathroom is appropriate but not in the office or at the public place. Anthropologists have documented many such examples from different societies. For instance, the deliberate killing of a child is considered murder in almost all societies, but in Brazil's Tenetehara society, it is a legitimate practice.

Cultural relativism is based on the philosophy that denies the existence of truth independent and outside of itself. It maintains that beliefs, values and theories are relative to time and place that produced them and not valid outside those circumstances. Accordingly, culture (ways of life) can only be judged in the context of age or society that has produced them. Some theories in sociology of knowledge are relativistic in that they suggest that all knowledge is socially produced.

Cultural relativism stresses that different social contexts give rise to different norms and values. As such, practices like polygamy, bullfighting and monarchy should be examined within the particular context of the cultures in which they are found.

Culture Shock

Culture shock is a term used to express a negative feeling experienced by persons moving from one society to another or within one's own society. Such persons find that the culture in which they move is not only different to their own but see things which are quite strange and opposite to the culture in which they have been brought up experience a feeling that is termed as culture shock. People feel horrified to see the custom of 'head hunting' as found in some tribes of Nagaland, and a custom of mixing of blood of two persons to make them blood brothers.

Xenocentrism

Xenocentrism is a culturally based tendency to value other cultures more highly than one's own. On the basis of this feeling, the products, styles, ideas and values of one's society are regarded as inferior to that of other societies. For example, people in India often assume that British lifestyle (dress pattern, etc.), French fashion or Japanese electronic devices (TV, tape recorders, mobile set, washing machines, etc.) and Swiss watches are superior to their own. This is why people give preference to foreign goods while purchasing. In brief, xenocentrism is the belief that what is foreign is best. It is interesting to note that xenocentrism on the one hand is an extension of cultural relativism and on the other hand, in a sense, it is a reverse ethnocentrism.

Xenophobia

Xenophobia is a culturally based fear of outsiders. It is often seen with the immigrant people into societies and communities. It is based on the genuine or sometimes fictitious fear of the strangers for competition of jobs, or ethnic, racial, or religious prejudice. This feeling has given rise to anti-immigration movements in many countries of Europe, USA and Australia. Recently, these countries have enacted many stringent laws to discourage people to come to their country.

Cultural Diversity

Culture differs greatly from one another. The focus of behaviour varies widely from culture to culture. The Indian ways of living and behaving are quite different from the Western/Arab/Chinese societies. In the West, for example, the marital partners are chosen through the practice of dating, while in India, till today, living aside a few, this is done by parents. Jews do not eat pork, while Hindus eat pork but avoid beef. Westerners regard kissing as normal part of behaviour in public places while in India it is refrained or avoided.

Universality of Culture

Despite differences in cultures, all societies have attempted to meet basic human needs (sex, shelter or protection and hunger). These needs are found, notwithstanding time and places, all over the world. In order to survive man has devised various cultural responses to fulfill these basic needs. These responses are shared, learned behaviour known as cultural universals. Behind the seemingly endless diversity in culture patterns, there is a fundamental uniformity in these universals. Anthropologists have termed them as cultural constants or common denominators. Cultural universals are believed to exist among all men and attributed in most cases to the necessity of meeting needs, as said above, common to all men. Famous American anthropologist George P. Murdock (1965) has given a list of such universals. Some such universals are marriage, family, food habits, food taboos, funeral ceremonies, games, sexual restrictions, language, housing, myths, religion, medicines, cultural practices (gift giving, cooking, dancing, etc.).

Popular Culture

Popular culture is the accumulated store of cultural products, such as music, dance, art, literature, film, television, videos, radio, etc., that are consumed primarily by non-elite groups. These groups consist of working and lower class as well as substantial segments of the middle class. It is sometimes, as such, referred to as the 'culture of the masses'.

Popular cultures have been studied from two points of view: Frankfurt and British. Members of the Frankfurt School (Germany) agued that popular culture is trivial, homogenized and commercialized. It dulls people's minds, making them passive and easier to control. In this perspective, popular culture has been equated with mass culture. It has also been said that because popular (pop) culture is controlled primarily by elites, it tends to reflect their interests. The mass media and other popular culture outlets are controlled through ownership over it by the elites.

The other view is of British along with some American sociologists who argued in just an opposite manner. They held the view that popular culture is creative and authentic. It is often a vehicle for rebellion against the culture of the dominant groups. In Britain, popular culture is viewed as an oppositional movement, challenging conventional taste, fashion and values. It is said that popular culture is not a steady, bland diet handed down from above in order to dull and pacify subordinate groups and reflect and promote elite interests. Lower classes, teenagers, women, racial groups and other subordinate groups do not passively absorb popular culture, but play a part in producing a vision of what their lives are about, including some consciousness of their disadvantageous position.

Popular culture is not necessarily a common culture; its diversity reflects the age, sex and class division within its audience. Sociological studies of youth culture, for example, suggest that there are series of sub-cultures relating to distinctive class, regional and sexual differences. Popular culture is often contrasted to 'high' or 'elite' culture which generally refers to the tastes of educated ruling minority groups.

Elite Culture

The term 'elite culture' in used usually to refer to the culture of a socially dominant group in a society. This dominant group is known by various names such as upper class, ruling class, aristocratic class, elite etc. Elites who form a minority group in a society have power and influence over others and are recognized as being in some way superior. This group has access to distinctive careers, entertainment and lifestyles generally closed to the rest of the population. The way of living of this group is different from those of the masses. Usually, their culture has snobbish overtones. Their consumption pattern has been termed as 'conspicuous consumption' by Thorstein Veblen. It is the practice of buying and displaying material possessions in order to indicate or enhance one's prestige in the eyes of others.

The term 'mass culture' is paired with 'elite culture'. The mass means 'the rest', those who are not elite. The word 'mass' is used to denote large number of people.

Cultural Globalization

Nowadays, there is much talk and discussion about cultural globalization, i.e., a common culture is developing across the globe. To some extent, it is true despite some resistance from national culture, as both are developing side by side. Generally, the word 'culture' is used to mean 'the total way of life' to include economic, political and social norms, values and behaviour. Globalization is seen as the intermixing of people, cultures, economies and technologies. Modern cultural globalization is a new phenomenon. It started with economic globalization—spread of transnational corporations and global commodities, especially food and drink items like pizza and coke, and dress material such as Levi jeans, Reebok and Nike shoes, etc. In this way, we are all sharing in a common transnational form of consumption. This developing consumerism has encouraged mass common consumer culture which reflects a powerful grip on societies throughout the world. As consumerism spreads, changes are visible in lifestyles, cultural tastes, food habits, dress patterns and in modes of entertainment also. As an example, gastroenteritis—a disease associated with eating habits—reflects the impact of globalization. The rise of eating disorder, use of more and more fast foods and irregularity in eating have contributed much to the disease of gastric disorder. Neo-Marxist sociologists argue that the process of globalization is not only limited to consumer articles, but it is also accompanied by ideas and more generally ideologies which sustain the consumer culture. Changes even in norms and values are quite striking. Globalization encourages a growing integration and convergence of cultural relations.

The concept of cultural globalization is closely linked with economic globalization. Mike Featherstone (1990) argued that as a result of the development of financial markets, the main actors share many business and lifestyles norms and values. As an example, he cited that there is a close relationship between leisure activities and work. Other scholars have stressed on the emergence of global patterns of consumption and consumerism, the cultivation of cosmopolitan lifestyles, the spread of popular culture (e.g., Madonna or Michael Jackson's latest songs) as the basis of the development of cultural globalization. Thus, increased economic linkages led to cultural influences across countries. The key agents of globalization of culture are transnational corporations, cultural and media agencies that go beyond the nation-state.

In spreading cultural globalization, technology has played a crucial role. Technology, in reality, has shrunk the world in our palm. Revolutions in electronic communication (such as radio, TV, cinema, telephone, mobile, fax, Internet, etc.) and rapid means of transportation have produced an indelible impact on local, regional and national cultures because these means can now reach swiftly even the remotest corner of any country. As a result, the world is slowly and slowly becoming as one place. Both the media and geographical mobility feed this perception. Giddens (1997) has called this phenomenon as 'time-space distantiation' meaning separation of time and space brought about by modern communication. Problems, like floods in Thailand or Indonesia, famine in Ethiopia, tsunami in Japan and events like World Football Competition or Olympics in China or England have a global dimension. Similarly, creation of international economic, political, social and other agencies like UNO, WHO, UNESCO, UNDP, IMF, World Bank, human rights organizations, and the complex interchange between world systems, have contributed to a large extent global cultural homogeneity.

Over and above, science and secularization of thought are the main factors in developing the critical and innovative character of the modern outlook and this in turn has helped in spreading cultural globalization. People no longer assume that customs or habits are acceptable merely because they have the age-old authority of tradition. On the contrary, our ways of life have increasingly based on rationality. In addition to how we think, the content of ideas has also changed. Ideals of self-betterment, freedom, equality and democratic participation are largely creations of the past two or three centuries. Such ideals have served to mobilize the process of globalization of culture.

Globalization has affected cultures in two ways: Firstly, it has tried to homogenize the cultures. We can see this in dress pattern such as pent and shirt and to some extent in food recipes—pizza, Chinese noodles, etc. On the other hand, globalization has helped in the resurgence of local culture. This we can observe in the revival of traditional cultures and reforming of the identity.

Cultural globalization is also marked with some new trends in human relations. Recognition of a worldwide ecological crisis, the development of worldwide concern about health problems such as AIDS and other diseases, extension of the concept of human rights and the creation of global democratic movements are a few examples of integration that is taking place between different nation-states.

Temporocentrism

Temporocentrism is the belief that one's own time is more important than the past and future. It is the temporal equivalent of ethnocentrism. Bierstedt (1974) stated, 'we are all inclined to assume that the present is more important than the past and that the whole of historical time is significant only for what it means to us'. Emile Durkheim has made a significant contribution to the analysis time in his sociology of religion. In modern times, Giddens (1984) has analysed the temporal dimensions of social relations through his concept of time-space distantiation, social action is stretched over time and space dimensions.

Globalization in India

Globalization is not new to India. It was enshrined in the philosophical traditions of India—the idea of *Vasudhaiva Kutumbakam* (let the whole globe be our family). But, the modern globalization is different from the ancient idea of globalization. The ancient idea was humanistic based on the principles of brotherhood, peace and coexistence while the modern globalization is competitive in character driven by selfish motives. It provides no answers to the problems it creates. Modern globalization involves some kind of homogenization, which was nothing but Americanization. Since India joined WTO in 1990s, its economy is being rapidly drawn into the economic network—a large rise in integration with respect to product and capital markets. Since 1991, there has been a sharp reduction in the barriers to international trade. With particular reference to India, Prof. Yogendra Singh observed, 'it (globalization) is perceived as a friendly process by traditional local artisans, craftsmen and artists, etc., because they find in it a scope for economic empowerment and social mobility. It encourages them to link themselves to the international market and capital. It helps to innovate their ethnic styles, forms and materialises in the cultural products. It adds new dimensions to their sense of cultural identity. In the realm of non-material culture values, beliefs, rituals and religious practices, it only enhances the consciousness of cultural identity'.

Chapter 3

Processes of Social Interaction

KEY FEATURES

- What is Social Interaction?
- What is Meant by Process?
- Explaining Social Process
- Classification of Social Processes
- Co-operation
- Competition
- Accommodation
- Assimilation
- Integration
- Conflict

There are sociologists like R.E. Park and E.W. Burgess (1921), who defined sociology as the study of social interactions and social processes. These sociologists viewed society as an ongoing process, as a series of interactions between human beings, each person stimulating another person and responding to the stimuli from the other persons. Interaction refers to an action done in response to another person's action. It is defined as interpersonal action. It becomes a social action when it is oriented to others or taking others into account. Social action is an action done by a social actor. It is always a response to another actor or an attempt to secure such a response. Social action becomes social interaction when the response occurs. Social interaction consists of that behaviour by which an individual influences the overt actions or the state of mind of others. It is an action that affects the recipient in some way and usually intended by the actor to result in a reaction back to him. Social interaction can take many forms. It may be regular and recurrent, ephemeral and short-lived, or fall somewhere in between. Similarly, it may be planned or spontaneous.

Social interaction is the essence of social life. Without interaction there would be no social or group life. It is the basic ingredient of social relationships which are the basis of the formation of society. This is why, it is often said that society is rooted in social interaction. Herbert Blumer (1969) argued that social systems exist through interaction among individuals without whom there is no society. Man becomes social animal only when he interacts with other members of society (family, community and many other groups).

What is Social Interaction?

The concept of interaction has become one of the fundamental and most nearly universal ideas almost in each of the fields of knowledge—physical, biological and social. But it should not be inferred that interaction as it takes place in the inorganic or organic order is the same in all respects as is interaction in the superorganic (human-social) realm. It is also the core datum of sociology. It has been defined as 'any event by which one party tangibly influences the overt actions or the state of mind of the other' (Sorokin, 1928). It is a reciprocal and interdependent activity. Defining social interaction, Gillin and Gillin (1948) wrote: 'By social interaction we mean the mutual or reciprocal influence, resulting in the modification of behaviour, exerted through social contact and communication which, in turn, are established by interstimulation and response.' This definition emphasized on two main conditions of social interaction: (a) social contact, and (b) communication. Social contact is the first place of interaction. It rather initiates interaction. Social contact refers to the connection between persons and groups.

For social contact, social proximity (mental contact) and not the physical proximity (bodily contact) is essential. Social contact differs from physical or bodily contact. Mere physical contact (proximity) of individuals does not constitute a group. This is why, it is said, 'where there is contact of human minds, there association exists; where there is no contact, there is a state of isolation'. Social contacts may be direct or indirect and positive or negative. Direct contacts involve immediate presence of persons (face-to-face) in the exchange of ideas or things. Other contacts are indirect as we find in the case of the writer and the recipient of a personal letter. Such contacts may be established through any means of communication (telephone, TV, Internet). Positive contact means associative interaction which leads towards assimilation through tolerance, compromise or cooperation. Negative contact means disassociative interaction, which gives rise to the feeling of hatred, rivalry, jealousy, indifference or lack of response.

The other condition for social interaction is communication. Society can only be conceived of through communication. It has a central place in society. It may vary from writing a letter to a friend, to all the modern methods of communication. Means of communication may be language, script, gestures, words or symbols, etc. Language is a symbolic communication because it consists of conventional cues or signs. Gestures and facial expressions like speech and language play a significant part in communication at human level. Hand-shake, head-nodding, waving the hand are good examples of gestures. Communication in either form of material or sensory medium is a necessity for social contacts. Communication plays an important role in personality formation, transfer of social heritage and social experience from generation to generation.

What is Meant by Process?

Before examining social process, we should know what is meant by a process. A process is a sequence of steps by means of which transition is made from one condition to another. In this sequence, each step is the outgrowth of what precedes and in turn gives rise to that which follows. It is a group of activities, each of which has a meaning in relation to all others. For example, the process of digestion includes various steps involved in the organism's transformation of food into the various elements of the body tissue. Process is essential to being: interaction is a necessary part of reality. Separate and disparate planets do not make a solar system. Life cannot be understood merely through inert, non-acting and isolated aggregate of cells. Every natural process involves the reciprocal interaction of diverse elements. Where there is no interaction, there is no process. So diverse elements and mutual interactions are the two essential factors that constitute any natural process. The processes have no beginning, and no end: no beginning because there were antecedent actions, and no end because there is continuity.

Explaining Social Process

When social interaction becomes continuous and repeated many times, it leads to some result, and then it becomes a social process. A social process is a group of related activities involved in the transition from one social condition to another. According to Horton and Hunt (1964), 'the term "social process" refers to repetitive form of behaviour, which is commonly found in social life'. Ginsberg (1956) stated: 'Social processes mean the various modes of interaction between individuals or groups including co-operation and conflict, social differentiation and integration, development, arrest and decay.' MacIver and Page (1962) observed: 'Social process is the manner in which the relations of the members of a group, once brought together, acquire a certain distinctive character.'

The essential elements of social process are:

1. Sequence of events or elements
2. Repetition of events
3. Relationship between the events
4. Continuity of events
5. Social result

Classification of Social Processes

Social process may be classified in three ways as under:

1. By the number of persons involved, i.e., one-with-one; one-with-group; and its reverse, group-with-one, and group-with-group.
2. By the degree of intimacy of the individual and groups in interaction. For example, primary, secondary and tertiary or marginal groups.
3. By the nature or types of the processes.

There are, of course, hundreds of social processes—political, educational, industrial, economic, religious and others. The specific social processes are also numerous. Among those of more general nature are association, cooperation, conflict, accommodation, assimilation, domination, exploitation, differentiation, etc. These processes may be grouped into two main categories: (1) integrative/conjunctive/associative, and (2) disintegrative/disjunctive/disassociative.

Integrative or Conjunctive or Associative Processes

These are the processes which bring the individuals and groups together. Such processes produce unity among members of a group or society. According to Max Weber, 'a social relationship will be called associative if and in so far as the orientation of social action within it rests on a rationally motivated adjustment of interests'. Co-operation, accommodation and assimilation are the examples of integrative or associative processes.

Disintegrative or Disjunctive or Disassociative Processes

These processes are quite opposite to the integrative processes. They breed contempt, tension and bring disunity among the members of a group or society. Competition, rivalry and conflict are the main disintegrative processes. Weber has also included 'communal' relationship under this category. For him, 'a social relationship is "communal" if and so far as the orientation of social action, whether in the individual case or on the average, is based on the subjective feelings of parties whether affectual or traditional that they belong together'. Such relationships may be seen in religious brotherhood, personal loyalty and in national community.

We shall here discuss only five fundamental types of interactions (social processes), viz., co-operation, competition, conflict, accommodation and assimilation.

Co-operation

It is a basic process of social life. Its nature is associative. Society cannot exist without co-operation. Human survival can only be accomplished if human beings act collectively. Society is produced by the cooperative activity of human beings and the human organism becomes human only in society. Co-operation generally means working together in the pursuit of common goals or common interests. It is a joint activity carried out for shared rewards. It is a coordinated effort to reach mutual goals. Co-operation implies a regard for the wishes of other people. Men may also find that their selfish goals are best served by working together with their fellows. Co-operation involves sacrifice, effort, subordination of private interests and inclination to the joint ends of the community. The tendency to co-operate seems to be fundamental. It is found in animals as mutual aid, in primitive people, in children and in civilized adults.

According to Merrill and Eldredge (1965), 'co-operation is a form of social interaction wherein two or more persons work together to gain a common end'. H.P. Fairchild (1944) observes: 'Co-operation is the process by which individuals or groups combine their effort, in a more or less organized way for the attainment of common objective.' Defining co-operation, Robert A. Nisbet (1974) writes: 'It is joint or collaborative behaviour toward some goal in which there is common interest.' It may be:

1. spontaneous/directed (planned as in bureaucracy)
2. voluntary/involuntary
3. contractual/traditional (joint family)
4. large/small in scale

Elements

Following are the main elements of co-operation:

1. Two and more than two persons.
2. Common end or goal.
3. Joint activity.
4. Conscious effort.
5. Restrain over ego-centred drives.

Types

Co-operation may be personal or impersonal, and direct or indirect, in character. There are many modes of co-operation in social life. Its principal types are: (i) deliberate primary group co-operation, and (ii) indirect secondary group co-operation.

Deliberate primary group co-operation

Co-operation by members of small groups (family, recreation groups, work associates) is very common in our society. The nature of this type of co-operation is personal and direct. Playing together, worshipping together, tilling the fields together are the instances of direct personal co-operation. In the direct co-operation, individuals do *like* things together.

Indirect secondary group co-operation

This type of co-operation is found in the secondary groups such as large organizations, industry, government, trade unions, etc. Consumer and producer co-operation are its good examples. The nature of such co-operation is generally indirect and impersonal. This type of co-operation is based on the renowned principal of division of labour and specialization. In such activities, people do *unlike* tasks for fulfilling a common goal/end. Indirect co-operation is the main characteristic of modern society. The individual of modern industrialized society is increasingly separated from face-to-face direct co-operation.

Importance

Co-operation can accomplish things no one person could manage alone. From the earliest period of human existence, providing food and shelter, while also taking care of the new born and teaching him/her what he/she must know, required that individuals co-operate with one another. By co-operative activity among humans learning from one another, skills are acquired, knowledge is accumulated, techniques and tools are developed and all are transmitted to the next generation.

'Society is co-operation crossed by conflict'. These words of MacIver and Page (1962) clearly highlight the importance of co-operation in society. The authors have equated society with co-operation but at the same time they have not ignored the incidence of conflict which takes place from time to time in society. All progress of mankind is attributed to the co-operative efforts in various fields but conflict is also necessary for the upliftment of society lest the people may become inert and life become inactive and eventless. Co-operation is a universal phenomenon found since birth to death. Rearing, caring and protection of the child is not possible without the help and co-operation of mother or any other person. Even on death some persons are required to carry the dead body to the cremation ground. All social groups—from the smaller family to the large international organizations—are based on the co-operation of their members.

Competition

Competition is an elementary, universal and impersonal form of social interaction. It is elementary in the sense that it is basic to all other forms of interaction. Each individual is involved in countless ways of which he is generally unaware in a vast web of competitive relationships. This lack of awareness on the part of the competing units gives competition its impersonal character. Of the various concrete expressions, the most obvious is *struggle for existence*. Every form of life is in constant struggle for life with the impersonal forces of nature that exist everywhere in the natural world. There is a ceaseless struggle between each form and its foes. In human society, the struggle of existence is seldom a brute struggle for the means of life as we find in the animal world. The typical struggle in human society is for livelihood rather than for the means of existence. The human struggle is for economic security and for place, power and status. It is present in almost every walk of life.

'Competition is the struggle for possession of rewards which are in limited supply—money, goods, status, power, love—anything' (Horton and Hunt, 1964). It is a process of seeking to obtain a reward by surpassing all rivals. In the words of Biesanz and Biesanz (1964), 'competition is the striving of two or more persons or groups for the same goal which is limited so that all cannot share it'. According to Sutherland, Woodward and Maxwell (1961), 'competition is an impersonal, unconscious, continuous struggle between individuals or groups for satisfaction which, because of their limited supply, all may not have'.

Regarding competition, one important point to be kept in mind is that the attention of the competitors is always focused on the goal or reward and not on themselves. When there is a shift in interest or focus from the objects of competition to the competitors themselves, it becomes rivalry which may sometimes lead to conflict in hard cases.

Characteristics

1. *Competition is a culturally patterned process:* It is present to some degree in all societies but it differs greatly from society to society. The fiercely competitive Kwakiutl society (a tribe of North America) and the relatively non-competitive Zuni (a pubelo Indian group of New Mexico) society offer an example of a striking contrast. American society though competitive, yet this competition is sharply limited.
2. *Competition is impersonal:* Competition is impersonal and is usually not directed against any individual or group in particular. Competition may be personal when the competitors know one another but generally its nature is impersonal.
3. *Competition is unconscious:* Competition takes place on the unconscious level. Competitors at many times are not aware about other competitors and even if they are aware, they do not pay any heed to the activities of their competitors. For example, candidates, appearing for IAS or any other competitive examination, do not know one another and their

whole attention is focused on their studies (reward or goal) rather than on competitors.

4. *Competition is universal:* Competition, though an important characteristic feature of modern society, is found in all societies—primitive, traditional, modern or in pre-historic eras and in every age.
5. *Competition is continuous:* It is a never ending process. It goes on consciously or unconsciously all the time. It is unstable and frequently yields either to co-operation or to conflict.
6. *Competition is restrained:* It implies that there are rules of the game to which all competitors must follow. When the competitors break the rules or when it turns into cut-throat competition (unrestricted), the situation transforms into conflict.
7. *Competition is for scarce goods (rewards):* If the object of competition is in abundance (unlimited) quantity or sufficient in supply, there would be no competition. There is no competition for sunshine and air, which are unlimited.

Types

There are mainly two types of competition:

1. *Personal competition:* When two competitors contest for an election to office, it is called personal competition. In this competition, competitors know each other.
2. *Impersonal competition*: When contestants are not aware of one another's identity as we find in university or civil service examinations, it is called impersonal competition.

Thus, competition is indispensable in social life. It is sociologically significant for the positive and negative effects it produces in social life. It performs many useful functions in society. Some of the main functions are: (1) It serves the function of allocating scarce rewards among the competitors. (2) It has the additional function of stimulating both individual and group activity in a manner to increase the total productivity of the competitors. It furnishes motivation to excel or to obtain recognition or to achieve reward. (3) It assigns place to each individual in the hierarchical social system. It determines who is to perform what function. (4) It tends to enhance one's ego and helps in satisfying it. (5) It is conducive to progress and welfare of the society. It spurs individuals and groups to exert their best efforts to fulfil their goals. (6) It increases efficiency.

Competition has negative functions also. For example: (1) It shapes the attitudes of competitors when persons or groups compete, they normally develop unfriendly and unfavourable attitudes towards one another. (2) It may turn into conflict if it is too acute and sharp (cut-throat competition).

Unfair competition has the most disintegrating effects on the individual and the society both. (3) It may create emotional disturbances. It may also lead to neurosis through frustration. (4) Unlimited competition may lead to monopoly. People try to protect themselves through their association.

Early sociological thinkers such as Herbert Spencer saw competition as a necessary mechanism for achieving social progress—a view that was very much in line with the emergent modern capitalist system and its beliefs in competition as an engine that promotes low prices and high efficiency. It is the main driving force of modern capitalistic societies. It is widely prevalent in every sphere of modern life and in its every activity. In its approach to urban life, the Chicago School of Sociology stressed the role of competition in urban growth patterns as various ethnic, class, racial, and other groups compete for space.

Max Weber saw competition as a peaceful form of conflict. Karl Marx also saw its relationship to conflict but in a less peaceful light. Marx argued that competitions among capitalists, workers, and between capitalists and workers were major sources of contradiction and struggle. Regulated competition is the sort of peaceful conflict which is resolved within a framework of agreed rules.

Accommodation

The antagonistic state of affairs produced by conflict is for a brief time and impermanent. Life cannot go long if individuals or groups are engaged in conflicts continuously. Conflict must be resolved as early as possible for making life peaceful and worth living. The conflicting parties arrange for alternatives to conflict to bring about termination of hostilities or conflicting relationships and to enable some form of co-operation. The cessation of hostilities usually occurs by means of two social processes of interaction—*accommodation* and *assimilation*.

The term 'accommodation' is derived from experimental psychology, where it denotes how individuals modify their activity to fit the requirements of external social world. Although accommodation has its origin in conflict situation, still it is radically different type of interaction. In a conflict situation there are always forces operating to its cessation because conflict does not continue indefinitely. The forces making for peace, as those making for war, are continuously operative. The transition from a state of war to a condition of peace may come in numerous ways. After sometime conflicting parties come to certain terms. This state is known as *accommodation*.

Accommodation is a form of social interaction in which we get used to the factors that are likely to lead to conflict either by force of habit, or sheer inertia, or a desire to 'live and let live'. It simply means adjusting oneself to the new environment. For adjustment (physical or social), one has to adopt new ways of behaving. In this process of adjustment, persons are required to take a sequence of steps by which they are reconciled to changed conditions of life through the formation of habits and attitudes made necessary by the changed conditions themselves. It involves conscious and tentative forms of subordination and superordination. Now, we will cite some definitions of the prominent sociologists.

According to Gillin and Gillin (1948), 'accommodation is the term used by sociologists to describe a process by which competing and conflicting individuals and groups adjust their relationships to each other in order to overcome the difficulties which arise in competition, contravention or conflict'.

Famous American psychologist J.M. Baldwin notes: 'Accommodation denotes acquired changes in the behaviour of individuals which enable them to adjust to their environment.'

According to Park and Burgess (1921) observe: 'Accommodation is a natural issue of conflicts. In an accommodation, the antagonism of the hostile elements is temporarily regulated and conflict disappears as an overt action. Even though it remains latent and may become active again with a change in the situation.'

Accommodation is 'a process of developing temporary working agreements between conflicting individuals' (Horton and Hunt, 1964).

Accommodation refers to 'a permanent or temporary termination of rivalrous parties to function together without open hostility at least in some respects' (Cuber, 1968).

'Accommodation is a term used by the sociologists to describe the adjustment of hostile individuals or groups' (Ogburn and Nimkoff, 1958).

Nature

Accommodation is both a condition and a process. As a *condition,* accommodation is the recognition and acceptance of a set of relationships that define the status of a person in the group or of the group in a more inclusive social organization. The state of accommodation does not represent a state of complete harmony. It is rather an acceptance of conditions in order to avoid or terminate conflict. In reality, this state represents the fact of equilibrium between individuals and groups. Conflict, out of which accommodation directly or indirectly arises, does not entirely disappear in accommodation. It continues to exist as a kind of potential opposition. In some cases, conflict appears in a disguised or sublimated form. Indifference, reticence and cynicism are some of the forms of accommodation. As a *process,* it refers to the adjustment by means of which overt conflict is resolved and competition restrained within fixed limits. The glaring example is the adjustment between husband and wife that enables each to realize personal wishes in a measure and with a minimum of friction and to carry on a tolerable common life. The person, who undergoes to a new social situation, has to develop new habits and interests in accordance with the new situation and his/her accommodation to it is then underway. The example of Indian bride is the most appropriate example to cite here. In order to accommodate herself in the family of her husband, she has to make many adjustments. For adjustment, conscious efforts are made by persons to develop working arrangements among themselves and try to make their relations more tolerable.

Characteristics

From the above description, we may sum up the characteristics of accommodation as follows:

1. It is the natural result of conflict (Park and Burgess, 1921). Even if conflict disappears as an overt action, it remains latent as a potential.
2. It is a universal process.
3. It is a continuous process. It changes with the changing environment.
4. It is a state in which the attitudes of love and hate coexist (Ogburn and Nimkoff, 1958).
5. It is generally a subconscious process.
6. It is an agreement to disagree (Jones, 1949).
7. It involves changes in habits, attitudes, patterns of behaviour, techniques, institutions and traditions, etc., according to the changed conditions of life.

Forms/Methods

Accommodation takes a number of forms. Some are deliberately planned, others arise as unplanned products of group interaction. It may be brought in many different ways. The more important of these are described below:

Coercion

Coercion means the use of force or the threat of force to terminate a conflict. It usually involves parties of unequal strength, the weaker party yields and submit itself to the wishes of the stronger group, because of the fear of being overpowered. This happens only when the parties are so unequal in power that resistance seems useless or impossible.

Compromise

Compromise is the adjustment of the opposed wishes of people in which each contender gives up part of his demands. When all the parties are of equal strength or powerful enough so that none of them want conflict, they may compromise their differences. It involves a limited surrender by all groups in order to end or avoid conflict. In compromise, each party agrees to make some concessions and yields to some demands of other in order to reach an agreement. In this type of accommodation the spirit of 'give and take' prevails. Politics may be seen as a continual round of shifting power positions and changing compromises. Illustrations of compromise in labour-management disputes are numerous. Family differences are often settled through compromise. Compromise is rarely an ideal solution because it does not last long.

Arbitration and conciliation

The techniques of arbitration, mediation and conciliation are generally used in arranging compromises. These involve the third party to bring about an end of the conflict between contending parties. Such techniques are often helpful in breaking deadlocks of hostile relations. The labour-management conflicts usually are resolved through the intervention of an arbitrator or a mediator. The UNO frequently serves in the role of arbitrator at an international level. The great difficulty with arbitration is the securing of a mediator who has the confidence of both sides in the controversy.

Arbitration differs from mediation in that a definite decision is handed down by the arbitrators and the decision is regarded as binding. In the mediation, the suggestions made by the mediator have no binding force.

Toleration

Where compromise is unacceptable yet agreement not absolutely necessary, people or groups may use toleration as an alternative to conflict. In this form of accommodation, interacting parties may agree to disagree. People accept each other's right to differ without demanding settlement. Each party holds its position, but respects the fact that the other party has an opposing viewpoint. Religious conflict, such as the demolition of Babri Masjid, is a classic example of this situation. Both parties to this issue 'tolerate' each other, despite the fact that the basic issue is not eliminated.

Conversion

In this form of accommodation, one of the acting parties accepts and adopts the views of the other on the ground that it has been wrong and its opponent is right. Conversion is frequently related to religious beliefs but it may also occur in politics and other fields.

Rationalization

Accommodation through rationalization involves plausible excuses or explanations for one's behaviour instead of acknowledging the real defect in one's own self. Recently, the American government has justified its attack on Iraq on the ground that Iraq has nuclear weapons.

Superordination and subordination

The fundamental pattern of accommodation is of reciprocal superiority (superordination) and subordination. The whole web of relationships between two persons is commonly complex series of subordinations in which one or the other is subordinated according to the character of the situation in which they are jointly involved. For example, in legal matters, the physician is subordinate to the lawyer whereas in medical matters the lawyer assumes the subordinate role. The organization of all societies is essentially the result of such a type of accommodation. From family to larger groupings (political, economic or religious), we can see such types of relationships.

Accommodation by subordination is effective under two conditions. The first is that the dominant party should be so strong as to force the other to submit. The second condition under which subordination as a form of accommodation may be successful is that relationships of subordination should be socially sanctioned as a part of the social structure and heritage of society. The hierarchical structure of military organization, with the clearly defined superior and subordinate ranks or the familial relationships between parents and children, are good examples of such type of accommodation.

Truce

A truce is an agreement to cease rivalrous interaction for a definite or indefinite period of time. The purpose is usually to give both parties time to review the issue in the light of proposals or suggestions for settlement. This form of accommodation is temporary, usually giving way to a more permanent form.

Displacement

Displacement involves termination of one conflict by replacing it with another. Use of a 'scapegoat' is a displacement technique; the problem of a group (a nation or a village) may be blamed on an individual or on a minority or on imperialists, etc.

Institutionalized means

The structure of various societies may provide institutionalized means for release of tensions. They work as safety valves for resolving of hostility. These means may provide us a form of accommodation in bringing about termination of antagonistic relationships. Community sports, wrestling and other tournaments (cricket matches between India and Pakistan), special feast days, religious and other festivals are its few examples.

Accommodation and Adaptation

Accommodation is to be differentiated from adaptation although both are forms of adjustment. Whereas 'adaptation' may be defined as structural change in the organism which takes place through biological variation and selection, the term 'accommodation' is reserved for functional changes in the habits and customs of persons and group changes which are transmitted socially rather than biologically.

Adaptation is a biological concept whereas accommodation is a social phenomenon. Accommodation is an outcome of conflict, while the adaptation is a natural issue of competition. Adaptation is an end-result in the process of biological evolution. It refers to the biological process of selection which operates through a series of generations and tends to produce organic forces better and better fitted to their environing circumstances. As a condition, it refers to the biological state of a species. Accommodation is not a selective process and involves no change in the organic type. It is a learning process that fits the person to the environing social conditions by way of changes in habits, sentiments and ideas. As a process, accommodation is a mode of transition from one prior condition, usually one of conflict, to another. It involves a sequence of steps by which persons are reconciled to the changed conditions of life.

The distinction between accommodation and adaptation is well illustrated by Park and Burgess (1921) in the difference between domestication and training. Domestication is a specific type of adaptation. It is a matter of selection, through generations, of variants and the gradual production of a new biological form. Training, on the other hand, is a specific form of accommodation. The tamed animal acquires a set of habits that allows it to live in association with man, it undergoes no organic change in so doing.

Thus, accommodation is one of the familiar and commonplace facts of everyday life. The situation into which a child is born is never one that satisfies the wishes of his original nature. He/she has to accept the arrangements that characterize the particular group and culture. Such accommodations are a part of the social heritage. They are accepted without question by the persons born and reared in the society. All through the life, the process of accommodation goes on, changing the person to the changing surroundings. It involves changes in habits, attitudes, patterns of behaviour, techniques, institutions and traditions, etc., according to changed conditions of life.

Society can hardly go on without accommodation. It checks conflicts and brings unity between opposing elements. Our society is by and large a complex of competing interests. It is also a fact that the competing individuals or groups are not always having equal power and resources. One may dominate and the result is conflict at many a time. It may be harmful to both the opposing parties if the conflict is not checked and hence accommodation comes to play. Besides, accommodation creates a background for another social process, namely, assimilation.

Assimilation

A term synonymous with acculturation, used to describe the process by which an outsider, immigrant, or subordinate group becomes indistinguishably integrated into the dominant host society (*Oxford Dictionary of Sociology*, 1994). Acculturation, on the other hand, is a process whereby a group (usually ethnic group) loses its cultural distinctiveness and acquires the language, religion and other cultural attributes of another group. It modifies cultures, without a complete blending of the two cultures. Acculturation, therefore, implies modification but not complete assimilation. Assimilation is also different from accommodation whereby the subordinate group simply conformed to the expectations of the dominant group. Assimilation implies that the subordinate group actually came to accept and internalise the values and culture of the group. In accommodation, the mental distance and 'inactive intolerance' continue. In assimilation, the psychological distance is completely overcome and perfect identity of shared experiences is a precondition. Accommodation is a first step to assimilation. Assimilation is also different from the analogous process of amalgamation, which is a biological phenomenon. It is a process of cross-breeding to the production of hybrid offspring and the blending of racial stocks through intermarriage and intermating. Assimilation, on the other hand, is a cultural, social and psychological phenomenon. On one hand, it involves the fusion of cultural heritages, and on the other hand, the modification of sentiments and attitudes and the gradual incorporation of the strangers into the cultural group. The two processes are thus quite different from each other. One is biological, the other is sociological; one is a fusion of cultures, the other is a blending of racial stocks. Like socialization, accommodation is also a process of learning.

According to Park and Burgess (1921), 'assimilation is a process of interpenetration and fusion in which persons and groups acquire the memories, sentiments, attitudes of other persons or groups and by sharing their experiences and history are incorporated with them in a cultural life'.

Ogburn and Nimkoff (1958) write: 'Assimilation is the process whereby individuals or groups once dissimilar become similar, i.e., become identified in their interests and outlooks.'

Horton and Hunt (1964) defined it as 'the process of mutual cultural diffusion through which persons and groups become culturally alike'.

According to Schaefer and Lamm (1992), 'assimilation is the process by which a person forsakes his or her own cultural tradition to become part of a different culture'.

Summarizing the above views, it may be said that assimilation is a process of fusion or blending, whereby cultural differences tend to disappear and individuals and groups once dissimilar become similar. It results in the modification of attitudes, values, patterns of thinking and ultimately behaviour. Husbands and wives, after marriage with dissimilar backgrounds, often develop a surprising unity of interest and purpose. In the long run, they become more or less similar in their attitude toward life and family.

Nature

Assimilation takes place slowly, and to a considerable extent without conscious effort and direction. The speed of the process of assimilation depends upon the nature of contacts. If the contacts are primary, assimilation occurs naturally and rapidly but if they are secondary, i.e., indirect and superficial, the result is accommodation and not assimilation. It takes quite sometime before individuals or groups dissimilar become similar, i.e., become identified in their interests and outlook. Children are gradually assimilated into adult society as they grow up and learn how to behave. Assimilation occurs through the mechanisms of imitation and suggestion.

Assimilation is a matter of degree. Complete assimilation of an individual into a culture takes considerable time and is seldom if ever achieved within his lifetime. Such a person exhibits behaviour that reflects elements of both cultures. He has been labelled as a 'marginal man'. In large society, complete assimilation is perhaps hypothetical.

Assimilation is a two-way process when it happens between two cultural groups, each group contributing varying proportions of the eventual blend. The alien group not only contributes to the host culture but retains many of their own ways. As a result, there is *cultural pluralism* which may reflect incomplete assimilation. Should the minority group be forced to assimilate the culture of the majority group is a very controversial question.

Levels

The process of assimilation takes place mainly at three levels: (i) individual, (ii) group, and (iii) culture.

Individual level

A socialized individual when enters or joins a new group having different cultural patterns, he or she has to adopt new patterns of values, habits, customs and beliefs of the other group in order to be fully accepted by the new group. In course of time, he or she becomes assimilated into the second group. For example, as mentioned above, an Indian woman after marriage starts with dissimilar backgrounds and develops a surprising unity of interests and identifies herself with the family of her husband. The tendency is to conform to other's behavioural pattern and differences in time may largely disappear.

Group level

When two groups with dissimilar patterns of behaviour come in close contact, they inevitably affect each other. In this process, it is generally seen that the weaker group would do more of the borrowing from and would give very little to the stronger group. For instance, when we came into contact with Britishers, being a weaker group, we have adopted many cultural elements of them but they have adopted a very few such elements from Indian society. The adoption of elements of dominant culture paves the way for total absorption, if not checked, of the new cultural group with the dominant culture. Similarly, immigrants in America or Britain usually adopt the material traits (dress pattern, food habits, etc.) easily in order to adjust themselves in the new cultural environment.

Culture level

When two cultures merge to produce a third culture which, while somewhat distinct, has features of both merging cultures. In western countries chiefly but also in developing countries to some extent, rural and urban cultures which were radically different are, with rapidly increasing communication, merging as differences continue to disappear although they still exist.

Types

Two types of assimilation have been identified: cultural assimilation and structural assimilation.

Cultural assimilation

Assimilation, as said above, is a two-way process: persons (such as immigrants) must want to be assimilated and the host society must be willing to have them assimilate. The immigrant must undergo cultural assimilation, learning the day-to-day norms of the dominant culture pertaining to dress, language, food, recreation, games and sports. This process also involves internalizing the more critical aspects of culture such as values, ideas, beliefs and attitudes.

Structural assimilation

It involves developing patterns of intimate contact between the 'guest' and 'host' groups in clubs, organizations and institutions of the host society. Cultural assimilation generally precedes structural assimilation, although the two sometimes happen simultaneously.

Conducive Factors

Factors that contribute or aid to assimilation are:

1. *Tolerance:* Without the attitude of tolerance, assimilation is not possible. Tolerance requires the feeling of sacrifice and elimination of strong prejudices. It is a democratic virtue which fosters sympathy.
2. *Intimacy:* Frequent close social contacts and communication are a prerequisite for the start of assimilative process. Intimacy dissolves the walls of ultra-individualism which separates man from man.
3. *Cultural homogeneity:* Culturally homogenous groups easily assimilate the values and goals of one another. Mutual similarity creates mutual affinities which bring two individuals or groups nearer to each other.

4. *Equal economic opportunity:* Equal economic opportunities are required to fill the gap of disparity in wealth. It implies that any increase in the availability of opportunities or equality in their distribution would create conditions favourable to the growth of assimilative process.
5. *Association:* Various associations, clubs, and other places of public meetings help in the assimilative process. When people live in the same vicinity, meet and come together, there is every possibility of the start of the process of assimilation.
6. *Amalgamation or intermarriage:* Amalgamation, though a biological process of cross-breeding, helps in cultural assimilation. Through intermarriages members of different racial stocks come together and adopt the cultural traits of other group.

Hindrances

There are also certain factors which retard or hinder the process of assimilation. Some of these are:

1. *Cultural dissimilarity:* Extreme differences in cultural background act as the most powerful impediment in the way of assimilation. Language and religion are usually considered to be the main constituents of culture. Same religion and language often help in early and speedy assimilative process. Customs and beliefs are other cultural characteristics, which can aid or hinder assimilation. When two cultures (or groups) share many common elements, assimilation is accelerated; the absence of such factors acts as a barrier to the process.
2. *Physical differences:* Differences in physical traits and skin colour present a formidable barrier to assimilation. This we can see between white and Negro (black) races in which discrimination is practised almost everywhere in the world. Physical differences are extremely visible and can be eliminated only by generations of intermarriage between cultural groups concerned.
3. *Feeling of superiority and inferiority:* Such feeling, along with the exploitation of the weaker section (minority group) of the population by stronger one, is contradictory to the assimilative process.
4. *Prejudices:* Stereotypes and ethnocentrism both can operate as barriers to assimilation. Prejudices (prejudgement) may create a social distance between the alien and dominant cultures.
5. *Isolation:* The absence of communicative interaction is isolation. It is a situation deprived of social contacts. Isolation signifies detached position or the act or process of attaining a detached position. It may be spatial separation or organic.

Importance

Thus, assimilation is a process of mutual interchange or diffusion of culture through which persons and groups come to share a common culture. It is a process of decreasing differentiation and increasing unification among people. It reduces group conflict by blending differing groups into larger, culturally homogenous groups. Anything which binds people into a larger group will tend to reduce rivalry and conflict between them. A study by Sherif and Sherif (1953) shows that even there are no real differences or issues to fight over, conflict still tends to develop wherever separate group identity is recognized. Assimilation removes some but not all possible pressures toward conflict.

The importance of assimilation rests primarily in its elimination of boundary lines as two groups, formerly distinct, assume a common identity. Boundaries help in developing 'in' and 'out' group feelings or the feeling of *ethnocentrism* (the attitude that one's own culture is superior to others, that one's own beliefs, values and behaviour are more correct than others). Boundary determination is accomplished through various means such as separate unions, using some distinctive marks (*tilak* on the forehead by Hindu males and red *bindi* and vermilion by Hindu females), dress pattern, special type of hair and beard, initiation ceremonies, etc. To lessen the effect of boundaries, systematic linkage is suggested. Systematic linkage is a process by which groups avoid isolation while maintaining their separate identities.

Integration

Integration, literally, means to make up whole out of parts. It presupposes diversities and the idea is to bind the parts together. Ogburn and Nimkoff (1958) observed: 'Integration is a process of creating a single unit by joining different parts.' In other words, integration is a process of establishing unity between the constituent parts of a structure which though different have organization in their relationships. The different parts of this structure are so systematically related to each other that the emerging whole becomes greater than the sum of parts. Thus, integration is more than collection of parts. In this connection, Gillin and Gillin (1948) aptly remarked: 'Integration is organization, rather than homogeneity.' It does not preclude differences between different parts altogether.

When we apply this view to society, it only means that different constituent groups that make the society, do not lose their identity. It is thus different from the concept of assimilation in which different groups (religious, racial or ethnic) submerge their identity to make a homogenous society. In assimilation, a person forsakes his or her own cultural traditions and forget his/her own history to become part of a different culture.

Integration should not be confused with 'homogeneity' through the process of assimilation. There is a difference between the three processes, viz., acculturation, assimilation and integration. *Acculturation* acquires and modifies the culture of a group through contact with one or more other cultures. *Assimilation* is a process in which one group (small) takes over the culture and identity of another (larger) group. It is a one-way process, whereas acculturation is a two-way process in which both the cultures come in contact taking something from the other. Assimilation involves merging of one group (subordinate) into the other (dominant) group. On the other hand, in *integration,* complete elimination of differences is not sought for. Different groups can keep their identity intact while adjusting with other groups. The main aim of integration is to maintain a harmonious and active relationship between different social and cultural groups or various structural components of society.

Assimilation is a higher social process of integration. This is a stage which is very difficult to obtain. At this stage different component parts (cultural traits) of a social and cultural system lose their identity. This is a very complex process and hardly any society reaches the stage of total assimilation.

Methods

How various elements of society are held together, and how they integrate with each other. The following are two methods of integration:

1. Assimilationist approach
2. Integrationist approach

The first method is commonly known as the assimilationist approach. According to this, all groups (religious, racial, linguistic or ethnic) should conform in major public to what they take to be the established way of life (Indian or British or American way of life). They do not believe in multiculturalism or pluralism. Assimilationists consider that minority groups (generally immigrants) should adopt themselves to the dominant culture of the society. There are people who even insist on assimilation in the area of public life and personal taste. Such people in cricket game expect that a true 'Indian' person would support the Indian team rather than say, the Pakistan team. This view tries to strike at the very roots of a person's identity as he or she seeks to gain full acceptance as an 'Indian' or 'American' or 'Britisher'.

The other method, generally known as the integrationist approach, emphasizes pluralist or liberal-pluralist view. According to this view, a variety of cultural groups can and do exist in a society (say, Indian society) within a common legal and democratic framework. In cultural pluralism, various groups maintain their distinctive cultural patterns, sub-systems and institutions. Whereas an assimilationist seeks to eliminate ethnic or racial boundaries, pluralist (integrationist) wants to retain them. Pluralists argue that groups can co-exist by accepting their differences. However, basic to cultural pluralism are beliefs that individuals never forget or escape their social origin, that all groups bring positive contributions that enrich the larger society, and that groups have the right to be different but equal. Cultural pluralism may be expressed with the formula:

A + B + C = a + b + c

The alphabets ABC represent various groups while their distinctive cultural patterns, institutions, etc., are represented by abc.

We can designate these two views as 'Indo-conformity' process and 'melting pot' process. Melting pot process represents the integrationist view in which each group contributes a bit of its own culture and absorbs aspects of other cultures such that the whole is a combination of all groups. Indo-conformity process is equated with 'Indianization', whereby the minority loses its identity completely to the dominant (Hindu) culture. After independence, integrationist policy has been adopted in India. Integration comes about when feeling of different race, religion, ethnicity, caste, etc., becomes insignificant and everyone can freely and fully participate in the social, economic and political mainstream.

Education serves the latent function of promoting social and political integration by transforming a population composed of diverse racial, ethnic, caste, and religious groups into a society whose members share—to some extent—at least a common identity (Touraine, 1974). From a functionalist perspective, the common identity and social integration fostered by education contribute to societal stability and consensus.

Social planning is the most effective method of achieving integration in a complex and rapidly changing society like India. For this purpose, programmes of social planning are to be launched. The avowed objective of all social planning is welfare and establishing harmony and unity in the society.

Multi-cultural societies like India maintain separate identities and try to keep multi-ethnicities, multi-languages, multi-religions, and multi-identities intact. In such societies, integration can be achieved only in a limited way as we see in our country. To attain integration in such societies, the old principle of 'live and let live' is to be followed.

Conflict

Georg Simmel (1955) writes: 'There probably exists no social unit in which convergent and divergent currents among its members are not inseparably interwoven. An absolutely centripetal and harmonious group, a pure 'unification', not only is unreal, it could should have no real life process ... society, too, in order to attain a determinate shape, needs some quantitative ratio of harmony and disharmony, of association and competition, of favourable and unfavourable tendencies.' In simple words, social conflict is always present in social life. It is a fundamental feature of human society. It does not occur because people are unreasonable or unco-operative or because they are unwilling to live properly and decently with others. It is rooted in social differences of class and status, of wealth and opportunity, of material interests, where scarce resources are unequally shared. Psychologists regard conflict as an instinctual response in humans, in the face of stressful situations. This response can be in the form of (1) fight, (2) flee, (3) simply freeze, or (4) turning sideways into the conflict.

It is said that human beings are for the most part quite selfish and that chaos and strife are both common and natural. This is why, conflict is the fundamental form of disassociative interaction or oppositional-oriented relationship. It is inherent in all social relationships and is also inevitable and universal. Bottomore (1962) observed: 'Conflict is an intrinsic part of our social life, sustaining, modifying or destroying the social groups in which it takes place.' Whenever and wherever there is a difference in the motives and interests (desire for prestige, economic benefit, power and defeat or destruction of the enemy) of different persons, there is bound to be some kind of conflict. It may be destructively or constructively directed. It may be between individuals, groups of individuals or two societies (or nations) depending whether the contradictory interests involved are personal or of group or of the whole community or nation. Thus, merely to deplore that it is destructive, it is to miss its significance as a force for social change.

Definitions

An analysis of the literature reveals that the term 'conflict' is defined in a number of ways. Followers of Georg Simmel, like R.E. Park, have seen conflict as one of the central forms of interaction. Simmel (1955) writes: 'If every interaction among men is a sociation, conflict must certainly be considered as sociation.' Park and Burgess (1921), likewise, treat conflict as a distinct form of competition. They wrote: 'Both are forms of interaction but competition is a struggle between individuals or groups of individuals who are not necessarily in contact and communication while conflict is a contest in which contact is an indispensable condition.'

According to Max Weber (1968), 'a social relationship will be referred to as *conflict* in so far as action within it is oriented intentional to carrying out the actor's own will against the resistence of the other party or parties'. Thus, the social interaction of conflict is defined by the desire of each participant to impose his will upon the other's resistence. These sentiments are well echoed in the words of A.W. Green (1956) who defined it as 'the deliberate attempt to oppose, resist or coerce the will of another or others'. As a process, it is the antithesis of cooperation in which a deliberate attempt is made to thwart the will of others. Gillin and Gillin (1948) wrote: 'Conflict is the social process in which individuals or groups seek their ends by directly challenging the antagonist by violence or threat of violence.' To sum up, it may be said that conflict refers to the struggle in which competing parties, attempting to reach a goal, strive to eliminate an opponent by making the other party ineffectual or by annihilation.

Characteristics

On the basis of foregoing discussion, the following characteristics (nature) of conflict, in brief, may be cited:

1. It is a *universal* process found in every society.
2. It is the result of *deliberate and conscious* efforts of individuals or the groups.
3. The nature of the conflict is *personal and direct.* In conflict the incumbents or participants know each other personally.
4. It is basically an *individual's* process. Its aim is not directly connected with the achievement of the goal or an objective but is rather directed to dominate others or to eliminate the opponent.
5. Conflict is of brief duration, temporary and *intermittent* in character. But, once begun, the conflict process is hard to stop. It tends to grow more and more bitter as it proceeds. Being temporary, it gives way to some form of accommodation.
6. It is a process loaded with *impulsiveness* of human emotions and violent passions. It gains force and then bursts open. Unlike fighting of animals, generally in human groups, the spontaneous fighting is inhibited. It is often avoided through the process of accommodation and assimilation.
7. It may be *latent or overt.* In the latent form, it may exist in the form of tension, dissatisfaction, contravention and rivalry. It becomes overt when an issue is declared and a hostile action is taken.
8. It is *mostly violent* but it may take the form of negotiations, party politics, disputes or rivalry.
9. It is *cumulative;* each act of aggression usually promotes a more aggressive rebuttal. Thus, termination of conflict is not easy.
10. It tends to be *more intense* when individuals and groups who have close relationships with one another are involved.
11. Groups previously in conflict may co-operate to achieve a goal considered important enough for them to unite despite their differences.
12. It may emerge as a result of opposing interests. It is layered in a history of binary perceptions: exile/homeland, outsider/insider, us/them, patriotic/unpatriotic.
13. It has both disintegrative and integrative effects. It disrupts unity in a society and is a disturbing way of setting issues. A certain account of internal conflict, however, may serve indirectly to stimulate group interaction. External conflict can have positive effects by unifying the group.

Conflict and Contravention

Contravention is the mild form of conflict in which contending parties (groups or individuals) strive to prevent each other from achieving the objective through indirect attacks on the opposite party. It does contain antagonism and hostility like conflict. The establishment and fostering to temporary political parties during national elections with the express purpose of dispersing votes and confusing the electorate is an illustration of contravention.

Forms

Conflict can be distinguished in so many ways. It may take place between persons or individuals and groups. Conflict between persons is the most direct and immediate form of conflict. It may involve intense personal animosities. It may take the form of a brute struggle on the physical level to destroy or eliminate the opponent. Personal conflicts arise on account of various motives—envy, hostility, betrayal of trust being the most predominant. In all societies there are at least two forms of conflict. First, there is conflict between men contending for positions of power. Second, there is conflict between the powerful and the powerless.

Group or corporate conflict

It takes place between two societies or groups within a society. When group loyalties and needs take precedence over personal individual feelings, it is group conflict. In such conflict, individual feelings become irrelevant. Groups attempt to impose their will on other groups in order to gain power, prestige, wealth and commodities of value. Such conflict is impersonal. Communal or race riots, religious persecution, labour-management disputes, and wars between two or more nations are some of the examples of corporate or group conflict.

Greek philosopher Heracltitus once said: 'All is incessantly changing and war is the father of all things.' War is the most characteristic and spectacular form of group conflict. In the first instance, it grows out of a clash of interests such as to destroy or weaken the competitor group, to snatch the land or to steal the women or the property. Primitive warfare was often operated selectively between the occupying peoples and the invading hordes. In later years, culture development over population has often been at the base of national conflict, although the direct and inciting causes often seem for removed.

Simmel (1955) has distinguished four types of conflict: (i) war; (ii) feud or fictional strife; (iii) litigation; and (iv) conflict of impersonal ideals. Simmel attributed war to a deep-seated antagonistic impulse in man. For him, antagonistic impulse is a foundation of all conflicts. Feud is an intra-group form of war which may arise because of injustice alleged to have been done by one group to the other. Litigation is a judicial form of conflict when an individual or group asserts its claims to certain rights on the basis of objective factors. Conflict of impersonal ideals is a conflict carried on by the individuals not for themselves but for an ideal. In such a conflict, each party attempts to justify truthfulness of its own ideals.

Direct and indirect conflict

Direct conflict occurs where individuals or groups thwart or impede or restrain or injure or destroy one another in the effort to attain the goal. Indirect conflict occurs where individuals or groups do not actually impede the efforts of one another but nevertheless try to attain their ends in ways which obstruct the attainment of the same end by others.

Gillin and Gillin (1948) have classified conflict in five groups: (i) personal conflict, (ii) racial conflict, (iii) class conflict, (iv) political conflict, and (v) international conflict.

Causes

Earlier scientists like Charles Darwin saw conflict as inherent in the principles of struggle for existence and survival of the fittest, while for Thomas Malthus, the champion of population theory, reduced supply of the means of subsistence is the cause of conflict. Some sociologists like Gustav Ratzenhofer and Ludwig Gumplowicz regard it as underlying social evolution and progress. According to Ratzenhofer, the struggle for life takes the form of conflict in interests. For Gumplowicz, it represents a primordial feeling of 'syngenism'—a feeling of belonging together. There are two main approaches which have analysed the causes of conflict in their own way:

1. *Psychological approach:* This approach tries to look for the causes of conflict in human nature and posits a 'fighting instinct'. This is exemplified in the views of Simmel, Freud and Lorenz. According to Freud, there is an innate instinct for aggression in man which is responsible for conflict in human society. Recent biological and anthropological studies have generally supported the notion that there is an 'aggressive instinct', resulting from natural selection. This theory has been criticized on various grounds. It is said that the theory which depends upon a permanent and constant aggressive instinct cannot explain the cycle of conflict and absence of conflict. It only explains the propensity to engage in aggressive behaviour.
2. *Sociological approach:* This approach is based on a theory of interests, i.e., conflict occurs, for example, when territory is invaded or property is looted or attacked. This approach has its roots in the Marxist tradition. This tradition assumes that social life is shaped by groups and

individuals who struggle or compete with one another over various resources and rewards. These shape not only the patterns of everyday life and interaction, but also large patterns such as racial, ethnic and class-caste relations. Marx argues that most conflict is economic and rests on the unequal ownership and control of property.

There are many other causes of conflict, which may be briefly stated as under:

1. *Individual differences:* No two men are alike in their nature, attitudes, ideals, opinions and interests. These differences lead them to some or the other sort of conflict to fulfil their individual interest. Because of these differences, they fail to accommodate themselves with each other.
2. *Cultural differences:* Culture differs from society to society and also from group to group. These differences sometimes cause tension and lead to conflict. The religious differences have often led to wars and persecution in history. In India, often, communal conflicts broke out as the results of religious differences.
3. *Clash of interests:* The interests of different people or groups (such as political parties) occasionally clash. For example, the interests of workers clash with those of the employers which leads to conflict in the form of strike, *bandh* or *dharana*, etc., among them.
4. *Social change*: All parts of society do not change with the same speed. This causes 'lag' in the parts which may cause conflict between different parts of the society. Conflict of generations (parent-youth) is the result of such social changes.

Types of Social Conflicts

In the struggle to change the structure of society, or to resist such a change, conflict takes various shapes. Some common types of social conflicts are:

1. *Social movement:* A strong sense of unjust suffering readily provides the rationale for a social movement, such as Gujjars' *Andolan* (2007 and 2008) for reservation in ST category in Rajasthan or *Namak Andolan* of Gandhiji.
2. *Riots and rebellions:* Riot is a situation in which a large crowd of people behave in a violent and uncontrolled manner, especially when they protest about something. Rebellion is an organized attempt to change the government/leader of a country using violent methods.
3. *Civil politics:* In modern democratic societies there is an effort to bring conflict into the political institution, to get people to work 'inside' the system instead of 'outside'. It is a principle of liberal politics that all classes and groups should have access to the political process and be encouraged to pursue their goals through conventional political means.

4. *Revolution:* A revolution is the ultimate form of struggle against the prevailing social structure, in which the intent is to alter the society's institutions and create a whole new social order based on a radically different set of principles. It is a sweeping, sudden and comprehensive change in the basic practices and ideas of an institution or society.

Nature of Conflict in India

In India, the following main forms of conflict are found:

1. Communal conflict (communalism)
2. Caste conflict (casteism)
3. Regional conflict (regionalism)
4. Rural-urban conflict
5. Class conflict
6. Value conflict
7. Inter-group conflict
8. Inter-generation conflict
9. Reservation conflict
10. Gender conflict

Role (Functions) of Conflict

Conflict has always captured the attention of people and the society. As other forms of social interaction, it has both positive and negative effects. Conflict both terminates and commences to serve the interests of man in society. Cooley (1902) maintained: 'Conflict of some sort is the life of society, and progress emerges from a struggle in which each individual, class or institution seeks to realise its own ideals of good.' Simmel (1955) observed that a conflict-free harmonious group is practically an impossibility. There is no denying the fact that society requires for its formation and growth both harmony and disharmony, association and disassociation. Sorel (1908) felt that a social system was in need of conflict only to renew its energies and revitalize its creative forces. His arguments that violent confrontations can be noble and civilizing and that there is nothing to suggest civilized men and women will ever wholly renounce violence to advance estimable causes. Young and Mack (1959) write: 'At its most rudimentary level, conflicts result in the elimination or annihilation of the opponent. In human society, however, most conflicts end in some sort of agreement or accommodation or in the fusion of the two opposing elements.' It is said that the origins of the state, social organization and many social institutions are the result of war and struggle.

Generally, conflict is regarded as disintegrative and its dysfunctions are highlighted but conflict plays constructive role also and it has positive functions for the individual and society both. For instance, inter-group conflict is a patent source of inter-group co-operation. It helps in unifying a society or a group when some external aggression occurs. Conflict prevents the ossification of the social system by exerting pressure for innovation and creativity. Horton and Hunt (1964) have distinguished the effects of conflict as under:

Integrative effects	*Disintegrative effects*
Define issues.	Increases bitterness.
Leads to resolution of issues.	Leads to destruction and bloodshed.
Increases group cohesion.	Leads to inter-group tension.
Leads to alliance with other groups.	Disrupts normal channels of cooperation.
Keeps groups alert to members' interests.	Diverts members' attention from group objectives.

As a form of interaction, sociologically significant both from the point of view of personality (individual level) and from that of social organization, both self-consciousness and group consciousness are the result of conflict. At the individual level, every problem in the life of a person is a conflict (struggle). Conflict plays a corresponding role in group organization. Groups reach the maximum of unity and solidarity in overt conflict. External conflict (conflict with another group) tends to integrate the group. On the one hand, it provides the members with an external outlet for their hostilities and resentments and thus removes a lot of internal tensions. On the other hand, it compels each member to co-operate and forge unity to face the external threat. While external conflict separates a group from its enemies, it also promotes alliances with other groups. Simmel (1955) writes: 'A state of conflict pulls the members so tightly together and subjects them to such a uniform impulse that the most completely get along with or completely repel one another.' Coser (1956) has also analysed in detail the role of conflict in promoting unity. Thus, the above discussion about the role (functions) of conflict may be summed up as under:

1. Conflict determines the status of the individual in the social organization. Rivalry, war and other forms of personal struggle determine superiority and subordination of men and groups.
2. Conflict is not always an unmitigated evil everywhere as it is generally assumed. It is a chief means of group contact, and it has played an important role in the development and spread of culture.
3. Conflict may eventuate in peace through victory of one contestant over others.
4. Conflict helps to define social issues and brings about a new equilibrium of contending forces. It may lead to the working out of non-violent

techniques for resolving crises. The end result of conflict is that the issues are resolved at least for a time.

5. Conflict tends to stiffen the morale, promotes unity and cohesion within the group and may lead to expanding alliances with other groups.
6. Conflict keeps groups alert to members' interests.
7. Conflict generates new norms and new institutions. It happens mostly in economic and technological realms. Economic historians often have pointed out that much technological improvement has resulted from the conflict activity of trade unions. It leads to redefinition of value systems.
8. Conflict within and between bureaucratic structures provides means of avoiding the ossification and ritualism which threatens their form of organization.
9. According to Marxists, conflict leads not only to ever-changing relations within the existing social structure, but the total system undergoes transformation through conflict.
10. Conflict between vested interests and new strata and groups demanding share of power, wealth and status have proved to be productive of vitality.
11. Conflict may lead to a new consensus.
12. Conflict theorists (e.g., Coser, 1956) believe that conflict is necessary for progress. They contend that societies progress to a higher order only if oppressed groups improve their lot.

Dysfunctions of Conflict

Conflicts, as we know, disrupts social unity. It is highly disturbing way of settling issues. Conflict within a group makes it hard for members to agree on group goals or to co-operate in pursuit of them. It often results in group tension. It increases bitterness and leads to destruction and bloodshed. Conflict disrupts normal channels of co-operation. It diverts members' attention from group objectives.

Conflict of Values

The conflict of values is a struggle of a different order and on a different plane from either the personal or the group conflict. It is an aspect of conflict that is purely objective and impersonal. In its simplest manifestation, conflict is merely a physical struggle between individuals or groups. But back of these physical facts is the social and psychological situation, i.e., the clash of interests and attitudes that leads the groups to physical struggles. The wars of nations may arise out of clash of attitudes and values. Value conflict between husband and wife sometimes results into mental stress which eventually may lead to divorce.

The values involved may be material or immaterial realities. Men and nations fight for food and lands and markets but they also fight for sentiments, beliefs and ideals. Some degree of actual or potential conflict between younger and older generations is inevitable in a changing world.

But above and beyond the physical struggles of individuals and groups and apart from the interests and attitudes that motivate or accompany them is the conflict of values. Many of the ideas and ideals prevailing among human beings are opposed and mutually exclusive such as democracy vs aristocracy, privatization vs state ownership, globalization vs nationalism, etc. Evolution and fundamentalism are contradictory interpretation of reality. There is no resolution of conflict between such logically incompatible ideas and beliefs. The only resolution of such a conflict is the disappearance of one or the other from the realm of human values.

Co-operation and Conflict

Society and civilization are the products of human co-operative labour. But, by some strange act of the nature of the things themselves, co-operation and conflict reside side by side, affecting each other and often are placed in position of cause and effect. Both are universal and inescapable elements in social life and they often go together. They sometimes resemble in this respect—the equivalent of linked emotions of love and hate. According to Cooley (1962), conflict and co-operation are not separable but phases of one process which always involves something both. Even in the most intimate marital or friendly relations, there is some point where interests diverge or where attitudes are not in accord.

Co-operation is a condition of conflict. There are many examples of co-operative enterprises in society within which conflict in some form is present. In this connection, MacIver aptly remarked that co-operation crossed by conflict marks society wherever it is revealed. In the co-operative culture of the Zuni tribe of South-West America, in the collectivized economy of *Kibbutzim*, in the formal club, etc., co-operation and conflict both were found side by side. It is difficult to eliminate conflict altogether from society. Though conflict threatens group solidarity, but despite it all conflict cannot be eliminated. Even if open conflict can somehow be eliminated, conflict in its partial or latent form continues to exist.

Competition and Conflict

Competition is a 'peaceful' conflict as argued by Max Weber (1968). He wrote: 'A peaceful conflict is "competition" in so far as it consists in a formally peaceful attempt to attain control over opportunities and advantages which are also desired by others.' Competition describes a conflict over the control of resources or advantages desired by others where physical violence is not employed. Thus, regulated competition is a sort of peaceful conflict, which is resolved within the framework of agreed rules. A competitive process is 'regulated' competition to the extent that its ends and means are oriented to an order.

The difference between conflict and competition lies chiefly in the focus or attention and manner of achieving the goal. In competition, the primary focus is the goal, and interaction is according to culturally defined rules of behaviour and procedure. In conflict, the focus is on the competitor or opponent (not on the goal) themselves with an objective of annihilation or incapacitation of them, so that the way is cleared for achievement of the goal. This distinction can be diagrammatically represented as under:

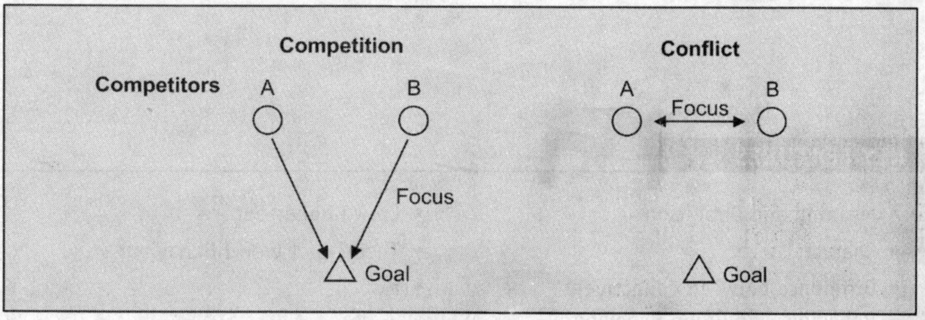

In competition the direct aim is the success of the actor in achieving the goal; indirectly, it may result in the failure of the competition but in conflict the direct result of the action of one person is to impede, prevent or destroy the act of another. For example, a running race is a competition, whereas a bull fight is a conflict. There are other distinctions also between competition and conflict, which may be presented as under:

Competition	*Conflict*
Unconscious process	Conscious process
Impersonal process	Personalized process
Continuous process	Intermittent process for a brief duration
Attention on the goal	Attention on the competitors (opponent) themselves
Non-violent	May involve violence or threat of violence
Regard for norms (rules and regulations of competition)	No regard for any norms

In the end, it may be stated that conflict and competition are sometimes difficult to distinguish, both being forms of rival behaviour. However, the difference in focus, as explained above, of the opposing parties serves as a generally useful guide. When the attention of the competitors is shifted from the goal to the competitors themselves, competition becomes conflict.

Chapter 4

Collective Behaviour

KEY FEATURES

- Meaning and Definition
- Characteristics
- Difference between Collective Behaviour and Group Behaviour
- Forms of Collective Behaviour
- Theories of Collective Behaviour
- Conditions of Collective Behaviour
- Crowd
- Process of Crowd Formation
- Classification of Crowds
- Crowd Behaviour
- Theories of Crowd Behaviour
- Mob
- Audience
- Some Other Forms of Collective Behaviour
- Publics and Public Opinion
- The Crowd and the Public
- Public Opinion

Social life is found practically at all levels of animal life. At the lower levels, however, it is more or less automatic, directed by physico-chemical forces. It is from the insects (ants and bees) level onwards that we find truly social life. Most facets of social life of human beings follow patterns of rules and norms. It is by and large orderly and well-structured. We generally have some type of daily routine and conform to the roles expected of us. There is, however, another dimension of social life in which activities are relatively spontaneous, loosely structured, transitory and uncertain. In sociology, this facet of social life is termed as 'collective behaviour'.

Collective behaviour is crucial for an understanding of human beings as social animals. It is through collective behaviour that one sees masses of people in motion, individuals affecting the group and being affected by it; one also sees some of the forces that contribute to intended and unintended social change. All societies constitute a social order, but there is disorder within the order and collective behaviour is frequently the form that this disorder takes or in which it manifests itself. Sociology is concerned with collective behaviour because it emphasizes on the communal nature of our social existence.

Meaning and Definition

The term 'collective behaviour' is commonly used in a generic or in wide sense to include all the facts and phenomena of associated life (or group life). In literal sense, it would incorporate all behaviours involving more than one person. From this viewpoint, practically, all group activity can be thought of as collective behaviour. But sociologists use this term in a limited sense. They have given distinct meaning to it to mean 'the behaviour of individuals under the impulse that is common and collective ... that is the result of social interaction' (Park and Burgess, 1921). N.J. Smelser (1962), a sociologist who specializes in this field of study, has defined collective behaviour as the 'relatively spontaneous and unstructured behaviour of a group of people who are reacting to a common influence in an ambiguous situation'. Mob, crowd, panics are prime examples of collective behaviour. Publics, lynchings, crazes, fashions, social unrest, social movements, and revolutions are other manifestations of collective behaviour.

Kurt Lang and Gladys Lang (1968) describe collective behaviour as 'the sequences and patterns of interactions that emerge in a problematic situation. They include, as examples, not only crowd behaviour, but also responses to disaster, the disorderly street mob, or the radical and social upheaval to the peaceful and comparatively trivial shifts in the orientations of individuals and small groups that, occurring en masse, can produce major changes in taste, fashion, or public opinion.' To this list, we can add panics, crazes, aggressive outbursts, masses, mass media, mass behaviour, etc.

Thus, collective behaviour is a term that covers too wide a field to encompass the whole of sociology. At one extreme, it includes the study of co-ordinated and organized social movements; at the other, it refers to the spontaneous eruption of any episodic event.

Characteristics

In general parlance, any behaviour that takes place between two or more persons is known as collective behaviour. But sociologists use this term to refer to that social behaviour which exhibits the following characteristics:

1. *Spontaneous and episodic:* Collective behaviour is spontaneous and takes place occasionally rather than regularly and routinely.
2. *Unstable:* It tends to be short-lived as long as the centre of attraction exists. It has no stable goals, values and expectations like institutionalized behaviour.

3. *Unstructured*: It has not set rules or procedures to follow like a regular and routine behaviour. Generally, it is loosely structured.
4. *Unpredictable*: The direction and outcome of such behaviour cannot be foretold.
5. *Irrational:* Usually such behaviour is guided by unreasoning, beliefs, hopes, fears and hatreds. In such situations, decisions are not generally made on the basis of logical or rational discussion.
6. *Emotional*: Sometimes such behaviour is emotional and based on considerable personal interaction.
7. *Non-traditional:* It is non-traditional in the sense that it is not clearly defined according to any culturally established norms and values. In such situations, conventional guidelines and formal authority fail to afford any direction for social action.

Difference Between Collective Behaviour and Group Behaviour

Collective behaviour is not group behaviour as is sometimes understood. The term 'collective behaviour' has been confined to relatively irrational, unplanned, disorganized, volatile activity that contravenes established rules and normative definitions in society. In short, it is the unified behaviour of collectivities that is neither expected nor accepted. Yet, this should not mean that collective behaviour totally lacks organization and random in its formation and direction.

It is contrasted with group behaviour or *institutionalized behaviour*. In the institutionalized group activities, interaction is routine or planned. It is recurrent, more enduring and follows an orderly pattern with a relatively stable set of goals, expectations and values. An example of group behaviour would be interaction within the family or in very formal complex organization or going to class or a temple or commuting on a train. In all these activities, the behaviour is more or less routine and predictable. Although literally the action is collective in the sense that it is shared communally but it is not spontaneous and unstructured activity as we find in collectivities. When people are confronted with an unfamiliar event, such as a highway accident, fire or disaster (train wreck), collective behaviour takes place. In such events people may behave in ways differ radically from their normal conduct because of lack of norms or established rules. The ordinary norms breakdown and are replaced by new ones during such event. People generally leave a cinema hall in a quiet, calm and orderly fashion without pushing and shouting, but if a fire breaks out or some other untoward incident takes place, their conventional behaviour would change. They start screaming, shouting, and may rush for the exists. Not only this, people may resort to rampage and violence.

Forms of Collective Behaviour

Sociologists have examined many forms of collective behaviour. Among these the important ones are crowds, mobs, panics and crazes, fads and fashions, rumours, public and public opinion, and social movements. All these forms of collective behaviour can be grouped into two major types as under:

1. *Spatially proximate collective behaviour:* There are situations in which people are in face-to-face contact (physically visible) or geographically close to one another. Crowds, violent mobs, riots, etc., are best example of this type of collective behaviour in which we find people in close proximity with one another.
2. *Spatially diffuse collective behaviour:* People engaged in collective behaviour may not always collect physically at one place and at a certain time but may be dispersed over a wide geographical area. Such groupings of people are not in close proximity and may not have a common focus of attention. Masses, publics, fads and fashions, mass hysteria and panics and social movements are some types of diffuse collective mass behaviour.

Theories of Collective Behaviour

What causes collective behaviour? Early social psychologists, such as Gustave Le Bon and Gabrial Tarde, suggested the origins of collective behaviour, especially crowds in both herd instinct and mass imitation. Different interpretations have been offered by modern sociologists to explain collective behaviour. Major theoretical perspectives that describe collective behaviour are as follows:

1. *The Classical View:* Perhaps the earliest formulation of collective behaviour we find in the most influential book written on collective behaviour is *The Crowd* (1895) by the French social psychologist Gustave Le Bon. In this book, he analysed crowd psychology and developed two key concepts: *collective (or group) mind* and *mental unity*. Describing crowd mentality, he said that 'crowds are impulsive, changeable, and irritable; incapable of sustained attention, criticism or perseverance and are governed by a sense of omnipotence and exaggerated feelings'. The sentiments and ideas of all the persons in the gathering take one and the same direction, and their conscious personality vanishes. A collective mind is formed, doubtless transitory, but presenting very clearly defined characteristics. Le Bon, the originator of the 'group mind' concept held the view that all individual responses were lost in crowds, and that a 'collective mind' emerged which made people 'feel, think and act in manner quite different from that in which each individual of them would'. Le Bon believed crowds cause people to regress. According to this view, crowds are guided by instinct, and not by rational decisions. Crowds do not listen to reason, they respond instantly to the immediate situation.

2. *Ignorant Mass View:* This is an early explanation which maintains that the masses revolt because they are uneducated, unreasoning, impulsive and uncivilized savages. This mass view, laid down by Gustave Le Bon in the 19th century, is now considered highly prejudiced and outdated and is no more accepted.
3. *Alienated Mass View:* According to this perspective, collective behaviour is the result of citizens set adrift in a large, complex, rootless world. People indulge in such activities because they experience hardships and frustrations. To seek remedies to their problems, people become ready to undertake collective action, which promises to provide solutions.
4. *Value-added View:* The most influential general theory of collective behaviour is that of N.J. Smelser (1962) which draws particular attention to the importance of 'generalized beliefs' and values in directing social movements. He argued that under conditions of rapid social change and political disruption or precipitated by such 'master processes' as economic development, severe 'strain' undermines the value consensus in society and give rise to sequence of steps culminating in collective action. These steps are:
   (a) *Structural conduciveness:* It refers to the existence of conditions or situations in which collective behaviour is possible.
   (b) *Structural strain:* It refers to some type of frustration, stress, conflict or dissatisfaction in society (such as economic deprivation). Structural strains may be caused by conflicts between goals and available means (a state of anomie) or by the gap between the social ideals (full employment, equality) and social realities (unemployment, poverty, inequalities and discrimination based on age, caste and sex).
   (c) *Generalized belief:* It means a shared understanding of reasons for the strain and stress that serves to guide our behaviour (for example, a mass hysteria, delusion or creation of folk devil).
   (d) *Precipitating factors:* A specific incident that triggers collective response (such as some communal happenings).
   (e) *Mobilization for action*: It is the fifth step in which individuals or groups encourage participation in collective behaviour. Once a precipitating event has taken place, people have to be persuaded (via effective leadership) to join the movement.
   (f) *The operation of social control*: It is the sixth and final step of collective behaviour. Social control can be exercised both formally (through government) and informally (through mass media or groups), which can suppress or influence collective behaviour. Social control may prevent, delay, or interrupt a collective outburst.
5. *Emergent-norm View:* This view have been offered by Ralph Turner and Lewis Killian (1972) which suggests that a collective definition of

appropriate and inappropriate behaviour emerges during episodes of collective behaviour. Like other social norms, the emergent norm reflects shared convictions held by members of the group and is enforced through sanctions.

The early writings on collective behaviour imply that crowds are basically ungovernable. However, this is not always the case. In many situations, crowds are effectively governed by norms and procedures and may even engage in such practices as queuing, or waiting in line. These new norms of proper behaviour (making queues) may arise in what seem at first as ambiguous situations.

6. *The Interactionist View:* Herbert Blumer (1939), a theorist of collective behaviour, rejected Le Bon's idea of group or collective mind. He focused on social interactions and a circular reaction process that generates willing, collective excitement and social contagion. He believed that crowd behaviour results from circular reactions operating in a situation of social unrest. In a situation of social unrest, interactions reinforce and heighten the unrest.
7. *The Assembling View:* Building on the interactionist approach, McPhail and Miller (1973) introduced the concept of the 'assembling perspective'. This perspective emphasizes to examine how and why people move from different points in space to a common location. These sociologists have given particular attention to the question of how people come together to undertake collective action. They have also observed that organized interactions occur during such diverse events as celebrations and revolutions. People may chant, sing, or gesture with respect to a common object.

Conditions of Collective Behaviour

Certain conditions in cotemporary societies tend to increase the likelihood of collective behaviour. Rising prices, shortage of drinking water and electricity, corruption, oppression, red-tapism, injustice, terrorism, rising graph of crimes, rape cases and suicides by farmers or increasing unemployment—all provide fertile ground for collective behaviour. These situations bring people into contact with others to get redress their day-to-day problems in a collective manner. Sometimes certain events like breaking some statue of a great leader trigger some kind of collective behaviour. Rapid social changes create tensions and conflicts that sometimes lead to collective actions and violence. Social diversity and the associated inequalities in the distribution of wealth and opportunities may produce social movements—the women's movement, the civil rights movement, right to information movement, Kisan Majdoor Sabha movement, etc. In activating these movements, the mass media play a very important role in dissemination of information of all types.

Crowd

A crowd in a popular usage is defined as a temporary gathering of people at one time and one place. But a mere chance grouping of people at any place is not a crowd in the sociological sense. A massed aggregation of individuals becomes crowd only when they have a common interest or focus of attention and exhibit a distinguishing set of behaviour characteristics. This focusing of attention and congregation of persons at one place help in the formation of a crowd. According to Horton and Hunt (1964), 'a crowd is a temporary collection of people reacting together to a stimuli'. For social psychologist, Kimball Young (1942), 'a crowd is a gathering of a considerable number of persons around a centre or point of common attraction'. Eshleman and Cashion (1983) defined it as 'temporary or transitory groups of people in face-to-face contact who share a common interest or focus of attention'. For Giddens (1997), 'a crowd is any sizable collection of people who are in direct interaction with one another in a public place'.

The conventional notion of crowd usually involves a large number of physically aggregated people for short duration, in close proximity, and with a common concern. This description of elementary crowd gatherings is of little use in exploring the dynamics of collective behaviour. Generally, this description includes passive crowds, casual crowds and conventional crowds and sometimes it would even include audiences. According to Blumer (1969), they are marked by 'lack of unity' (social isolation), 'loose organization', and an extremely fleeting life span.

Process of Crowd Formation

Close proximity and focused attention of individuals at a single point in a group becomes highly suggestible. This situation is in itself stimulating. It increases the emotional strain and nervous excitement, hence suggestibility. A common mood is built, intensified, and maintained. The members develop a high degree of emotional like-mindedness, stimulation and responses. The centring of attention on one object or idea shuts out for the time being all consideration of other things. This mental isolation is the most characteristic and important feature of crowd organization. The conventional inhibitions are forgotten in the crowd situation. They have for the time being ceased to exist for the members of the crowd. In these conditions the impulses commonly repressed or sublimated.

The final element in the fully organized crowd is some form of collective representation, such as a banner, a slogan, a war cry, etc. This helps in focusing the attention, symbolizing the sentiment or passion and embody the objective of the group. In every true crowd, the above mentioned process takes place in its formation. From the above discussion of the definition and the process of crowd formation, we may discern the following elements of the crowd in brief:

1. Temporary physically aggregation of considerable number of people at a public place.
2. A common interest or a focus of attention, such as fire, accident or natural disaster.
3. Close proximity between the members participating in the crowd.
4. Reacting together to the stimuli.

Classification of Crowds

Crowds differ one from another in numerous ways. They differ in size and duration, in objective and behaviour, in mode of origin, in degree of organization, etc. Each concrete crowd is a historic phenomenon. No two crowds are identical. Various writers have classified crowd in their own way. For instance, sociologist Herbert Blumer (1939) identified four types as under:

1. *The casual crowd:* It is an aggregate of onlookers viewing a common event, such as fire or an accident on the street or people gathered around a street fight or to listen to a street musician. Such crowds have little unity, a very loose internal organization and a momentary existence. They are high in anonymity, but low in suggestibility, contagion and emotional arousal.
2. *The conventional crowd:* It consists of individuals pursuing a clear and mutual goal, such as fans watching a cricket match in a stadium or attending a rally or concert or the passengers in a train. Because the behaviour of participants in such crowds is more established and regularized, they are known as conventional crowd. They are expected to follow established social norms, and rules and procedures. Nevertheless, a conventional crowd has all of the characteristics of crowd: it is proximate, temporary and focused on a single spot.
3. *The expressive crowd:* This is one in which participants gather together for self-stimulation. People who sing, dance and rejoice at a religious festival or carnival are examples. Blumer also term it 'dancing crowd'. He maintains that expressive crowds usually begin as conventionalized crowds, but as emotions become intense, the social organization guiding member behaviours become ineffectual.

   Such types of crowds are also termed as passive crowd or inactive crowd because they do not act but are often content simply to feel. They are purely feeling groups rather than active. The audience is an example of passive crowd. Audience consists of those individuals who come together to witness a sporting event (as spectators), see a performance, and the like. Unlike the other types, the expressive crowds are introverted in that its impulses and feelings are spent in mere expressive actions—singing or dancing which provide an outlet for tensions and emotions. The members of an expressive crowd are interested more in voicing their grievances than in destruction.

4. *The active/action crowd*: The gathering of crowds in intense situations always presents the possibility of action crowds of mobs and riots. Such crowds engage in direct action towards individuals and objects whereas casual and conventionalized crowds generally do not take part in the associated event. It is aggressive (to some extent, destructive), hostile, volatile and sometimes dangerous and is directed towards a certain purpose. It exhibits all the features of crowd—uncertainty, a sense of urgency, suggestibility, emotionality and permissiveness. In such crowds, participants react immediately and directly to the remarks and actions of others without thinking about the consequences or any alternative course of action. Mobs and riots are most dramatic forms of acting crowd.

The characteristics of above mentioned four types of crowd overlap in many situations. In reality, it is very difficult to draw a line of demarcation between these types, especially between active and expressive, as can be seen in the case of riots. Some have argued that riots are expressive and emotional, while others have suggested that riots are instrumental. Such distinctions are not always clear.

Crowd Behaviour

Each crowd is a unique phenomenon of brief duration. It has no past, hence no sentiments or traditions, and no future. It has a beginning, a period of development and organization and a stage of decline and dissolution. Because of its uniqueness, it is difficult to generalize about the nature of crowds. Since it varies dramatically, yet sociologists have tried to delineate the following common characteristics of the crowd behaviour:

1. *Anonymity*: Crowds are anonymous, both because they are large and are temporary. Usually, the members of a crowd behave in a manner as if they do not know each other. The anonymity of the collective gives each person in a crowd a feeling of invincible power which allows him/her to yield to instinct. During a riot, this characteristic of anonymity of crowd members makes it easier for people to loot, kill and steal. In a lynch mob, brutal and atrocious acts can be committed without feelings of shame and responsibility.
2. *Suggestibility:* The participants in a crowd become highly suggestible as if they had been hypnotized. People become highly responsive to the suggestions of others, especially the leader of the crowd and thus their

behaviour often becomes unpredictable. The tendency of individuals to go along with the crowd heightens leaps and bounds.

3. *Contagion:* A contagion sweeps through the crowd like a virus that passes from one person to another. Turner (1978) defines this aspect of crowd behaviour as 'interactional amplification'. As people interact, the response of the participants in the crowd increases in intensity towards the common event or situation. If some people in the crowd start throwing stones at police, or somebody else, their behaviour is likely to motivate others to do the same thing.
4. *Emotionality:* Crowd behaviour is emotional and mostly impulsive. The participants in a crowd become highly emotional. Anonymity, suggestibility and contagion tend to arouse emotions. In crowd situation inhibitions are forgotten, and people become 'charged' to act. The members of the crowd do not know what they are doing. There can be no prediction what it is likely to do at any moment.
5. *Loosely structured:* Though crowd is an unorganized group, it does not totally lack in structure. Individuals come together not deliberately but it happens that there is some object of attention which attracts each individual. This focus of attention later on helps in the emergence of some kind of structure. Even during riots, participants are governed by identifiable social norms and exhibit definite patterns of behaviour. When people says, 'Let us carry the injured man to a hospital and inform his people at home', the crowd transforms itself into an organized group.
6. *Unpredictable:* It is very difficult to predict the behaviour of people, especially in acting crowd. A crowd in action can be a terrifying thing. In such crowds, the behaviour of members approximates most closely to the packs and herds of the lower animals. Crowd members act uncritically upon suggestions as such their behaviour becomes utterly unpredictable.
7. *Impersonality:* The sense of individuality is almost removed in the crowd. Persons do not behave as individual members. The individual losses his/her personal restraints and sense of personal responsibility.

To summarize the idea of crowd, it may be written that a crowd is temporary grouping. It has no rules, no traditions and no formal controls and as such it is unstructured. Crowd behaviour is generally irrational and unrestrained, it is spontaneous and utterly unpredictable and has no established patterns for the members to follow. The above characteristics may be seen in any crowd but their intensity may vary. Some crowds permit great anonymity (because of the largeness) than others, some have higher levels of suggestibility, contagion and organization, and yet one or more of above characteristics may not appear at all. The combination of characteristics mentioned above makes the behaviour extremely volatile and sometimes frightening.

Theories of Crowd Behaviour

The study of collective behaviour started with the study of crowd behaviour. In the 19th century, crowd behaviour was a significant area of study in the field of psychology. Early social psychologists such as Gustavo Le Bon and Gabrial Tarde suggested the origins of crowds in herd instincts and mass imitation. On this basis, Le Bon proposed 'mob psychology' as a theory of crowd. Since then sociologists have largely replaced psychological point of view of crowd behaviour. They have shown that behaviour in crowds is far more mindful, rational and socially organized than Le Bon believed. Not only this, they have broadened the field and coined the new term 'collective behaviour' to include mob, riot, panics and craze, rumour, audience, public and mass (social) movements, along with crowd.

Many theories have been propounded by various psychologists and sociologists to explain why the crowd behaves in a particular way. We will below examine a few of them.

The behaviour of the crowd is always emotionally determined. The things common to all people are such fundamental emotions as fear, anger and rage. In terms of these common elements, crowds form, feel and act. These provide a common bond and a basis for interaction in all conditions.

In the crowd the emotional tone is heightened by the concentration of attention, the suggestions of leaders, the use of verbal and other symbols, the excited gestures of the crowd members, and other circumstances of the occasion. On the basis of these emotional characteristics, the crowd is easily led. In the crowd, mostly critical faculties are in abeyance. Individuals accept as true the most improbable of statements.

Le Bon's Theory

According to Le Bon, the earliest and main exponent of crowd behaviour, the individual yields 'to instincts which had he been alone, he would perforce have kept under restraint'. Like the hypnotized person, 'he is no longer conscious of his acts … . At the same time that certain faculties are destroyed, others may be brought to a high degree of exaltation … . He is no longer himself, but has become an automation who has ceased to be guided by his will … . In the crowd he is barbarian. He possesses the spontaneity, the violence, the ferocity and also the enthusiasm and heroism of primitive beings'.

While explaining the crowd behaviour, Le Bon developed his most important notion of 'group mind'. Group mind makes people feel, think and act in a manner quite different from that in which each individual would feel, think and act where he in a state of isolation. The group mind is not a mere collection (or the sum) of the minds of all the individual members of a group. It is a mind of its own distinct from minds working on different levels. Its working is based on emotions, appeals, suggestions and slogans. Its acts are less rational and more emotional. It is an irresponsible mind focusing its attention on some immediate object. Its mental level is very low. It becomes easily excited and acts in a hypnotic way. It is on this account that individuals behave most irrationally in a crowd than otherwise behave individually. Le Bon's ideas may be summarized as follow: (i) crowds emerge through the existence of anonymity (which allows a decline in personal responsibility); (ii) in contagion (ideas moving rapidly through a group; and (iii) through a suggestability. In the crowd, the individual psychology is subordinated to a 'collective mentality' which radically transforms individual behaviour. Le Bon said that in periods of social decline and disintegration, society in threatened by the rule of crowds.

McDougall's Theory

Psychologist William McDougall's theory of the behaviour of unorganized groups or crowd is practically the same as Le Bon's. He explains the two central phenomena of crowd behaviour, namely, the intensification of emotion in a crowd and the lowering of intellectual level, as follows: The former is due to the principle of direct induction of emotion by way of 'primitive sympathetic response'. He says, the greater the number of people in whom the same emotions can be simultaneously observed, the greater the contagion. The individual under the influence of emotion losses the power of criticism and slips into the same emotion. The collective emotion becomes intensified by mutual interaction. The intensification of emotion and unpreparedness for opposing the authority of the crowd, in their turn, inhibit intellectual processes and the lowering of intellectual level in a crowd.

McDougall described the behaviour of the crowd in the following words:

> A crowd is 'excessively emotional, impulsive, fickle, inconsistent, irresolute and extreme in action, displaying only the coarser emotions and the less refined sentiments; extremely suggestible, careless in deliberation, hasty in judgment, incapable of any but the simpler and imperfect forms of reasoning; easily swayed and led, lacking in self-consciousness, devoid of self-respect and of sense of responsibility … . Hence its behaviour is like that of an unruly child or it is like a wild beast.

Freud's Theory

McDougall's theory of sympathetic induction to account for the intensification of emotion is not accepted by all scholars. Sigmund Freud in his essay on *Group Psychology and Analysis of Ego* remarks, 'There is no doubt that some thing exist in us which, when we become aware of signs of emotion; … how often do we not successfully oppose it, resist the emotion and react in quite an opposite way? Why, therefore, do we invariably give way to this contagion when we are in group?' Freud traces it to our indirect impulses.

Freud suggests that what holds any group together is a love relationship, i.e., emotional ties. This explains what he considers to be 'the principal phenomenon of group psychology'. Using psycho-analytic approach of Freud, E.D. Martin interpreted crowd behaviour as the release for repressed drives. Through a crowd, the restraints of a superego are relaxed and primitive ego-impulses come into play. The 'censor' within the individual is set aside in the crowd and the 'instinct' or basic 'id' impulses, which are normally confined to the inner depths of the personality, come to surface. The crowd thus provides a momentary release of otherwise repressed drives.

How far the Freudian theory is helpful in explaining crowd behaviour, it is argued that it is not substantiated by factual observation. Sometimes, the crowd behaviour may be the expression of repressed drives, but it may not be true of all the crowds. Moreover, it is unable to explain all the features of crowd behaviour.

Allport's Theory

F.H. Allport has also criticized McDougall's theory of sympathetic induction of emotion and behaviour. He offered the explanation of crowd behaviour by two principles, of which one is the *principle of social facilitation.* According to this principle, a common stimulus prepares two individuals for the same response and when they are so prepared, the sight of one making that response releases and heightens that response in the other. The second principle is that of *interstimulation.*

Turner's Theory

Sociologist Ralf Turner has gone beyond inadequate psychological explanation of the crowd behaviour as discussed above and developed an emergent norm perspective. The central thesis of this perspective is that even in the most violent and dangerous crowds, there is also social interaction, in which a situation is defined, norms for sanctioning behaviour emerge, and lines of action are justified and agreed upon.

Thus, all above explanations throw light on either one or the other factor of the complex phenomenon of crowd behaviour. As such, they are incomplete and insufficient. There are multiple factors, such as anonymity, stimulation, emotionality, suggestibility, initiation, contagion, lack of volition, force of unconscious impulses, etc., which are responsible for the emergence of the typical behaviour of the crowd.

The theory of crowd behaviour has moved away from the older perspective (McDougall, Le Bon, etc.) that viewed the individual as coming under the sway of the crowd and losing its capacity for rational judgement before the sweep of an overpowering emotional contagion. Instead, sociologists now explain crowd behaviour by the same sociological concepts that explain social group behaviour.

Mob

Mob is a solidaristic and focused form of active crowd. It is an emotionally aroused group taking aggressive and violent action. It is generally spontaneous, short-lived and highly unstable. Riots, orgies, panics are different types of mob. Mob groups engage in violent behaviour such as throwing stones, firebombs, hanging people in effigy or destructive orgies.

The behaviour of the mob is an avert expression of a strong hidden dissatisfaction, extreme discontentment about something such as existing policies of government or any institution or about social conditions. Mobs reflect widespread feelings of frustrations and hostility or inhibited emotional attitudes. Such crowds have a defined objective and the mass surges to this achievement. Charles Tilly (1978) emphasized that mob action and rioting characteristically express the frustration of people who cannot gain access to orthodox channels to express grievances or press for reforms they think necessary.

Audience

Audience is also categorized as a crowd (in some sense) which gather for some peaceful purpose, at certain appointed time and place, for example, to seek information or to attend religious congregation. It is primarily a listening and more or less a passive group whose members use their ears more than their eyes or tongues. It is a crowd in the sense that its interest is centred on stimuli outside themselves. This stimuli is one way to a single stimulus—a lecture, a movie or a dance, etc.

The audience differs from a (acting) crowd in that it is highly structured or organized than a crowd. In audience it is thought and not feeling that predominates. It also differs in respect of their leaders. The audience leader puts forth facts quietly, starts the give-and-take, and keeps ideas scintillating. He guides and directs the discussion and nurtures creative thinking. The leader of a crowd, on the other hand, may shout, gesticulate, become oratorical and fume, and thus instead of guiding, he may sway the group. An audience's best size is generally smaller than that of crowds.

In audience, there may be certain amount of communication between members as they cheer, applaud, boo, whisper, mutter, doze or snore. Audiences may become unruly and at times may even become converted into a mob when a clash of ideas takes place or when there is a free play of feelings. Some scholars have used the word 'assembly' for audience. There are two main characteristics of an assembly: (1) restraint, and (2) thoughtfulness. Committee meetings, public lectures, forums and religions congregations to listen sermons or to participate in 'Hari Kirtans' are the main examples of audience.

Some Other Forms of Collective Behaviour

Besides crowd, mob, audience, there are other forms of collective behaviour, such as riots, panics and crazes, rumour, fads and fashions, mass hysteria, etc. In these forms, people may not be in close proximity but are dispersed over a wide areas.

Riots

A riot is a form of mob which is violently aggressive and destructive. It may lead to violent acts against any object or person who happens to be in the wrong area at the wrong time. It is 'a sudden upsurge of collective violence often directed at property, sometimes at persons in authority' (Oxford Dictionary of Sociology). The incident that triggers a riot can be relatively trivial, as sometimes exchange of some hot words between the members of two castes, races or communities about something may led to a riot. During riots, human behaviour become immediately violent and unpredictable. In the mob, people engage in such activities as destruction, burning and looting which are generally indiscriminate.

Panics and Crazes

Panics and crazes both represent responses to some generalized belief which may and may not be accurate. The name 'panic' is generally given to that condition in which a group is disintegrated. For example, when a fire breaks out in the theatre, every individual is so overcome by dread that each cares for his/her own safety and loses all consideration for others. The mutual ties cease to exist and a gigantic and senseless dread is set free. There is also a feeling of fear which spreads like contagion.

Defining panic, Smelser (1962) writes, 'A panic is a collective flight based on hysterical belief ... in order to preserve life, property, or power from threat.' Smelser cites instances such as sinking ships, burning buildings and fluctuations in the money market (stock market crashes) as events that give rise to panic behaviour. Any crowd may turn into panic. It represents behaviour following the sudden breakdown of an organization or of group. It leads to mass hysteria and a situation of an animal-like stampede. In the panic the basic emotion is fear which spreads like contagion and the activity is an attempt to escape impending danger. People run hither and thither to save their lives.

In contrast to panic, a craze is 'mobilization for action based on positive wish-fulfilment belief' (Smelser, 1963). It is a rush towards some satisfaction. Manias, booms and fads are provided as examples of craze. But it differs from the fad in that it becomes an obsession for its followers. According to Lofland (1981), 'A craze is an exciting mass involvement which lasts for a relatively long period of time.' In contrasting crazes with panics, Smelser (1962) draws the analogy of objects that attracts and those repulse people who are affected. In a sense, one rushes towards the object of attention when in the grips of a craze, and away from the object when in the throes of panic. In other words, the key distinction between the two is that panics are escapes from something whereas crazes are movements to something.

Rumour

A rumour is a piece of information gathered informally which is used to interpret an ambiguous situation. It arises in such a situation where people want some verifiable information but do not get or cannot get it. Rumours are frequently, but not always, false. According to Horton and Hunt (1964), 'A rumour is rapidly spread report unsubstantiated by authenticated fact.' Much of our casual conversation or gossip consists of rumour mongering. It is very tempting to accept a story or some juicy tale about people's private affairs when it is unable to confirm or deny it—especially if it is vague and entertaining. Usually, the contents of rumour get distorted in the course of its transmission from one person to the next.

In both panics and crazes, a rumour may be significant factor. It is also enough to cause a riot. People are likely to believe a rumour if the bearer is credible. Outlining the general function of rumour, Lang and Lang (1961) contend that it 'is an attempt to bring the orientations of others sufficiently in line with one's own to make collective activity possible'.

Fads and Fashions

Fads and fashions are specific types of collective mass behaviour that people enthusiastically pursue. They refer to periodic changes in styles and patterns of our behaviour. Generally, both arrive suddenly and also disappear quickly, but they may attract great interest from large numbers of people during their period of stay. There is an almost endless list of objects and behaviour patterns come under the category of fads and fashions but some lifestyle or particular taste in jewellery, clothing, music, recreation, hair style, etc., catch the fancy of people more than anything else.

Fads are usually trivial, short-lived variations in speech, decoration or patterns of behaviour or activities involving large number of people, whereas fashions, although similar to fads, change less rapidly, are less trivial, and tend to be more cyclical. According to Lofland (1981), 'fashions are pleasurable mass involvement that feature a certain amount of acceptance by society and have a line of historical continuity'. Some examples of fads are crowding into telephone booths, chewing the chewing gum, dancing the twist, wearing T-shirts, playing TV games, etc.

Mostly, fads are harmless and have no long-range social consequences. Typically, when people think of fashions, they generally think of styles of dress and behaviour, but there are also fashions in adornment, music, art and literature. To be 'in fashion' is to wear the types of clothes and having the style of hair (cricket player Dhoni style or filmstar John Abraham style or in ladies Sadhna style) that are currently in vogue and the advertisers are pushing. At anytime, hemline ladies' skirt may be long or short, trousers may be long or short, trouser's bottomline or neckties may be wide or narrow, and hair styles may be short or long or straight or curly. In reality, fads and fashions enter every aspect of life where choices are not dictated by sheer necessity—sports, children toys, vehicles, TV sets, beverages, architecture, cameras, wedding invitation cards and decoration, etc.

Unlike fads and crazes, fashions change relatively gradually. There is a clear commercial motive behind these forms of collective behaviour. Nowadays, they are also big business.

Fads and fashions allow people to identify with something different from the dominant institutions and symbols of culture. They provide many people with a sense of excitement, feeling of belongingness, or a source of identification and self-esteem. Fashions can sometimes falsely give the impression of wealth and status. Sociologists are interested in fads and fashions because they are indicators of trends of change in society. They throw light on class behaviour.

Mass Hysteria

Like panic, mass hysteria is also a type of diffused collective mass behaviour. It is some form of irrational, compulsive behaviour spreads among people. Mass hysteria takes place when a potentially destructive or threatening event causes a widespread, highly emotional fear. Sometimes these fears are accompanied by panic, mass movement or attempts to escape from the perceived danger.

Publics and Public Opinion

The least organized and most individualized form of collective behaviour is represented by *publics*. In ordinary discourse, one speaks of the public as synonymous with people, residents, and sometimes citizens. In sociology, the term, particularly in the plural form (publics), is given a more specific sense.

Sociologically, a considerable number of people who share common opinion on a specific issue but are not organized and scattered all over, is known as the public. Since all persons may not feel similar on every issue, there may be as many publics as there are issues such as the movie public, the sporting public, the public of voters, consumers, magazine subscribers, stockholders, etc. Members of a public will interact with one another to arrive at a position on a concerned issue, out of such debate may emerge a collective voice, *public opinion*. As issue changes, so do publics. It can grow and decline as events change.

Meaning and Definitions

The term 'public' refers to a dispersed group of people, not necessarily in contact with one another, who share interest in an issue. Different from crowd, it is a geographically separated collectivity which also exhibits some characteristics of collective behaviour. It is a group of people so large that individuals are not in physical contact with one another but are bound together by common opinions or interests on certain issues on which all are interested.

According to Reuter and Hart (1933), 'The public is any group, aggregate, non-aggregate, that achieves corporate unity through critical interactions.' For Horton and Hunt (1964), 'A public is a scattered group of people who share an interest in a particular way.' Blumer (1939) defined it as 'a group of people who are confronted with an issue, who do not agree on how to address the issue and who discuss the issue'.

A public comes into being when there is an issue, such as consumer rights, right to information, abortion, terrorism, unemployment, corruption, etc. Since there are innumerable social issues that may evolve and hence an uncountable number of publics that will be formed. A public is not a united group, even though there has to be some degree of consensus on the issue around which it is formed. It lacks the structure that one associates with well-organized groups. It has no officials, though there may be some opinion leaders.

The size of the public is determined by the available means of discussion and means of communication. In the present time publics are not always congregate groups. The development of mass media of communication (printed material, electronic media, TV, Internet, etc.) has created a public of very considerable size. The new means of communication enable persons to participate in the discussion of an issue without being in direct face-to-face contact with each other. They have enormously increased the size of publics. In the present era great numbers of widely distributed people may follow the course of happenings and promptly register their reactions, for example, on the killings of Nithari or Atari train's bomb blasts or the recent gangrape happenings in Delhi and other parts of the country. These reactions after wide discussions take the form of public opinion. Public opinion is a consensus on the issues/matters of common interest.

Nature and Characteristics

From the above discussion, the following characteristics of publics can be delineated:

1. It is a spatially diffused collectivity scattered all over.
2. It is an amorphous (shapeless group) and enormous aggregation of people whose size and membership varies with the issue.
3. Its composition is constantly changing, some new people join and the old members retreat to dormancy. It seldom has a definite membership.
4. It has no internal organization. People do not have fixed status and roles in it.
5. It has a specific common issue or interest around which it is formed. It comes into existence only when some issue arises.
6. It is not necessarily a face-to-face group like a crowd. The members of a public may not know each other.
7. It is formed on the basis of deliberation and discussion—arguments and counter-arguments on the issue and exchange of ideas.
8. It has no culture and no consciousness of themselves.
9. Though the members of a public have common interest, they are not like-minded—a group mind as in a crowd. They show difference of opinions over common issues.

The Crowd and the Public

Public is different from crowd. The two collectivities differ in the following respects:

1. A crowd is transient and impulsive whereas the public does not exhibit emotional intensity and impulsiveness.
2. In the crowd there are expectancy, enthusiasm and excitement; in the public there is an absence of excitement and tension.
3. Public is a scattered group of people whereas the members of a crowd collect at one place—a scene of incident or accident.
4. Public is a critical group whereas in a crowd no critical discussion is possible. In the public, discussion is essential which is generally free and unimpassioned.
5. The members of a public have common interests but are not like-minded as in crowd. They show differences of opinion over common issues.
6. In the crowd, the contact between its members is personal and face-to-face while in the public the contact is through communication by means of press, TV, radio, etc. Public is not necessarily a face-to-face group.
7. In the crowd, there is contagion through contact; in the public, there is contagion without contact.
8. A public is a much bigger group than a crowd.
9. The crowd is more suggestible than the public.
10. The crowd is an ecstatic aggregation while the public is a rational group.
11. The crowd generates and expresses emotion and nulls to a dominating collective impulse; the public deliberates in regard to issue on the basis of facts and evidence.

12. The crowd reaches unanimity through the development of rapport; the public arrives at a consensus through the clash and modification of opinion.
13. Public have long life than crowds which dissolve through fatigue or discom -fort of the members. People disperse as soon as the objective is achieved.

Public Opinion

An opinion is simply an interpretation placed upon a fact or a set of facts about which there are doubts and discussion. It is often a complex, confused and heterogeneous thing, not the definite and unitary it is sometimes assumed to be. The term 'public opinion' is defined variously. Sometimes as an opinion held by a substantial member of people or as the dominant opinion in a given population. As said by L.W. Doole (1935) 'public opinion refers to public attitudes on an issue when they are members of the same social group'. The presence of an issue is the first condition for the formation of public opinion. Depiction of differing reactions on an issue also reveals public opinion. 'A public opinion refers to the differing opinions held by a public upon a issue' (Horton and Hunt, 1964). The term is also often used to refer the opinions of the public—of everybody. Herbert Blumer (1939) identifies it as the collective product of the public known as public opinion. This can be visualized as the product of the exchange of opinion among the members of a particular group. According to Schaefer and Lamm (1992), the term 'public opinion' refers to expression of attitudes on matters of public policy which are communicated to decision-makers.

Public opinion thus means the mass of ideas and judgements, operative in a community which are more or less definitely formulated, which have certain stability, and which are the results of many minds acting in common.

One must be clear enough that the opinion of majority does not always mean public opinion as long as that majority forms a special group in opposition to the minority group. The opinion in order to be public must be the opinion of a homogeneous group. And moreover, it must also be a co-operative product, the results of the meetings of many minds. Thus, it is different from private opinion. Hearsay, hasty empirical generalizations, accepted traditions and deliberate propaganda act as the main ingredients in the formation of public opinion. Public opinion is influenced by attitudes and stereotypes.

For research purpose, public opinion consists of the aggregated views of members of a population on various issues. Knowledge of public opinion is generally obtained through the use of polls, which are a form of survey research. The surveyor asks sample population a series of questions about the issue of concern, for example, do you favour legalizing abortion? or are you in favour of birth control? Measuring public opinion, on any current issue of importance, has become a mass industry in recent years.

Chapter 5

Social Control and Deviance

KEY FEATURES

- Social Control
- Means of Social Control
- Social Control and Socialization
- Social Control and Social Change
- Deviance
- Main Elements of Deviance
- Forms of Deviance
- Explanations of Deviant Behaviour
- Conformity, Deviance and Social Control

All societies constitute a social order, but there is disorder within the order. Sociology is concerned with social order and disorder both in order to understand the functioning of a society. The study of social control begins with the study of the social order within which people interact. Order is a state in which social life—actions and interactions—can be conducted without major disruption. Social order means a system of people, relationships and customs operating smoothly to accomplish the work of a society. It depends upon the expectations of others and conformity to social norms or rules. A society must have some social order if it is to function smoothly and properly. Societies cannot function if massive members of people defied standards of appropriate conduct. The orderliness of a society rests upon a network of roles according to which each person accepts certain duties towards others and claims certain rights from others. An orderly society can operate only as long as most people will generally be observing most norms and fulfil most of their duties towards others.

Social Control

In very simple terms, the system or the organization by which the social relations or behaviour is controlled is called social control. The word 'control' may refer to two types of acts:

1. to an act of controlling; or
2. to the process, technique, device by means of which changes in the behaviour is affected.

As applied to human relationships, the term 'control' may carry either of these meanings. Sociologists are generally interested in social controls (second meaning of control) rather than in the act of controlling. Not all control in human society is social; it is physical in so far as the relation between persons is purely external. It is social to the extent that it involves communication. The control becomes social only when it brings modifications in behaviour resulting from act of communications and not from arbitrary applications of physical force.

According to Roucek (1947), 'Social control is a collective term for those processes, planned or unplanned, by which individuals are taught, persuaded, or compelled to conform to the usages, and life-values of groups'.

MacIver (1937) observes, 'Social control is the way in which the entire social order coheres and maintains itself how it operates as a whole, as a changing equilibrium'.

Parsons (1954) defined social control as 'the process by which, through the imposition of sanctions, deviant behaviour is counteracted and social stability is maintained'.

Horton and Hunt (1964) write: 'Sociologists use the term social control to describe all the means and processes whereby a group or a society secures its members' conformity to its expectations.'

In the words of Peter L. Berger (1963), 'social control refers to the various means used by a society to bring its recalcitrant members back into line'.

According to Roberts (1991), 'the term social control refers to the techniques and strategies for regulating human behaviour in society'.

In *Oxford Dictionary of Sociology* (1994), social control refers to the social processes by which the behaviour of individuals or groups is regulated.

For Bottomore (1962), 'the term social control refers to the social regulation of human behaviour'. In the end, we conclude this section with the definition of Gillin and Gillin (1948), which is quite exhaustive and easy to understand: 'Social control is the system of measures, suggestions, persuasion, restraint and the coercion by whatever means including physical force—by which a society brings into conformity to the approved pattern of behaviour of a sub-group or by which a group moulds into conformity its members.' All the above definitions of social control emphasize on three things: (1) it is a system of devices or processes or means and techniques through which (2) society brings its recalcitrant or deviant members back into the line, and (3) forces them to conform to the accepted standard behaviour.

Why Social Control?

Why there is need for social control? Many explanations have been given for this question. Generally, it is said that to satisfy peacefully the basic drives of humans—sex, shelter (security) and hunger—some kind of regulation is needed. This regulation acts as a check on the individual desires of persons so that they cannot fulfil them the way they wish as we see in animals. Human beings have to adhere to certain norms (folkways, mores, rules and regulations of the group) to satisfy their wants (needs and desires) without any clash. These norms act as means of social control. Thus, for the mutual welfare and well-being, some kind of control (inner as well as external, i.e., social control) is an almost necessity. Through social control, personal, cultural and social mal-arrangements are properly balanced and the struggle among the persons to satisfy their unlimited wants is eliminated or reduced to a manageable extent. According to Gillin and Gillin (1948), the main function of social control is to realize certain purposes of the group, including maintaining the social equilibrium for the continued existence of society.

Functionalists contend that people must respect social norms if any group or society is to survive. They stress that order is necessary for effective social life. In their view, societies literally could not function if massive numbers of people defied standards of appropriate conduct. To maintain unity, stability, continuity and the balance in the group or the society, some kind of social control is needed. By contrast, conflict theorists are concerned that the successful functioning of a society will consistently benefit the powerful and work to disadvantage of other groups. Marxists argue that not only does the law protect the powerful and perpetuate inequality but common people have unequal access to the law.

Objectives

Kimball Young (1942) stated that the social control aims to 'bring about conformity, solidarity and continuity of a particular group or society'. It is essential for the continued existence of the society. On the basis of above analysis, the main objectives of social control may be stated as under:

1. To regulate the individual behaviour and avoid clash in the society.
2. To maintain and re-establish the social order.
3. To establish unity and solidarity among the members.
4. To ensure the continuity of the group or the society.
5. To secure member's conformity to the group expectations.
6. To bring society's recalcitrant and deviant members back into the line.
7. To check cultural degeneration and social disintegration.

Functions

The major functions of social control are:

1. It forces persons to get obeyed social decisions.
2. It maintains the equilibrium and stability in the society.
3. It helps in choosing behaviour and fulfilling one's desire for social status.
4. It helps in proper socialization of the individual.
5. It helps in performing social roles.
6. It helps in mitigating tensions and conflict among members.
7. It breeds conformity in society.

Social control operates at three levels:

(i) Group over group.
(ii) Group over its members.
(iii) Individuals over their fellow members.

Thus, social control takes place when a person is induced or forced to act according to the wishes of others, whether or not in accordance with his/her own individual interests. It operates on the basis of the individual's desire for social status, induces him/her to conform to group standards of conduct whatever his/her personal inclinations or situational temptations. Social control occurs in every aspect of society—in the family, in the peer groups, in bureaucratic organizations, NGOs and in the government of every society.

Forms

Analyses of forms of social control differ. Different authors have used different terminology to refer different forms of social control as we see in the following table:

Authors	*Forms of Social Control*
E. A. Ross	Formal and Informal
C. H. Cooley and Barnard	Conscious and Unconscious
Karl Mannheim	Direct and Indirect
Kimball Young	Positive and Negative
Gurvich and Moore	Organized, Unorganized and Autonomous
R. T. Lapiere	Authoritarian and Democratic
Horton and Hunt	Planned and Unplanned

The common distinction is between the formal (repressive or coercive) and the informal (persuasive or softer) forms of control. It has the universal sanction and acclaimed by many sociologists. Social control may be positive or negative, i.e., consisting of rewards or punishment and repressive measures respectively. Similarly, social control may be planned (deliberate) or unplanned (incidental). If it is planned, it may be either formal (organized) or informal (unorganized).

Informal and unplanned (incidental) control

Informal social control, as the term implies, is used by people casually. Norms are enforced through the informal sanctions. These norms include folkways, customs, mores, values, conventions, fashions and public opinion, etc. Ritual and ceremony also act as instruments of informal control. But ceremony plays a less important role in modern society than in the traditional societies. Informal control often takes the form of a look, nudge or frown which says 'behave yourself ' or 'get into line'.

Methods and techniques of informal control are numerous. They vary with the purpose and the character of the group in question. For example, in a homogeneous primary group type of village community, the gossip may be a potent means of enforcing conformity but would be of little importance in the personal life of a metropolis like Mumbai. They also vary greatly from one social situation to another. They are positive and negative both. Awards, prizes, wealth and power over others are examples of positive control through physical medium. Gossip, smiles, praise, persuasion, badges and titles are examples of positive control by symbolic means. Negative social control is represented by satire, laughter, raising of an eyebrow, opprobrium, name calling, negative gossip and ridicule, threats, physical torture and ostracism, etc. Words and phrases (epithet, watchwords and slogans) are other means of informal control. They serve as collective representations symbolizing the emotional attitudes of the group.

The above techniques of informal control are typically employed within primary groups such as families. Individuals learn such techniques early in their childhood socialization to cultural norms—folkways, mores, values, etc. Other than the family, these methods and techniques are also exercised by personal friends, colleagues and co-workers at the workplace.

Informal social control is based on this popular belief that 'the all-seeing eyes of Gods are everywhere'. It acts as mores (a controlling device). A belief in spiritual persons, who are omnipresent and omniscient, introduces an imagined presence which serves as a powerful controlling device.

Formal and planned (deliberate) control

Informal methods of social control are not adequate in enforcing and conforming of obedient behaviour in all cases and in every situations. It can serve as a last resort when socialization and informal sanctions do not bring about desired result. In secondary groups and mass society where relations between individuals are impersonal, the primary group controls are not so effective. Control is then exercised through some agencies and formal institutions such as state, law, education, government, courts, police, military, administrators, corporate managers and bureaucrats, etc. There are formal controls of licensing boards, professional organizations and trade unions also. As against the informal social controls, which grow out of necessities of the group or the society and which are the outcome of spontaneous growth, the formal social controls are deliberately created and imposed by man themselves. But, these are less powerful forms as they are not based on human instincts and basic necessities of life. Thus, they have not much importance in primary groups. Only one example will suffice to clarify this point. The law banning child marriage was passed as early as in 1929 in India but the thousands of child marriages are still performed on a single auspicious day of *Akshay Tritiya*. Thus, laws are not all-powerful. Laws which go against widespread customs are resisted and customs carry the day as it comes. Laws that are unpopular, such as prohibition of *gutka* (mixture of tobacco and flavoured betelnut), or use of plastic carry bags become difficult to enforce.

The primary group type of rural community is fast disappearing as a result of industrialization, urbanization and globalization. The ineffectiveness of informal means of social control (mores, tradition, primary group, group opinion, etc.) of personal behaviour in modern secondary society accounts for the increasing resort to such means as law, police, courts, etc. To make formal means (law) more effective the technique of propaganda is used.

Distinction between informal and formal social control: A synoptic view

Informal Control	*Formal Control*
Operates mainly in primary groups and simple society.	Operates mainly in secondary groups and mass society.
Spontaneous growth or gradually emergence.	Consciously created or expressly enacted.
Mostly unwritten.	Written and codified.
More powerful.	Less powerful.
Punishment by society or the group concerned.	Punishment by the state or the institution concerned.
Important means—folkways, customs, mores, morality, religion, public opinion, leadership, etc.	Important means—law, courts, state and government.
Administration is impersonal.	Administered by persons.

Means or Agencies of Social Control

There are many means of social control. They work either severally or simultaneously to maintain social order. Bottomore (1962) has enlisted them as the agencies of social control. On the basis of the above analysis of forms of social control, the means of social control may be grouped into two classes:

(i) institutional, and
(ii) non-institutional.

Institutional means

Following are the institutional means of social control:

(a) Political institutions—state, law and government
(b) Religion
(c) Marriage, home and family
(d) Education
(e) Social classes

Non-institutional means

Following are the non-institutional means of social control:

(a) Ideologies, legends and myths
(b) Beliefs, ceremonies and rituals
(c) Art and literature
(d) Folkways, customs and mores, taboos
(e) Leadership
(f) Violence and terror
(g) Social suggestions—conventions, traditions, symbols, fashion, craze, public opinion.

Law and Society

Some norms are considered so important by a society that they are formalized into laws controlling people's behaviour. In a political sense, law is the 'body of rules made by government for society, interpreted by courts, and backed by the power of the state' (Cummings and Wise, 1989). Laws or legal rules have a sanction which cannot be evaded. Sanction means the penalty attached to the violation of rules.

Legal and political system is a potent means of social control under which one is obliged to live. This is the system that, quite against one's will, will tax one, make one obey its innumerable rules and regulations, and if need be put one in prison and in the last resort will kill one.

Social Control and Socialization

Functionalists claim that order in a society is achieved partly through socializing members into the accepted values and norms. Socialization is the means by which value consciousness (agreement) is brought about, and this is achieved through internalization of norms. We learn expectations of others through socialization and develop a desire to conform to them. The basic values members learn in a given society will generally lead them to conform and therefore behave in an orderly manner. Those who are not successfully socialized and become 'deviant' may be controlled by more coercive means such as police. Through socialization social control becomes *ipso facto* effective.

The various agencies of socialization like family, neighbourhood, community, school, working place, peer groups, etc., are also the agencies or means of socialization. They exercise regulatory influence over the behaviour of the individuals. The family, which used to be most important agency of social control, has now lost much its age-old public support in the battle of social control especially in urban areas. In 'mass society' where relations between individuals are impersonal, the primary group or family controls are not much effective. In such societies, control is exercised through institutions like state, law and government.

Social Control and Social Change

With social changes, the ideology, direction, methods and techniques of social control also change. Many a time and at several places, the negative controls instead of positive controls are given importance and free will is crushed. Gillin and Gillin (1948) stated, 'too rigid social control means repression of that dynamic person or minority group in any population supplying the ideas and actions on which social change depends'. Excess regulation and rigidity often results in bad results as we have seen during the emergency imposed by the then Prime Minister of India, Indira Gandhi.

Deviance

Deviance is directly related to social order and control, i.e., how it is structured and how its moral, economic and political interests are protected. When a society functions in an orderly way, most people will generally be observing most norms. But when some people do not conform to established ways of behaving and violate social expectations and social rules, and act contrary to established norms of society, which other uphold, they are known as deviant person and their behaviour is termed as deviant behaviours. Deviance occurs when conduct norms are broken or violated. Deviance connotes only those violations that make a person objectionable or at least significantly discredited. It arises when the departure from accepted norms involves action about which the community feels so strongly as to adopt sanctions to prevent or otherwise control the deviant behaviour. Thus, 'deviant behaviour is a conduct that the people of a society generally regard as aberrant, disturbing, improper, or immoral and for which specific social control efforts are likely to be found' (Smelser, 1962). In its widest sense, it is a generic term referring to the activities described in such conceptional expressions as 'crime', 'alcoholism', 'immorality', 'cheating', 'sexual perversion or assault'., suicide, drug abuse, and occasionally, other topics.

Changing Concept of Deviance

The concept of deviance like all other aspects of social life is not frozen into a place forever but is subject to redefinition and change. There was a time (Middle Ages), when a theological definition of deviance prevailed, and accordingly deviance was a sin. After the advent of industrial revolution and the emergence of the nation-states in the 19th century, most deviance was defined as *crime*. In the 20th century and now in 21st century, when science more often guides our conceptions of reality, deviance is increasingly designated as a social problem, or as *illness*—physical and mental. Medicio has achieved the authority to define many deviant individuals as 'ill' rather than as 'immoral' or 'criminal' (the conceptions of 18th and 19th centuries).

However, sociologist Howard Becker (1932) did not accept the above conception of deviance and deviants. He asserted that it is society who label deviants. According to him, 'deviant behaviour is behaviour that people so label'. It does not reside in acts or behaviours *per se*, but in the meaning attached to them. People are labelled as deviants by others and thus become 'outsiders'. Becker says: 'Social groups create deviance by making the rules whose imposition constitutes deviance, and by applying these rules to particular people and labelling them as outsiders.' From this point of view, deviance is not a quality of the act the person commits, but rather the consequence of the application by others of rules and sanctions to an offender.

Deviance is universal and normal. It exists in all societies (folk-urban or traditional-modern) wherever people interact and live in group. The notion of 'deviance' or 'deviant', as we shall see, is actually not easy to define. It meant different things to different people. Generally, it is defined as any 'failure to conform to the customary norms of the society'. According to Wickman (1991), 'deviance is behaviour that violates the standards of conduct or expectations of a group or society'. Being late for class is categorized as a deviant act; the same is true of dressings gorgeously for a funeral ceremony. Giddens (1997) defined it, 'as non-conformity to a given set of norms that are accepted by a significant number of people in a community or society'. On the basis of these definitions, we are all deviant from time to time. Most of us on some occasions transgress generally accepted rules of behaviour. None of us are all rule breakers as well as conformists. In this context, Jack Dougles (1970) words are relevant to quote: '... All of us, except those who live alone in caves, run necessary risks of being publicly denounced as deviants.' The opposite of deviance often is called conformity, conventionality, normality and morality. All of these terms imply obedience to norms.

Main Elements of Deviance

There is no fixed agreement on the substance of deviance—even murder or incest is accepted at times. But there are a few interrelated elements which help characterize the phenomenon:

1. *Deviation is relative, not absolute:* In this sense, most people are deviant to some degree. When we say that deviance is relative, it only means that what is defined as deviant varies because different cultural groups have different norms. Thus, to consume alcohol would be a deviant act in an orthodox Muslim community, but not in Rajput community of Hindu society. Not only this, the relative nature of deviance also varies historically within a given culture. An act considered deviant in one time period may be considered non-deviant in another. Thus, deviance not only varies by time but by place also. Behaviours viewed as deviant in one location, society, or culture may be considered non-deviant in others.
2. *Deviance refers to norm violation:* There are wide range of norms—religious norms, legal norms, health norms, cultural norms and so forth. Sometimes, there is a conflict between these different norms. In such situations, it becomes very difficult to decide about deviance or deviant behaviour. It should be noted that norm violation is somewhat broader conception than deviant behaviour since it connotes breaking any standard of expected conduct in a particular social setting.
3. *Deviance is also viewed as a 'stigma construct':* It is a label bestowed upon certain classes of behaviour at certain times. This characteristic can also be seen as very wide ranging. People may make friends deviant simply because they belch or talk too much. Terrorists at times may become political martyrs.

Because of its relative character, wide range of norms, and stigma construct, deviance is a shifting, ambiguous and volatile concept. This is why, Colin Sumner (1994) proclaimed that the concept of deviance is now dead and the focus should be on why some forms of deviance are socially censured whereas others are not.

Forms of Deviance

Deviance takes many forms. It can vary from political terrorism to failing to observe accepted eating habits. The juvenile delinquent, the hermit, the ascetic, the mentally ill, the hippie, the sinner, the homosexual, the saint and the miser gloating over his wealth all have deviated from the conventional social norms.

But only those forms of deviance are considered deviant which are disapproved by the society or the culture. So, the scope of the concepts of deviant and deviance is very wide. More recently, sociologists have begun to advocate a relativistic view of deviance. This view suggests that like other behaviour, deviance can also be interpreted in the socio-cultural context in which it occurs. This view avoids the problems of the absolute, moral, medical and statistical models of deviance. According to this view, an act that is deviant in one context may not be deviant in another. A behaviour considered sick (mentally ill) in one society could be thought healthy in a different society.

Thus, deviance does not consist merely of acts or behaviours, but of group responses, definitions and the meanings attached to behaviours. Definitions of deviance vary with circumstances, time, place, situation, and even with social status. Sociologists almost always recognize socio-cultural relativity in deviance. As stated earlier, an act considered deviant in one time period may be considered non-deviant in another. Behaviours or social practice such as polygyny viewed as deviant in one society or culture may be considered non-deviant in others. Behaviour defined as deviant in one situation (e.g., wearing woman's clothes by a man to act in a play or consuming alcohol at public place) may not be deviant in another, even the same time period and place. Deviance also varies with social status. The status associated with person's sex, caste, age and income will influence which of his or her behaviours are considered deviant. To understand deviance, we must focus not only on people or acts but also on the conditions in which deviance occurs and how others react to it.

In a nutshell, there are two major forms of deviance: individual deviance and group deviance. Deviance does not refer only to individual behaviour; it concerns the activities of group as well. Deviance may be individual, in which a person deviates from the normal behaviour of his/her group or it may be group deviance, in which the entire group deviates from social norms. The individual deviates from the norms of his/her sub-culture. He/she is thus an individual deviant. In a complex society, however, there may be a number of deviant sub-cultures, whose norms are condemned by the conventional morality of the society.

Explanations of Deviant Behaviour

Why do people violate social norms? Earlier explanations for deviance identified supernatural causes or genetic factors. The oldest theory to explain deviant behaviour (criminal conduct) was 'diabolical possession and instigation'. Throughout much of mankind history, explanations for criminal behaviour tended to be *demonological.* Crime was the result of a person succumbing to the blandishments of the evil spirits. Even today, when science has gained ground as a plausible method of explanation of facts, some of the day-to-day phenomena still are subject to magical and religious treatment. Though the 'devil' no longer serves this function to a broad scale, but the belief in spirit or 'demonism' still persists in our culture. In rural India, we can easily find cases of such women who have been beaten to death because they were thought to be possessed by some evil spirit or devil.

Later on, the demonological approach to deviant behaviour was replaced by genetic factors. Attempts were made to associate deviant behaviour with inherited traits, body and mental types. It was claimed that certain body types were more prone to deviant behaviour than others. Earlier social scientists were quite sceptical about these genetic theories of deviant behaviour. Although these theories were supported by impressive empirical evidence, critics had noted serious errors in methods which cast doubts upon their findings.

Durkheim's Theory

Emile Durkheim was perhaps the first to analyse deviance or 'social pathology' as he called it in a different way. He argued that deviance is universal (and normal), relative and functional. His influence on the sociology of order and deviance has been immense. Before Durkheim, it was generally regarded that deviance is an attribute, as something inherent in a certain kind of behaviour or person: the delinquent, the homosexual, the mentally ill, and so forth. For earlier writers (social pathology theorists) like Cesare Lombroso, Charles Goring, Hans Eysenck and others, some individuals are psychologically or physically predisposed to deviant behaviour (crime) as a result of their biological inheritance. This view is still important in some clinical and criminological researches. But sociologists reject any emphasis on genetic roots of crime and deviance. For them deviance is best viewed, not as a type of person but rather as a formal property of social situations and social systems, i.e., how social structures (familial, economic or political) are organized.

Durkheim, in his works, raised two major but somewhat antagonistic issues about deviance. One is his focus on *anomie,* which is a state of normlessness and breakdown which emerges most conspicuously at times of rapid social change.

Durkheim's Model of Anomie

Sudden change		Breakdown of normative structure		Development of the state of irrationality		State of normlessness and de-regulation
(Because of progress, regression, technological change)	→	(Slackening of collective order and regulating force)	→	(Lack of knowledge of right and wrong)	→	(People use this state to satisfy their excessive impulses)

Durkheim had argued that deviance is likely to increase in circumstances of anomie, i.e., circumstances in which social norms are no longer clear and people are morally adrift. This concept suggests that deviant is not a special type of person but a product of certain kinds of social structure.

It is an idea later on followed by many theorists of criminal (deviant) behaviour like Robert Merton (1957), Albert Cohen (1955) and Cloward and Ohlin (1960). Their theories have been discussed later on.

Durkheim's second concern is his focus upon the functions of deviance. In *The Rules of Sociological Method* (1895) he suggests that 'crime is normal because a society exempt from it is utterly impossible'. For him, deviance is bound up with the very conditions for a society; far from deviance being abnormal or pathological in itself, every society needs deviance. Why deviance is universal? Answering this question, Durkheim suggests that deviance fulfils a number of important functions. Citing Socrates, he argues that one of these functions is to bring about change: today's deviants are signs of tomorrow's world. Durkheim's this argument has not been accepted by all. This is not true of all deviance. In contrast to the function of facilitating change, there is also a major function of solidarity and cohesion secured by deviance: people unite against a common enemy.

Merton's Theory

Robert Merton followed Durkheim but modified his analysis of anomie and deviance both. Merton used the term 'anomie' to describe the strain which occurs when individuals experience conflict between pursuit of society's goals and the means society provides to achieve them. Where such strains existed, individuals would be more likely to adopt deviant means to achieve their goals. In the broad sense, it is the social structure which exerts pressure upon individuals, causing some of them, under certain conditions to engage in deviant behaviour. While contextualizing deviance or non-conformity within the total social structure, Merton proposed a descriptive typology of deviant behaviour in the following diagrammatic form:

Cultural goals	*Institutional means*	*Type of deviance*	*Examples*
+	+	Innovation	Economic offenders
–	+	Ritualism	Bureaucrats (Bureaucratic Work)
–	–	Retreatism	Bohemians, Vagabonds, Chronic drunkards, drug addicts, etc.
+	+	Rebellion	Revolutionaries

N.B.: (+) = Acceptance; (–) = Passive Rejection; (+) = Rejection and Substitution.

In terms of the typology, a criminal is one who accepts the cultural goals of monetary success but adopts illegitimate means for pursuing it, and thereby indulges in 'innovation'.

Despite its popularity, Merton's theory of deviance has had relatively two applications. Moreover, this theory has no answers to the questions—why do some disadvantaged groups have lower rates of reported crime than others? Why is criminal behaviour not viewed as a viable alternative by many people faced with adversity? Nevertheless, Merton has made a key contribution to sociological understanding of deviance.

Sutherland's Theory

Members of the so-called 'Chicago School' examined deviancy as a part of a normal learning process of cultural transmission. Following this line of thought, Edwin Sutherland (1939) formulated a general theory of criminal behaviour known as *the theory of differential association.* The theory states that criminal behaviour is learned; it is not inherited, contrived, nor invented by the actor. Individuals learn to be deviant through their association with others who are already so, principally in small, intimate (primary) groups. An association with other deviants provides support for the deviant behaviour. They are socialized to deviant norms. This learning includes the techniques of committing the crime and 'the specific direction of motives, drives rationalizations and attitudes'. People become criminal as a consequence of an excess of social definitions favourable to violation of law over definitions unfavourable to violation of law. This is the main principle of differential association. The central thesis of this theory is that criminal behaviour results from the same processes as other social behaviour. The integral parts of this theory are contact, interaction, communication and learning.

Differential associations are not of all equal weight; some have more impact than others. This weight varies with *frequency, duration, priority* and *intensity.* Persons become criminal because they apparently have more contacts in their daily lives with criminals or quasi-criminals than with non-criminals and their milieu is heavily weighted by individuals who are crime-motivated and crime-oriented. Differential association is a logical consequence of the principle of learning by association. It is really another way of saying that he who runs with thieves is very likely to become a thief.

Sutherland denies that criminal behaviour can be explained by 'general needs and values'. This is not because they do not help to determine criminal behaviour, but because both criminal and non-criminal behaviours are expressions of the same general needs and values. Thieves steal for money, honest labourers work for it. To explain it, we must find differences.

The theory is important as a critique of explanations which treated criminals as abnormal persons (some biological types) because it located the cause of crime in general social process. While the theory is valuable in the study of professional criminals who have a deviant career, it is less relevant in the case of crimes like homicide or suicide which are typically single, isolated acts.

Theory of Delinquency Area and Subculture

Since 1920, with the emergence of the scientific school of sociology developed under R.E. Park and E.W. Burgess, the sociologists have focused much of their attention on the community and its impact on the individual. As a result, many new theories, approaches and concepts developed such as 'delinquency area' (Clifford Shaw), 'subculture' theory (Albert Cohen), 'differential opportunity' theory (Cloward and Ohlin) and many others. Shaw's 'delinquency area' approach rests upon the idea that there are certain areas in the cities which act as breeding ground for the delinquency. This concept was born out of the study of Chicago. These areas are characterized by physical deterioration, high proportion of population (often congested and disorganized) and high patterns of ethnic and racial minorities. The people who live in these areas (generally known as 'slums' or 'ghettos') are marginal, having mere subsistence level, and often clash among themselves. In Frederic Thrasher's work *The Gang,* this delinquency area approach was utilized to study 1,313 gangs in Chicago. While criticizing the 'delinquency area' concept, Albert Cohen (1955) stated that much delinquency flows from a subculture that persists in certain social classes (lower income groups), primarily in many urban areas, generation to generation. These classes he described as non-utilitarian, malicious and negativistic. According to his theory, it is the delinquent subculture which emphasizes on the existence of norms and values that place positive value on delinquent behaviour and confer status on gang members for delinquent acts. Such a subculture also defines the altitudes and behaviour towards those outside the group. The mere motivation to steal or to indulge in some other criminal activity is inadequate to account for deviant behaviour. Deviant subcultures provide learning experiences and opportunity structures parallel to those provided in the legitimate areas of society.

Cloward and Ohlin (1960), in their attempt to explain deviant behaviour, proposed a concept 'differential opportunity'—differential access to illegitimate means. The point is that some individuals through their social backgrounds and spheres of interaction find it easier than others to learn and utilize illegitimate means. They have the 'know-how' and the contacts. The kinds of illegitimate opportunities and their distribution determine the content of the deviant behaviour. Delinquent subcultures, according to Cloward and Ohlin, typically take one of three forms: (1) criminal subcultures, (2) conflict subcultures, and (3) retreatist subcultures. This typology is an extension of Merton's typology of non-conformity. Whereas Merton highlights that access of legitimate opportunity is unequal, they point out that the same applies to illegitimate opportunity. Young people from lower socio-economic classes and minorities, impoverished and ill-educated, who are denied the means of fulfilling their aspirations instilled in them by society, band themselves together to achieve by illegitimate means what they cannot hope to obtain legitimately. According to Cloward and Ohlin's theory, most juvenile delinquents do not aspire to the middle class, they merely want to improve their lot.

Marxist Theory

Recently, there have been attempts to see deviance as a form of social conflict and to link it to Marxism. Marxists argue that conflict not consensus is the fundamental social reality. They see two main points about deviance. First, deviance is partly the product of unequal power relations and inequality in general and for this capitalistic system is responsible. Second, it is because people with power protect their own interests and define deviance to suit their own needs. The 'rules' operate broadly in favour of the dominant class, some of its members often break and 'bend' the rules for their own gains. Marxists point out that many crimes committed by the rich and the powerful go unheeded. Not only this, the criminal justice system also serves the interests of the rich and the powerful. Many conflict theorists argue that law-making is often an attempt by the powerful to coerce others into their own morality.

Deviant behaviour cannot be assigned to any single universal source. It may be the result of manifold causes. It springs from a wide variety, and usually from a multiplicity of alternative and converging influences. The nature of these factors, and their varying combinations, differs greatly from one individual to another.

Deviant behaviour is not peculiar to some people but in fact experienced by all people. Most probably, people commit one or more deviant acts in their lifetime, particularly when young. But most of them do not follow a deviant career. Instead, they become 'committed' to conventional rules and behavioural patterns of their own groups in society. However, once they come under the category of deviants, the label of deviants stick to them, regardless of anything else they may do.

Conformity, Deviance and Social Control

Conformity and deviance are two responses to real or imagined pressures from others. Conformity means going along one's peers—individuals of a person's own status. A recruit entering military service will typically conform to the habits and language of other recruits. Conformity is opposite to social deviance which implies obedience to the norms that make a person acceptable in a particular society, group, or social setting. The concept of conformity was also used by Robert Merton (1957) to refer to acceptance of cultural goals and the legitimate or approved means of achieving them. In his scheme of adaptations to the goals and means, only conformity to both indicates non-deviance.

Deviance is a behaviour that violates the standards of conduct or expectations or social norms of a group or society. Alcoholics, gamblers, sex deviants, drug addicts or late comers in the class are all classified as deviants or deviant acts. Deviance involves the violation of group norms. It is a very comprehensive concept that includes not only criminal behaviour but also many actions not subject to prosecution. Standards of deviance vary from group to group and also vary over time. Moreover, deviance can be understood within its social context.

A society must have social order if it is to function smoothly. But no society succeeds in getting all its members to behave as expected all the time. When a person fails to conform to the social norms of society, social deviation arises. If societies are to survive, they must have ways of making people conform to social norms. This situation gives rise to different types of controls—planned and unplanned or persuasive and coercive. Control works two levels: internal and external. Internal controls are those that exist inside individuals. It is sometimes referred to as self-control. It differs from social control. Self-control works from within while social control is from without. The working of internal controls can be explained through the process of socialization that we have discussed earlier in this chapter and in the chapter on socialization as well. External controls are those that come from outside the individual. They can be either formal or informal. All these types of social control have been explained in the beginning of this chapter.

Chapter 6

Kinship and Family

KEY FEATURES

- What is Kinship?
- The Family
- Forms of Family
- Different Perspectives of Family
- Changes in Family Patterns
- Factors of Change
- Indian Joint Family
- Changes in the Joint Family
- Future of the Family

The phenomena of kinship, marriage and family are interrelated. In spite of differences in social, economic and political institutions, kinship, marriage and family have central place in all societies. In all societies, we find some general norms for defining these institutions and groups. These norms consist of such matters as who marries whom, how mates are selected, who lives together, who is the head of the group, which relatives in family and kin groups are most important, and children are to be raised and socialized by whom. These norms vary greatly around the world. This is why, a tremendous variety of marriage, family and kinship patterns exist.

What is Kinship?

Kinship is the most universal and basic of all human relationships. It is one of the main organizing principles of human society. It is based on ties of blood, marriage or adoption (some societies recognize varieties of fictive kin also). The state of being related to others on the basis of blood ties (real or imaginary) and marriage are collectively referred to as *kinship*. According to Anthony Giddens (1997), 'kinship ties are connections between individuals, established either through marriage or the lines of descent that connect blood relatives (mother, father, offspring, grandparents, etc.). Kinship is culturally learned and is not totally determined by biological or marital ties. For example, adoption creates a kinship tie which is legally acknowledged and socially accepted.

Anthropologists often distinguish between ties based on descent and those based on affinity, i.e., ties resulting from marriage. Relationships established by marriage are usually known as affinal relationships. The relationship between spouses and their relations on either side comes under this category. Relationships based on blood ties are called consanguineous (same blood) relationships. The relationships between parents and their children and that between siblings, i.e., children of the same parents, are known as consanguineous kin (agnates). In determining consanguineous kin, it is not the biological fact that is important but social recognition. Such relationships may or may not be actual but may be based on supposed ties of blood as we find in the universal practice of adoption. An adopted child is everywhere treated as if it were one's own biologically produced offspring.

The family and the kin group are not necessarily the same. Family is only one type of kinship association. It is the social organization of reproductive activity. While family is a household unit, kin groups do not always live together or function as a collective body on a daily basis. Kin groups include aunts, uncles, cousins, in-laws, and so forth. The members of kin group meet together only on certain occasions, such as feasts and festivals, marriage or funeral, etc. In small tribal societies, kinship is the basis of social organization. In other words, the kin group and the society are one and the same thing. As societies become more complex, kinship ties become relatively unimportant, as we find in industrial societies. Kinship is socially important because of its connection to social rights, responsibilities and obligations, power, the social inheritance of property and status. Kinship and affinity rules may also affect residence, relationship between individuals, modes of addressing, and economic and political behaviour.

The concept of kinship is vital to anthropologists not only because it exists in smaller non-industrial societies as a major part of social organization, but it is less important in industrial (modern) societies. As such, sociologists treat this topic as important mainly in the form of sociology of family.

The Family

Anthropologist George Murdock (1949) has observed that there are only two truly units of human organization—the family and the community. Philosophers and social analysts have also noted that society is a structure made of families and these have been observable throughout man's history. It is unlikely that any society has ever existed without some social arrangement that could be termed 'family'. Even in most primitive societies, it existed in some or the other form. It has remained present in all cultures despite variations in its composition, descent, residence and authority patterns.

The family is the basic social institution from which the other institutions—political, economic, religious and educational—have grown as increasing cultural complexity made them necessary. It is the institution which links the individual to the large social structure and thus performs the mediating function in the large society. It is through the family that the society is able to elicit from the individual his/her necessary contribution. It grows out of biological needs, such as procreation, protection of the expectant mother and the infant child, and old and the sick who cannot support and live by themselves. Not only this, it also helps in the socialization of the young, the production and distribution of food and the exploitation of environment which is essential to permit the satisfaction of the more intimate biological needs which cannot take place without organized cooperative efforts.

What is meant by the term 'family'? The term 'family' has been defined in various ways in a narrow and broad sense both. In a very narrow sense, Elliot and Merrill (1961) defined it as 'a biological social unit composed of husband, wife and children'. Almost, in similar terms, Ogburn and Nimkoff (1950) stated, 'family is more or less a durable association of husband and wife with or without children or of a man or woman alone with children'. However, in modern times, one of the most notable features of the Western society has been the increase in the single-parent family, i.e., a family where one parent, usually the mother, resides with, and takes responsibility for parenting her children. Not only this, there are instances of pairing in which unmarried people are living together or homosexual couple rearing children. Such people call their pairing as families.

In a broader sense, family has been defined by Burgess and Locke (1963) as '... a group of persons united by the ties of marriage, blood or adoption, constituting a single household, interacting and intercommunicating with each other in their respective social role of husband and wife, mother and father, son and daughter, brother and sister, creating and maintaining a common culture'. Similarly, *Oxford Dictionary of Sociology* (1994) defines family as an intimate domestic group made up of people related to one another by bonds of blood, sexual mating or legal ties. According to MacIver and Page (1959), 'the family is a group defined by a sex relationship sufficiently precise and enduring to provide for the procreation and upbringing of children'. In the two definitions cited above, the roles, functions and relationships between different members have also been taken into account besides the associational aspect of the family. Looking to the possibility of its polygamous character as found in many primitive and even modern societies, anthropologist Edward Westermark defined it as 'a relation of one or more men to one or more women which is recognized by custom or law and involves certain rights and duties both in the case of parties entering the union and in the case of the children born of it'. This definition seems to be most exhaustive as it includes its associational and institutional aspects both.

Recently, Anderson and Sabatelli (1999) have defined family as 'an interdependent group of individuals who have a shared sense of history, experience, some degree of emotional bondage and devise strategies for meeting needs of individual members and the groups as a whole'. This definition locates the crucial roles and responsibilities of the family members as a linked entity.

Family can be studied as a group, a social system and a social institution. As a social group, it consists of spouses and their children with or without other nearest blood relatives. It is the primary social group in which early childhood socialization takes place. As a social system, it is composed of interdependent parts, it has a characteristic organization and pattern of functioning, and it has sub-systems that are part of larger system. The family is also considered as a social institution because it is an area of human social life that is organized in discernible patterns. It helps in meeting our crucial societal goals and needs. As an institution, it places emphasis on household, marital and kinship relationships, along with norms and values that govern inter- and intra-familial relationships.

Forms of Family

Families throughout the world vary in many different ways. There are tremendous variations in family structures around the world. Variations in family structures include variations in accepted modes of mate selection (endogamy and exogamy), forms of marriage (monogamy, polygamy), rules of authority (patriarchal or matriarchal), rules of descent and inheritance (patrilineal or matrilineal and sometime bilateral), rules of residence (patrilocal, matrilocal or neolocal) as we find in modern society. We here explain the important forms of family based on structure and marriage.

Nuclear Family

It is a unit generally composed of married couple (in the statuses of husband and wife) in the role of 'mother' and 'father' or 'parent' and their unmarried dependent children, either natural or adopted, living together. It is called nuclear as it serves as the core or nucleus upon which larger family groups are built. It is also sometimes referred to as 'conjugal family'. Such type of family is relatively independent of the wider kinship network because the social emphasis is placed primarily on the marital relationships. William Goode (1959) observed that spouses in the nuclear family have to rely heavily on each other for the companionship and support that might be provided by other relatives in an extended (joint) family system.

The term 'nuclear family' is sometimes used for such families also which may and may not include husband and wife. They consist of any two or more persons related to one another by blood, marriage or adoption who share a common residence. Thus, a brother and sister or a single parent and child would be nuclear families but not strictly speaking conjugal families. In conjugal family the emphasis is primarily on conjugal bound, i.e., marital relationship.

In virtually all societies we can identify this type of family. In most traditional societies, including India, the nuclear family was part of a larger kinship network of some type. Anthropologist G.P. Murdock (1949) asserts that it is a 'universal human grouping'. However, there are several categories of evidence against this position. Family units comprising step parents as a consequence of divorce or remarriage is known as 'reconstituted family'. It is a form of nuclear family in which one or both parents have had children from a previous relationship.

Extended Family

When nucleus of the conjugal family is extended by the addition of other closely related kin (grandparents, aunts, uncles, nephews, brothers and their wives, cousins, sisters, etc.), it is called an extended family. Giddens (1997) writes: 'When close relatives other than a married couple and their children live in the same household or in close and continuous relationship with one another, we speak of extended family.' As stated above, an extended family may include grandparents, brothers and their wives and children, sisters and their husbands, aunts and nephews. The term refers to a family system in which several generations live in one household. It consists of several related individual families by blood or marital ties. In most traditional societies, the extended family is the norms which go beyond the nuclear family unit. But, the old structure of extended family is crumbling and fast changing everywhere and in its place a modified extended family is gradually coming up.

The form of extended family differs from society to society. Indian joint family is also one of the forms of extended family. It is an extended form of consanguine family in which many blood relatives together with their mates and children reside. It is different from conjugal family which has a married couple as its core, surrounded by a fringe of blood relatives, whereas the consanguine family has a group of brothers and sisters at its core surrounded by a fringe of husbands and wives. Generally, it is defined as, *when two or more lineal or collateral nuclear families live together in one household, it is called joint family* (in reality, 'joint families are an amalgam of what have otherwise been several families of origin and procreation') (Majumdar 1956).

Families formed on the basis of marriage are of two types: *monogamous family*, in which one man marries one woman at a time, while *polygamous family* is formed by the concurrent marriage of one sex to two or more members of the opposite sex. Polygamous family is of two types:

(a) *polygynous family*, in which a man may be married to more than one woman at the same time, and (b) *polyandrous family* in which a woman may have two or more husbands simultaneously. This type of family is much less common.

Families Based on Descent, Inheritance and Residence

Norms of descent, inheritance, authority patterns and residence also decide the forms of family. The most common norm of descent is *patrilineal*. In this type of descent, lineage is traced through father's kin: offspring owe a special allegiance and loyalty to father and his kin. It indicates that only the father's relatives are important in matters of property, inheritance and the establishment of emotional ties. Conversely, in societies which favour *matrilineal descent,* the mother's relatives assume the important role among offspring. This pattern of descent is not common, but they do exist as we find in Khasi and Garo tribes of North-East India. When both sides of a person's family are regarded important, this system is referred to as *bilateral descent*. In this system, kinship lines are traced equally through the biological relatives of both the mother and the father and inheritance is passed on in equal proportions to children regardless of sex.

Now, the question arises: Who rules? Who has the power to make a decision? Societies vary the way the power within the family is distributed. Most societies are *patriarchal,* i.e., the men have the power and authority and are dominant. They dominate in all family decision-making. Women hold low status in such societies. By contrast, in *matriarchal* societies, the authority rests with the females, especially wives and mothers. This system is rare and even in such societies male members are seen exercising power through female members. The least common pattern of authority is the *egalitarian* model in which spouses are regarded as equals and decisions are equally taken by husband and wife. In modern times, the egalitarian family has begun to replace the patriarchal family as the social norm.

Norms of residence are very many. When a married couple chooses its own place of residence or decides to establish a separate household, it is known as *neolocal family*. This type of residence pattern seems to be linked most closely with norms of monogamy and individualism. In many societies, the bride and groom live either with groom's parents (the *patrilocal family*) or with bride's parents (the *matrilocal family*). In such cultures it is felt that the new couples need the emotional support and especially the economic support of kinsfolk. Usually it is seen that the young couple begin their married life not as an independent household (neolocal residence) but with parents of either spouse and later on after sometime they set up an independent household of their own.

Sociologists also distinguish families of orientation and families of procreation. The family (usually nuclear) in which one is born and reared is termed as *family of orientation*. This is the family in which the most basic early childhood socialization occurs. Contrary to this, when a person marries, a new nuclear (or conjugal) family is formed, it is known as *family of procreation*. It is a family in which the person procreates after being married. This family consists of oneself and one's spouse and children. Thus, a person becomes member of two different but overlapping nuclear families. Marriage is a dividing line between family of orientation and family of procreation in terms of the nature of roles one performs in two families.

Different Perspectives of Family

There are various perspectives to study family—functionalist, conflict, exchange, interactionist and feminist. We shall in the following paragraphs analyse family from these perspectives one by one:

Functionalist Perspective

Functionalist perspective analyses the functions of the family in relation to society and the adaptation of the family to historical change. As a social institution, the family is defined by social functions it is expected to perform. Functionalists regard the family as an important 'organ' in the body of society and believed that the nuclear family is universal. Friedrich Engels (1884), a close colleague of Karl Marx, questioned the need of the family. He described the family as the ultimate source of social inequality. Following this line, some conflict sociologists argued that the family contributes to societal injustice, denies opportunities to women and limits to their freedom. On the contrary, functionalists maintain that families perform vital functions for their members, and for society. Despite the variations that exist in family structure around the world, families everywhere perform many of the same functions. In spite of many changes and modifications in its constitution that the family has undergone some of its functions has remained with it since the remote historical times. These functions are mostly the primary functions of the family and have also been active ingredients in the evolution and development of the family.

George Murdock (1945), an early functionalist, considered the four basic (universal) functions of the family to be sexual, reproductive, educational or socializing and economic. Murdock argues that without the sexual and reproductive functions society would become extinct; without economic cooperation among family members, life would cease; and without the education of children, culture would end. Now, we will describe these functions along with some other functions that a family performs:

(i) Reproduction (biological function)

In all societies, primitive or modern, simple or complex, human sex urge requires established and socially-recognized regular channels of satisfaction. Procreation of the human specie (indirectly replacement of dying members) is generally a consequence of satisfaction of sex urge. In this sense, the family contributes to human survival through its function of satisfaction of the sexual impulse and reproduction. Cohabition leads to conception and children satisfy the psychic instinct of parental love.

(ii) Protection

Unlike the young of animal species, human infants need constant care and economic security. In all cultures, the family assumes ultimate responsibility for the physical, economic and psychological protection and upbringing of children. Not only the parents provide above mentioned protection to their children, but children also provide some social and economic protection against physical and psychological needs to their parents in old age.

(iii) Socialization

The family is one of the most important agents of socialization. All children everywhere get their earliest instruction in the family. It is the agency through which the child is made familiar with the patterns of social behaviour. The transmission of cultural tradition proceeds from generation to generation through family.

The family is the first primary group where child's personality development begins. Parsons and Bales (1955) suggested two essential functions of family: (a) the primary socialization—children learn to speak a particular dialect (language), to prefer certain foods and dress, and to pursue certain types of professional activities in the family; and (b) the stabilization of adult personalities of the society—which teaches and transmits to its members the knowledge, skills, values, expectations and the set of norms of the society and subculture. It is here that the child learns to assume the role models of a husband/wife and a father/mother through role-taking play.

(iv) Sexual regulation

The family defines socially approved and disapproved sexual outlets. There is an almost universal taboo against incest, whereas marriage is the most universally approved outlet for sexual behaviour. Both are linked to the family system. Sexual relationships are generally defined in terms of the family and marriage, as pre-marital or extra-marital relationships.

(v) Affection and emotional support (psychological function)

Cry is the only language of a child and it is the family which guarantees that the language of that cry be understood. Humans are social animals who depend on their families at every stage of the life cycle for affection and emotional support. We expect our relatives to understand and to care for us. Lack of affection actually damages an infant's ability to survive. Ageing persons also need emotional support from their children which proves a major source of life gratification.

(vi) Social placement (identity)

One important function of the family is providing social status in the society. We inherit a social position because of the family background and reputation of our parents and siblings. The family serves as a basis for ascribing several statuses—age, sex, birth order, caste and class. Even statuses that are achieved such as marriage, occupation, and education are also influenced by one's membership in a particular family. In brief, it helps in influencing and determining the many roles and statuses children will occupy in society.

(vii) Economic security

The family is the basic economic unit in many societies. Even in primitive societies, it used to be a self-sufficient unit in which members of the family consumed primarily what they had produced. This situation, however, has changed or changing gradually. Occupational skills, science and technology have greatly affected this function. Now, anybody can learn the skills and intricacies of any occupation.

(viii) Legitimacy of the children

The family is the most widely approved social institution which helps in providing legal status and social approval to parenthood and reproduction. Renowned anthropologist Malinowski (1936) called it the 'principle of legitimacy'. The principle states that every society has a rule that every child should have a legitimate father to act as the child's protector, guardian and representative in the society. Legitimacy also helps in deciding matters related to inheritance and succession.

(ix) Religious function

Much of the religious attitudes used to be formed in family circle, but this is not a trend today. Take the cases of Barack Obama (US President) and A.R. Rahman (a noted musician).

Conflict Perspective

According to the conflict perspective, family members continually struggle for power and control. Conflict theorists contend that social systems, including family, are not static structures that maintain equilibrium and harmony among their parts. They argue that social systems, along with family, are constantly in a state of conflict and change. Conflict stems from unequal distribution of power over scarce resources. This inequality exists not only in economic and occupational realms but also in the family. Conflict is as inevitable in the family as it is in society, and it leads to change. The theorists view the family as a bolster for a capitalist society.

Friedrich Engels' book *The Origin of the Family* (1902) remains the starting point for most conflict (Marxist) analyses of the family and of gender relations. He claimed that the family, the basic unit in a capitalist society, serves as the chief means of oppressing women. The major contribution of Engels' was to assert 'women's oppression as a problem of history, rather than biology'. This is the basis of Marxist and most conflict analyses of the family. Using the Marxist terminology, conflict theorists regard the husband as the bourgeois and the wife the proletariat. Some Marxists regard the sexual possessiveness of marital partners as just one expression of the possessive and self individualism of capitalist society. Collins (1977) argues that the basic institution of sexual gratification is the notion of sexual property – the belief that one has eminent exclusive sexual rights to a particular person. In societies (patriarchal) dominated by males the principal form of sexual property is male ownership of females, or husband ownership of wives. The status of women is also evident in wedding ceremonies, just as in India, in which the father 'gives away' some of his property—the bride—who is told not just to love but to honour and obey her new owner (the groom).

Marxists further argue that the liberation of women depends on a change in social system from capitalism to socialism. They suggest that the structure of domination shifts as resources shift. Thus, women today have a better bargaining position because they hold jobs and are economically independent. 'Women become at least potentially free to negotiate their sexual relationship' (Collins, 1977). However, the changes involve much more than just sexual relationships. Conflict in families also occur over issues other than inequality between men and women. It can arise over a variety of issues such as inheritance rights, decision-making, selection of mates, etc. In every case, the issue is likely to give rise to inequality of power, authority or resources, which may lead to conflict. Marxists believe that to abolish sexual property riots in females, the socializing and other functions of nuclear family could be pared down and done more effectively by other institutions.

Exchange Perspective

The exchange perspective assumes that all human relationships, including those between husbands and wives or parents and children, can be viewed in terms of social exchange, i.e., there are rewards and costs in all relationships including those in marriage and family. This view suggests that when selecting a spouse, people try to get the best they can with what they have to offer. The complementary need theory (Winch, 1958) proposes that people seek mates who will meet their needs without causing conflicts. For example, if both people are dominant, the relationship would not succeed, but if one is dominant and the other is submissive, the relationship is complementary and the needs of both parties are met smoothly.

Interactionist Perspective

Interactionist perspective emphasizes the influence of role expectations and how people define situations. In this view, marriage, like other relationships, is a dynamic process of reciprocal interactions. According to this view, husband and wife have reciprocal influence on each other. Each partner continually affects the other and thus adjustment is a process, not an end result. In the process of adjustment, the couple tries to share role definitions, meanings and perceptions. Adjustment is the result of shared expectations. For successful marriage, a process of adjustment of continual adaptations to shift in shared meaning is required.

Following this perspective, Willmott and Michael (1973) made some interesting observations on changes in family roles and relationships. They argued that the direction of change in the familial roles is towards *symmetrical family,* i.e., a joint or shared approach to married life rather than one which is segregated into largely separate roles. The symmetrical family is not wholly egalitarian but 'a measure of egalitarianism' does exist. The reasons for the development of symmetrical family are two-fold: Firstly, immense improvements in household technology are assumed to have reduced much of the drudgery of housework and to have simplified it to the extent that any member of a household can do it. Secondly, as more women are doing paid work, there is practical logic and fairness in men becoming more involved with domestic work.

Feminist Perspective

Feminist perspective stresses the subordination and oppression of women within the family and society. In many respects it is similar to the conflict perspective which we have dealt earlier. Feminists recognize that sex, reproduction, socialization and economic production 'need' to occur but not necessarily in ways that 'exploit' female labour and leave them relatively powerless. This perspective rejects the naturalistic approach of functionalist theories and emphasizes that the gendered division of labour which allocates domestic work overwhelmingly to women is seen as socially constructed, not as the product of nature. French social scientist, Michael Foucault viewed females as positioned in subordinate situations by being drawn into discourses (stories, images, myths, ideologies) which place them there. Discourses such as the myths of domesticity or submissive feminity help to create real gender and other inequalities. Secondly, the view that the family is a sphere of personal autonomy and free affective expression is seen as a convenient myth which helps to subordinate women. Radical critics Michelle Barrett and Mary McIntosh (1982) regarded family as not only oppressive to women but also an anti-social institution. Some feminists believe that the conjugal family oppresses and represses individuality.

Changes in Family Patterns

The 18th and 19th century industrial revolution, which has been largely technical in nature (brought changes in technology), has also brought with it the spirit of materialism and hedonism. This spirit has greatly affected the society as a whole—its economic and social values and ideology. Any change in the society has some bearing on the system of family—a basic institution of society. Today, the family is not the same as it was before industrialization. Industrialization has changed the concept of the family largely. About a half century back, Burgess and Lock, in their book, *The Family* (1953) said that the family is moving fast or slowly 'from institution to companionship'. It is united not by work and external pressures but by shared interests and affections. The direction of change is from the traditional family system—usually extended or joint family system to some form of conjugal family system (neolocal and nuclear form) of which the kinship network is not strong. Commenting on this new form of family, William J. Goode (1963) argued that this nuclear family pattern is in itself a world revolution. As a part of the revolution, the nuclear family emphasizes the importance of the freedom of the individual to choose his/her own life and control his/her own destiny, released in good part from the one's rigid controls of extended kinship structures. At the same time, we are experiencing the shrinking ties among kinship groups and reduction of the sense of responsibility that family members used to have for one another. Such a family is moving in harmony with the rest of our institutions.

Everywhere in the world, the family is changing from its old pattern and adapting to the new emerging society in accordance with the time. It is changing in size or perceptions, norms and role structures also. In pre-industrial era, the (agrarian) family was necessarily the centre of life for the individual. It possessed major economic functions as a production unit, organized by a division of labour mostly based on sex and age. It not only socialized the young, it provided much other training of the child as well. A boy learned his occupation by working with his father at a younger age. Furthermore, in an agrarian society the kinship group maintained the aged, nursed the sick, buried the dead and provided for the mentally ill or physically crippled. It also ensured support for widows and orphans and made a place for stray cases of unmarried men and women. As a result, kinship became a most binding and obligatory relationship, regardless of personal feelings, requiring that family interests take precedence over individual one.

The family is no longer the all-encompassing social group; it once was. It has lost its age-old valued functions of rearing and caring (child-raising) and education of the child. Such loss of function reduces the dependence of the young on the family at an early age. Thus, the family loses its authority and control over the young. The major changes that have occurred in the family after industrialization can be summarized in the following points:

Decline of Extended Family System

With the impact of technology and industrial change, there is a worldwide movement towards small, nuclear family maintaining a separate and independent household and breaking down of the traditional extended (joint) family system and other types of kin groups. Their influence is declining in every field of life. A modified extended family structure is emerging in which individual nuclear families retain considerable autonomy and yet maintain connections with other nuclear families or so-called 'joint family'. The traditional pattern, i.e., extended or joint family, rarely exists anywhere in its purest forms. Now, there is a trend towards smaller family, i.e., fewer uncles and aunts and other relatives. But it does not mean that the extended family is totally dead. Mutual support between generations at times of birth, marriage or death still exists in some or the other form but in a modified form.

Fissioned families are increasing day by day which are generally formed after marriages. Newly married couples establish their own family either in the same house or in the same city or in some other city or village. But relations are not totally severed.

Changing Authority Pattern

There is a change in the division of labour and authority in the family. Male authority is declining in the modern family. The concepts of 'symmetrical family' (Young and Willnott, 1973) and 'egalitarian family' are taking place of traditional patriarchal family. The authority is slipping from the hands of family elders because of new economic and political opportunities. Young couples do not rely on family elders for job instructions or education of their children. Because of the dual-career marriages (husband and wife both working), there is a significant change in the attitude towards equality between married partners.

Changing Status of Women

The rights of women are becoming more recognized in respect to both initiation of marriage and decision-making in the family. The 'quite revolution' in women's employment along with the feminist movements has changed the status of women in the family. Now, they are no more chattel or deaf and dumb like animals.

Changing Economic Functions

The modern family is no longer united by shared work on the farm. It is now a unit of consumption instead of a unit of production as it was in the agrarian society. It is now united by feelings of companionship, affection and recreation only.

Free Choice of Mate Selection

A new freedom of personal choice, of freer opportunities for romantic love and sexual intimacy have now entered the society. The individualism, which industrialism had created, permeated all spheres of social life, not just economic; it encouraged the ideal of romantic love and free choice of mate. Young people began to give more attention to their own feelings, and less to parental wishes. They also started paying court to whom they liked rather than whom their parents thought best. Kin arranged marriages, thus, are becoming less common. Even in India, which is a traditional society, this trend is increasing day by day in urban areas due to free mixing opportunities available in educational institutions and at workplaces.

Decline in Family Size

Most married couples want to have children, but economic considerations force them to have smaller family with one or two children. Young people believe that reproduction is not the duty of all married couples. Today, a joint family of ten or more children living under one roof is rare to find. Children are no more economically necessary, unlike in an agrarian society. Neo-localism is developing in which married couples live alone wherever they wish. Couples prefer to have a 'car' rather than a 'child' these days.

Changing Attitudes Towards Sex and Marriage

There is a revolution in sexual attitudes and practices. Higher levels of sexual freedom (open expression of pre-marital and extra-marital sex) are developing in societies that were earlier very restrictive. For the young, sex has become as casual as having a cup of coffee together. Pre-marital pregnancies have increased considerably in Western countries and America. There is an increase in male-female couples who choose to live together without marriage. This has given rise to the concepts of 'living together,' 'living arrangements' or 'live-in relationships'. Such couples engage in what is commonly called 'cohabitation'. Because of these changes, some new forms of families have emerged such as families of unmarried couples, families of single or lone (single) parent and families of homosexuals.

Declining Trend in Non-essential Functions

As stated earlier, most of the socializing functions today, like child raising, education, occupational training, caring of elderly, etc., have been taken over by the outside agencies, such as creches, media, nursery schools, hospitals, occupational training centres, hospice institutions, funeral contractors, etc. These tasks were once exclusively performed by the family.

The protective functions of the family are on the verge of decline. For example, the function of providing help and shelter to the sick, aged and handicapped has been taken over by agencies like health institutions, old-age houses, deaf and dumb institutions, etc. However, these functions are still performed to some extent by the family in India because of the persistence of old traditions and values.

As the society is becoming more and more industrialized, parents can less and less transmit occupational succession to their children, especially in the case of the wage-earning working class and the salaried clerks and professionals. But where there is a family business, this is possible but that too is also changing because of specialized nature of many modern businesses.

The affectionate and companionship functions have emerged as the most valued aspect of the modern conjugal family today. The tie between husband and wife is viewed as the most important bond holding the family together. Though most of the other functions might have been taken over or being performed by other agencies, it is the only function which is still performed by the family. The other relationships like father/mother-in-law with daughter-in-law have become subordinate relationships. These are interactional changes in the family.

Commenting over the family life in the modern space age in the 14th International Family Conference held at Rio de Janeiro, Christensen declared that family is, 'little more than a "service station" for its members where they call in for sleep, food and other services, but in which they do not spend a lot of time and towards which they do not feel a great deal of loyalty'. Not surprisingly, it is widely perceived that a radical change is occurring in one of society's key institutions. It is perceived by many that the institution of family is 'in trouble'. New forces of change are gradually undermining the traditional system of family. The old size of the family is giving way to the smallest unit (nuclear family) of human association, which is essential for the prime act of procreation, rearing and caring of the new-born child. Available evidence suggests that blood and marriage alone cannot bind families and communities together; some other adhesive is required, either common acceptance of gendered hierarchical relationship, or love and solidarity. In the absence of both families tend to break down, renowned social philosopher Eric From once remarked about the declining trend of family: 'We tend to love things more than people and to use people for personal advantage very much as we are things … . Frequently today people are valued for what they acquire or achieve more than for what they are.'

Commenting over the declining functions of the family, Talcott Parsons remarked that the family has shed some of its less necessary functions, such as economic, political, health, education, recreation, but it still performs the most important functions of socialization and 'tension and emotional management' which are keeping alive the institution of family in face of so many onslaughts on it.

Factors of Change

Changes in family patterns are being produced by many factors. The important among these are science and technology (industrialization), expansion of towns and cities (urbanization) and employment of men and women both within organizations outside family influence. The material condition of industrial-capitalist society is the main cause of change in the family. Greater affluence, geographical and occupational mobility and economic independence of (some) women are the main contributing factors for the change in patterns of residence and family life.

The global factor (technology and industrial change) is nearly encompassing everything. Since it is everything, naturally it causes everything. Industrial change or industrialization includes not merely machines, but the science and engineering that produced them, the secular attitudes of the modern era, anti-traditionalism, job placement on the basis of competence, an open-class system, high geographical mobility and urbanization. Industrialization in this enveloping sense does 'cause' the modern social and family patterns. These changes are tending to produce a worldwide movement towards nuclear family systems, eroding extended (joint) family forms and other types of kinship group. It is opined that there is a 'fit' between industrialization and the conjugal (nuclear) family. There is also some sort of natural harmony between the modern complex of industrialization and the conjugal system. The industrial system has increased the demand of emotional satisfaction which is provided by conjugal bond only. Thus, this family system is attuned to serve the needs of industrialization. The extended family system is unfit to the demands of industrialization. Decreasing emphasis on land ownership also increases the ease in mobility. The conjugal family is neo-local and its kinship network is not strong, thus it puts fewer barriers in geographical mobility.

W.F. Ogburn (1922) saw a wide range of new elements as sources of family change, from ideology to airplane. He argued that the development of formal agencies like schools, hospitals, hotels, etc., for handling major functions of the family have greatly affected the institution of family. Labour-saving devices have reduced the number of hours of the housewife. This has offered more freedom and has relieved them from many household tasks. The young ones need not now rely on family elders for job instructions, since the schools and the factory teach them new skills.

The growth of romanticism, the high premium on individual attachment along with individualistic and liberal values of industrial-capitalist society encourage people to change their partners as they want. In this connection, Giddens (1997) observed, 'for many in the West commitment is "for now," not necessarily "for ever".' Relationships depend on feelings, not an externally imposed moral frameworks. These values have led in the rise of divorce rates and as a consequence single-parent households, reconstituted family or living with step families are increasing. Cohabitation (where a couple lives together in sexual relationship without marriage) has become increasingly common in many developing and developed countries. The situation in India and other traditional societies is bit different where the institutions of marriage and family are still rooted in religion (in India, marriage is regarded as a *samaskar*, a religious sacrament). Baring a few metropolitan cities, people still do not resort to divorce as a common remedy for the ills of marriage.

Indian Joint Family

There are certain technical differences between the joint and the extended family. In Western society, what is called 'joint family' meant one uniting both father's and mother's lines. In this sense, Indian joint family is different from Western joint family. It is not only the extended form of nuclear family as is generally supposed, but it has other ingredients of jointness also. Co-residentiality, i.e., living together of nearest kin relatives with the conjugal family, is only one characteristic of Indian joint family and that too has lost much importance these days. What is meant by 'jointness' that makes a family 'joint' in Indian context, we start with much quoted definition of Irawati Karve (1953). She defined it as 'a group of people who generally live under one roof, who eat food cooked at one hearth, who hold property in common, who participate in common family worship and who are related to each other as some particular type of kindered'. Karve has defined the family in historical context: the family that seems to have existed in Vedic and Epic period or in medieval times. This definition emphasizes on five characteristics of the joint family: (1) common residence; (2) common kitchen; (3) common property and income; (4) common worship; and (5) some kind of kinship relations. If we apply these characteristics to the present Indian families, it would be very difficult to call a handful of families to be joint in the above sense.

According to I.P. Desai (1956), it is the relationship between the members of a household that determines the type of the family. What distinguishes nuclear family from the joint family is the difference in the role, relations and the normative patterns of behaviour among different members. He defined it as under: 'We call that household a joint family which has greater generation depth (i.e., three or more generations) than the nuclear family and the members of which are related to one another by property, income and mutual rights and obligations.' Desai thinks that when two nuclear families having kinship relations are living separately but function under one authority, it will be a joint family. For him, generational depth, rights and obligations and property relations are the main criteria for explaining joint family.

Some sociologists have given importance to commensality and fulfilment of obligations as the criteria of joint family, irrespective common residence and common kitchen. It is the authority of the elder in matters of family and religion, joint investment of capital, joint enjoyment of profits, and of incurring birth, marriage and death expenses out of joint funds that determines a family to be joint. Thus, the main basis of joint family is the subordination of narrow individual interests to the larger interest of the family as a whole. It is the co-operative spirit among the members to help each other at the time of any calamity and their attendance at family functions and the observation of obligations or responsibilities towards other members of the family rather than the facts of co-residence, commensality and the size of the group that keep the family joint. Due to the exigencies of modern times, it is not possible to place undue emphasis on common residence and common kitchen as dimensions of jointness. In its modern form, the nuclear families as the units of a joint family retain considerable autonomy and yet maintain connections with the other nuclear families of brothers and their parents to change gifts, goods and services. This type of family differs from a traditional joint family in that its members may live separately in the same household or in different parts in a city or in different cities in India or outside India and choose their occupations independently rather than following the traditional parental occupation, yet it may be joint family if its members contribute their mite to the feelings of jointness by rendering financial and other kinds of help, performing a various reciprocal obligations and following joint family norms. Physical jointness (common property, purse, common land or business) has more or less weakened, but sentimental jointness still exists. This we can see at the observance of any family ritual—birth, marriage and death—when all members gather. When a joint family grows so large as to be intend to split apart, brothers start new joint families of their own. The Indian joint family has probably always gone through such cycles of formation and fission. To conclude, it may be said that it is a set of relationships and rights and obligations that make a family to be joint rather than its mere structure. 'Instead of large joint families, we will have only locally functioning effective small joint families of two generations and so. At the same time, even the majority of those nuclear families in which a man, his wife and unmarried children live separately, will continue to be "joint" with their primary kin like father or brother in terms of "functioning"(Ahuja, 1993). At the level of interaction, if the actions are oriented towards the husband, wife and children, it should be understood as nuclear family, but if they are oriented towards to a wider group of relatives (brothers, sisters, uncles, aunt and grandparents, etc.), then, it should be understood as a joint family. The basic elements of the traditional joint family may be summarized in the following points:

(a) Responsibilities of members—duties and rights.
(b) Authority structure based on status.
(c) Affectional pattern—intimacy.
(d) Sentiments—mutuality of interest and mutual assistance.
(e) Primary group controls.

The family has been one of the most important institutional pillars of Indian society. 'If there is an "ism" that governs Indian society and its institutions, it is familyism' (Kakar and Kakar, 2007).

Changes in the Joint Family

In the last quarter of the 20th century, the concept of family solidarity began to face the challenge of the individualism inherent in the Western thought. The joint family in India is also crumbling fast as a result of the impact of the forces of modernization which hardly any society in the world can escape today on account of the rapid improvement in communications, thanks to the advance of science and technology. 'Ideally, the joint family is based on the authority and sharing of relations among adult males rather than on conjugal bonds between a married couple. The love and affection between spouses, which might break the joint unit into nuclear families, does not play a major role, since marriages are arranged before a love relationships can develop.' This picture of the traditional joint family was drawn by W.J. Goode (1963) is now not applicable because of the various forces stemming from education, economic progress and new avenues of employment. Even the mate selection procedure has undergone much change. Pre-arranged marriages have become less popular among educated and wealthy class, especially in urban areas. The 'traditional' joint family is passing through a 'transitional' stage which is characterized as under:

1. Nuclearity or jointness of a household is now understood in terms of its interactions and interrelationships among its members. The relationships between members of joint family still exist but with different degrees of intensity.
2. The rights and obligations enjoined with particular relationship among the members of the family and those outside are not fulfilled with the same vigour and zeal as used to be.
3. The large joint family is giving way to the small units of nuclear type. Thus, the number of fissioned families is increasing. Sons prefer to live separately (neo-local residence) from their parents either due to separate occupation or because of other reasons.
4. Instead of structurally jointness, the functional type of joint family is emerging. The married sons though living separately, continue to fulfil their traditional obligations towards parents and siblings, though with lesser and indifferent feelings.
5. Authority of the elders in matters of choosing occupations, mate selection and other matters is weakening.
6. The existence of joint property is now not an essential requisite to keep the family joint. Where there is joint estate and the members of the family become separate in estate, the family sometimes ceases to be joint in terms of common property but still it may function as joint family if its members fulfil their respective obligations and responsibilities towards members of the family wider than the nuclear family.
7. In the traditional joint family, the female role was confined inside the household and the male outside to income-producing work. But, due to industrialization, the housewife and the wage-earning employed labourer as the two basic roles of the new form of family emerged.

According to a recent survey, only about 17 per cent of the households in India now consist of more than one couple and their children. But even the joint family property is broken up, and when couples go away to live separately, emotional ties remain strong, and family solidarity continues. Important decisions may still be made by the eldest male, and the extended family still has a specific geographic centre—the old joint family home, usually in the village.

Writing about joint family, Kingsley Davis long back (1949) observed that joint familism tends to limit social mobility and social change because it binds the individual to others by duties inherent in birth. It ties the young to the old, and forces them to support their indigent relatives regardless of their own efforts to help themselves. Also it is supported and upheld by the caste system in India. Moreover, joint family is largely antithetical to the problems of overpopulation and complete modernization of economy.

What is the future of the traditional Indian joint family? In this context, more than a half century back, eminent sociologist K.M. Kapadia (1966) observed that 'the general assumption that the joint family is dying out is invalid'. He concluded that the traditional joint family has not disintegrated but is passing through severe stresses and strains and its future is not bleak. How far Kapadia's observation is relevant today in the face of rapid changes that are occurring in India due to modernization and the other global forces of change? As we see today that the structure and functions of the traditional joint family are not the same as these were a few years back. Modern forces of change have disintegrated the large joint families to a great extent into smaller units to which today we term 'nuclear family'. These nuclear families are not totally conjugal and in such families old parents, unmarried brothers and sisters also live. It is seen that the families of brothers or the parental family (living separately) do not come into contact over a long period of time. This phenomenon weakens the emotional attachment and even the feelings of family obligations and the authority of the former patriarch also lessons. When this happens, there remains very little feeling to call this reduced unit (family) a joint family. When there remains no feeling or very little feeling and desire for identity within the larger kinship group (Ross, 1961). Thus, the word 'joint family system' cannot be applied anymore to Indian family except as a local term with no unique meaning.

Thus, we may conclude that the traditional joint or semi-joint is no longer the most frequent pattern of family in urban India. But, in the rural areas and smaller cities and towns, the functional and sentimental jointness still persists to some extent; it indicates that as a cultural element, the feeling of jointness may exist for some decades. Increasing urbanization and materialization of life is continually affecting the residential composition (i.e., residential nuclearity) of the family but the cultural elements like the concept of *rin* (debt) and our moral and spiritual duties towards parents and other members of wider kin group will keep the joint family intact in some altered form. It is definite that the Indian family is not going to be of Western type of nuclear family in the near future where relations with the extended kin (parents and siblings) more or less do not exist as we find in India. In India, the social relationships between members of a fissioned joint family are based on binding obligations and emotional attachment. The conjugal, filial and fraternal bonds continue to remain intact to some extent even after disintegration. The members of the joint family, because of the exigencies of modern life, may not live at one place under one hearth, but they still maintain some relations with the members of the wider family group and try to come together on significant events and occasions like wedding, anniversary or death of a family member and also on some festivals such as Holi and Diwali.

Future of the Institution of Family

The existence of the twin institutions of marriage and family, which used to be pivot of all community life, seems to be in peril because of the changes in the attitude and norms of associational living. There have been loud claims that families are in decline and there have even been those who welcome the so-called demise of the family, because it is viewed as oppressive and bankrupt institutions. Scholars of Marxian leanings advocate that there is no need of marriage and stable traditional family. They regard these institutions as the outcome of patriarchal structures, which represent capitalism. Critics of modern family life suggest that a woman's inferior place in the home compound, female inequity in society at large and virtues of intimacy and emotional attachment, in fact, unveils a system of exploitation of wives by husbands and children by parents. Commenting on the modern family, Edmund Leach (1967) wrote, 'The parents and children huddled together in their loveliness take too much out of each other. The parents fight; the children rebel.' Leach further argues that the 'isolation and close-knit nature of contemporary family life inculcates hate which finds expression in conflict in the wider community.'

Since industrialization and its attendant harmful consequences and the disorganization of family life (breaking of family ties, open attitude about sex, increasing divorce rate, a general tendency for seeking personal happiness, mental and emotional disturbances, delinquent behaviour and illegitimate children) and the increasing tendency of 'living together' without marriage after the advent of IT revolution in the mid-20th century, it had become much common to forecast pessimistic future of marriage and family. Whether the family is breaking up or adapting to the modern needs? Traditionalists affirm the idea of breaking up or declining or to use David Cooper's word 'dying'. Feminists and other critics of the conventional family have an interest in derogating it in some way or the other.

Some experts are concerned about the ultimate outcome of the profound changes that occurred after industrialization and IT revolution of the 20th century and are afraid that there will be a complete breakdown of the family. It is rather premature to tell the 'demise' of the family and not to expect that the family will adapt itself to the new situation. Nonetheless, it is but definite that the family is fast changing and its old format is crumbling and is being replaced by a new one.

In spite of the constant prediction of its demise, the family remains a significant institution. It is the only refuge in a brutal society. The family has become the sphere of personal life at a time when people are increasingly looking to themselves, outside of productive work, for meaning and purpose. Resilience and elasticity are the most potent characteristics of this institution, which are keeping it alive. It is certain that there are changes underway, and possibly more to come, which will not only change the structure and functions of family but also its meaning. The loss of traditional functions was the basis for defining the family which used to be the source of emotions and sentiments. These are not found in an impersonal, competitive world of today, for making it a haven in a heartless world.

There are scholars, on the other hand, who are quite certain about the continuation of the institution of family in the face of many damaging attacks on it. Lucien Guibourge, President of the International Union of Family Organization, commented in its 17th conference in 1966, 'the institution of the family would remain as long as humanity existed because its values were universal and they were transmitted from generation to generation'. Indian sociologist G.C. Hallen, in one of his article 'The Future of the Family' (1967), has written that 'the family is an eternal truth and an eternal social reality; its disintegration and degeneration at any stage is only a temporary phenomenon'. The ancient trinity of father, mother and child has survived more vicissitudes than any other family structures. Although more elaborate family (joint family) patterns can be broken from without or may even collapse of their own weight. Expressing confidence in the existence of the family, H.E. Barnes as long back as in 1922 observed, 'If civilization survives the present world crises, we may safely predict that the family will be greatly modified, but the marriage will continue to be as popular as ever, though undoubtedly readjusted in terms of social rationality.' The above observation seems to have come true if we go through the recent studies on marriage and family. Divorces are high both in Western countries and the United States. True, that young people choose to live alone (without marrying) above the age of 30 years and more or they prefer to have 'live-in-relationship' with some partner and marry after long periods of experience. In spite of this, both marriage and family are not unpopular in these societies. Robert Chester (1985) argued that the family (nuclear) and marriage still remain the normative experience for the great majority of Britons where the family is passing through severe stress and strains. Most people live in nuclear families. Most children are brought up in nuclear families. Most marriages end with death, not divorce. Divorcees are usually keen to remarry again. Similar opinion has been expressed by eminent Indian sociologist Andre Beteille on the rising divorces in India (but not to the extent as find in United States and European countries) that 'this does not in any way indicate the end of family as an institution. It only means the family is changing in character. It will be reconstructed and based more on choice'. Majority of married people still do not get divorced even if there is trouble in marital relationships, but remain committed, more or less happily, to one partner for life. Though there is a significant change in attitude towards marital ideal of life-long marriage, still family commitment is a part of our cultural outlook. The basic attitudes of the husband and wife towards each other and towards the family system have changed.

All societies develop myths about their present family systems, as well as about the past ones. It is a well-established tendency to glorify the past. How can we assume that modern family system and the morals attached to it are really worse than the golden past, if we go deeply in the details of individual lives of 18th and 19th centuries? The traditional family as it was usually thought of in its purest form never existed. There are too many oppressive facets to families in the past to make them a model for today. The theme of bemoaning the rapid pace of modern change, as against the harmonious unaltered family behaviour of the past, is an old one. We cannot, however, prove that life was much more harmonious a century ago, or people were more contended in it. There is no doubt that the structure of the family and the norms of associational living are changing. The traditional expectation that the marriage will last for a lifetime has become an ideal of the past. In this regard, Anthony Giddens has suggested that terms like 'broken marriages' and 'broken homes' embody the traditional ideal and have unfortunate negative connotations, especially regarding children whose parents are separated or divorced. Thus, the changes in the family as discussed above may be viewed from the point of view of reorganization of the family.

To conclude, it may be said that the future of the family and marriage is not bleak. Both institutions, which are rooted in the basic emotions of love and affection, will survive in some form or the other. Their structure may differ from place to place but the content (functions) shall keep the trinity of father, mother and child together. The form of the new emerging family may be the 'neo-conventional family'—a family which suits to the needs of the modern man. The social changes that have transformed earlier forms of marriage and family are mostly irreversible such as the modern women would not like to return to the old domestic situation, confined to the four walls of his house. This was quite painful for them. The norms of family living and sexual partnership have also undergone a sea change. Emotional communication between the members of conjugal family is becoming more and more central both in the personal and family domains. Because of the emphasis on the modern values of individual freedom, personal happiness, satisfaction and self-fulfilment both partners now do not want to live in a miserable marriage and thus there is every possibility of the steep increase in divorces in near future. This may be a cause of concern for those people who advocate for the old values of family stability. In reality, the family is not collapsing or dying as is generally said by the traditionalists; it is merely diversifying in its form and functions. Transitional families (neo-local, functionally joint, based on equality of sexes) are increasing and may become the order of the day.

Chapter 7

Marriage

KEY FEATURES

- Defining Marriage
- Forms of Marriage
- Norms of Mate Selection
- Marital Choice
- Emerging Patterns of Marriage and Family
- Divorce in India

Human beings, like all mammals, mate, copulate and have children. Like other creatures too, they rear families which survive until the young become independent. However, humans, unlike animals, mate and procreate in some 'orderly way' to which they have given the name 'marriage'. Marriage is the basis of human society. Marriage forms society as our social forms are reinforced by marriage. It is a basic institution found in all human societies because no other union of men and women meets all the requirements of mating, home-making, love and personality development at the level of biological, psychological, social, ethical and spiritual evolution. Casual intercourse suffices for sexual satisfaction up to a point, but it does not and cannot create marital or family life. Man and woman constitute two parts of a complete whole—the one complementary to the other with corresponding distinctions and relations. To regard marriage as mere means of sexual satisfaction is to reduce it to a sub-rational level of instinctive mating. Moreover, sexual relations between a man and woman do not constitute marriage in some parts of the world, such as Australia. The institution of marriage makes human beings subjects of rights and duties, which finds expression in the man-woman relationship. As a legal institution, marriage confers various rights on those who enter into it, for example, to be regarded as next-of-kin to one's partner. There is a bit difference of point of view between anthropologists and sociologists about marriage. Anthropologists like Lowie, Murdock and Westermark emphasized on social sanction in the union and how it is accomplished by different rituals and ceremonies; sociologists like Bowman, Baber and Burgess, on the other hand, view it as a system of roles and as involving primary relationships.

Defining Marriage

In almost all societies, marriage is understood as a legally and socially recognized sexual relationship, always between a man and woman (or more than one woman or one man) and usually with other restrictions of race, ethnicity, religion, caste, etc., implicitly specified. Depending on the society, marriage may require religious or civil sanction (or both), although some couples may be considered married simply by living together for a prescribed period.

Westermarck (1891) defines marriage 'as a relation of one or more men to one or more women, which is recognized by custom or law, and involves rights and duties both in the case of the parties entering the union and in the case of children born of it'. The *Concise Oxford Dictionary of Sociology* (1994) defines it as, 'Marriage is traditionally conceived to be legally recognized relationship, between an adult male and female, that carries certain rights and obligations.' Giddens (1997) states, 'Marriage can be defined as a socially recognized relationship and approved sexual union between an adult male and female, that carries certain rights and obligations.'

In the above definitions it is stipulated that marriage is a relationship between adult members but there are societies like India where child marriages are also allowed by the custom of the society, though it is banned by law. Not only this, even in so-called modern societies like Britain where age at marriage is falling dramatically, adolescent marriages are on the rise. Marriage bond not only connects two adult individuals but also a wider range of kin people. Parents, brothers, sisters and other relatives of one partner become relatives of other partner through marriage. Many new statuses and roles, such as mother-in-law, daughter-in-law, father-in-law, sister-in-law, etc., come into existence after marriage.

Although in most societies marriage is defined in heterosexual terms (between male and female), marriage involving partners of the same sex is not unknown and is becoming increasingly acceptable in some so-called modern societies. For example, gay (male homosexuality) and lesbian (female homosexuality) marriages are legal in Denmark and in some parts of the USA. According to Adrienne Rich heterosexuality is not so much the natural form of sexual preference but is imposed upon individuals by social constraints. In many Western countries and America, movements by homosexuals have started to get legalize their marriages.

Forms of Marriage

Every society has certain forms of pairing arrangements to which we call marriage but remaining single or pairing without marriage (living together) is fast emerging as an acceptable form of lifestyle in the modern world. The trend towards maintaining an unmarried lifestyle is related to the growing economic independence of young people. Singleness is an attractive option for those who do not want to limit their sexual intimacy to one lifetime partner or have the burden of children over the past 50 years, living alone has become one of the most rapidly increasing social trends. The single life—for both men and women—is not viewed as a social taboo anymore. Eric Klinenberg, professor of sociology at New York University, in his recently published book *Going Solo* (2012) revealed that there is a fascinating rise in the numbers of 'singletons' (people who live alone). Such people regard solitary living as a sign of accomplishment. This is appealing to millions of people around the world. India, along with China and Brazil, has recorded the fastest growth of single-person households. This change has affected families, communities, cities and personal lives.

The main forms of marriage are:

1. *Monogamy*: It is a form of marriage in which one man is married to one woman at a time. It allows one wife to have one husband till death and only divorce separates them apart. This form of marriage is the only universally recognized form and is the predominant even in societies where other forms exist. In Western countries and the United States, an increasing number of married people end their relationship with one spouse (leading to subsequent divorce) and remarry another. This pattern of marrying is called *serial monogamy*. It means a person is allowed to have several spouses in his or her life at a time.
2. *Polygamy:* Some cultures allow an individual to have more than one spouse at the same time. Having more than one marriage partner at a time is known as *polygamy*. It was practised in most of the societies of the world but now the trend is towards monogamy. However, as anthropologist George Murdock (1959) found, 80 per cent of societies had some type of polygamy. There are three basic forms of polygamy:
    (a) *Polygyny:* It refers to plurality of wives or having more than one wife at the same time. In many societies, having several wives is a mark of prestige, distinction and status. It is very common among Muslims in Africa and in Middle East and Asia.
    (b) *Polyandry:* It is a type of marriage in which a woman can have several husbands (plurality of husbands) or two or more husbands simultaneously. It is very rare form of marriage. Wherever it is practised, the co-husbands are usually brothers, either blood brothers or clan brothers and are of the same generation. It is known as adelphic or fractural polyandry. The Todas (South India) and Khasa (North India) are the famous examples of polyandry. One

motive in this case would be the maintenance of land and property within one family.

(c) *Group Marriage:* It is one more type of polygamy, in which several or many men marry to several or many women. It is practised in some indigenous societies.

Norms of Mate Selection

All human societies have explicit or implicit social rules which specify certain categories of persons who are regarded as eligible marriage partners. These norms can be distinguished into two categories as under:

1. *Exogamy,* a rule of marriage which compels a person to marry outside the immediate group, usually one's own family or certain kinsfolk. It requires that marriage partners should be from a different group. In Hindus, for example, the rule of *gotra* or *pravar* or *spinda* exogamy is practised, i.e., one has to choose a mate outside one's *gotra* or *pravar*. Many societies forbid marriage within the clan, the village or sometimes even the tribe.

   Certain exogamous norms are almost universal. The *incest taboo*, a social norm common to virtual all societies, leaving aside stray examples of Egyptian and Inca royalty, prohibits sexual relationship between certain culturally specified relatives, such as one's mother, father, brother, sister, son or daughter.

2. *Endogamy,* a rule which specifies the zone of marriage or a rule which permits or prescribes marriage within a specified group. This group can be a clan, caste, class, village, tribe or based on religion, race or ethnicity. According to this rule, a Hindu is expected to marry within his own caste. Endogamy is intended to reinforce the cohesiveness of the group.

   Every society practices both exogamy and endogamy, as it specifies the limits of group closeness (exogamy) and the limits of group distance (endogamy) within which mates must be selected. Both exogamy and endogamy, therefore, restrict the eligibility of available marriage partners for both the sexes. In Indian society, these rules are still followed but with some changes. Following rules of exogamy, now, four or six *gotras* are not avoided strictly as was done a few years back. Similarly, the rule of caste endogamy is bit loosened but largely followed. In reality, this is the only attribute which is still keeping alive the caste system in India though in its modified form.

Marital Choice

There are a fascinating range of possibilities in the choice of marital partners. Some of these are:

1. Preferential marriages in which children of certain socially designated kinsmen marry each other as we find in cross-cousin and parallel cousin marriages practised in many societies, including India. In such societies, a person has to marry one of his mother's brothers' daughters or one of his father's sisters' daughters.
2. Arranged marriages are those in which choosing of marital partner is accomplished by parents or certain relatives, with or without considering the couple's wishes. In India, the mate selection was done by elders of the family till recently and freedom was totally denied to the couple in this process. In rural uneducated and traditionalist families, this system still prevails though with declining trend, yet western type of courtship practices are almost discouraged. Generally, traditionalists still favour arranged marriages for their children.
3. Self-choice marriages are those in which couples can do their own selection sometimes with parental guidance or parental veto. At certain times, it is seen that children select their own partner and settle marriage after consulting or sometimes just informing their parents.

In Western countries and the United States love plays an important role in marital (courtship) process. The people in these countries value love highly as a rationale for marriage and they encourage it to develop among the young. Quite contrary to this, in India, feelings of love are not a prerequisite for a marriage. Marriages are arranged by parents or relatives and there is little freedom for mate selection. The Indian male/female of marriageable age does not engage in the kind of dating behaviour so typical of American or British youth. In mate selection, many other factors are given priority than just romantic feelings. In India, the concept of 'love after marriage' is valued. The newly married couple is expected to develop a feeling of love only after a formal marriage. Economic consideration (dowry) also plays a significant role in mate selection. But gradually this situation is changing and the western type of courtship and dating phenomena have replaced them, particularly among the educated urban youths.

Emerging Patterns of Marriage and Family

Family and marriage patterns are becoming more and more varied in contemporary societies. When we look at the trends in family patterns, we find it has gone from joint families (extended) to nuclear (conjugal) ones, from nuclear to live-in-relationship and what more live-in-relationship to just lovers. All over the world, monogamy still remains the only legally permitted form of marriage, but many other forms of associational living have dramatically emerged during the last few decades, especially in Europe and the US. There is tremendous increase in couples who choose to live together without marriage.

The virus of this trend has also entered the Indian metropolitan cities as reported by two popular magazines—*India Today* (2006) and *Outlook* (2007). From their accounts, it was observed that the popularity of marriage had begun to plummet down as that of 'cohabitation' increased. This phenomenon has affected the family also. Not only familial relations are becoming weak but also limited to just one generation. The present generation does not want to have any relation with the members of earlier generations, even their grand-parents, aunts and uncles. Some emerging trends in marital and family lifestyles may be summed up as under:

Consensual Unions

As said above, there is an increasing trend in Western countries in which the partners live together without being legally united by a formal marriage. It is commonly called cohabitation. This is linked to greater acceptance of pre-marital sex and delayed entry into marriage and beginning of the family life. People, who are wary of marriage and its legal and emotional commitments, opt for 'living together arrangement' without legal marriage. For some people, living together may represent a kind of 'trial marriage' or 'sexual experimentation'. Actually, words like 'intimacy' and 'commitment' in one's personal or social life have become obsolete in such pairs or even conjugal family. Studies show that such arrangements are generally found in working couples. In Western countries including the US, it is also seen among college students. One report notes that in Sweden, it is almost universal for couples to live together before marriage. In Denmark, this practice of living together is called 'marriage without paper' and in Australia, these couples are known as 'de facto couples'. This trend has also entered into India through some metropolitan IT centres like Bangalore, Pune, Hyderabad, Chennai, Mumbai and Delhi.

In such arrangements, in place of legal marriage contract, unmarried couples enter into a private conjugal (informal/unwritten) contract, defining rights and obligations of both. Such contracts are only binding and cannot be upheld in a court of law. Recently, the Maharashtra government has taken step to legalize live-in-relationship to protect women from cheating and harassment by the male partner. It is learnt that such proposal is also underway in the parliament. Under this proposal, if a man and a woman live together as husband and wife for a reasonable long period, the man shall be deemed to have married the woman according to customary rights of either party.

The introduction of such private conjugal contracts is but one effort in the present time to find new ways of associational living. It seems that we are redefining the meaning of marital relationship—a matter very relevant concerning the future of marriage and the family. Such relationships are giving rise to childless marriages or reproduction of children without formal marriage. Such children will possibly have to be content with parents who never entered into wedlock at all. After all, the cost of getting divorce far exceeds the expenses we incur in getting married. Not only this, such arrangements are skirting around the issue of morality altogether. Many a time, couples in live-in-relationships face social humiliation and rejection by their relatives and friends in India but this is not the case in Western societies where this arrangement has become well established.

Single-parent Families

The pressing exigencies of the modern life have given rise to one-parent or single-parent families. In many cases, this is the result of the death of a spouse or divorce or sometimes because of the developing a new custom of live-in-relationship. But, in many cases, it is the result of deliberate choice because of some or other reasons. The rising divorce rate is one of the main reasons for this developing trend. It has become a significant phenomenon in many developed and developing countries. According to one estimate, in US alone, almost four in ten marriages end in divorce. After divorce, generally children live with their mother who goes out to work. She takes on the roles of both parents. An increasing number of men in the West divorced or widowed are choosing to bring up their kids single-handed. Single dads do not mind double roles. What does it mean is a change in the dynamics and rhythm of relationship for both child and the father?

Teenage Marriages

Studies show that there has also been a trend towards teenage marriages in the Western societies, including USA and Canada. There was a news that a 17 years old girl was to be married to the 18 years old father of the baby. Recently, Barack Obama, president of USA, expressed serious concern about the rising number of early pregnancies among teenagers in America. Many teenage marriages involve a pregnancy at the time of marriage. Teenage marriages generally take place during studying which forces them for dropout. The main cause of teenage sex is the higher exposure to sexual content in movies, TV, music and magazines along with the extreme openness and liberal norms and values about sex and also disintegration of family. Recently, it is reported in the newspapers that in Britain during sex education session in schools contraceptives were distributed for safer sex. Most of these marriages end in divorce because people marrying young unprepared for the process of selecting a mate and assuming a marital role, so they derive little satisfaction from marriage and this situation leads them to divorce.

This trend has affected the median age at first marriage in these countries. It is dropping and moving backward towards the younger ages possibly because of the maturity of the young and partly because of the general breakdown in family controls. Now, the movement is towards individualism and away from family and community controls. British sociologists have shown concern that the traditional system of marriage first and then reproduction is on the brink of end. Astonishingly, the studies report that the cases of unmarried mothers are rare among British Indians who are living there for one or two generations.

Contrary to this trend (lowering of age at marriage), the age at marriage is rising in India, the Arab countries and in sub-Saharan Africa. In India, there is a reverse trend regarding the age at marriage. In past few years, the age at marriage is rising in urban areas, especially in metropolitan cities. Nowadays, there is a trend of postponing marriage and remaining single until they are older, which reflects a decision on the part of young people to live independently as they pursue higher education or job opportunities. Not only this, there are instances where people opt to remain single throughout their lives. The trend towards maintaining an unmarried lifestyle is related to the growing economic independence of young people. Such people neither want to produce children nor do they like to burden themselves with the responsibilities of the family. Moreover, from a financial point of view, it is often no longer necessary for a woman to marry in order to enjoy a satisfying life. Recent economic liberalization has enhanced the pay packets of both male and female workers. This has given liberty to enjoy sex without wedlock.

Homosexual Marriages

Lately, there has been a trend towards homosexual marriages in many countries. Gay and lesbian couples are living together though their number is very meagre. Since 1970s homosexuals, both male and female, began to claim the right for the homosexual marriages in many Western countries including America. In these countries, they have started a sort of movement for the approval of such relationships. Denmark is the first country to formally recognize homosexual marriages. Techniques of artificial insemination mean that gay women may have children and become gay-parent families. Demands for legalizing gay/homosexual marriages and live-in-relationships are threatening the existence of traditional marriage and family system. This forces either to broaden the concept of family or dismantle the marriage altogether or relegate it one way of living rather than only one. Gay marriages or live-in-relations are considered as digression of gender norms.

It is recently reported that fourteen nations in the world have legalized the homosexual marriages. France is the last nation which has enacted law to legalize such marriages in May 2013.

Future of the Institution of Marriage

With increasing marital breakdown and subsequent divorce, especially in Western developed societies, there are growing fears that marriage as an institution is in decline. Compromise, sacrifice and adjustment are no more the ideals of modern marriage. Self-sufficiency and individuality are best aspirations of modern couples. Living together but feeling to be alone have become the ideals of modern couples without marriage. The controls regarding pre-marital and even extra-marital sex relations have loosened. Now, the marriage vow 'till death do us part' has become anachronistic in the same manner as did a few years back, not to go long in the past when marriage was regarded as a holy sacrament. The ideas of sacramental union or even of expected life-time monogamy have now been abolished in many parts of the Western world.

In recent years, cohabitation before marrying has virtually become a norm in Western countries. Marriage is going out of fashion with an increasing number of people cohabitating and even rearing children outside matrimony. Marriage is sometimes interpreted more liberally and the phrases like 'living as married' or 'live-in-relationship' are used in place of the term marriage. Some feminists who see 'marriage' as an oppressive, authoritarian and capitalistic institution have urged women not to marry. In their opinion, the inequalities of marriage are reflections of the inequalities of the sexes in society. The trend is towards what is called 'factual familism' or social relations between the sexes considered to have no fundamental meaning beyond present company and the present moment. This is the question which the sociologists of today are facing. Will we continue in the same age-old virtues of mother's love, parental obligation and spouse loyalty?

Looking to these conditions, one might easily say that the future of marriage (and for that reason family also) looks bleak. Marriage has ceased to be (as it ever was) the condition for regular sexual experience for either sex. It is no longer the basis of economic activity and rearing and caring of the young. Moreover, some couples choose not to have children and regard themselves child-free. They do not believe having children automatically follows from marriage, nor do they feel that reproduction is the duty of all married couples. In spite of all these problems of marriage and changed attitude towards associational living, marriage still remains the preferred way of life for the vast majority of world population. Despite the dire statistics of divorce, marriage seems to be rather resilient institution. We agree with Giddens (1997) when he says, 'Marriage and family remain firmly established institutions, yet are undergoing major stress and strains.' Or, in other words, both the institutions are passing through a critical stage of transition.

Divorce

For many centuries, marriage was regarded as virtually indissoluble in many societies, including India, where it was regarded as 'sacramental' (religious). Divorces were granted only in limited cases in extraordinary circumstances.

But now almost all societies have made some provisions for divorce in certain situations. Today, marriage is less often seen as a sacred spiritual union, but more as a personal and practical commitment which can be broken if it fails. The trend is towards making marriage consensual. Attitude to divorce is changing rapidly. It is no longer treated as an unpardonable sin. Even a few years ago, there was more of a stigma attaching to divorce. Now, it has become a more practical option for marital discord. It is believed to relieve married partners and their children from stress.

Though divorce is common in world's societies, it is still seen as unfortunate. Even in societies with relatively high divorce rate there is no substantial approval of divorce. Rather, various procedures or mechanisms are evolved by which divorce is kept at a lower rate than would occur without these patterns. But, due to marital dissolution, divorce rate is rising not only in Western countries, but also in India. At the same time, there are many countries like Japan and in certain Arab countries like Algeria where it is being dropped. However, the institution of divorce is gaining ground slowly and slowly and becoming respectable in almost all societies. The ease of divorce also reflects that it ceases to be a stigma, especially for women. This attitude encourages divorce among those dissatisfied with their marriage. Women now have more options and less dependent on men. Changes in the traditional structure of sex roles have altered the perceptions of both men and women about what they want from marriage. In this almost disposable age, people used to throw everything—lighters, tea cups, dress, furniture, curtains, etc., so they feel they can throw out a marriage too.

Now, a question arises: What is divorce? Actually, all marriages do not succeed; some also end in disharmony. Divorce is a formal (legal) and permanent form of breakup—termination of bonafide marriage. Another form of breakup is desertion. It is illegal and unofficial on the part of either husband or wife or both to decide to leave each other and cease to discharge their role obligations. Mostly it is husbands who desert their wives. Desertion may be temporary or permanent. Both forms (divorce and desertion) ultimately lead to family disorganization. It is the breakup of a family unit, the dissolution or fracture of a structure of social roles when one or more members fail to perform adequately their role obligations.

Divorce is the socially recognized and legal dissolution of marriage. According to the *Concise Oxford Dictionary of Sociology (1994)*, 'the formal legal dissolution of legally constituted marriage' is called divorce. What constitute marriage and divorce varies widely. Like marriage, it is governed by a variety of cultural rules and differs widely from society to society and over time. In countries such as Spain, Brazil and Peru marriage is indissoluble except by death. The laws of Islam and Judaism give a husband the power to terminate his marriage by simple renouncing his wife or wives. In many Western countries, including the USA, a divorce is granted if it is shown that the marriage has failed or on the basis of certain grounds or mutual consent.

Six Stations of Divorce

Divorce is nearly always a tragedy, for it generally means blighted faith, broken truth and severe disillusionment. It is a complex and difficult experience for all family members. Anthropologist Paul Bohannan (1970) has identified six overlapping experiences which arise from divorce. Bohannan calls them 'six stations of divorce'. These are:

1. Emotional divorce, which represents the problem of the deteriorating marriage.
2. Legal divorce, based upon the grounds on which the marriage will be dissolved.
3. Economic divorce, which deals with the division of money and property.
4. Coparental divorce, which includes decisions regarding child custody and visitation rights.
5. Community divorce, the changes in friendships and institutional ties that a divorced person experiences.
6. Psychic divorce, focused on the person's attempt to regain autonomy and self-esteem.

Causes of Divorce

Why divorces take place? There is no satisfactory answer to this question. Whenever any two people interact, disagreement sometimes leading to conflict may arise on any point at any point of time and one person or both may go to the extent of breaking relationship. This is true for all types of relationships including marital relationship. Unlike most relationships, however, marriage involves civil, legal or religious ties that specify if and how the relationship can end. All marriages cannot succeed and some end in disharmony and break and culminates into divorce. Generally, divorce is the outcome of the failure of marital adjustment between a husband and a wife.

Many studies carried out in India and elsewhere found that the important causes of divorce are domestic disharmony, ill-treatment of wife by husband or vice versa or by their relatives, cruelty (physical or mental), adultery, impotency, barrenness, immoral conduct of the spouse, illicit relations, alcoholism, etc. Besides, there are many other factors involved which may lead to divorce such as financial problems, emotional immaturity, difficulties in adjustment with new environment and relationships, discrepancies in role expectations, etc. When people from quite dissimilar backgrounds (different religion, caste, class, culture, educational status, ethnic group, etc.) marry, the necessary adjustments in role expectations are more difficult and a divorce is more likely. The main reason of divorce among such couples is often poor interpersonal communication. This happens more in conjugal family than extended (joint) family where communication and other problems are sometimes solved by other members of the family. Lack of proper communication may give rise to tension and conflict between the spouses, leading ultimately to divorce. Increasing involvement of women in paid work (outside home) has resulted in contradictory demands of two roles (housewife and working woman) which can produce tension between husband and wife and leads the wife eventually to seek divorce.

The changing aspirations and a strong desire for greater independence and individual expression among men and women causes conflicting expectations. It has become the main basis for the increasing divorce rates. Besides, changing aspirations, it is generally alleged that the tolerance levels of couples have gone down considerably. Modern society attaches utmost importance to individuality and personal self-fulfilment. It evaluates marriage in terms of the level of satisfaction of personal ambitions it offers. The single lifestyle can offer certain freedom that married people may not enjoy. This feeling has also contributed much in the breakdown of marital relationship.

Moreover, there is a great decline in the feeling of commitment to marriage and family. This is because of the growing erosion in the old formal religious belief that marriage is a permanent and binding commitment and it is a God ordained relationship which cannot be broken. Moreover, too much importance was attached to the monogamy. It was often said that this is the only true form of marriage. But this is not correct. Recent studies of zoologists have discovered that faithfulness is a fantasy even in the animal world. Almost every species of animals cheats on its partners—males a little more; females somewhat less. Sexual prostitution is rampant even among the animals. At some basic level humans are animals too, and therefore there is breakdown of marriages. Statistics prove that in western countries slightly more than half married couples remain monogamous.

Not only this, perhaps the most important factor in the increase of divorce is the greater acceptance of divorce itself. Divorce is regarded as an appropriate response to marital disorganization. This attitude to marriage has resulted in a series of changes in law, making the ground for divorce less strict and easier. To obtain a divorce in Western societies, it is enough merely to prove irretrievable breakdown of marriage. Thus, liberalization of laws has also increased the propensity for divorce proceedings to be initiated by women.

One more factor which has helped in increasing the number divorces is the transitory romantic love (having no real emotional attachment) on which the marital relations are found in modern societies. A high rate of marital breakdown, or the death of these romances, is an inevitable consequence of building relationship on such an unstable and fragile basis. When the romantic love dies, it is seen that people resort to such action as divorce as a remedy to marital disadjustment. Improved birth control technology may have further contributed to sexual attitudes and behaviour based on pure personal gratification rather than any wider norms or morality.

It is estimated that in Britain over one-third of all marriages end in divorce and in the United States, the proportion of marriages to divorces is about two to one, i.e., one out of every two marriages ends in divorce. While in the Western countries, most of the divorcees remarry with other persons, in India, only a negligible number of divorcees remarry.

In March 2007, in one case (Ghosh vs Ghosh), the Supreme Court of India granted divorce on the basis of 'mental cruelty'. The apex court has defined mental cruelty as:

- Withholding sex without reason.
- Unilateral decision not to have a child.
- Abortion or sterilization without consent of spouse.
- Nagging behaviour.
- Indifference and frigidity.
- Denial of company.
- Filthy language and verbal abuse.
- False allegations.

Commenting on this verdict, the activist and writer Madhu Kishwar said, 'The verdict reveals that the institution of marriage is under crises … . The squabble at the level of the mind reflects the increasing complexity of man-woman relationship that challenges the very idea of marriage. So how different is divorce in the new millennium?' 'The essentially private nature of modern marriages makes it difficult for those outside to understand, legislate, prove or judge what's going on inside,' says Andre Beteille, the eminent Indian sociologist. 'But it's increasingly clear that saying goodby to a spouse is no longer the dismal climax to protracted misery that it once was. The shift expresses the increasing recognition of men and women as individuals' (*India Today,* April 16, 2007).

Impact of Divorce

Divorce may be seen as a personal misfortune for one or both spouses in any society. It may happen at any time in the life of the family—even within a week or month after the marriage. It makes deep impact on the lives of marital partners, their children and the society as a whole. It is difficult to draw up a balance sheet of the social advantages and costs of divorce. More tolerant attitudes towards divorce mean the couples can terminate an unrewarding relationship without incurring social ostracism. (In India, however, such tolerant attitude has not yet developed.) On the other hand, marriage breakup is almost emotionally stressful for all the parties involved, i.e., husband, wife, children and other members of the family. (In India, the members of in-law family are also involved.) Emotional disturbance may lead to personality disorganization. (Sometimes people become mad, lunatic or mentally derailed.) Old values, old definitions, old schemes of life organization all shatter and lose their validity.

Divorce may also create financial hardships for one or both parties. When a man divorces his non-earning wife, it seriously jeopardizes her life along with children. It brings many economic problems to women, especially those depended on their husband. It forces her either to find work for herself or send children at the tender age for earning. Women and children who have never worked before often face severe economic hardships. Divorce leads to the formation of single-parent family, usually mother household family, since the wife usually obtains custody of the children following a divorce. Because of economic hardships, some divorced women take to an immoral life (prostitution). They may sometimes contract illicit sexual relationships just to earn a livelihood. This situation further may lead to many other associated problems like child labour, juvenile delinquency, disorganized personalities, neurotic disorders, depression and so on.

Disruption of family life caused by divorce affects the children very badly. Children reared in a happy home are more likely to grow up happy and psychologically healthy themselves. Psychiatric studies emphasize the difficulties experienced by people who as children lived in 'broken homes' or 'chaotic families'. At many times, after divorce children face the very first problem and that is of custody. Many children become the custody of a single parent. Not only do they lose the regular company of one parent, they may also have to move away from friends and family surroundings. Living with one parent means losing other parent's love and affection. For balanced personality development, supervision of both parents—mother and father—is essential. If parents remarry, children often face the problem of stepparenting treatment. The stepmother or stepfather cannot take the place of a real mother or father. They will always be fundamentally a stranger. Whether it is a single parent going it alone, or the remarrying parent creating a new household, such new living arrangements require new forms of parental relations to children as well as new problems.

Researches indicate that children do often suffer emotional anxiety after the separation of parents. Life in the single-parent family is extremely difficult, stressful, insecure and unhappy for them. The children of the divorced couple often face the social criticism when they are condemned, teased or taunted by their playmates.

Divorce in India

In India, there are references in ancient Hindu literature about permitting divorces under certain circumstances but in actual practice divorces and remarriages were almost non-existent. However, in recent years, 'sacramental' nature of Hindu marriage is gradually being replaced with modern secular beliefs. These beliefs refer to the declining influence of the religious attitudes and values which in turn affects the marital ties. As a result of secular beliefs and the impact of Western civilization, the government enacted Hindu Marriage and Divorce Act of 1955 (amended in 1976 and 1981). It contains provisions for both judicial separation and divorce. The grounds for the dissolution of a Hindu marriage are adultery (immoral conduct), unsound mind, conversion to other religion, desertion and cruelty, incurable leprosy and venereal disease, barrenness of wife and renunciation and bigamy. It also permits divorce by mutual consent. People aspiring for divorce have to wait for the period of judicial separation of one year. This period is meant for reconciliation but if it does not happen during this period, one gets the decree of divorce.

The changed social values, which allow divorce as an appropriate response to marital disorganization, have also led in the increases of divorces in India. The altered position of women has also contributed to this rising trend all over the world, including India. This is why more and more women are seeking divorce today. It is important to note that three-fourth of divorces in USA are granted on the petition of wives and two-fifth are granted to couples married less than five years. However, compared to the US and UK, the divorce rate in India is still considerably low. *Time* magazine (October 2007) reports only one in one hundred marriages here ends in divorce compared to a much higher percentage in the West, including America. But, nevertheless, divorces are on the rise, especially in metropolitan areas.

Dual-career (earning) marriages (both spouses working as wage earners) lead to conflicts and contradictions between marital expectations. Employment of women outside the home has changed the status and the aspirations of women. Some observers associate the increase in divorce with this change of status. Such women are no longer willing to tolerate a subservient position in the home. In her book, *Families on the Fault Line* (1994), Lillian Rubin comments: 'Among young women there is a desire for autonomy and self-fulfilment, through work as much as family and valuing of risk, excitement and change.' There is also a growing tendency towards freedom of women to work and control their reproduction, freedom of mobility for both sexes and freedom to define one's own style of life. The young generation is much pleasure seeking and not much concerned about sexual behaviour, marriage and gender divisions. Thus, dual earning marriages and changing attitudes towards sex, marriage and family life are sowing the seeds of divorces. But, the increasing number of divorces does not mean that the institution of marriage is going out of fashion. After divorces, it is seen that most of the families in the West are reconstituted by remarriages.

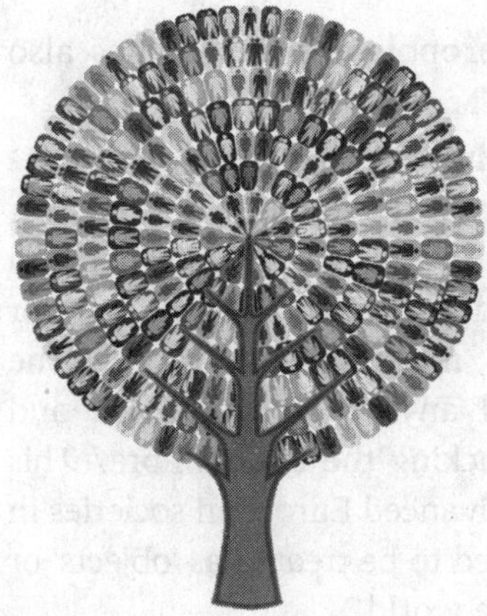

Chapter 8

Status of Women

KEY FEATURES

- Status of Women in India
- Empowerment of Women in India
- Women in Politics
- Problems of Women in India

The concept of status is central to sociology which reflects a person's evaluation of his or her position in the status hierarchy (i.e., prestige) in terms of occupation, education, income, inheritance and the like. Status denotes the relative position of a person in relation to other person or in a group of persons on a hierarchy of social worth. It is closely linked with honour or prestige. Broadly speaking, status refers to the position which a person occupies in a social structure or a group or a social system. In this sense, 'wife' and 'husband' are statuses in a martial system.

Descriptions of status as high or low often amounts only to making very generalized statements. According to R.H. Lowie (1950), an eminent anthropologist, 'Status may mean four different things: (1) actual treatment, (2) legal status, (3) opportunity for social participation, and (4) the character and extent of work; all determine in a specific sense and manner the status of women in society. All these determinants are independent of each other and causally related.'

It is generally argued that in the relation between man and woman, it is an individual with a powerful personality (physical prowess and mental qualities) who acquires a position of dominance. It is generally seen that in all mammals, including human, it is the male who commands power over a female, though in a few cases, a female also might exercise control over a male. Looking to the history of relationship between man and woman, it has been seen that women have always been dominated by men since the very early periods of history in all cultures. The anthropological researches also prove this fact.

All over the world and particularly in South and East Asia, gender disabilities and discrimination are widespread. Women are considered to be the weaker section of society almost everywhere, including India. Neera Desai (1957) observed: 'Ideologically woman who was considered a completely inferior species, inferior to the male, having no significance, no personality; socially, she was kept in a state of utter subjugation, denied any right, suppressed and oppressed; she was further branded as basically lacking the ethical fibre.' This state prevailed everywhere including all so-called advanced European societies in ancient times. Even a few centuries back women used to be treated as 'objects' or 'chattel' by the male-dominated societies all over the world.

The concept of status of women has changed with the change of time. Working of women with men in the fields was once considered honoured one but today withdrawing womenfolk from manual work on farms is a symbol of high status in the countryside. But this is not true of working women belonging to the lower-middle classes in towns and cities. Working women—both married and unmarried—are considered an asset today. Time has changed and today men and women are considered equal in all fields.

Why does society tend to devalue women and the work they do? Why do women have lower status in comparison to men in society? Answering these questions, some scholars, mostly physiologists and psychologists, have taken refuge in biological differences between men and women. According to them, males and females differ from the moment of conception when sex is determined. Sex hormones affect the central nervous system and many other capabilities—mental and physical—that influence how males and females behave. For such scholars, biological differences are the main basis for their gender-role differences. If we survey different types of societies like simple and complex industrial societies, we find that generally women had traditionally stayed at home as housewives, caring for home and family and men had provided the family income needed to sustain their lives. Sociologists do not agree with this biological explanation. They have studied many societies and contended that it is the socialization processes that are responsible for gender-role differences. Both men and women are capable of meeting the demands of almost all positions or statuses without being constrained by biological factors.

To measure the status of women, the following criteria have been used:

1. To what extent women enjoy freedom in and outside home in matters relating to their education, marriage and occupation?
2. How far their opinion is honoured?
3. How far they are given equal treatment at the workplace regarding power, pay and other matters in relation to their job?

4. To what extent society allows women for widow remarriage, participation in politics and other social activities and forbid veil system (*purdah*), *sati* system and child marriages?

Status of Women in India

The position of women in ancient India has been a very complicated one because of the paradoxical statements in different religious scriptures and sometimes in the same text at different places. Some have described their status as 'equals to men', while others have held not only in disrespect but even in positive hatred. This is why it has presented many problems to sociologists while evaluating women's status in India. The cultural history of India reveals that in India theoretically women enjoyed the status of *devi* (goddess) as described in many religious texts of Hindus, the majority community in India. Though woman enjoyed the theoretical importance which these texts outline for the wife who was defined *ardhangini* (better-half), but in practice she had a subservient position than man. She was regarded as a 'chattle' (a corporal moveable property) with no rights. It was generally seen and believed that women had lower status with reference to power and influence than men in all spheres of life—family, community, religion and politics. Till recently, it was held that up to marriage, she is protected by her parents, during married life, she is looked after by her husband, and after the death of her husband, she was used to spend remaining years of her life under the roof of her children without any will or desire and rights in the family. She was not allowed to decide how money would be spent or invested. She did not have any money at her disposal. She had to take permission to spend money from her elders—father, brother or husband or any other male or female elder person in the family. In brief, she had no personality of her own. Some scholars have explained this inferior status of women as a result of patriarchal code of living. The rigid codes of behaviour as outlined for women in Brahmanical texts were also responsible for the low status of women in India. In the following paragraphs we will survey, in brief, the position of women in India from Rigvedic period to modern times.

Rigvedic Period

It is generally upheld on the basis of the instances depicted in religious texts (e.g., Vedas, Upanishads, Smritis, epics like Ramayan and Mahabharat and other Dharmasastras) that in ancient India, especially in Rigvedic period, women enjoyed equal status with men. They had an honourable place in the society. They were not secluded from men and freely participated in public life. They attended great assemblies and state occasions. They studied the Vedas and composed hymns. They also distinguished themselves in science and learning at their times. They were considered intellectual companies of their husbands, as the friends and loving helpers in the journey of life of their partners, in their religious duties and the centre of their domestic bliss.

In Vedic times, women were not treated as inferior or subordinate but equal to men in all matters of life. They were given education and had a voice in the selection of their husband. Marriage was regarded as a religious bond. Child marriage was unknown. Often there were love marriages known as *Gandharva Vivaha*. Monogamy was a general rule. Polygamy was almost unknown. Women enjoyed complete freedom in household matters. In the religious field, women enjoyed all rights and regularly participated in religious ceremonies. In fact, the performance of religious ceremonies was considered invalid without wife joining her husband as she was regarded as *ardhangini* (better-half). The references in the Rigveda to the life of a widow are very few but it was not characterized by restrictions and austerities as in the post-Vedic days. Remarriage of widows was allowed. There are a number of references to the custom of *Niyoga* where a brother of the deceased husband/or any other person could marry the widow. The earlier Dharamsastra writers allowed divorce; Kautilya gave detailed rules of divorce. As regards *sati*, burning of the widow, Shakuntala Rao Sastri writes that the Rigveda does not mention anywhere the practice of the burning or burial of widows with their dead husbands. As regards property rights, according to Vedic hymns, both husband and wife were joint owner of the property. Women inherited and possessed property, but their rights were limited. As a daughter, she had no share in her father's property. Similarly, as a wife, a woman had no direct share in her husband's property. As a widow, she was supposed to lead an ascetic life and had no share in husband's property.

Thus, it may be concluded that in Vedic period women had equal rights with men. Their status was fairly high and they were treated as equals with men in almost all spheres of life.

Post-Vedic Period (Upanishads, Puranic and Smriti Periods)

The position enjoyed by women in Vedic period deteriorated in post-Vedic period. It was gradually degraded in the Puranic and Smriti periods. The description of position before BC 300 shows that she enjoyed a fairly high status, though not to the extent that she enjoyed in Vedic period. It appears that several drastic changes that took place in the Indian society from about BC 300 to the beginning of the Christian era led to the curtailment of freedom of women. Imposition of Brahaminical rules and code of conduct, rigid restrictions imposed by caste system and joint family system were the main reasons for lowering of status in this period. A daughter began to be regarded as curse. They were denied the right of inheritance and ownership of property. Pre-puberty marriages came to be practised. She was forbidden to offer sacrifices and prayers and undertake pilgrimages. Practice of polygyny came to be tolerated. Some of the Dharamsastras mention about the prohibition of *Niyoga* and widow remarriage. The widow was asked to devote herself to an ascetic life at home. Marriage became an irrevocable union as far as the wife was concerned. The Smriti writers preached that the wife should look upon her husband as God. Widows were required to spend a life of penance and austerity. *Sati* had become popular by the 7th century AD. In this period, women were regarded just as a means of satisfying the physical desires of men. Just to refer one instance of Mahabharata, it is said that 'there was no creature more sinful than man ... woman is the root of all ills'. This simple quotation is sufficient to prove that how disrespect was shown towards women. However, it is not out of place to mention here that Indian scriptures are full of paradoxical statements. At one place, women were regarded as goddess, held in high esteem, where at other place in the same scripture, in some other context, they were regarded, no better than just slaves or chattels. Disregarding what was practised at any particular time, the ancient Indian scriptures and documents (Mahabharata, Ramayana, Vedic hymns, and various codes of the law of Manu) gave women a very high and protected place in their basic moral codes. Husband and wife stood as equals before God. Up to this period *purdah* (veil) was not commonly observed by women. Divorce was, however, not permissible to them. But then, it was not permissible to men either. Their position was not one of complete disability but one dictated by justice and fairness. Women used to help their male members of their family in economic pursuits. They sometimes accompanied their husband or other members of the family in hunting and agricultural pursuits.

Medieval Period

The period between 11th century to 18th century witnessed further deterioration in the position of women due to the impact of Muslim culture. In this period, female infanticide, child marriage, *purdah* system, *sati* and slavery were the main social evils affecting the position of women. The birth of a female child began to be regarded as curse, a bad luck. They were almost confined to the doors of their homes. There was further curtailment of freedom of women in matters of education, mate selection, public appearances, etc. *Purdah* system came to be rigorously followed. Women education was almost banned. More and more feeling of conservatism increased about women. She not only continued to hold low status in and outside home rather her position worsened in this period.

It is often said that in India the *purdah* (veil) system came into existence only after the arrival of Moghuls. A.S. Altekar, in his book, *The Position of Women in Hindu Civilization* (1962) writes: 'This for nearly 2000 years from BC 20 to 1800 AD, the position of women steadily deteriorated though she was fondled by the parents, loved by the husband and revered by her children. The revival of Sati, the prohibition of remarriage, the spread of Purdah and the greater prevalence of polygamy made her position very bad.' Thus, there was a vast difference between the status of women in the early Vedic period and the subsequent periods, stretching from post-Vedic to the medieval period. The dual standards of morality set by *Manu Smriti* and other *Smritis* continue to prevail right up to now though some changes are visible in urban educated women.

British Period

During the period of British rule of about 200 years (early 18th century to the first half of 20th century) some substantial progress was achieved in eliminating inequalities between men and women in matters of education, employment, social and property rights and so forth. *Sati, purdah,* female infanticide, child marriage, inheritance, slavery, prohibition of widow remarriage and the lack of women's rights in different fields were some of the problems which attracted the attention of British Raj. Though the British rulers initially decided not to interfere with the traditional social fabric of Indian people (Hindus) and as such they took no steps to bring any change in the status of women in India. It is only in the later half of the 19th century and the first quarter of the 20th century that they took some steps to abolish or change some social customs through legislative measures. For such measures incentive was provided to them by some social reformers, such as Raja Ram Mohan Rai, Ishwar Chandra Vidyasagar, Dayanand Saraswati, Kehab Chandra Sen, Swami Vivekanand, Maharashi Karve, Justice Ranade, Mahatma Gandhi and others. Through the efforts and the various movements launched by these great social leaders of the 19th century before independence, it had been possible to get many legislations passed and public opinion mobilized in favour of some issues of social reforms. These steps have paved the way in removing the obstacles in the progress of women. Not only this, it had helped in eliminating inequalities between men and women and giving proper respect to the other-half of the society.

The most significant legislations relating to the problems faced by the Indian (Hindu) women passed during British period were as follows:

1. Abolition of Sati Act, 1813.
2. The Hindu Widow Remarriage Act, 1856.
3. Civil Marriage Act, 1872.
4. Married Women's Property Act, 1874.
5. The Child Marriage Restraint Act (Sharda Act), 1929.
6. Hindu Law of Inheritance Act, 1929.
7. Hindu Women's Rights to Property Act, 1939.
8. Hindu Marriage Disabilities Removal Act, 1946.

Besides these Acts, many provincial governments also enacted some legislations. In 1779, infanticide was declared to be a murder by the Bengal Regulation XXI. In 1804, this was extended to other parts of the country.

Another significant feature of the 19th century was the attempt made by social reformers to educate Indian girls. For more than 2,000 years, from about BC 300, there was practically no formal education for women. Only a few women of the upper castes and classes were given some education at home. The ideas of imparting education in a formal manner first emerged during the British period. Christian missionaries took great interest to impart education to the girls. It was in 1824 when the first girls school was started in Bombay (Mumbai). In 1882, girls were allowed to pursue higher education. Since then, to pursue there has been a continuous progress in the field of education of girls in India.

In the last decades of 19th century, a marked change took place in the outlook of both men and women about the education and employment of women as teachers, nurses, doctors, etc. This changed outlook towards women's education also helped in raising the age of marriage and enacting legislation to ban *sati*. Thus, the ground prepared by the 19th century social reformers and their untiring efforts led to the emancipation of women. This also helped them to take their rightful place in society.

After Independence

In addition to the measures to uplift the status of women in India initiated by Britishers, many vigorous steps (legal, social, economic and political) have been taken by Government of India after independence by removing the hurdles put in their way by traditional past. The efforts of the social reformers and their movements launched in the pre-independence period also bore fruits. The Indian National Movement also led to the emancipation of Indian women.

The leaders of the national movement realized that the liberation of the country from the bondage of imperialism was impossible without the active participation of women who constituted half of the population of the country. Most of the social reformers and thinkers of the 19th and 20th centuries were influenced by the tenets of the liberal philosophy of the West, which emphasized the principle of contract rather than status, a rational outlook of life and problems, freedom of speech, criticism of authority, questioning of accepted dogmas and finally the recognition of the value of the individual and insistence on the rights of man as opposed to his duties. They also got impetus from Upanishads and other Hindu scriptures.

The decades after independence have seen tremendous changes in the status and position of the women in Indian society. The Constitution of India has laid down as a fundamental right the equality of sexes. But, the change from a position of utter degradation of women to a position of equality is not a simple case of the progress of women in the modern era. To uplift the status of women, many legislations pertaining to women were enacted after independence. These were mainly related to marriage, divorce, inheritance of property and employment. Some of the important Acts are mentioned below:

1. The Hindu Marriage Validity Act, 1949.
2. The Special Marriage Act, 1954.
3. The Hindu Marriage Act, 1955 (amended in 1986 and 2010).
4. The Hindu Succession Act, 1956.
5. Immoral Traffic (Prevention) Act, 1956.
6. The Sati Prevention Act, 1987.
7. The Dowry Prohibition Act, 1961.
8. Indecent Representation of Women (Prohibition) Act, 1986.
9. Prohibition of Child Marriage Act, 2007.
10. Protection of Women from Domestic Violence Act, 2005.
11. Compulsory Registration of Marriage Act, 2006.

Besides, the Acts especially related to employment are:

1. The Factory Act, 1948.
2. Employees Insurance Act, 1948.
3. The Maternity Benefit Act, 1961.
4. The Equal Remuneration Act, 1976.

The above legislations and many other emancipatory actions of the social reformers have no doubt raised the status of women in India but still much is to be done in this field. The institution of bigamy (man marrying any number of women) has almost come to an end; if detected, it has become a punishable offence. Today, both sexes have the right to a civil marriage. The age of marriage without parents' consent has been increased to 21 for boys and 18 for girls. Thus, monogamy along with facility of judicial separation, nullity and divorce (even on mutual consent), inheritance (equal share in paternal property), adoption, widow remarriage and *sati* abolition are some of the salient features of post-independence era which put men and women on equal footings from the point of view of legislative measures.

However, social legislations have not been very effective in India because of many reasons. One important reason is that most of the women are not fully aware of the measures adopted by the state for their upliftment and even if aware they do not use them because of the old social values that are still persisting. These traditions and values inhibit them to take any revolutionary steps. Legal or legislative sanctions alone cannot bring any substantial change in the downtrodden position of women unless there is a marked change in their attitude and consciousness of men and women both. In this regard, their illiteracy is one of the great hindrances. According to the 2001 Census, 45.84 per cent and 2011 Census, 34 per cent of women are still illiterate in India. Even literate women also do not exercise their right of equality wherever it is required.

Thus, the status of women has been raised in the eyes of law, but they are still far from equal to men in every sphere of life. In practice, they continue to suffer discrimination, harassment, humiliation and exploitation in and outside home. Theoretically, women might have been given more freedom but in practice, they still suffer many hardships, inhuman dignities and unworthy treatment everywhere. Within the home, she is still not treated at par with her male counterpart. Barring a few urban educated families, a baby girl is never welcomed with as much éclat and happiness as a baby boy. Sometimes, the birth of a girl is regarded as a bad omen. They are not treated as equals to men, and not given due respect in the family (75 per cent women are in labour force but only 0.01 per cent has property rights). Male's roles as father and husband still dominate over both his children and wife. The power to govern the home and the authority still rests in the hands of male head of the household. The dominant father model still persists in most of the middle and lower class families. Leaving aside a few, in the so-called modern families wives have not become equal partners to their husbands even if they are well-educated or more educated to their husbands. Most of the decisions of the household—from purchasing daily household items to decide about the education and marriage of their children—are taken by father/husband. There is no significant change in the attitude of the males even in the families where females are working outside the home. Women as daughters or wives have to seek permission from their fathers/husbands for going outside home or for receiving higher education. In some families, it is seen that husbands do not allow their wives of the same caliber and education to take up any job assignment of the same status outside the home. They prefer their educated wives should utilize their energies just in home management and rearing and caring of children or old parents. Women's lower status in Indian society contributes to early marriages, lower literacy, poor nutrition and high fertility and mortality levels, especially during the reproductive age.

In professional field their condition is also not better. Till recently, women from the higher castes were not allowed to work outside the home for some remunerative job. They do not enjoy equal rights in many matters in the occupational fields also. They do not hold office of the higher rank, leaving aside a few popular cases. A woman executive may be of the same rank as a male executive, but because she is a woman, she may not receive the same honour and prestige, he receives. The case of super cop Kiran Bedi is well known. She was superseded for the post of Delhi Police Commissioner by a man two years junior to her in service. Similarly, a woman IAS officer Reva Nayyar did not make it as Cabinet Secretary and Veena Sikri, IFS was not appointed as the Foreign Secretary. There are still any numbers of other victims who wither unseen. Twenty-one years ago *Wallstreet Journal* had coined the term 'glass ceiling' to refer to apparent barriers that prevent from reaching the top hierarchy that still hold true, barring a few exceptional cases. Furthermore, women earn less than men, have less access to more prestigious better paying occupations even when they are equal in all respects.

The best example is provided by the rural India, where in theory women are equated with goddess, but in actual practice, they are treated as drudges. The problems of inferiority, inequality, dependence and the exploitation experienced by women have not much changed in the villages, where most of the India lives, even after 65 years of independence. Ill-treatment is coupled with no equal opportunity for social participation in spite of the immense amount of work which is expected of them in the home as well as in agricultural field or in some employment. One of the main characteristics of women is her multi-tasking dexterity. She is usually the one who handles home as well as occupational field or office.

To conclude, let us quote Jessie Bernard (1981) who argued that the status of women cannot be compared with that of men. It is generally said that men have higher status because they are usually better educated and have more organizational skills and experience than women. In addition to these, women acquire their status from their husbands, that they are socialized to think themselves as inferior, and they are physio-psychologically conditioned, to use the modern term, they are programmed to be wives and mothers, non-competitive with men because they are less able to compete. Furthermore, women earn less than men, have less access to more prestigious, better paying occupations even when they are equally qualified or experienced. Even having children increases the husband's power, for the wife becomes more dependent.

Empowerment of Women in India

The subject of empowerment of women has becoming a burning issue all over the world including India since last few decades. Many agencies of United Nations in their reports have emphasized that gender issue is to be given utmost priority. It is held that women now cannot be asked to wait for any more for equality.

Inequalities between men and women and discrimination against women have also been age-old issues all over the world. Thus, women's quest for equality with man is a universal phenomenon. What exists for men is demanded by women? They have demanded equality with men in matters of education, employment, inheritance, marriage, politics and recently in the field of religion also to serve as cleric (in Hinduism and Islam). Women want to have for themselves the same strategies of change which menfolk have had over the centuries such as equal pay for equal work. Their quest for equality has given birth to the formation of many women's associations and launching of movements.

The position and status of women all over the world has risen incredibly in the 20th century. We find that it has been very low in 18th and 19th centuries in India and elsewhere when they were treated like 'objects' that can be bought and sold. For a long time women in India remained within the four walls of their household. Their dependence on menfolk was total. A long struggle going back over a century has brought women the property rights, voting rights, an equality in civil rights before the law in matters of marriage and employment (in India women had not to struggle for voting rights as we find in other countries). In addition to the above rights, in India, the customs of *purdha* (veil system), female infanticide, child marriage, *sati* system (self-immolation by the women with their husbands), dowry system and the state of permanent widowhood were either totally removed or checked to an appreciable extent after independence through legislative measures.

Two Acts have also been enacted to emancipate women in India. These are: Protection of Women from Domestic Violence Act, 2005 and the Compulsory Registration of Marriage Act, 2006. The Domestic Violence Act recognizes that abuse be physical as well as mental. Anything that makes a woman feel inferior and takes away her self-respect is abuse. Compulsory Registration of Marriage Act can be beneficial in preventing the abuse of institution of marriage and hindering social justice especially in relation to women. It would help the innumerable women in the country who get abandoned by their husbands and have no means of proving their marital status. It would also help check child marriages, bigamy and polygamy, enable women to seek maintenance and custody of their children and widows can claim inheritance rights. The Act is applicable on all women irrespective of caste, creed or religion. It would truly empower Indian women to exercise their rights.

To what extent legislative measures have been able to raise the status of women in India? Are women now feel empowered in the sense that they are being equally treated by men in all spheres of life and are able to express one's true feminine urges and energies? These are the important questions to be investigated with regard to women's empowerment in India.

We all know that girls are now doing better at school than boys. The annual results of Secondary and Higher Secondary Board examinations reveal this fact. More women are getting degrees than men, and are filling most new jobs in every field. There was a time when women's education was not a priority even among the elite. Since the last quarter of the 20th century and more so after the opening up of the economy, post-1991, a growing number of women have been entering into the economic field, seeking paid work (remunerative jobs) outside the family. Women are playing bigger and bigger role in economic field: as workers, consumers, entrepreneurs, managers and investors. According to a report of *The Economist*, 'Women and the World Economy', in 1950, only one-third of American women of working age had a paid job. Today, two-thirds do, and women make up almost half of American's workforce. In fact, almost everywhere, including India, more women are employed, though their share is still very low. Manufacturing work, traditionally a male preserve, has declined, while jobs in services have expanded, reducing the demand for manual labour and putting the sexes on equal footing.

We can now see women in almost every field: architecture, lawyers, financial services, engineering, medical and IT jobs. They have also entered service occupations such as a nurse, a beautician, a sales worker, a waitress, etc. They are increasingly and gradually seen marching into domains which were previously reserved for males (police, drivers army, pilots, chartered accountants, commandos). In spite of their increasing number in every field, women still remain perhaps the world's most underutilized resources. Many are still excluded from paid work and many do not make best use of their skills.

The rapid pace of economic development has increased the demand for educated female labour force almost in all fields. Women are earning as much as their husbands do, their employment nonetheless adds substantially to family and gives family an economic advantage over the family with only one breadwinner. This new phenomenon has also given economic power in the hands of women for which they were earlier totally dependent on males. Economically independent women feel more confident about their personal lives. Hence, they are taking more personal decisions, for instance, about their further education, marriage, etc. More and more women want freedom of work and control their own reproduction, freedom of mobility and freedom to define one's own style of life. It is contended that freedom leads to greater openness, generosity and tolerance. This new pattern of working wives and mothers has affected the status of women in many ways. Women's monetary independence leads them to the way to empowerment. Sociologist Robert Blood (1965) observes, 'Employment emancipates women from domination by their husbands and secondarily, raises their daughters from inferiority to their brothers' (Blood and Wolfe, 1965). In brief, economic independence of women is changing their overall equations, perspective and outlook.

Economic independence of women has also affected the gender relationships. New forms of gender relationships (live-in relationship, lesbian and gay marriages) are challenging the long-rooted conception of marriages as a permanent arrangement between families and communities. In traditional marriages the relationships were hierarchical and authoritarian. The modern conjugal relationships are based on freedom and desire rather than convention. People's attitudes about marriage are also changing. Educated women now feel that there is more to life than marriage. They can get most of the things they want (income, status, identity) without marriage, while they find it harder to find a suitable accomplished mate. This is why their marriage is delayed.

With increasing literacy among women in India, their entry into many types of work, formerly the preserve of men, women can now look upon the bearing and raising of their children not as a life's work in itself but as an episode. It women have started taking men's work, it could be said that men have taken over women's. Young fathers could be seen wash up and making beds, caring of the young and doing many other domestic works. The division of labour between sexes has changed somewhat. They do similar work and share both household activities and tastes. Women wear trousers, jeans, suits and put on ties.

The facts about working wives suggest a basic change in Indian family. The traditional (nuclear) household, in which the husband works and the wife remains at home to care for the children, though still a dominant pattern, is changing gradually but steadily. A new pattern is emerging in which both partners work outside the home but do not share equally in housework and child care as we see in Western families. In India, the paternalistic attitude of the male has not undergone much change. In spite of such drawbacks and hurdles that still prevail, Indian women (especially educated) are no longer hesitant or apologetic about claiming a share and visibility within the family, at work, in public places, and in the public discourse.

Women in Politics

A new dimension of women in politics emerged in recent years all over the world. More and more women have now been entering into politics. Conventional politics reflected male concerns and hence women were notably absent in politics. Welfare policies had been constructed and reinforced women's traditional position as wives and mothers. Women have struggled over issues affecting them, especially their rights to property and vote in the 19th century and to abortion, equal pay and nursery provision in the 20th century. In India, reform movements before and after independence have helped women to gain some power in politics also. After independence they have achieved an unprecedented political breakthrough with the reservation of seats for them in panchayats and other public bodies. It is heartening to note that Indian women were among the earliest to get their political rights (right to vote) without any political movement like in the United States and many Western countries. They were among the foremost to take active part in politics even in pre-independence times. Indian women have a distinction to become UNO Secretary (Vijaylaxmi Pandit), Prime Minister (Indira Gandhi), Chief Minister (Sucheta Kriplani, Jayalalitha, Uma Bharati, Mayawati and Vasundhara Raje) and even President (Pratibha Patil). By becoming Pradhan or a ward member in a Gram Panchayat or any other civic body, or a member of State Assembly or Parliament, it augments respect within the family as well as in the community at large besides increasing their self-esteem, confidence and decision-making ability.

If we take the women's participation in politics as one of the measurements of their emancipation, we find at present their number is very low in comparison to men in State Assemblies and Parliament. It is about 11 per cent only (26 women in upper house—Rajya Sabha consisting of 245 members and 59 women in lower house—Lok Sabha consisting of 543 members. There are only 8 women ministers out of total 75 in the government of Dr Manmohan Singh). In Sweden 45 per cent seats are occupied by women in parliament. So far as the administration is concerned, there are only 592 women IAS officers out of 4,671 officers. The demand for special concessions and privileges along with the reservation of posts in assemblies and parliament (the bill is pending for the last more than ten years) and other civic institutions are a few steps towards women empowerment in India. Women have started writing and reading what other women have written. During the last two decades the writings of many women writers (such as Arundhati Roy) have been acclaimed by the institutions of international repute. There are many women in the field of journalism which was previously dominated by men. Now, she blogs and networks using it for the freedom denied so far to voice her angst, express outrage and disapproval, fulfil the need for acceptance and approval.

In spite of many gains, much remains to be done to improve the status of women in India. The female work participation rate in India is only 26 per cent whereas it is 46 per cent in China. Some 34 (2011) out of every 100 women are illiterate as compared to only 13 in China. Female foeticide accounts for an estimated half-a-million missing female births in India every year, lowering the female sex ratio to a dismal 914:1000 (2011). It is worst since independence. According to the report of UNICEF, India ranks at 115 out of 162 countries in matters of gender development.

Though the above changes signify positive gains from the point of view of equality for women, but the reality is beset with many problems and tensions. The observation about the gains in equality applies only on a meagre number of Indian educated women living in urban areas. Many studies conducted in India and elsewhere (in so-called developed countries) revealed that equal sharing of housework is still a nightmare for women. Working wives find that housework and care of children is still largely their task, quite unequally wives shared with husband as on an average working wives/mothers are compelled to work at least 14 hours a day and even more. The weekend is less a time for rest and more to catch up on unfinished and pending tasks of the household.

The status of women in a society cannot be secured by her economic power alone as is generally supposed. It depends on culture also. As a micro study reports that 'women's participation in the job market is more intensive when they come from poor and very poor households. Women's income in particular becomes a means to survival of the poor people.' Does this crucial income of poor women enhance their status? The study further reports, 'They are empowered as far as earnings are concerned but not with respect to spending the earnings. The very attitude of considering women's income supplementary and something not preferred ... raises problems for women's empowerment. Furthermore, 'the limited empowerment that we have seen has been nurtured within the socio-economic-political empowerment process of people, including women, through the Panchayat system' (Bagchi, 2000).

Problems of Women in India

Many empirical studies have been conducted to assess the problems faced by women in and outside family and to know the quality of change in the status of women in India. Almost all studies reveal that sexism still prevails everywhere. Women often encounter prejudice, discrimination and abuse from both men and women both in the family and at workplace. Almost daily we come across some or the other incident of dowry death, domestic violence, exploitation, rape cases, harassment, etc., reported in newspapers or magazines. Most of these incidents or accidents are reflection of the problems still faced by women in India.

Apparently, women are now fully emancipated and free to choose their profession, life partner and the way of life. But, the fundamentally deep-rooted feeling of inequality and discrimination still persists due to domineering attitudes of males and the age-old customs and traditions. A few urban educated women may look upon themselves as emancipated, enlightened and progressive. They may ape the western way of life but the deep-rooted inhibitions and age-old restraints always cram their mind. In public women might get a lot of lip respect, especially on 'women's day' or 'mothers day,' but at home their equal rights and privileges are a mere myth. Most husbands and fathers took upon their wives and daughters as their own possessions. Obedience to her husband is still expected from a good Hindu wife even in the so-called well-educated families. True and full expression of her individuality, unfettered by restraints, is unheard of. The normal Indian wife's thinking is conditioned in such a manner that she cheerfully accepts any amount of domination. She takes it for granted that her likes and dislikes, her wishes and ideas will never be placed on the same level as her husband. Working wives are however treated with a little more respect and consideration. Economic dependence of Indian women on her husbands has kept them in a state of perpetual bondage. This is the crux of the whole problem of Indian women. The condition of women narrated above is still true for rural India. Exploitation of women in the countryside still prevails. She is still identified as a daughter, daughter-in-law, mother, mother-in-law, wife, etc., and not as a person. She has no independent connections, friends and relatives outside the family. Earlier sociologists stressed that a change in the structure of the family, e.g., from joint to nuclear, would automatically lead to a change in the status of women. But it has not come true. It is a very simplistic approach because the socialization of a woman ensures that she remains in a subordinate position irrespective of family structure. Hence, the institutions of family and marriage both need a reorientation.

To conclude, it may be said that considering the long history of suppression of women under patriarchy, women seem to be on the path to empowerment although at a slower pace. The fact that women come forward to contest elections for various civic bodies from panchayat to parliament and hold positions in these bodies and work as Collector, Chief Secretary, I.G., Professor, Vice-Chancellor, engineers, doctors, business and bank executives, pilots and many other responsible posts is itself a step on the road to empowerment. In raising the issue of women's autonomy and right to go out to work, they challenged entrenched gender roles, and even suggested that not getting married might be valid choice for women. Christensen, President, National Council of Family Relations once remarked that sex has suffered much from giving married women complete equality with their husbands. It has encouraged her to become more aggressive and hence more masculine … . Furthermore, she sometimes has confused equality with identity, and in her effort to be equal with man she has tried to copy man—in dress, mannerisms, even vulgarities … . At the same time, man has tended to soften both because of women's inroads and because of the comforts of modern culture which means that he is be coming less masculine.' Women's equality with man in this sense is harming sex. And, there is a growing tendency to love things more than people.

Chapter 9

Economic Institutions

KEY FEATURES

- Economic Institutions: Sociologists and Economists Perspectives
- Concept of Economic System
- Economic Determinism
- Classification of Societies
- Types of Economic Systems
- Capitalism (Market Economy)
- Socialism (Planned Economy)
- Models of Development
- Planning and Development
- Requisites of Planning
- Types of Planning
- Social Planning
- Development
- Social Development
- Sustainable Development
- Planned Development in India
- Community Development Projects
- Panchayati Raj
- Schemes of Rural Development
- Some other social schemes
- Development Programmes: An Evaluation
- Women and Development
- Globalization and Women
- Sociological Determinants of Economic Growth
- The New World Economy
- Division of Labour
- Economic Development and Social Change

From the time of Karl Marx, Max Weber and Emile Durkheim and other sociologists of 19th and early 20th centuries have had a long and deep interest in economic institutions, especially as these relate to non-economic aspects of social life such as the family, education and the state. The term 'economic institutions' is usually used for socially sanctioned such concepts and structures which men have developed in the process of satisfying their material needs. Economic institutions provide basic physical subsistence for society and meet needs for food, shelter, clothing and other necessities of life. These institutions include production—agriculture and industry and the distribution, exchange and consumption of commodities, goods and services necessary for human survival. Secondary economic institutions are credit and banking system, advertising, co-operatives, etc. In detail, these institutions are studied by the science of economics. Economists study the internal workings of economic system—production, distribution, supply and demand and consumption of goods, taxation, borrowing, saving and spending, and so on.

Sociologists are not economists. Therefore, they are not much interested in the mechanisms of production and distribution but they have surely an interest in the relations of men incident to a particular economic order. All human and social life has an economic basis, the nature of which determines the formal structure of society. Economic institutions arise out of the determinants we make with respect to the goods we need. Sociologists study economic systems to better understand how the production of goods influences social life. They study types of economic systems, the size and power of corporations, the occupations in economic systems, and how work affects the rest in one's life. Not only this, sociologists study the role of values and preferences in affecting production and consumption of goods, the influence exerted by prestige or custom on the price of goods, the origins and motivations of entrepreneurs and managers, the contribution of education to productivity and similar issues. In brief, sociologists study how the economic system interacts with other social institutions or how the non-economic aspects of social life affect the economic aspects. By knowing the political conditions of different societies, for instance, it is possible to predict some of the economic activities that will occur in them. Even something so intimate as friendship may condition economic processes. If workmen in a clique do not accept management's goals of production, they often try deliberately to slow the output. Moreover, they use the lever of friendship and loyalty to enforce these restrictive practices in their group. Members often 'go along' with the norms because they wish to remain in good standing in the clique (Smelser, 1962).

Sociologists and Economists Perspectives

Although sociologists and economists do not study the same subjects, they actually cover much of the same material, but with different interests and points of view. Economists cannot understand the success or failure of an economic system without considering how it interacts with the rest of the society. Sociologists cannot understand how systems interact unless they understand the functioning of each system. Nevertheless, the disciplines have different goals. Economists specialize in studying the economic system—the study of the production and distribution of goods and services. It is just one of society's important interacting parts whereas sociologists study the whole of society, including the economic system. Economists think, as do sociologists, in terms of systems and sub-systems; they stress the relations between parts, especially patterns of dependence, dominance, exchange, and the like. Sociologists consider the economy as a sub-system of society, then they shall ask how it is related to other major sub-systems—the cultural system (for example, values and ideologies), the political system, the stratification system, and so on.

Concept of Economic System

Every society must provide some organized way for satisfying those material wants—food, shelter, clothing and health care—without which life could not be sustained. To be accepted in modern society, however, we need many more things—soap, hair oil, face cream, deodorant, powder, toothpaste, shoes, and various types of clothes for different occasions. Not only this, we also like to have some luxuries of our society such as car, television, radio, washing machine, heater, geyser, sporting equipments and so on. All these things, from the most basic necessities to the most expensive luxuries, are produced by our economic system. A society's economic system provides for the production and distribution of all the necessities, comforts and luxuries the society uses. The basic function and problem of all economic systems is to maximize satisfactions through an economical allocation of various resources which are limited for the satisfaction of various needs which are unlimited. The term 'economic system' refers to the social institutions and their arrangements through which goods and services are produced, distributed and consumed. According to Anthony Giddens (1997), 'the economic system consists of institutions that provide for the production and distribution of goods and services'. It influences our lives from before we are born until we die. It even influences how we are buried. So, with all other social institutions such as the family, religion and government, the economic system shapes other aspects of the social order and is, in turn, influenced by them. Sociologists study the economic system because it interacts with all segments of society. An economic system may be represented in different ways. The economy may be treated as a social sub-system like political system. There is continuous interaction among these sub-systems.

Economic Determinism

It is a term which has a great bearing on the social system as such requires explanation. It is generally used in the sense of economic reductionism that asserts all social, political and cultural activities have their roots in the economic base. It denies the 'superstructure' any independent significance. This assertion is associated with Karl Marx who said that the relations of production constitute the base upon which legal and political superstructures rest. This and similar propositions have been the source of much debate about the nature and source of economic institutions.

Classification of Societies

Human societies may be distinguished on the basis of different ways in which men make a living and the different forms and extent of their control over the material environment. Societies with a technology which gives them little independence from, or control over, the environment—societies where people are at the mercy of the natural world, a prey to hunger and disease, where they die easily and usually too young—these are often called 'simple societies' (primitive and peasant societies). The economic organization of the simple societies is of the subsistence type, i.e., production-consumption economy. A classification scheme which categorizes societies on the basis of their economic system may be developed as under:

Hunting and Gathering Society

The hunting and gathering society is a social system having the simplest minimal technology and mostly unsophisticated mode of production. People are constantly on the move in search of food (generally termed as *nomadic society*), and there is little division of labour based on gender. There is no scope for specialization. The entire society is organized around kinship ties which serves as the source of authority and influence. In such societies many roles are included in or subsumed under kinship roles. It may be difficult to distinguish between kinship, political, military and economic roles. Production is communal and cooperative and the distribution system is based on sharing. Social inequality is at minimum and social differentiation is based on such ascribed characteristics as gender, age and family background.

Horticultural Society

It is a society based on horticulture, a mode of production in which people plant seeds and crops using digging sticks to cultivate small gardens. In contrast to the hunting and gathering society, members of horticultural societies are much less nomadic and develop settlements that have larger populations. Some accumulation of food and goods was done in such societies because of social surplus. A more complex division of labour, more substantial dwellings and a small amount of trade was developed in such societies.

Agrarian Society

An agrarian society focuses its mode of production primarily on agriculture. Because of the introduction of new technological innovations such as the plough, farmers can increase their crop yield. The ability to produce great surpluses allowed the emergence of larger and permanent settlements. The comparative and greater surpluses of agrarian society make it more feasible to create artifacts and art objects.

Industrial Society

The technology of the agrarian society continues to rely on the physical power of humans and animals. With the use of machines and non-animal sources of energy, industrial society came into existence. It is a society that relies chiefly on mechanization for the production of its economic goods and services. It involves changes in the social organization of the workplace. The division of labour became increasingly complex. Industrial societies also promote the rationalization of social life, increased literacy and the growth of science, formal education, and mass media. Bureaucracy becomes a ubiquitous form of social organization. Industrial society is frequently associated with mass society.

Post-industrial Society

The significant changes in the occupational structure of industrial societies as their focus shifts from manufacturing to service industries have led social societies to call technically advanced nations post-industrial societies. Sociologist Daniel Bell (1973) defines it as 'a society whose economic system is based on the production of information rather than of goods'. He suggests that, in modern societies, theoretical knowledge forms the 'axial principle' of society and is the source of innovation and policy formation. In the economy this is reflected in the decline of goods producing and manufacturing as the main forms of economic activity, and their replacement by services. Larger numbers of people become involved in occupations devoted to the teaching, generation or dissemination of ideas. In such societies the technicians and professionals occupy the pre-eminent position.

The term 'post-industrial society' was first used by Bell in 1962 to describe economic and social changes that took place in the late 20th century. According to him, a post-industrial society is one where knowledge has displaced property as the central preoccupation, and the prime source of power and social dynamism.

Types of Economic Systems

To produce goods and services for a society, an economic system requires land on which it produces food and builds factories. It also needs raw materials, tools and machinery to process them, and labour. Economic systems in modern societies vary according to who owns the land, the factories, the raw materials, and the equipments. These means of production may be privately owned (owned by individuals), or they may be owned publicly by the state. On this basis, there are currently two basic types of economic systems—*capitalism* (system based on private ownership) and *socialism* (system based on state ownership). No society is purely capitalist or purely socialist. Mixed economies in which private and state ownerships are both practised have a system called 'democratic socialism'.

Capitalism (Market Economy)

Capitalism is 'a system of economic enterprise based on market exchange'. The *Concise Oxford Dictionary of Sociology* (1994) defines it as 'a system of wage-labour and commodity production for sale, exchange and profit, rather than for the immediate need of the producers'. 'Capital' refers to wealth or money used to invest in a market with the hope of achieving a profit' (Giddens, 1997). It is an economic system in which the means of production are largely in private hands and the main incentive for economic activity is the accumulation of profits. From the perspective developed by Karl Marx, capitalism is organized around the concept of CAPITOL implying the ownership and control of the means of production by those who employ workers to produce goods and services in exchange for wages. Max Weber, on the other hand, considered market exchange as the defining characteristic of capitalism. In practice, capitalist systems vary in the degree to which private ownership and economic activity are regulated by government. It has assumed various forms in industrial societies.

In common parlance, these days, capitalism is known as a *market economy*. The goods sold and the price they are sold at are determined by the people who buy them and the people who sell them. In such a system, all people are free to buy, sell and make a profit if they can. This is why capitalism is often called free market system. It gives freedom to entrepreneur (of opening industry), to worker (of selling labour), to trader (of buying and selling goods), and to the individual (of buying and consuming).

Main Characteristics of Capitalism

Capitalism involves new attitudes and institutions—entrepreneurs engaged in the sustained, systematic pursuit of profit, the market acted as the key mechanism of productive life, and goods, services and labour become commodities whose use was determined by rational calculation. The main characteristics of capitalistic organization in its 'pure' form may briefly be described as under:

1. Private ownership and control of the economic instruments of production, i.e., CAPITOL.
2. The gearing of economic activity to making profits—maximization of profits.
3. Free market economy—a market framework that regulates this activity.
4. The appropriation of profits by the owners of capital. It is the income derived by the capitalist from selling in the market.
5. The provision of wage labour, which is created by converting labour power into a commodity. It is this process which produces the working class and inherently hostile relationships in capitalist society: worker (proletariat) versus capitalist, employee versus employer.
6. Business firms are privately owned, and compete with each other to sell their goods to consumers.
7. Commercialization of agricultural and industrial production.
8. Development of new economic groups and expanding across the globe.
9. Capital accumulation by the capitalists as an obligatory activity, for unless there is capital to invest, the system will fail. Profits produce capital when they are reinvested.
10. Investment and growth are accomplished by using accumulated capital to expand an enterprise or create a new one. Capitalism, thus, is an economic system that requires constant investment and constant economic growth.

What has impressed students of modernity is the huge and largely unregulated dominance of capitalist enterprise across political and religious control with its related monetary and market networks.

Historical Development of Capitalism

Historically, modern capitalism has mainly developed and expanded in Great Britain and the United States. Early industrial capitalism in Great Britain and the United States in the 19th century is regarded as the classical model that approximates the pure form most closely. Modern (industrial) capitalism differs in a fundamental way from pre-existing production systems, because it involves the constant expansion of production and ever-increasing accumulation of wealth. In traditional production systems, levels of production were fairly static since they were geared to habitual, customary needs. Capitalism promotes the constant revision of the technology of production.

The impact of science and technology stretches beyond the economic sphere. Scientific and technological development, such as radio, television, computers and the other electronic media (modern forms of communication), have also come to shape how we live, how we think and feel about the world. In the face of these developments, traditional debates between the advocates of free market capitalism and state socialism have become more or less outdated or are becoming outdated. As we have moved into a 'postmodern' world (information society) from the 18th and 19th century modern society, some philosophers like Francis Fukuyama predicated about the 'end of history'—meaning that there are no future alternatives to capitalism and liberal democracy. Capitalism has won in its long struggle with socialism, contrary to Marx's prediction and liberal democracy now stands unchallenged (Giddens, 1997).

Socialism (Planned Economy)

According to the *Oxford Dictionary of Sociology* (1994), 'an economic and political system based on collective or state ownership of the means of production and distribution is known as socialism'. This approach has its roots in the writings of Karl Marx and Friedrich Engels. These thinkers were disturbed by the exploitation of the working class as it emerged during the industrial revolution. In their view, capitalism forced large numbers of people to exchange their labour for wages. The owners of an industry pay workers less than the value of the goods they produced. They pocket the difference between the value of the labour and the value of the product—*surplus value* as Marx called it. Marx was struck by the inequalities the capitalist system creates. A socialist economic system represents an attempt to eliminate such economic inequalities and exploitation. The goals of socialist system include destroying the class system and thereby ending the exploitation, oppression and alienation of workers, replacing greed and the profit motive with concern for collective well-being.

Socialism differs from capitalism in a sense that the means of production and distribution in a society are collectively rather than privately owned. The basic objective of the socialist system is to meet people's needs rather than to maximize profits. Socialism also differs from capitalism in that it is not controlled by the market—it has a planned economy. The government controls what will be produced and consumed. It sets prices for goods, decides what goods the society needs, and what would be the luxuries. Thus, there is no free market. Socialists reject the laissez-faire philosophy that free competition benefits the general public. As a result, social life would be regulated democratically in ways that put human needs first and make more efficient and effective use of human and other resources. Socialist societies also differ from capitalist ones in their commitment to social service programmes. Contrary to capitalist societies, socialist societies typically offer government financed medical care, housing, education and other key services for all citizens.

In practice, however, like capitalism, the socialism takes many and diverse forms. It has worked quite differently. Authoritarianism rather than democracy has been the predominant form of political power, inefficient central planning has generally failed to meet the needs of the people, a privileged class of bureaucrats has perpetuated the class system, and chronic (until recently) conflict and competition with wealthier and more powerful capitalist nations have drained both attention and resources. In fact, no socialist society has met Marx's main preconditions for successful socialism.

Main Characteristics of Socialism/Socialist Societies

While there are various strands of socialist thought, most socialists identify the following as the important characteristics of socialist societies:

1. There is a common ownership of the means of production and distribution. It is collectively owned system of production.
2. Economic activities are planned by the state and the market plays little or no role in the allocation of resources.
3. There is no place for exploitation, oppression and alienation in a socialist society.
4. With the disappearance of private property, economic classes also disappear and hence the state has an administrative rather than repressive function.
5. The structural changes will also vanish the ideology, especially religious.
6. Socialism emphasizes the abolition of markets, capital, and labour as a commodity.
7. The socialist state or government of each nation will eventually 'wither away' as will inequality and class differentiation.
8. In a communistic state (a brand of socialistic state found in the erstwhile Soviet Union and Eastern Europe) most of the industry and agriculture was owned by the state—only a few businesses were in private sector.

Socialist thought, emerged as a powerful and credible alternative to capitalism in USSR, Eastern Europe, Asia (China) and Africa, faded away with the collapse of Soviet communism in 1989. Some commentators believe European socialism is dead and buried. Communist parties in West and East have given themselves new names and distanced themselves from the heavy-handed, state communism of the past. However, the concerns that have been addressed by those who espoused or eschewed the cause still remain. The dichotomies of freedom and equality, individual and collective rights all remain very much to the fore. Liberal capitalism fails to see the uneven and unequal impact that globalized economy has.

As written earlier that socialism emerged in response to and as a challenge to the inequalities of capitalism. Since capitalism has now been globalized, there is always a potential for this challenge to re-emerge, but perhaps via a different sort of language and organization, perhaps based on ecology, gender, anti-consumerist movements, and so on.

Thus, capitalism and socialism serve as ideal types of economic systems. In reality, the economy of each industrial society (Great Britain, the United States, and the Soviet Union including India) includes certain elements of both capitalism and socialism. All industrial societies rely chiefly on mechanization in the production of goods and services. In almost all countries, some property is private and some is owned by the state. In India, before the introduction of liberal economy in 1990, there was mixed economy—railways, airways and many other industrial units like BHEL were owned by the state but now the wind is changing towards privatization of these units also. Before adopting the liberal model of development, Indian model, based on socialist ideology, was known as 'democratic collectivistic model'.

Models of Development

Stages of Economic Growth

In primitive societies economic activity was almost entirely devoted to satisfying the biological requirements for survival. When men were able to move beyond the stage of subsistence and started using more time and effort to produce tools and other kinds of capital equipment, it resulted into increased productivity of labour. Consequently, some societies had attained a level of affluence. The historic process of development from the subsistence economy to the affluent society has been conceptualized by the American economic historian Walter W. Rostow. He postulated a five-stage sequence of economic and social development as given below:

Stage I: Traditional society

This is the subsistence level achieved by pre-literate or 'primitive' societies. It is characterized by a high concentration on agriculture and consequent restriction on geographical mobility. This stage is characterized by 'primitive technology,' hierarchical social structure and behaviour conditioned more by custom and accepted practice than by the systematic application of reason.

Stage II: Preconditions for take off

When scientific thought develops and begins to be applied to practical problems, either through conquest, imitation or internal processes, then, the precondition for 'take-off' exists. At this stage, economic growth is seen by certain people as an end in itself as well as a means of attaining other ends. They are motivated to invest money for profit in manufacturing, commerce and trade. Max Weber has beautifully explained this point of motivation in his celebrated work, *The Protestant Ethic and the Spirit of Capitalism* (1930).

Associated with this development, it is expected that the entrepreneur must, to some extent, be free from the attitudinal and social constraints of traditional society. To stimulate economic growth, there should also be centralization of political power which enables economic activity to proceed within a framework of law and order.

Stage III: The take off

When the emerging forces of change become predominant and economic growth is cumulative, then, the crucial 'take-off' stage is reached. The successful completion of this stage requires: (a) surplus of consumer goods; (b) technological development; and (c) active political encouragement and financial aid. Some kinds of capital equipments (infrastructural facilities), such as roads, schools, public health services and so on require high initial investment. The profit motive being inadequate to provide for such things. The huge amounts of capital investment needed to make the transition to industrialism may be obtained in three basic ways as under:

1. By forced saving.
2. By voluntary saving as in stock exchange investment or as the cultivation of abstinence as a moral duty.
3. By obtaining aid from other societies in the form of investment, credit facilities or ready-made capital equipment.

Stage IV: The drive to technological maturity

At this stage, called 'the drive to technological maturity' some 10 to 20 per cent of the national income is regularly invested so that economic growth outstrips the inevitable growth of population as the standard of living rises. The economy is then able to move beyond its dependence.

Stage V: Age of high mass consumption

This is the stage of 'high mass consumption' or affluence. Increased efficiency at this stage permits a decreasing number of workers to satisfy primary needs and the occupational structure shifts increasingly to the production of 'non-essential' consumer goods and services for a mass market. In the context of mass consumption, advertising may be seen as a necessary means of maintaining the balance of supply and demand.

The above stages suggested by Rostow may or may not be applicable everywhere because of national and/or territorial differences. These differences make for a variety of patterns of development. Processes of economic development may differ in the following ways:

1. *Variations in the pre-existing conditions of the country:* A society's value system may be congenial or antipathetic to industrial values. The society may be tightly or loosely integrated. Its level of wealth may be low or high. This wealth may be evenly or unevenly distributed. From the standpoint of population, the society may be 'young and empty' (e.g., Australia) or 'old

and crowded' (e.g., India). The society may be politically dependent, recently independent or altogether autonomous. Such pre-existing conditions shape the impact of the forces of economic development.

2. *Variations in the impetus to development:* The pressures to development may stem from (a) the internal implications of a value system (as in Weber's theory of ascetic Protestantism); (b) from a desire for material prosperity; (c) from a desire for national security and prestige; or (d) from a combination of these. Such differences influence the adjustment to modernization greatly.
3. *Variations in the content and timings of dramatic events during development:* Wars, revolutions, rapid migrations and natural catastrophes (flood, famine, earthquake, etc.) may influence the course of economic and social development.
4. *Variations in the path towards modernization:* The tempo of industrialization may be fast or slow. The development sequence may be different at different places. The government may play an active or passive role in shaping the pattern of investment.

Because of these sources of variations, it is very difficult to predict about the processes of economic development.

Core-Periphery Model

It is a model of the spatial organization of human activity based upon the equal distribution of power in economy and society. The core dominates (although it may in turn be dominated from outside) whilst the periphery is dependent. This dependence is structured through the relation of exchange between core and periphery. J. Friedmann (1966), with whom the core-periphery model is most closely associated, outlined the following four stages of the development: (a) pre-industrial society with localized economics; (b) core-periphery; (c) dispersion of economic activity and, to a lesser extent, control into certain parts of the periphery; and (d) the emergence of spatial integration in which the various parts of the economy relate in a more truly interdependent manner.

In recent years, the core-periphery model was used by Andre Gunder Frank in his analysis of underdeveloped nations of Latin America, including Honduras and Mexico. Analysing the underdevelopment of the Third World countries, he used 'dependency theory'. It challenges modernization theory by arguing that underdevelopment is not an early stage in a country's evolutionary process, but a condition resulting from their exploitation by modern First World countries. He argues that though some of the nations have become independent from colonial rule but they are still dependent for their development on modern First World countries—United States, Britain, etc. For him, development is a myth which obscures the reality of exploitation—the capitalist powers have never seriously intended to give up their economic domination over their erstwhile colonies. Frank had noted that this exploitation is done through unequal trade and exchange keeps them (Third World countries) in a permanent state of socio-economic dependency on dominant capitalist states, or the 'metropolitan' countries of the world. Dependent states are merely satellites whose surplus is extracted, especially by powerful multinational corporations. In this metropolis (core)-satellite (periphery) relationship, the majority—overwhelmingly peasant—remains poor and only the elite and a small urban middle class develops in a situation of 'uneven' development.

Planning and Development

Social behaviour is partly rational and partly non-rational. A man behaves in a particular way because such behaviour is looked upon as the 'right way' of behaving and because he can achieve some tangible result. In our day-to-day life, we perform many rituals connected with birth, marriage or death ceremonies and do many things which have no reasons. They are based on sentiments, values and our traditions or they may be just habitual reactions of the man. They are not governed by considerations of efficiency and are not amenable to rational considerations. In this connection, it will not be out of place to mention the views of Vilfredo Pareto who pointed out two types of social action: rational and irrational. Economics studies only rational action while sociology studies rational and irrational both.

There is yet another aspect of social behaviour which is of great significance. This aspect of behaviour is based on realistic considerations and rational calculations which is known as *planning*. Planning is a methodical way of assessing the needs and priorities and working out sound procedures to fulfil these needs. It is a rational activity which presupposes that an endeavour is made to bring about certain changes which are considered to be more efficient and more worthwhile. Planning aims to answer the questions of what, how much, where, when and by whom the project or programme is to be executed. Any planning involves a clear identification of the (a) goals, (b) a concrete specification of the targets, and (c) the methods and means to achieve them. Thus, any planning (economic or social) involves deliberate thinking, deliberate action and evaluation to determine the extent to which the planned programmes have to be implemented in the whole society or community. It is always based on scientific thinking and facts. It implies vision, design and wisdom. It is an attempt to shape the future by deliberate action.

Requisites of Planning

To make any planned programme a success, the following requisites are to be fulfilled:

1. Drawing out the blueprint of the planned programme, i.e., laying down concrete details of the plan. This blueprint must include the goals or objectives, the means, methods and techniques to achieve the goals, period of the plan (time limit), physical and human resources, etc.
2. To enlist cooperation and participation of the people so planned for and for this public opinion must be educated and mobilized before hand.
3. An indomitable will, a missionary zeal, sustained effort and an abiding interest on the part of the planners.
4. The schemes and ideals must conform to the social consensus and background of the people so planned for.
5. The diversity of local conditions, traditions, customs, manners and other sociological factors must be given due consideration.
6. Co-ordination, co-operation and systematization between different wings of planning department should be made. It should be emphasized that the best use should be made of poor means, rather than the poor use of the best means.

Types of Planning

Planning can take two forms: (1) democratic planning, and (2) totalitarian planning. The only important difference between these two is that in totalitarian planning people have faith or fear in the dominant minority which draw the blueprint of planning, i.e., set the goals and decides the means to achieve them. While in democratic planning there is participation by the people through the representative institutions in setting up the goals and in deciding the means to achieve them. However, whether it is democratic planning or totalitarian planning, once the goals and means are decided and accepted, these are enforced by the agency of planning—government or any corporation or institution.

Social Planning

Till sometimes back, the word 'planning' was generally used in the economic sphere only to control and direct economic activity. Or, in other words, its use was delimited to economic development. But recent sociological studies have proved that there are social aspects of economic development also. It was experienced that economic development was slowed down by the social-structural features of the society. There is no doubt that people want to have better material conditions of living. But even the activity which is necessary for achieving such an end is not forthcoming due to social-structural frameworks. Some of the important characteristics which contribute to inactivity within the realm of planning and development are: (a) tradition, (b) religious values, (c) caste system, (d) joint family system, (e) vested interests, (f) charismatic movements, etc. These favour structural stability rather than change.

Thus, besides economic planning, there is social planning too. Social planning is a conscious interactional process combining investigation, discussion, agreement and action in order to achieve those conditions, relationships and values that are regarded as desirable. In a sense, it is an intelligent direction of social change. Sociologist can work as a change agent. He can direct social change in such a way that change becomes less disruptive, painful and costly to the people.

The aims of social planning are: (1) to bring change or reform social institutions, such as caste system or institutions of marriage and family; and (2) to solve social problems like alcoholism, poverty, prostitution, unemployment, terrorism, delinquency, etc. Social planning involves a certain consensus in the whole society or at any rate in a large majority. People must consider that the situation in which they live is unsatisfactory, and it is possible to change the situation so that it becomes more satisfactory. Such a consensus is necessary both in democratic planning and totalitarian planning.

Development

The terminology of social change reflects a variety of ideological perspectives such as development, underdevelopment and undevelopment. Development implies some positive progress in society's condition. It can be viewed as 'organized social changes'. Undevelopment implies decline or stagnation. Underdevelopment is a term used especially by Marxists to indicate that the operation of international capitalism tends to prevent or retard development in the poor world. What is viewed as development varies somewhat from society to society. The goals of socialists are not the same as those of capitalists ones. The former tend to stress egalitarian and communal objectives, whereas the latter put greater emphasis on individuality and personal freedom.

Development is a dynamic concept. It has different meanings to different people. For some people it means increase in income, while for others it lays emphasis on employment, income, quality of life, happiness and so on. Still others give stress on meeting the basic needs of the life of the people. It is indeed so many things to so many people. In common usage, 'development' has the implications of economic growth, modernization, improvement in levels of material production and consumption, and changes in social, cultural and political structures to resemble more nearly those displayed in countries or economies deemed 'developed'. Economists focus their attention exclusively on economic development. Sociologists, on the other hand, pay much attention to the relationship between economic development and social change or its consequences.

The idea of 'development' was invented in the post-Second World War period to describe the process by which 'backward' countries would 'catch up' with industrialized world. Literally, development means gradual unfolding, growth, expansion or realization of potential. In the context of human development, it refers to a process of change through which an increasing proportion of a nation's citizens are able to enjoy a higher material standard of living, health, and longer lives, more education and greater control and choice over how they live. Broadly, development is a movement towards desired goals and objectives over which there is an overall near agreement between the members of a society. Nearly all societies seek to improve their technology, increase their wealth and develop the skills of their people. How this should be done (or what should be the methods) and who should most benefit from development are, of course, matters of wide disagreement.

The achievement of a state of development would enable individuals to make their own histories under conditions of their own choosing. The process of development is the means by which such conditions of human existence might be achieved. They, in turn, would necessarily involve people in a productive, crisis-free and non-exploitative set of relations with nature and in the struggle to remove oppression and exploitation from the relations between themselves. In a nutshell, it is an increasing attainment of one's own developed cultural life. What constitutes a developed cultural life, there may be differences about it. It may include the level of popular culture, i.e., the quality of everyday life and the 'high' culture—classical music, literature and the rests of the arts.

The above conceptualization of development emphasizes the following notions:

(a) That development is a process, not a state.
(b) That development implies change, but change always does not imply development or progress.
(c) That this process is ultimately related to (cultural) values of the people involved.
(d) That development is not something which can be given; it is to be acquired and worked for by those who are to benefit from it.
(e) That development is a continuous process which changes in space and time.

Social Development

Generally, the term 'development' is used and understood in terms of economic development. But it is more than purely economic and physical. It is directly related with satisfaction which may have little or nothing to do with objective statistical measures, such as GNP, GDP or per capita income. Economic development with no concern for social development is dubbed as 'development without human face'. 'Social development is the process of planned institutional change to bring about better adjustment between human needs and aspirations on the one hand and social policies and programmes on the other' (Ahuja, 1993). It encompasses a wide range of issues—social and economic equality, universal education, health and food security, provision of housing and sanitation conditions, safeguarding environment, upliftment of weaker section of society, redistribution of wealth, moral development, etc. All these may be regarded as indicators of social development.

Development cannot be understood in isolation. It is part of a more general process of social transformation. At no point in that process are we simply concerned with the attainment of economic goals or the creation of a new economic system. The goals and priorities, and the phasing of economic development, are deeply affected by overall social transformation requirement. An important aspect of development is that it is concerned with improving the overall welfare of human beings. It includes more than just increased productivity; it includes the resulting rise in the ability of people to consume the things they need to improve their level of living.

Social development entails changes in everything at once to achieve the following:

1. Elimination of poverty.
2. High literacy.
3. Social justice—equal distribution of opportunities.
4. Improvement in social welfare amenities.
5. A safe environment.
6. Opportunity for personal growth.
7. Protection and improvement of health—security in old age.
8. Upliftment of weaker sections of the society.
9. Providing security against various contingencies of life.
10. Enrichment and access to goods and services beyond the absolute minimum to sustain life.
11. High expectation of life at birth and low fertility.
12. Increase in level of employment—low proportion of labour engaged in agriculture.

According to Ram Ahuja (1993), social development involves four things: (i) assessing the needs of the people; (ii) introducing some structural changes in society such as discarding some old institutions and creating some new institutions, or changing some existing institutions; (iii) making institutions responsible to people; and (iv) associating people with decision-making.

S.C. Dube (1988) argued that 'development that makes no visible change in the degraded lot of common man—the majority in the country's population—is no development. Growth that permeates a small segment of the society to wallow a vulgar high living is immoral.'

Thus, the above and similar non-economic criteria constitute the main basis of development. The achievements of development must also be seen in terms of individual and collective well-being.

Sustainable Development

Concerns about the acute pressure of population growth, modern technology and consumer demand on the planetary fabric had been smoldering away since the 1970s. This has given rise to the concept of 'sustainable development' in the report of Harlem Brundtland (*Our Common Future*, 1987), who chaired a World Commission on Environment and Development (WCED) constituted by the then UN in 1983. The Brundtland Report, as it is popularly called, attracted huge attention. It also led to the Earth Summit—the UN Conference on Environment and Development—at Rio de Janeiro in 1992. This conference put the concept on the map and since then the world 'sustainable' has been applied to everything done in the name of development. The word 'sustainable' has now been absorbed into the development lexicon and is used for everything from 'environmentally sensitive' to 'respect of indigenous ways of doing things'. In common parlance, sustainable development aims at securing better life—food, clothing, shelter, education, medical aid and other primary requirements for all people. It refers to all-sided development of all sections of the society. Sustainable development was a big new idea which brought environmentalism into poverty reduction and poverty reduction into environmentalism in a neat and simple formula.

A new generation of environmental worries—species loss, global warming, deforestation, toxic wastes—has begun to capture scientific and popular attention. The world's natural resources are being rapidly depleted, often in the name of development. Commenting on this state of affairs, Vinay Lal (2005) said that 'in the name of development alone millions of underdeveloped people around the world have been killed, maimed, pauperized, displaced, culturally categorized and museumized'. Almost all population growth is among poorer people. But it is not they who are consuming the earth's supply of fossil fuels, warming the globe with their carbon emissions, depleting its ozone layer with their CFCs, poisoning soil and water with their chemicals, or wrecking ecological havoc with their oil spills. In fact, their consumption of the world's resources was minute compared to that of the industrialized world. Brundtland in his report declared that poverty in developing world was less cause than effect of contemporary environmental degradation—the outcome of insensitive technology transfer that pauperized people and natural systems. Only 'sustainable' development could blend the fulfilment of human needs with the protection of air, oil, water and all forms of life.

Thus, the concept of 'sustainable development' connotes not only social and economic advancement of people in order to assure them a healthy and productive life, but also that could not jeopardize the right of coming generations to their own slice of the world's pie.

Planned Development in India

Before independence, not much was done neither by Muslim rulers nor by Britishers for the development of Indian masses. Britishers, however, did launch some development programmes and enacted some laws to bring changes in the social and material life of the people of India.

The major problem that confronted India immediately after independence was how to remake, and how best to reconstruct, renovate, regenerate and reorient the vast multitude of humanity living in rural areas (about 82 per cent in 1947). Rural reconstruction means the adoption of a new pattern of life, which should be based on the habits, traditions and institutions of the villagers. For such rural reconstruction, following some other nations' footsteps, India had also adopted the course of planning, mainly economic planning. A Department of Planning and Development was created as early as 1944, following Bombay Plan. However, at this stage, the planning could not take concrete shape because of lack of resources and necessary means and skills to achieve it.

After independence, in accordance with the general and long-term goals of the Indian nation and the Directive Principles as laid down in our Constitution, the national government took an immediate initiative to appoint the Planning Commission in 1950 to coordinate all state and central plans and suggest ways and means to remove social inequalities and to bring social change in the desired direction. The first government, led by Pandit Jawaharlal Nehru, accepted the socialistic pattern of society as its goal to modernize India. Up to V.P. Singh and Chandrasekhar governments (1988–91), there was not much change in the Nehru's policy. But, the Narasimha Rao's government discarded this policy in early 1991 and launched a new model based on the policies of liberalization, marketization and privatization. This new model of development is still continuing. It has not only affected economic development but also brought enormous changes in the social structure.

The main aims of the Planning Commission are to:

1. to determine priorities;
2. to make an assessment of the material, capital and human resources of the country;
3. to make balanced utilization of the country's resources;

4. to assess the progress achieved from time to time and recommend readjustment; and
5. to identify factors that retard economic development.

It was in 1951 that the Commission submitted its report to the government, suggesting the formulation of five-year plans with a particular aim of developing rural India because at that time about 80 per cent India's population lived in villages. Moreover, the father of the nation, Mahatma Gandhi, also reiterated the need for rural development and for this supported the idea of planning. As a result, the First Five-Year Plan was launched in April 1951. Since its inception, the Planning Commission has prepared 11 five-year plans, each focusing on different objectives as under:

1. First Five-Year Plan (1951–56): In this plan top priority was given to agriculture and irrigation.
2. Second Five-Year Plan (1956–61): It was concentrated on relatively underprivileged sections of society and gave importance to heavy industrial development.
3. Third Five-Year Plan (1961–66): It emphasized on securing self-sustained growth.

   Plan Holiday (1966–69): To rectify the ills of the bad economy that had crippled in the planning process and to finish the unfinished tasks of the Third Plan.
4. Fourth Five-Year Plan (1969–74): It aimed at creating economic stability, reducing inequalities and to increase national income by 5.5 per cent.
5. Fifth Five-Year Plan (1974–79): Its main objective was to remove poverty, increase employment opportunities and attainment of self-reliance.
6. Sixth Five-Year Plan (1980–85): In this plan too the main stress was on the removal of poverty, elimination of unemployment, strengthening the public distribution system, control of increasing population and to achieve economic growth.
7. Seventh Five-Year Plan (1985–90): It emphasized on increasing food, work and productivity with improvement in the quality of life of the poor. Top priority was given to human development as the core of all development efforts in this plan.

   Yearly Plans—1990–91 and 1991–92.
8. Eighth Five-Year Plan (1992–97): Its main emphasis was on employment generation.
9. Ninth Five-Year Plan (1997–2002): It was the most ambitious and growth-oriented plan. It revived the First Plan objectives, i.e., agriculture and irrigation, and were given top priority. Along with agriculture, employment generation, poverty removal and infrastructure development were the main planks of this plan. It is also known as 'delivery oriented' plan.

10. Tenth Five-Year Plan (2002–07): In this plan, social sector was given priority. Many schemes of social welfare, such as elementary education, primary health care, nutrition, water supply and programmes of development for women and children, were launched. The major emphasis in this plan was on Green Revolution.
11. Eleventh Five-Year Plan (2007–12): It aims to achieve improved quality of life for the citizens of the state and contribute to the larger national goals of socio-economic development. It envisages an average of 9 per cent GDP growth. But the plan achieved 8.2 per cent growth.
12. Twelfth Five-Year Plan (2012–17): Its main theme is 'faster, sustainable and more inclusive growth'. The growth target of the plan is 8–9 per cent.

Thus, notwithstanding the primary aim of all the successive five-year plans being economic development (mainly increased productivity and provision of adequate income) along with social justice, due importance was given to social aims, i.e., provision of education, social security and social welfare schemes.

While up to the Eighth Plan, all plans were concentrated either on agriculture or industrial development, but since the adoption of the policy of liberalization in 1991, the priorities and the structure of the Ninth and Tenth Plans have gone major sea change.

Except the First and the Sixth Plans, no other plan attained the target. In spite of so much emphasis on different issues such as agriculture and industrial growth and social justice, etc., poverty and unemployment have increased. While the government claimed the number of people below the poverty line (BPL) has decreased from 40.72 crore in 2004–05 to 35.46 crore at present (March 2012), the number of unemployed has increased (the last reported in December 2010 was 9.4%). The UN Human Development Report, 2012, paints a dismal picture of social development in India and has put it among the medium human development countries. It has ranked India at 134th out of 188 countries. Human Development Index (HDI) is based on life expectancy, health and educational opportunities. Amartya Sen, the Noble laureate, also stated that India was a failure in economic development because of its tightly regulated economy. It was only in 1991 that India took a u-turn and began applying global experience (liberalization) by tackling its economic backwardness. Liberalization of the private sector has transformed economic growth. It is encouraging that in the last 15 years we have made amazing progress.

Community Development Projects

The phrase 'community development' is made of two words—'community' and 'development'. 'Community' is a social group, a cluster of people, who have some degree of 'we feeling,' share a common way of life and living in a contiguous limited area. Members of a community have a feeling of belonging together and a sense of common membership which is known as 'community sentiment'. The word 'development' refers to a process of change for better way of living (healthier life, more education, greater control over life, etc.). It implies some positive progress in society's condition. Thus, in simple terms, community development means development of the people of a community. It is a term which refers to the assessment of the needs, problems and resources of the community and try to solve them to the best of their efforts with the active participation of all. The United Nations has defined the term *community development* as 'a process by which the efforts of the people themselves are united with those of the governmental authorities to improve the economic, social and cultural conditions of communities, to integrate these communities into the life of the nation and to enable them to contribute fully to national progress'. It is a movement designed to promote better living for the whole community with the active participation and on the initiative of the community.

In India, Community Development Project (CDP) was launched under the Five-Year Plans on the birth anniversary of Mahatma Gandhi on 2nd October 1952 to carry out the objectives outlined in the draft of the plan. According to Planning Commission of India, 'CDP is the method and the rural extension the agency through which the Five-Year Plan seeks to initiate a process of transformation of the social and economic life of the villagers.' In one of the reports of UNDP, Dag Hammarskjöld, the then Secretary General, described the aims of Indian community projects in the following words: 'The aim of Community Projects and National Extension Services (NES) is not merely to provide ample food, clothing and shelter, health and sanitation facilities in villages. More important than the immediate material improvement is the change in outlook of the people instilling in them an ambition for a richer and fuller life and developing the capacities of the individual so that he can master matters for himself.' In the beginning only 55 projects for intensive development, covering about 18,500 villages with a total population of about 15.2 million were selected. The essence of the programme was to ensure people's participation right from the start. The basic aims of CDP in terms of its immediate and ultimate goals have been summarized by renowned social scientist S.C. Dube (1955) as under:

(i) To provide for a substantial increase in the country's agricultural production, and for improvements in the system of communications, in rural health and hygiene, and in village education.

(ii) To initiate and direct a process of integral culture change aimed at transforming the social and economic life of the villages.

The main target areas of the projects were: (1) agriculture and related matters, (2) irrigation, (3) communication, (4) education, (5) health, (6) supplementary employment, (7) housing, (8) social welfare, and (9) training.

Since the launching of CDP in 1952, the programme has undergone many changes. Some of the concepts related to the programme have been refined. It is to be noted that the nomenclature has also changed now from 'community development' to 'rural development'. Summarizing the ethos of the whole programme of CDP, R.N. Saxena (1956) observed, 'The foundation on which the whole superstructure of CDP is to be built is essentially the human factor—self-help, self-reliance and community life.' Hence, the people's active participation is the most essential factor for the success of the programme.

The programme (CDP) was evaluated at two levels: (a) government level, and (b) private agencies, institutions or by individuals. The Government of India established a Programme Evaluation Organization (PEO) under the Planning Commission to make appraisal of the ongoing projects and to identify the weaknesses and provide explanation for the response given by the people to the projects. Evaluation of the CDP's was also done by a number of Indian and foreign social scientists like A.R. Desai, S.C. Dube, Oscar Lewis, J. Mandelbaum, M. Opler, Carl Taylor, etc. Some of the major criticisms are as under:

1. The main criticism was that the whole programme of CDP became highly bureaucratized. Renowned social scientist S.C. Dube noted that the planning was from the top (bureaucrats) down. The people of the below (villagers) were passive receivers and onlookers of the programme. There was least involvement of the people at all levels—from planning to the execution stage.
2. A.R. Desai, a renowned rural sociologist, held that the sociological assumptions on which the CDPs were based, viz., that all individuals, groups, sections and strata forming the village community had common interests to bind them together, that the common interests will create enthusiasm, that interests of different sections of the community were not irreconcilably conflicting, were not correct.
3. Oscar Lewis maintained that there were considerable confusions and conflicts with regard to powers and duties among the staff of different departments. As a result, there was much overlap in the programmes.
4. Carl Taylor said that the government machinery failed to assimilate the true spirit underlying the whole programme. Bureaucrats worked like bosses, not as friends or guides of the people.
5. It was observed almost by all evaluators that corruption was widespread in the implementation of the programme at all levels. Only a meagre part of the budgetary allocation was actually spent for the people. In 1985 the then Prime Minister Rajiv Gandhi opined that only 15 paise in a rupee reach to the needy people.
6. Most of the benefits of CDP and allied schemes went to the big farmers.
7. Food production did not show any marked increase in spite of huge investment on agricultural development.

In a nutshell, it may be mentioned that all evaluators had felt that the CDPs were desirable and it was a good technique of rural reconstruction but almost all of them concluded that the rural people could not be mobilized as was envisaged in the programme. They did not actively and willingly participate in any schemes of the programme at any stage. They considered the whole programme as government programme—government sponsored and government executed—and not of their own. Even, the government could not instil the required confidence in the people about this programme.

Not only this, it was acutely felt that there was a great lack of coordination between different schemes of development. The whole structure of the programme was fragmented and overlapping. As such, the whole programme of CDP was seen as failed. Its man objectives could not be fulfilled. Then started a search for its failure. The main aim of this search was to find the answer of this most potent question—how could the enthusiasm of the people aroused and their active participation enlisted in this programme? It was suggested that there should be unified planning and integrated functioning of all schemes of rural development. Besides integrated planning, an integrated administrative structure (a combined agency at the district level) too was suggested for implementation of the planned programmes.

To find out the answer of the question posed above and to search the ways and means to make the programmes a success, in 1956, the Balwant Rai Mehta Committee was constituted to study and review the working of CDP. The committee submitted its report in 1957 suggesting the establishment of Panchayati Raj—a scheme of democratic and decentralization. The panchayats were expected to tackle village problems at the grassroots level and mobilize local manpower resources for purpose of economic and social progress. The Mehta Committee felt that active participation of the rural people in the schemes of development can be persuaded only when the developed machinery works under the elected representatives of the people. The committee has, therefore, recommended devolution of development and decentralization of machinery of administration. It recommended the setting up of elected democratic bodies at the village, block and district levels and the entrusting of all planning and developmental activities to these bodies.

These recommendations were later on accepted by the National Development Council (NDC) in 1958 and various states in India started the implementation of the scheme of Panchayati Raj. Rajasthan is the first state where this scheme was launched on the birth anniversary of Mahatma Gandhi on October 2, 1959. This scheme was inaugurated by Pandit Jawaharlal Nehru, the then Prime Minister, at Nagaur (Rajasthan).

Panchayati Raj

Mahatma Gandhi, the father of the nation, often emphasized that India lives in villages (at the time of independence, about 82.7 per cent population of India lived in villages) and unless the village life is revitalized, the nation as a whole cannot make progress. These ideas and the Article 40 of the Constitution of India, which declared that 'the state shall take steps to organize Village Panchayats and to endow them with such powers and authority as may be necessary to enable them to function as the units of self-government,' paved the way for the introduction of Panchayati Raj—a scheme of 'democratic decentralization' in India.

In India, the system of panchayats has a long history. Its structure however varied from time to time. In village India, the concept of 'Panch Parmeswar' is very old and very prominent. We also find references of Gram Panchayat in ancient and medieval literatures. As we know, India is a caste-ridden society. Along with Gram Panchayats we also find Caste Panchayats in every caste to solve their social problems like marital discord and disputes. During the British period, an effort was made to revive the Village Panchayats but it could not make any success.

The present Panchayati Raj system is the result of the failure of the Community Development Projects (CDPs)—a kernel programme of rural development launched in 1952 as an arm of five-year plans. The two successive plans had failed to not only produce desired results but also generate real enthusiasm among the people. It was felt that the scheme of CDP failed because of the lack of proper governance. In the context of this crisis of governance (inefficiency, corruption, lack of accountability, mounting disillusionment of the citizens towards government institutions and officials), decentralization was widely accepted as a powerful means to instil confidence and revive trust of people in government programmes. Democratic renewal through reorganizing the power structure would bring the government closer to people. It was seen as a means to deepen democracy, make governance accountable and responsive. Not only would it enhance the effectiveness of public policies and service delivery, but also give greater voice to citizens. It is against this backdrop, the idea of 'democratic decentralization' emerged which was based on the Gandhi's cherished vision of 'self-governing' villages. This was a transfer of power and initiative for social and economic development of villages. The then government constituted a committee headed by Balwant Rai Mehta to review the CDP and suggest changes. Thus, the Panchayati Raj came into being.

Indeed, the prosperity of entire country depends on the prosperity and self-sufficiency of the villages. The Panchayati Raj system fulfils the long felt need of making the village administration truly independent and genuinely representative of the popular will, and putting village people in direct charge of their affairs. It mainly aimed to foster democratic participation, involve villagers in the development efforts and ease the administrative burden on the states. This system was also considered necessary for the growth of a sturdy democracy in India. This could be possible only when the villagers are able to organize themselves to think, plan, work and pay for the necessities and amenities for their welfare. To those, who have considered the villages the real India, the innovation is rational, overdue and beyond criticism. It was hoped that the experiment of the Panchayati Raj will be able to harness and develop the better characteristics of the average villagers in spite of their illiteracy and restricted range of experience. It was also expected that this system will bring new aspiration and fresh stimulus to national self-respect. In the present scheme of Panchayati Raj, the villagers have been held responsible for all-round improvement in the village life, including education, sanitation, medical relief—curative and preventive, lighting, housing, maternity and child welfare along with the administration of civil, criminal and revenue justice. It was thought that this system would be powerful means for self-preservation in the arena of social life.

The main objective behind the Panchayati Raj is that the people in the village should undertake the responsibilities of governing themselves. Pioneer rural sociologist A.R. Desai spelled the objectives of PR system as follows: 'Panchayati Raj is claimed as a real democratic political apparatus which would bring the masses into active political control from below, from the vast majority of the weaker, poor sections of rural India.' People in the villages should actively participate in the development activities regarding agriculture, irrigation, animal husbandry, public health, education, etc. In a nutshell, the whole idea of this scheme is based on the dictum that 'rural development is for the rural people, of the rural people, and by the rural people themselves'. It is based on self-help, as an old adage says, 'God help those who help themselves'. This scheme of rural development confers on the rural people the power of decision-making regarding developmental activities. This is democracy at the grassroots. It will 'decentralize' democracy. This system has got a very important role to play in the social, economic and cultural life of the village community of India.

The Panchayati Raj system has many benefits. These can be summarized as under:

1. Panchayats can best carry out the uplift programmes, such as mending roads, terrace, and embank the fields, building bunds, digging drains, provide fresh drinking water, etc.
2. They are best constituted to organize voluntary labour for social uplift and economic amelioration.
3. Panchayats are the best agencies which can supply the political talent. They are the potential schools of political training for the rural masses.
4. They can also serve as the schools of social service, health care, popular education and social progress.
5. Panchayats can impart cheap litigation, speedy and substantial justice to the villagers.
6. Panchayats are best fitted to be representative and spokesperson of the villagers.

Phases of Development

Self-governing rural local bodies are described in Indian context as the institutions of democratic decentralization or Panchayati Raj. The story of Panchayati Raj has been a story of ups and downs. It seems to have passed through four distinct phases in its short span of life:

1. The phase of ascendancy (1959–1964)
2. The phase of stagnation (1965–1969)
3. The phase of decline (1969–1983)
4. The phase of revival (1983 onwards)

Revival and renovation of Panchayati Raj is associated with the government of Rajiv Gandhi (1985), the then Prime Minister. He infused a new blood in this institution by removing certain hurdles and handicaps. He constituted a committee under the chairmanship of L.M. Singhvi to write a concept paper on Panchayati Raj. About its revival there were two main schools of thought. One believed that Panchayati Raj is a God that had failed. The other suggested that Panchayati Raj, in fact, had not been tried in its true spirit and as such the question of a final verdict on its success or failure did not arise. The Singhvi Committee found that the PR system was not functioning owing to the lack of political will, lack of proper evaluation and feedback, and indifference to corrective measures. The apathetic attitudes of the bureaucracy and the elected representatives have crushed the spirit of the PR system. The official hierarchy failed to inspire confidence among the village people. Bureaucrats were unwilling to transfer power to elected representatives. They did not release funds in time.

The Janata Party government (1990) appointed Ashok Mehta Committee to enquire into the causes of decline of the PR system and suggest changes in the pattern of the PR system recommended by B.R. Mehta Committee. This committee has offered a balanced appraisal of PRIs in the context of two schools of thought referred to above. It opined, 'Panchayati Raj should not be viewed as a God that has failed. It has many achievements to its credit, the more important of which may be identified here. Politically speaking, it became a process of democratic seed-drilling in the Indian soil, making an average citizen more conscious of his rights than before. Administratively speaking, it bridged the gulf between the bureaucratic elite and the people. Socio-culturally speaking, it generated a new leadership which was not merely relatively young in age but also modernistic and pro-social change in outlook. Finally, looked at from the developmental angle, it helped a rural people cultivate a developmental psyche' (Report of the Committee on Panchayati Raj Institutions, Government of India, 1978).

However, it was felt that there were some shortcomings in the structure and functions of the PR system. The performance of PRIs had been vitiated by political factionalism, corruption, inefficiency, political interference, parochial loyalties, motivated actions, power concentration, arrogant attitude of bureaucratic officials, lack of feeling of service, etc. All these had made the common villagers averse towards the PR system.

To revitalize the PR system, the Rajiv Gandhi's government (1989), V.P. Singh's government (1990) and Narasimha Rao's government (1991) proposed some amendments in it. As a result, the 73rd Constitution Amendment Act, 1993 was passed. After this, PRIs have got the constitutional legitimacy. It was, therefore, adopted by all the states. The present Panchayati Raj differs from the B.R. Committee's pattern mainly in two respects. First, the earlier PR system was not a political institution but only an implementing body. In the previous system of Panchayati Raj there was no role of political parties. People used to contest election on individual basis. The new Act allows political parties to enter into election fray. Second, the present system is not an implementing body of the development programmes. It is a decision-making body that rules over the governance of the village. One very conspicuous aspect of this Act is that the present system empowers the women and the weaker sections (SC and ST people) of village by giving them representation by a fixed quota at all three levels.

In brief, the main changes brought out by the Act are:

1. Establishment of panchayats at two or three levels and a Gram Sabha is made mandatory in each village.
2. Tenure of PRIs is fixed as five years. Direct elections of all members in all the three tiers are made mandatory. The elections have to be conducted regularly.
3. Elections of chairperson at intermediate and district levels are to be indirect.
4. At least one-third of the total seats at all levels are reserved for SCs, STs and for women separately.
5. PRIs are given powers to impose taxes, duties, and fees and were given share in taxes collected by the state government.
6. The reservation of OBCs and association of MPs and MLAs in panchayats is made discretionary.
7. The Act also provides for the constitution of District Planning Committee.
8. It is obligatory on the part of Centre as well as the states to provide adequate funds for the PRIs to enable them to function properly.
9. Some sates like Bihar, Himachal Pradesh, Uttar Pradesh, Haryana and Karnataka have also made provision for Nyaya Panchayats to settle the disputes at all the three levels. But this is not obligatory as per the provisions of this Act.
10. States like Haryana, Orissa and Rajasthan have debarred the candidates, having more than two children, from contesting elections, with a view to contain population.

11. A list of 29 functions was prepared to be carried out by PRIs. Some of the important functions are: (a) agricultural development and irrigation facilities, (b) land reforms, (c) eradication of poverty, (d) dairy farming, poultry, piggery and fish rearing, (e) rural housing, (f) safe drinking water, (g) social forestry and fuel, (h) primary education, adult education and informal training, (i) roads and buildings, (j) markets and fairs, (k) child and women development, and (l) welfare of weaker sections—SCs and STs.

Looking at the above functions and some special provisions made in the Act, it is amply clear that the new PR system has undoubtedly empowered the villages to take steps for their all-round development.

Structure and Functions of Panchayati Raj Institutions

As said before, the structure of Panchayati Raj (PR) varies from state to state. Some states have three-tier structure (Gram Panchayat at the village level, Panchayat Samiti at block level and Zilla Parishad at district level), whereas some have two-tier structure (Gram Panchayat at village level and Panchayat Samiti at block level). A few states have only single-tier structure at the village level. In Rajasthan, the Panchayati Raj model is of three levels, viz., Gram Panchayats (village level), Panchayat Samitis (block level) and Zilla Parishads (district level). The chairperson of Gram Panchayat is known as Sarpanch, of Panchayat Samiti, Pradhan and of Zilla Parishad, Zilla Pramukh. Their nomenclature, composition and tenure vary from state to state. The structure and functions of the PRIs in terms of Gram Panchayat, Panchayat Samiti and Zilla Parishad are spelt out as under:

Gram Panchayat

Gram Panchayat is the base or bottom tier of the PR system. It is the first executive tier having jurisdiction over a village or group of villages. The members of the Gram Panchayat—the Panchas and Sarpanch (chairman)—are directly elected. Their number in each panchayat varies from 5 to 31 according to population of the concerned village(s). In addition to the elected Panchas and Sarpanch, there is a provision for co-option of two ladies, and one SC and ST member each, if they have not been elected as Panchas.

The main functions of the Gram Panchayat are:

1. *Law and order:* Maintenance of peace and harmony in the panchayat circle.
2. *Civic:* Construction of wells, ponds, water reservoirs and distribution tanks; construction of public streets, public latrines and maintenance of roads, etc.
3. *Welfare:* Famine and flood relief work, welfare programmes for women, children, handicapped and weaker sections.

4. *Administrative:* Collection of funds, maintenance of records, budget and accounts, registration of births and deaths, etc.;
5. *Commercial:* Supervision of community orchards, grazing ground, etc.
6. *Developmental:* Preparation and execution of plans for the promotion of agriculture, irrigation, co-operatives, cottage and small-scale industries.

The main sources of income of panchayats are the grants from government, taxes on buildings, vehicles, etc., octroi on goods and animals, pilgrim tax, etc.

Panchayat Samiti

It is the middle tier of the PR system—between Gram Panchayat and Zilla Parishad. This tier was coterminous with the tehsil or taluka. This is composed of Sarpanchas (ex-officio members) of all the Gram Panchayats within a block along with MLA of the area (without right of vote). In addition to these ex-officio members, there are some co-opted members—two women, one SC and ST representatives each, if they have not already been elected as primary members. The chairperson of the Panchayat Samiti is called Pradhan. He is elected by the members of the Panchayat Samiti amongst themselves. At certain places, such as in Rajasthan, Panchas of Gram Panchayat also take part in the election of Pradhans.

The main functions of the Panchayat Samiti are: (i) agriculture—formulation of plans of development of agriculture, tree plantation and soil conservation; (ii) animal husbandry; (iii) health and sanitation; (iv) education—running primary schools; (v) communication—construction and maintenance of inter-panchayat roads, etc.; (vi), co-operation—promotion of co-operative societies; (vii) development of cottage and small-scale industries; and (viii) miscellaneous work.

The main sources of income of Panchayat Samiti are annual grants by state government, share from land revenue, proceeds from taxes, fees and loans, contributions, etc.

Zilla Parishad

It is the apex body of the PR system located at the district level. It is also known as District Development Council in some states (such as Tamil Nadu). It is composed of (i) Chairpersons/Presidents of Panchayat Samitis within its jurisdiction; (ii) MPs, MLAs, and MLCs of the area; (iii) members representing women, SCs and STs are co-opted if they are not otherwise members; (iv) representatives of co-operative societies, municipalities of the area; and (v) some persons having experience in the field of administration, public life or rural development are also co-opted. The membership of the Zilla Parishad remains in the range of 40 to 60 persons. The elected head of Zilla Parishad is known as Zilla Pramukh (President). He is elected either directly or indirectly from amongst the members of the Zilla Parishad. Zilla Pramukh works through committees which look after specific works like education, planning and finance. The main sources of income of the Zilla Parishads are grants-in-aid from the state government, share in the land revenue and other taxes like the cess.

The above structure and functions of all the PR bodies have been changing over the years. It has aroused a spirit of self-help and popular participation to some extent among the rural people. The process of decision-making has come close to the rural people. It has also helped in the emergence of a new democratic leadership at the local level. But, the competitive elections have politicized the environment of all villages. This spirit has even entered into the family circles also. It is alleged that panchayat elections have given birth to caste politics (casteism), communal politics (communalism) and groupism and factionalism in the villages.

It is also alleged that due to panchayat elections, a 'cold war' atmosphere prevails among various sections of the village people. Some studies made on the PR system revealed that functional tensions are on the increase and this can be seen during elections and panchayat meetings. The so-called harmonious relations of the villages have almost vanished. People did not extend full cooperation from the core of their heart to the panchayats and as a result developmental activity has slowed down. Theoretically, the decisions had to be taken by the non-officials at all the three tiers of the PR system, but in practice, it was the government officials who used to take the decisions. The non-officials (Panch or Sarpanch) being illiterate and uneducated could not wield their power. Most of the benefits of development programmes initiated by PRIs were cornered by the high castes and big peasants. The poor segments of society remained neglected as before. There was a great lack of coordination among the three tiers.

Thus, to conclude, it can be stated that the devolution of power to the people without requisite development of character, training and capacity had been found to be a curse in the functioning of democratic institutions in our country and there were apprehensions that this new step in democratic decentralization, designed to be blessing, would turn out to be a curse to the people in the villages. The success of the step more than anything else depended on the quality of elected representative—Panchas and Sarpanchas—of these institutions.

No institutional change can bring about climatic change or strengthen the roots of democracy in this country, if it is divorced of the spirit behind it. In the absence of this basic change, which is a *sine qua non* to all other changes, we doubt, if institutional changes alone will take the country very far. In the beginning, responsibility for the planned development of the country through CDP and cooperative institutions was imposed on the people who were expected to discharge them in PRIs who were mostly uneducated and untrained mass of people. But there is a great change now in this condition.

Obviously, such a step, though basic and pregnant with great possibilities to strengthen the roots of democracy, was fraught with grave risks, disappointments and failures in its traditional phase.

Schemes of Rural Development

The main objective of rural development has been to remove poverty of the people and fill the widened gap between the rich and the poor. This has been also vocalized in the policy of the government which says: said, 'Rural poverty alleviation has been the primary concern in the economic planning and development process of the country … rural development which encompasses the entire gamut of improvement in the overall quality of life in the rural areas can be achieved through eradication of poverty in rural areas.'

Keeping in view the planning policy in mind, various schemes of development, especially the development of agriculture, the main occupation of the rural people, have been introduced. The major early programmes were:

1. Intensive Agricultural Area Programme (IAAP)
2. Intensive Agricultural District Programme (IADP)
3. High Yielding Varieties Programme (HYVP)
4. Rural Industries Projects and Rural Artisans Programmes (RIP and RAP)

Besides the above programmes, several poverty alleviation programmes have also been launched by the central and state governments for the rural people. These are discussed in the following paragraphs:

20-Point Programme

This has been a major programme of rural development encompassing various aspects of rural people. This programme is associated with former Prime Minister Indira Gandhi, who introduced it in July 1975 for reducing poverty and economic exploitation and for the uplift of weaker sections of society. She gave the slogan 'Garibi Hatao' during parliamentary elections. The important goals of this programme were:

1. Welfare of the rural masses.
2. Increase in rural employment.
3. Minimum wages to landless labourers.
4. Uplift of the SC and ST people.
5. Growth of housing facilities.
6. New programmes of family planning.

7. Extension of primary health facilities.
8. Making primary education more effective.
9. Welfare of women and children.
10. Some other programmes—drinking water facilities, public distribution system, increasing power production, etc.

The programme was discontinued with the change in government (during Janata Party government). However, it was revised in 1982 after the coming of congress government at the centre with an emphasis on eradicating poverty and reducing income inequalities, removing social and economic disparities and improving the quality of life.

Integrated Rural Development Programme (IRDP)

The programme was launched by the Centre in March 1976 as a major instrument of the government to alleviate poverty. Its main feature was to enable selected families to cross the poverty line in a given time-frame by taking up self-employment in various activities like agriculture, horticulture, animal husbandry, weaving and handicrafts and services and business activities. The target group consisted of small and marginal farmers, agricultural labourers and rural artisans having annual income below Rs 11,000 defined as poverty line in the Eighth Plan. Among the selected families, it is stipulated that at least 50 per cent of assisted families should be from SCs and STs. Furthermore, 40 per cent of the coverage should be of women beneficiaries. In spite of its many important features, the programme has also been criticized widely. The main criticisms against the programme are:

1. There was much corruption, misuse and malpractice in the implementation of the programme at every level—from selection of beneficiary families to the distribution of loans. Bribing was a *sine qua* non for obtaining a loan.
2. The poor people were not well conversant about the programme. They took less interest in the programme because they were afraid of being cheated. Moreover, they were unable to fill up complicated forms and find the 'guarantors' for themselves.
3. The bank officials, through which loans were to be given, were often reluctant towards these poor borrowers.
4. It was found that this scheme also could not make any significant impact in the generation of employment in rural areas.
5. Several studies indicated that IRDP loans neither raised the living standard of the beneficiaries, nor does it had any impact in the alleviation of rural poverty for which this scheme was launched.

Training Rural Youths for Self-Employment (TRYSEM)

This scheme was launched in 1979 to provide technical skills (training) to rural youths (between 18–35 years) living below the poverty line, to enable them to seek employment in fields of agriculture, industry, services and business activities. As in other schemes of poverty alleviation, in this scheme also, youths belonging to SCs and STs and ex-servicemen, who had passed ninth class, were given priority. One-third seats were reserved for women. The beneficiaries of this scheme after completion of training were absorbed in the IRDP scheme.

According to an estimate, up to 1995–96, about two lakh youths were being trained every year, of whom about 45 per cent became self-employed and 30 per cent got regular employment.

In spite of being a good scheme, it has many shortcomings. For example, (1) its coverage is very small in relation to need; (2) the amount of stipend given to the trainees (about Rs 75 to 200 per month) to motivate the youth is very meagre to join training programme; and (3) skills imparted in the training are of very low level and not linked with rural industrialization process.

Food for Work Programme (FWP)

This programme was introduced in 1977 by the then Janata government with the objective to provide employment to the unemployed/underemployed village persons during the slack season. The wages paid to the workers were in kind, i.e., food grains. The works undertaken were flood protection, maintenance of existing roads, construction of new link roads, improvement of irrigation facilities, construction of school buildings, medical and health centres and Panchayat Ghars (community halls) etc.

National Rural Employment Programme (NREP)

This is redesigned programme of FWP, planned for creating additional employment opportunities in the rural areas with the help of surplus food grains. It was started in 1980 as a part of the Sixth Plan (1980–85). This programme was especially for those rural people who largely depended on wage employment but had no source of income during lean agricultural period. PRIs were actively involved in this programme.

Later on, this programme was merged with Jawahar Rozgar Yojana (JRY).

Rural Landless Employment Guarantee Programme (RLEGP)

Special schemes were formulated by some states such as Maharashtra and Gujarat to provide increasing employment opportunities to rural people, especially landless people. Maharashtra started the Employment Guarantee Scheme (EGS) for the unemployed in rural areas. The Gujarat government's scheme provided for unskilled jobs to the unemployed workers on different projects. This scheme was later on merged into JRY along with NREP.

Jawahar Rozgar Yojana (JRY)

This programme came into existence in April 1989 with the merger of the NREP and the RLEGP. Under this scheme, it was expected to provide at least one member of each poor family (BPL family) an employment for 50 to 100 days in a year at a work near his/her residence. About 30 per cent of the jobs under this programme were reserved for women. The scheme was implemented through Village Panchayats.

Antyodaya Yojana

The Hindi word 'antyodaya' is a combination of two words—*ant* meaning end or bottom level and *udaya* meaning development. Thus, as a whole, it implies the development or welfare of a person standing at the end of the queue (lowest level), that is, the poorest of the poor. This programme was initiated by the Government of Rajasthan on 2nd October, 1977 for special assistance to persons living below the poverty line (BPL). It was later on picked up by the then Janata government at the centre in 1978. The idea was to select five of the poorest families from each village every year and help them in their economic betterment. For the selection of beneficiary families, a few economic criteria were laid down, in order of priority: (1) families under severe destitution without any productive assets with no member in the age group of 15–59 years capable of any economic activity; (2) families without any productive assets of land or cattle but having one or more persons capable of working and with a per capita income up to Rs 20 per month; (3) families having some productive assets with per capita income upto Rs 30 per month; and (4) families having per capita income upto Rs 40 per month.

Under this scheme, assistance was given in the form of allotting land for cultivation, monthly pension (Rs 30–40 per month), bank loan for purchasing bullocks, buffaloes, cows, goats and pigs, basket making, carpentry tools, opening a tailor's shop, a tea shop, a barber's shop or a grocer's shop and manufacturing activities like niwar-making, soap-making, etc.

Following the footsteps of the Government of Rajasthan, UP and Himachal governments also launched it on the same lines in 1980. The scheme has seen much ups and downs with many shortcomings, such as delay in the payment of loans, apathy on the part of government officials, etc. 'Antyodaya,' as preached by Mahatma Gandhi, has disappeared into 'ananta' or eternity and is replaced with 'swantyodaya', meaning one's own development. It places emphasis on 'myself mentality'.

Mahatma Gandhi National Rural Employment Guarantee Scheme (MNREGS)

After independence, for the development of rural society, particularly to develop the socio-economic life of the rural poor, many schemes and programmes were launched from time to time but unfortunately the fruits of these programmes reached to a very low proportion of these people. It was estimated about 70 per cent of rural population was still deprived of the basic necessities of life. For the purpose of extending the benefits to rural people, a new scheme was launched and a legislation was enacted under the name 'National Rural Employment Guarantee Act' (NREGA). This scheme was initially started in 200 districts of the country from February 2006 and from April 2008, it has been extended to cover all the districts of the country. The main objective of the scheme is to provide 100 days employment to rural unemployed people. In this scheme, employment to women is also provided.

Like other rural development schemes, this scheme is also plagued with many problems—workers' identification and registration, muster rolls, works attendance, calculations and disbursement of wages and overall transparency. In recent months, people from all circles have also voiced great concern about the rampant corruption in this scheme.

Some Other Development Schemes

1. *Pradhan Mantri Adarsh Gram Sadak Yojana (PMAGSY):* It focuses on integrated development of 100 villages with a 50 per cent population of SCs.
2. *Bharat Nirman Yojana:* It was launched in 2005 for building infrastructure and basic amenities in rural areas. It comprises of six components—rural housing, irrigation, drinking water, rural roads, electrification and rural telephony.
3. *Indira Awas Yojana:* It is one of the six components of Bharat Nirman Yojana. It was introduced in 1985–86. It aims to help built or upgrade the households of people living under BPL.
4. *Jawaharlal Nehru National Urban Renewal Mission (JNNURM)*: It was launched on 3rd December, 2005. The main objective of this scheme was fast track development of cities across the country. It was focused especially on developing efficient urban infrastructure service delivery

mechanism, community participation and accountability of urban local bodies and other agencies towards citizen.

5. *Rajiv Awas Yojana (RAY):* This programme was announced in June 2009 with an objective to make the country slum-free.
6. *National Rural Health Mission:* It was launched to make basic health care facilities accessible to the rural people.
7. *National Rural Livelihood Mission:* It is meant to eradicate poverty by 2014–15.
8. *National Food Security Scheme:* On the pattern of MNREGS, the central government is trying hard to bring a bill in the monsoon session (2013) to provide guarantee for food to the poor people, although it has already issued an ordinance in this regard.

Development Programmes: An Evaluation

After independence, the task for the national government was two-fold: dismantling the traditional and colonial economy and erecting in its place the base for modern, independent and self-reliant economic and social order. To achieve this goal, many schemes and programmes were launched by different governments at the central and state levels from time to time. At many times it was seen that only the names of the programmes were modified with just some minor changes in the actual contents of the programme. The core objective of almost all programmes was to bring change in the quality of human life and remove poverty. The history of modern systematic rural development programmes in India starts from 1952 when CDP was launched as a part of the five-year plans. Our first Prime Minister Pandit Jawahar Lal Nehru championed the cause of CDP along with V.T. Krishnamchari, the then Finance Minister, and S.K. De, the then Minister of Rural Development. These three persons conceptualized the CDP and painted it on the large canvas of India's 5,50,000 villages. For them, the CDP was the means—the vehicle, the way to remove from the villages the heavy burden of poverty, disease and ignorance.

Till now scores of schemes of rural development—from CDP to IRDP and MNREGS—have been launched/implemented and crores of rupees have been spent, but to our surprise not much have changed in rural India. The progress made by the people is no way much demonstrable. The rural people *(aam admi)* along with political leaders, have disillusioned with the schemes of development. There is no marked improvement in the living conditions of the landless farmers, small and petty land owners and the common masses who earn their livelihood through physical labour or some manual works. A large number of villagers languish without satisfying the basic needs of life. It is said that much of the money spent on (village) development programmes and various schemes went in the pockets of village officials, development personnel, technical hands (engineers), political leaders, etc. This bare fact was even acknowledged by Rajiv Gandhi, when he became the Prime Minister of India. The larger beneficiaries of these programmes were big farmers and village moneylenders who lent money to the small farmers or landless labourers on high rates of interest.

The main flows of various developmental programmes can be summarized in the following points:

1. Village development or rather all types of development has been politicized. Generally, every programme is launched with an eye to the next election. The programme is carried out in a half-hearted manner, in a piecemeal fashion. Thus, many programmes either wither away after sometime or merged with some other schemes.
2. Most of the development programmes, especially CDP, were considered as programmes of development from above, i.e., the government. The people for whom these programmes were made, lack the necessary awareness needed for the success of these programmes. The initiative should have come from below, i.e., from the people themselves.
3. Most of the programmes were made at the sheer whims of the politicians and bureaucrats rather than by compulsions of ground realities and requirements of the rural people. These programmes were framed at the state or central headquarters by such persons (ideologues of the ruling political party) in consultations with the bureaucrats who have either never visited villages or were not very well conversant to the reality of social and economic day-to-day life of the rural people.
4. Coordination between the different welfare schemes and their implementing agencies was lacking. Officials attached to these programmes did not appear to have faith in the objectives of these programmes at the core of their heart. They lacked commitment to the roles assigned to them. Moreover, there were many bureaucratic bottlenecks.
5. Almost at the heart of all programmes of development were the removal of poverty, enhancing the quality of life and reduction in income inequalities, but after the implementation of many schemes the gulf between the rich and the poor has widened. The backward have become more backward.
6. Misuse of funds, oppression of the powerful, terror against dalits, denying opportunities to women and subversion of elections are the main ills of PRIs—the agencies of development.
7. Religion and caste both have acted as important barriers to all schemes of development. India is a caste-ridden society and caste-based prejudices, stereotypes and animosities are well known. Moreover, there were varying customs of different communities, sects and groups resulting in putting hurdles in various schemes of development. The presence of deep-rooted beliefs, age-old superstitions, customs and traditions has brought planning and development in disrepute. People were also discriminated on the basis of religion in providing help to the minority people.

Proper implementation of all developmental schemes requires the following three main things:

(i) Correct and clear visualization of the goals and methods of achievement of the programme.

(ii) Transparency in implementation.

(iii) Accountability at every level.

Women and Development

Women play a crucial role in development but they have largely been ignored. Much of women's work remains unrecognized, uncounted and unpaid in the home, in agriculture, in food production and in child care. Former UN Secretary General Kofi Annan once remarked, 'Study after study has shown that there is no effective development strategy in which women do not play a central role. When women are fully involved, the benefits can be seen immediately; families are healthier, and better fed; their income, savings and reinvestment go up. And, what is true of families is also true of communities, and in the long run, of whole countries.'

In the last decade, all over the world, including India, women have participated in development processes on a wider scale than ever before, even if only at small-scale level. For example, they have been main actors in micro-credit schemes all over the world; they ran their own businesses (e.g., a women cooperative society in Gujarat which prepares a well-known brand of Papad 'Lijjat,' and recently developed 'Self-Help Group' in Rajasthan and elsewhere are some of the examples of contribution of women in development). A recent wealth management study says that 'by 2020 women millionaires would outnumber their male counterparts and that within 20 years, 60 per cent of the world's wealth would be managed by women'. It is evident that more and more companies in our country now have women in powerful positions. In so many companies the person at the top is now a woman, like Indra Nooyi of Pepsi Co., Kiran Majumdar Shaw of Bicon and Chanda Kochar of ICICI bank. Capitalism has benefited an elite group of educated, urban women who are enjoying unprecedented opportunities—from heading to Western countries and America for MBAs to launching their own companies.

Besides running businesses, they are also involved at local level institutions in many different countries. In India, 30 per cent seats are reserved in for women PRIs, urban local bodies and other civic institutions.

Globalization and Women

While globalization has brought an explosion in the jobs market, the benefits for women have been mixed. It has brought one major benefit to most women—more paid work. Since 1980 the growth in the labour force of women has been substantially higher than that of men in every region of the world except Africa. In India too, the number of female workers was 7.2 crore in 2001, which is attributed to women's increasing participation in activities outside home. Prof. Sand Choudury (Trent University, Canada) notes, 'The economic independence that these jobs provide has for the first time given Third World women the ability to contribute to their families financially; the opportunity to delay marriages and child-bearing; even the means to end oppressive marital relationships.' But, while more women may be working, they are still paid less than men. Even in the US, which is a highly developed country, women get less than men for the same work. In 2000, on an average, women earned 73 per cent of men's wages. Black and minority women fared even worse. In India, women labour earns about 50 per cent of the wages paid to their counterpart. Not only this, generally women are assigned to the worst paid, shortest contract, most monotonous jobs. They are the first to be dismissed from work in any economic crisis. While in developed countries, there are many part-time jobs for women, in India such jobs are negligible. Moreover, such jobs are also vulnerable and have little security. Although globalization has resulted in some women gaining employment in IT, service and manufacturing sector, the majority of Indian (Asian) women are still in the informal economy, rural farming and in the subsistence economic activities. The World Bank's 2000 report 'Gender in Transition' highlights differences between men and women by commenting that globalization has increased gender inequality, hampering socio-economic progress. In many Third world countries, including India, the average working woman earns just over half the income of the average man. Girls are more malnourished than boys. Less than half as many girls as boys are enrolled in higher education. Nearly half the pregnant women do not receive any form of prenatal care, resulting in very high infant mortality rates.

Globalization has also increased migration across borders and this has provided women with new opportunities, financial independence and higher status in their home country. Many women are moving to other countries either for higher studies or in search of jobs. There are regions, like Kerala from where women are working abroad in abundance. Women migrants often send remittance back home. At the same time, globalization has contributed to worldwide growth in the numbers of women and girls being trafficked for forced sexual services.

Globalization has changed the face of the world, making us all into global consumers and giving us access to instant information. This has deeply affected women's lives. Women have become products for sale in the form of advertisements. Women's bodies are used to sell from men's underwear, perfumes, motorbikes to cars. Their bodies have become simply objects now as other objects. The ways that women have been marketed at, and used for marketing, have changed considerably in the last decade.

Trafficking has become one of the fastest growing criminal activities in the global economy. Widespread poverty in some regions of India forced parents to sell their young daughters (wife buying) to the men of foreign countries, particularly Middle East, where they are forced to work as prostitutes or concubines. Young girls are lured by the promise of a good job or for marriage in another country. Traffickers exploit women's desire to make a better life for themselves with promises of jobs as waitresses, dancers, models, maids and nannies.

Sociological Determinants of Economic Growth/Development

Behind the immediate economic behaviour and attitude lie a host of non-economic determinants such as cultural, social and psychological, etc. Economic behaviour includes entrepreneurial spirit, cosmopolitan habits and style of life, thrift and austerity that promote saving. People's attitude to work, time, money, saving, their occupational choices and commitment and their ability to adjust themselves to the bureaucratic organization depends to a great extent on the values and interests that arise out of religious ideas which may either promote or hinder many aspects of economic activities.

For an analysis of how sociological variables impinge on economic growth, we here discuss the interaction of economic variables (savings, consumption, productivity, entrepreneurship, etc.) and sociological variables (kinship, family, social structure, stratification system, religious values, etc.).

The Saving-Consumption-Investment Complex

The saving-consumption-investment complex is conditioned in particular by the kinship and stratification systems. Inflexible gift-giving rituals may 'tie up' consumption in traditional forms and thus make for a low level of savings. The style of life of an aristocratic or multimillionaire family may make for higher levels of consumption. Their style of life, moreover, may emphasize savings in the form of jewellery, gold ornaments or heirlooms which 'freeze' savings so that they cannot be invested in economically productive enterprises.

The economists have identified that economic development is based on capital formation. Capital formation depends on savings. There are two aspects of savings which are important in the initiation of development; namely the level of savings and the form of savings. The amount of wealth that is diverted from the current consumption needs constitutes the level of savings. The second aspect, i.e., the form of saving generally constitutes the jewellery, gold or silver vessels, coins, etc. which are not available for any economic enterprise. While the level of savings may be high, but if it is 'frozen' in the above mentioned things, as we find in India, it is of no use for economic activity.

Moreover, various traditional rituals connected with the rites of passage of the life cycle (birth and wedding ceremonies, burial ceremonies and feasts for the dead) also divert wealth from investment. The graduated elaboration of ceremonies can absorb a major portion of surplus income or past savings which might otherwise find economically more productive uses. Such rituals—rooted in family, community, and religion—often die hard.

Sociological variables such as the stratification or kinship system have a great impact on saving and investment behaviour. With regard to the stratification system, most rural peasant societies are dominated by centring on the land. In a summary of studies on savings in southern Asia, Richard Lambert and Bert Hoselitze (1956) show how this kind of stratification (status based such as caste system in India) affects investment behaviour.

Labour Commitment

Another very important factor leading to economic development is labour commitment. Mere capital investment is not enough. The right kind of labour should be recruited and trained and there should be commitment on the part of the labour towards this new method of working. Peasant societies, like Indian society with their close kinship relations and their attachment to the land, frequently offer resistance to the recruitment of labour into industrial urban settings. Writing about the kinship system in non-industrial societies, Wilbert Moore (1951) says: 'It perhaps offers the most important single impediment to individual mobility, not only through the competing claims of kinsmen upon the potential industrial recruit but also through the security offered in established patterns of mutual responsibility.'

Because of the attachment with land and the kinsmen, industrial labourers do not become permanent city dwellers. Their regular migration not only increases absenteeism in the industry but also affects their health, efficiency and the commitment to industrial work. Apart from the pull of the village, their life in the city is so bad (inadequate and shabby housing, unbalanced diet, etc.) that they may not be attracted to settle down in the city. Discipline of factory life, long hours of work, the environment of personal human relations, lack of wrath of the life all make them depressed and homesick. All these factors impede productivity and in turn the economic development.

Entrepreneurship

One of the peculiar features of many traditional peasant and tribal societies is their being kinship/community/religion/based. Complex of institutions offers serious obstacles to the effective appearance of entrepreneurs. Ragnar Nurkse (1962) argues that the innovations of entrepreneurs are essential in the initiation of economic growth. The entrepreneur is a man who undertakes risk in reorganizing factors of production. Thus, his place in economic development is critical. If any society has to transform itself from underdevelopment economy to developed economy, with all other factors of production, the entrepreneur is essential. He is that hardworking and energetic man who reorganizes the factors of production and initiates the industrial activity.

Psychological Factors

We generally overlook the importance of the cognitive factors in development and growth. Man is a future-oriented animal. It is his vision of the future, his hopes, fears and expectations along with his mentality that determine his actions in the present, through his awareness of the past influences him as well. It is difficult to understand the dynamics of development unless one also has an understanding of these hopes and aspirations as well as of the self-image and sense of identity of the people. Until we take into account how man in a given society perceives his own problems, his interests and his goals, we really have no clue as to how and why he will react in a particular way and not in another. We should, therefore, concern ourselves with the perception of values, goals, purposes underlying the organization of a society. Psychological factors emphasize attitudinal and behaviour changes that initiate as well as sustain economic growth. The attitudinal facet implies transformation of traditional attitudes based on customs and religious belief systems into some form of rationality based on science. Other elements include greater achievement, motivation, entrepreneurial spirit, higher educational aspirations, etc.

Max Weber asserted that among other things, it is the ascetic spirit of Protestantism that had encouraged the entrepreneurial activity in Western Europe and the United States. Competitive nationalistic values may encourage entrepreneurship. On the other hand, aggressive nationalism becomes a vehicle for the destruction of traditional patterns of economic activity and for entrepreneurial innovation. Cultural values, such as rationalism and Protestantism, however, do not by themselves produce entrepreneurs. There is also a personality (psychological) determinant. According to David McClelland (1961), individuals have to be motivated to undertake entrepreneurial activity in the name of these values. Early socialization of the child is critical in motivating individuals.

Political Factors in Development

Development does not occur in political vacuum. Social change and development is bound to have political implications. Unless there is a government that has a strong commitment to development (economic/social), no sustained development is possible. Likewise, the degree of power a government is able to exert significantly influences the range of economic policy options open to her. Given adequate initial power, success will very much depend on the quality of its political leadership and its capability. Political factors like communalism, regionalism, lingualism also affect economic development. The effects of nationalism also cannot be ruled out. Bert F. Hoselitz (1956) wrote, 'Nationalism, like many traditionalistic religious systems, my hinder economic development by reaffirmation tradionally honoured ways of acting and thinking.' Knigsley Davis (1957) argued that secular beliefs, especially nationalism, exert more direct force on economic development than religious values as argued by Weber.

Religion and Development

Since the publication of Max Weber's celebrated work, *The Protestant Ethic and the Spirit of Capitalism* (1930), a very interesting and thought-provoking debate started on the relationship between religion and economic behaviour (economic development). In examining this, it is necessary to see what values and interests, arising out of religious ideas, either promote or hinder which aspects of economic activities and to what extent.

Weber in his above mentioned treatise significantly pointed out that religion (Protestantism) was responsible for the rise of capitalism (economic behaviour) in some of the countries of the West where Protestantism was found. He argued that the themes of this-worldly asceticism developed so highly in Protestantism (especially in Calvinism) encouraged man to value highly the rational and methodical mastery of the social and cultural, and in particular, the economic behaviour.

This Weberian thesis was not accepted in toto by many scholars like H.M. Robertson (1933), R.H. Tawney (1926) and J.B. Crauss (1961). Robertson was of the view that the spirit of capitalism is not the creator but the creation of the class of businessmen. Similarly, both Tawney and Crauss believed that economic transformation of the 16th and 17th centuries had transformed the religious outlook of the people which paved the way for a more expansion of capitalism. There are people like Kurt Samuelsson (1961) who found no relationship between religion and economic action. There are some authors who have not totally rejected the Weberian thesis but have considered other factors as more crucial. Thus, H.R. Trevor-Roper (1963) emphasized the local origin of the entrepreneurs as more crucial than the religious affiliation.

With regard to the non-European application of Weber's argument, many studies were conducted in Asian countries (e.g., Clifford Geertz, 1956 and Ralf Pieris). With particular reference to India, two major studies have been attempted by two economists—K.W. Kapp (1963) and V. Mishra (1962)— in which the relationship between Hinduism and economic growth has been explored. Examining this relationship, Kapp reached to this conclusion that certain general beliefs and values (rebirth, law of *karma*, cosmic causation, etc.) of Hinduism stand in the way of the emergence of one basic requisite of economic development, namely, the conviction that man makes his own history. These values and beliefs lead to increased feelings of helplessness, to fatalism and to the belief that human experience is transitory and illusory to reliance on magic and astrology. Mishra has also expressed similar views to those Kapp. He finds that the notions of otherworldliness, transcendentalism, cycle of life and death and *moksha* of Hinduism drive the believers away from economic activity. Along with these values and beliefs, the stress on minimization of wants and minimum interest on the capital have hindered the habit of savings, which is a sine qua non for capital accumulation and capital formation needed for economic development. All these traits of Hinduism have affected adversely the economic growth in India.

Refuting vigorously the above charges of Kapp on Hinduism, Milton Singer (1972) has expressed his skepticism against Kapp's hypothetico-deductive approach to economic development. In his empirical study of cultural values in India's economic development, Singer points out how the values and motivations, usually associated with the materialism of the West, are also common places in India. Unlike Kapp and Mishra, he emphasizes that the Indian view encompasses both material and spiritual values. In this connection, Singer discussed Mahatma Gandhi's views who discovered a discipline of action in the service of others as the basis of philosophy of renunciation. He suggested that asceticism may indirectly perform positive social and economic functions in the transfer of property from one generation to another, in redistributing wealth from the right to the poor and even in the accumulation of wealth.

Many other scholars have also dispelled the misunderstanding about the Hindu notions of rebirth, *karma* and *moksha*. For example, G.S. Ghurye, in his book, *Gods and Men* (1962), has clearly demonstrated, contrary to the ordinary belief in the otherworldly nature of Hinduism, that religious ideas are product of newly discovered social interactions and they are the expressions of needs and activities of cultural groups. Similarly, M.N. Srinivas also pointed to the secular role of ascetics and showed how Tilak sought sanction for positive action in the Gita, as against the otherworldly and fatalist meaning of *karma*.

Investigating relationship between Hinduism and economic behaviour, Kingsley Davis (1957) writes: 'One trait of Hinduism that presumably permits, if it does not favour, economic change is its syncretic, non-dogmatic and rather tolerant character. Being so diverse it has no bitter sectarian animosity, no objection to doctrinal non-conformity. This tolerance, however, does not extend so fully to social behaviour. While Hinduism, often called a system rather than simply a religion, gives absolute liberty in the world of thought, it enjoins a strict code of practice.' This trait of Hindu social system has been affirmed by Indian thinkers as well.

From the above analysis, it can be deduced that religion is not a hindrance to economic development as is generally assumed. Contrary to Weber's belief economic growth has occurred in many Catholic countries and, therefore, Weber's view that only Protestant ethic is responsible for economic development is not valid. From this it becomes obvious that Hinduism—accepting for the sake of argument that it is otherworldly—also cannot be regarded as a hindrance to economic development. Moreover, we do not find any significant change in Hinduism as after the publication of Weber's book, India (Hinduism) has made strides in the field of economic development. To conclude, it may be said that some types of values encourage economic development while others discourage it; and still others seem to have different significances at different levels of development.

Caste System and Development

Stratification system has a great role to play in the economic development, particularly in a closed society, like Indian society, where castes used to be the major units of the society. These castes were the deciding factor in the choice of occupation of the individual, which acted as a great barrier in economic development of India. Kingsley Davis (1951) remarked, 'the conception of hereditary occupation is exactly the opposite of the idea of open opportunities, free competition, increasing specialization and individual mobility associated with a dynamic industrial economy'. Restrictions of the caste system on interaction with people of other castes hindered the mobility of the people to urban areas, which was needed for fast industrialization. William Kapp (1963) has also pointed out that Hindu culture and Hindu social organizations are determining factors in India's low rate of development.

Social structure continues to be hierarchic based on birth with the members of the backward classes continuing to suffer social handicaps especially in rural areas. In urban areas, mostly in metropolitan cities, some changes seem to have occurred because of education and some legislations. But there is not much change in the personality structure of backward classes (so-called dalits). The members of the backward classes in rural areas continue to be submissive, though the Panchayati Raj system and other democratic institutions along with education have affected the outlook, aspirations and behaviour of these classes to some extent. Now, they can provide the minimum necessities to their families, namely, nourishing foods, adequate clothing and proper housing and see that their children enjoy good health and upbringing and education and are well-equipped to achieve rightful place in society.

Disagreeing with William Kapp's arguments, Milton Singer, in his study of entrepreneurs of Madras, shows that caste and joint family have positively contributed to business and entrepreneurship. He finds Gunnar Myrdal's idea of 'obstacles' created by institutional factors in the modernization of India immaterial due to the resilience of caste, family and Hindu religion. Caste has made inroads in secular fields like politics, elections and government jobs. Members of a family help each other in economic and other pursuits. This has helped them manage their economic and business enterprises better. One should keep in mind that caste as an institution now, i.e., in 2013, is not the same as it was before independence. Much has changed in every aspect of caste.

The New World Economy

Modern economies are units of a worldwide complex economic system. Recently, social scientist Immanuel Wallerstein (1974) described and analysed world economy and termed it as 'capitalist economy' which has become a world system. He believed that capitalistic development never stops at national boundaries. Now, the growth and change of national economy does not seem to depend on national concerns and objectives, but more on how the economy fits into a world system. The markets for most goods are worldwide. Every nation is caught up in a worldwide market structure. Today, any remote event in the larger world alter the fate of peasants in the village. The price of wheat or cotton or rose flowers is now no more governed by village *mandi* (market) or state market but by the world market. So, too, the job of a software engineer is also affected by the demand and supply of these people in America or Britain.

Division of World Economy

The main dimensions of global stratification are income, social inequality and human development. On the basis of these, the world economy may be divided into three groupings. This three-way division reflects both historical differences in development as well as differences in social organization and ideology.

1. The *First World* is made up of capitalist nations of North America and Europe, including Japan. They wield enormous economic and political control over poor nations and maintain a flow of raw materials from the formal colonies. These are rich nations producing 60 per cent of world's wealth with only 20 per cent of its people. The small number of powerful technologically developed societies are the core – the dominant, organizing centre – of the world system.
2. The *Second World* is the erstwhile communist bloc of nations in Europe dominated by Soviet Union and China but after the disintegration of USSR, this bloc has also largely been disintegrated. China, though outwardly professes the philosophy of communism, has also embraced capitalism.
3. The *Third World* is not clearly identifiable in regard to specific geographical region or political regime. It is a complex of mostly new

nations, formerly European colonies, located primarily in Asia, Africa and Latin America. They have achieved political independence but are economically poor and industrially underdeveloped. Among the Third World nations, some have made progress and thus they are known as developing nations while there is a group of nations which are still very impoverished and solely dependent on developed nations.

The periphery of the world system is built by these so-called undeveloped (poor) nations/societies of the Third world. There is also a semi-periphery, the economies of which are between the others—more diversified than peripheral ones, but much less so than the core economies. Mexico and Brazil are examples of such economies.

Division of Labour

Division of labour denotes 'any stable organization, co-ordinating individuals, or groups carrying out different, but integrated activities' (*Oxford Dictionary of Sociology*, 1994). Co-ordination is a complex concept. Division of labour could take place on a number of levels, between different sectors of the economy, between occupations, or between individual tasks. Modern societies, as a whole, are characterized by an extensive social division of labour, involving the specialization and interdependence of whole institutions and social processes.

Human beings have divided labour since earliest organization of society. All societies have at least some rudimentary form of division of labour—a range of tasks is assigned to women and another set of tasks given to men, and still others may be performed by either sex. This is popularly known as sexual division of labour. Very little of this division is required by the biological peculiarities of the two sexes. A man cannot bear a child or nurse it though some experiments have been done contrary to this popular belief. Men are stronger and can run faster than women who are in turn somewhat handicapped at times by pregnancy and menstruation. Women, however, have strength and speed to perform almost all tasks in every society. Equally important, what is defined as a man's task in one society may well be classed as a woman's job in another, thus indicating that most of the division is culturally defined, or based on a complex of factors in which the biological is only a part. However, in most of the societies (about three-fourth), women used to carry out these tasks—grinding grain, carrying water, cooking, preserving food, gathering food, repairing and making clothing, weaving and making pottery. In most of societies men are assigned these tasks—herding, hunting and fishing, lumbering, mining and quarrying, metal working, manufacturing of ceremonial objects, wood working and house building. Some of these require strength, and others demand some wandering from the hearth. Notice that the tending of crops calls for endurance and some strength, but it is as likely to be female activity as a male activity.

The division of labour is based neither on biology nor on simple equality. Another factor is significant as an element in the husband's position and the position of men in society. Whatever strictly male tasks are, they are defined as more honorific. The division is justified by various rationalizations and by moral precepts and these are part of the socialization experience of boys and girls in the society. In early socialization the young begins experience to acquire the values and skills of their parents.

With the development of industrialization, however, the division of labour became more complex than in any type of production system. Work has become divided into an enormous number of different occupations in which people specialize. Until the onset of industrialization, one person was a farmer, another made shoes, another spun cloth, still another backed or butchered. While society's labour was divided, each person performed a whole task and each of these tasks usually involved a number of developed skills. In traditional societies, non-agricultural work entailed the mastery of a craft, craft skills were learned through a lengthy period of apprenticeship, and the worker normally carried out all aspects of the production process from beginning to the end. Such a division of labour what Marx called the 'social division of labour'.

The days of the old crafts—man who made a total object with a few tool and his remarkable skill—have gone. With the rise of modern industrial capitalism, most traditional crafts have disappeared altogether, at least in so-called developed societies. Now, the human-made object is the end-product of a vast system of production that involves many special tasks. Each person contributes but one small part to the finished product. An electrician working in an industrial setting today, for instance, may inspect and repair only a few parts of one type of machine; different people will deal with the other parts and other machines.

As against the social division of labour that existed in traditional societies, there stands the manufacturing division of labour. In this type of division of labour, two things are involved: (1) the replacement of the human hand by the machine, which is a technological change; and (2) the sub-dividing of the whole task into many small, detailed tasks, which is a social change. These technological and social changes have not merely replaced the craftsmen with the machine-tending workers. Gradually, the worker lost control over tools, quality of work, hours of work, the pace and rhythm of work, and the like. A major consequence of this minute industrial division of labour is the alienation of the worker from his labour as well as from the product he has produced. Marx maintained that the worker typically feels that he is not in anyway fulfilled by work itself, that it is not a rewarding activity. Alienation of the worker occurs when work becomes a thing apart from the worker, an alien force beyond his control. According to Marx, capitalism reduces labour to a commodity to be traded in the market, rather than a social relationship, thus alienation of the worker from the reduction and from the act of production itself takes place. The work becomes a meaningless activity, offering little or no intrinsic satisfaction to the labourer.

Social Aspects of Division of Labour

While Marx stressed on the idea of alienated labour as an outcome of division of labour, for Durkheim, the principal interest of the division of labour is its moral consequences, that is, its effect on the underlying solidarity of the society, which should restrain individual egoism, ruthlessness and licence. Durkheim argued that traditional societies are integrated by so-called mechanical solidarity, in which emphasis is placed on the values and cognitive symbols common to the clan or tribe. Individuals and institutions are thus relatively undifferentiated. Modern societies, he claimed, require the development of organic solidarity, in which beliefs and values emphasize individuality, encourage specialist talents in individuals, and the differentiation of activities in institutions. But, although the economic division of labour may have initiated such a way of life by itself, the unregulated market loosens restraints on individual desires, undermines the establishment of social trust, and produces abnormal forms of division of labour. This situation creates anomie, and the forced division of labour associated with class and political conflict in society.

Recent feminist analyses have drawn attention on both power and moral types of explanation to explore invidious distinctions made between men's and women's social labour and social position, and the form of division of labour by gender has taken in industrial (modern) societies.

Economic Development and Social Change

It is generally said and understood that economic changes bring social changes (changes in caste, family, marital relationship, community structure, etc.) in their train. This type of relationship has been shown in the studies of rural and urban India and many other undeveloped countries like modern Africa. But, in reality, economic changes can occur only when the social conditions are favourable. Why industrial revolution has started in Europe and not India, China or Japan though these countries were far ahead in same crafts, such as silk weaving and ceramics. In replying to this question, Max Weber in his analysis gave greater weight to religion than other factors. For him, it was 'the Protestant ethic' which was closely linked with 'the spirit of capitalism'. This spirit places emphasis on honesty, trustworthiness, diligence, sobriety, modesty of personal tastes and the ability to save. This has made for the success in businesses of a class of people.

These were essential features of industrial capitalism, which developed in the 19th century in England, Europe and America. It could not have happened elsewhere. In India, for example, its emergence was fatally blocked by the caste system and the structure of joint family, which led to the conservation of traditional crafts in closed hereditary groups. In India, industrial development came later and that too as the result of the arrival of Europeans. How far this analysis of Weber is correct? It is a matter of serious investigation. Some studies substantiated the Weber's argument of religion and economic development, whereas supporters of economic determinism criticized it severely.

Most fundamentally, economic development depended first and foremost on the psychology of people, i.e., change in man's mind—a change in man's worldview and their place in it. It was this chage that led to a scientific attitude, a readiness to experiment, the acceptance of experience (empirical data) as the only test of the truth or falsify the ideas about the world. It was associated also with an acceptance of individual responsibility, individual risk and individual reward, which were essential to the spirit of capitalistic enterprise. This entailed in turn a disposition to accept change—an acceptance that changes will occur, and the readiness to accept the dislocation and re-arrangement of social relation (such as joint family to nuclear family and working together of members of different castes in industries) which always go with technical and economic change.

In the end, it may be said that economic, religious, scientific and technical changes took place together and reacted upon one another. Thus, there is no reason to say that economic changes come first and determine others as economist believes. The relationship between economic and non-economic (social and cultural) elements is reciprocal. Social and cultural elements that affect economic activity are also affected by it.

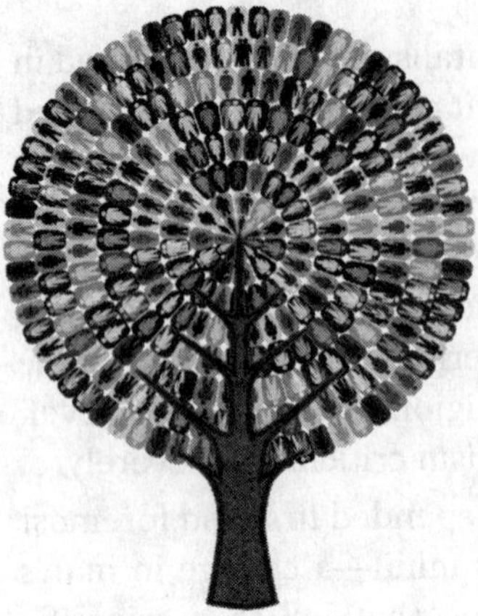

Chapter 10

Political Institutions

KEY FEATURES

- Approaches to Study Political Institutions
- Political Systems: Totalitarian, Oligarchic and Democratic
- Democracy: Participatory and Monarchical
- Problems of Democracy
- Globalization and Democracy
- State
- Political Participation
- Non-Participation: Causes
- Voting Behaviour
- Power: Economic, Social, Political, Knowledge, Military, Ideological, Distributional and Collective.
- Authority: Traditional, Legal and Charismatic
- Politics
- Power Structure: Elite and Pluralist Models
- Political Process and Political Parties
- Interest/Pressure Groups
- Political Mobilization
- Globalization and Politics

Sociologists study political institutions with the particular aim to understand social causes and consequences of given power distributions within or between societies, and with the social and political conflicts that lead to changes in the allocation of power. A major focus of sociology is the study of: (i) political conflicts and struggles between different nation-states; (ii) the nature and organization of the state within society; (iii) the nature and organization of political movements and parties; and (iv) the participation of individuals in politics, such as voting behaviour.

Approaches to Study Political Institutions

Political institutions are mainly concerned with the exercise and distribution of power and have the monopoly on the legitimate use of force. Institutions involving relations with other societies, including war, are also considered to fall in this category. For a sociologist, a society's political institution, or politics, is, like other institutions, a means of dealing with social problems. In this connection, political sociologists have offered two opposite approaches of how order arises, is maintained and motivates members of any given society. These approaches are: structural-functional approach, and conflict approach.

Structural-functional Approach (Consensus Theory)

This approach stresses on co-operation and stability. Theorists of this approach believe that political institutions hold the values of the dominant society and arbitrate conflicts when they arise. One person may act on a value of freedom by marrying more than one spouse, or members of a sub-culture may feel free to use drugs. It is the political system that decides which value must be upheld or limited to maintain social order.

Conflict Approach

This approach differs radically from structural-functional approach. It stresses on conflict and change as the centre of political life. It does not assume that societies are based on a set of values, but, rather, that they are drawn together by people's need for resources—food, shelter, and other necessities. Some groups get a larger share of resources to gain power. They use their wealth and power to influence and control political leaders and mass media to support their economic interests. Unlike the structural-functionalists, who believe that the values of the society shape political systems, conflict theorists believe that political systems are run by elites who shape the values of society.

There is also disagreement among sociologists on the nature of political power. Some sociologists claim that power involves the exercise of one's will over the opposition of others in society; others maintain that truly powerful often arrange to have their will carried out without arousing opposition. Sociologists have also distinguished between power and authority. In the following pages we have discussed these elements of political institutions—state, power, authority, politics, government, etc. But, before this, we will concentrate our attention on political system first.

Political Systems

Each society must have a political system in order to maintain recognized procedures for allocating valued resources. In large complex societies, many decisions must be made about the duties and responsibilities of citizens and also about the rights and privileges. If the society is to be orderly, people must obey the rules that are made. The political institution determines and enforces the laws and punishes those who disobey them. Even in stateless societies which had no developed formal central institutions were seen having some kind of decision-making and rule-making processes which were dominated by some members. As societies become wealthier and more complex, political systems develop and grow more powerful.

According to renowned political scientists, Gabriel Almond and James Coleman (1960), 'Political system is that system of interactions to be found in all independent societies which performs the functions of integration and adaptation by means of legitimate physical compulsion.' *The Concise Oxford Dictionary of Sociology* (1994) defines it as, 'a political system in any persistent pattern of human relationship that involves (to a significant extent) power, rule and authority.' It is a collectivity of political institutions (e.g., government), associations (e.g., political parties) and organizations performing roles based on a set of norms and goals (like maintaining internal order, regulating foreign relations, etc.). Sociologically, the term 'political system' refers to the social institutions which relies on a recognized set of procedures for implementing and achieving the political goals of a community or society.

Functions of a Political System

Almond and Coleman (1960) have described the following three main functions of a political system:

1. To maintain integration of society by determining norms.
2. To adapt and change elements of social, economic, religious systems necessary for achieving collective (political) goals.
3. To protect the integrity of the political system from outside threats.

They have grouped these functions into two categories: (1) input functions—political socialization, interest articulation, interest aggregation, and political communication; and (2) output functions—rule making, rule application and rule adjudication. Eisenstadt (1966) has classified the functions of a political system as (i) legislative, (ii) decision-making, and (iii) administrative.

Types of Political Systems

According to Edward Shills, there are three main types of political systems. These are discussed as under:

Totalitarian system

A system in which the state controls and regulates all phases of life considered essential for perpetuating its power and for carrying out programmes arbitrarily. It is the most extreme form of authoritarianism. Unlike democracies, where a variety of groups struggle for a voice in government, the government dictates the society's values, ideology, rules and form of government. Societies having totalitarian system do not permit dissent. The centralized authority always dominates over the autonomy of individual or sub-groups within the society. Mussolini's Italy, Hitler's Nazi Germany and Stalin's Soviet Union are often quoted as examples of totalitarian states. Totalitarian states are ruled by one political party that organizes the citizens into a unified group. In practice, the state is represented by a politically powerful ruling class or elite that dominates all other interest groups.

Oligarchic system

Any form of government in which there is a 'rule by a few', for example, by members of a self-regulating elite having domination over a large society is known as an oligarchic political system. It is a system in which a small group (elites) rules and holds supreme power over a larger society.

Democratic system

In its broadest sense, democracy is a way of life in which an individual feels free to act within accepted boundaries of norms and also equal in respects of his/her rights. In the narrower sense, it is a form of government, a power structure in which people govern themselves. People participate in the government through their representatives that they elect. In other words, people represent themselves and take their own decisions. It is an imagination of the replica of an equalitarian society.

Democracy

The word 'democracy' has its roots in the Greek term '*demokratia*,' meaning 'rule by the people' (*demos* means 'people' and *kratos* means 'rule'.) It is a political system in which people not monarchs (king or queens) or aristocracies (like lords) rule. Theodore Parker defines it as 'government of all the people, by all the people and for all the people'. Seymour Lipset (1960) gives a working definition of democracy as 'a political system supplying regular constitutional opportunities for changing the government by allowing the population to choose between alternative sets of policy makers'.

Democracy is a type of social system in which everyone has an equal share of power. In large complex societies, however, it is impossible for every citizen to be involved in the political process. Thus, when we refer to 'democratic' power structure, we mean those structures in which people are allowed to vote for elected representatives. Most societies that describe themselves as political democracies are actually representative democracies in which citizens elect politicians who actually hold and exercise political authority. Pure democracy is quite rare. This is because the definition of 'everyone' always excludes some portion of population.

The origins of democracy as an idea and a practice go back to the city-states of Greece in the 5th century BCE. But contemporary democracies are very different from the ancient Greek model. It is a paradox that though the modern democracy first emerged in the Greece, yet the Greeks were suspicious of democracy. They felt that people often made bad decisions that went against their interests. People could be manipulated by demagogues and vested interests. The pattern that emerged in England in the 17th century and slowly became the model for the entire world was one of representative democracy or parliamentary democracy. Here, citizens elect leaders by ballot who promise to represent the interests of those citizens in debates and decisions, which typically take place in some central national forum such as parliament or Congress. Thus, ideally, the parliament becomes a miniature *demos*. In India, this type of democratic political system developed after independence. It is said that in ancient India the people led a democratic way of living (Ram Rajya) but the political democracy of the modern form did not exist.

In practice, politicians in a democracy usually belong to parties which propose general policies or programmes, rather than responding to citizens on issue-by-issue basis. Parties thus become independent centres of power. The experience of the 20th century seems to show that citizens' interests are best represented by either two, or at the most three parties—as in Britain or the United States. Although there are many one-party systems in the world which claim to be democratic on the basis that they represent the collective will of the people. Political processes (elections, political socialization) are the lifeblood of all types of democracies. Political organization, political competitiveness, the big political gesture—all these are integral to democracy. It is widely agreed that for the real democracy, following necessary conditions must be fulfilled:

1. Free and fair elections
2. A genuine choice between candidates and policies
3. Real parliamentary power
4. The separation of powers between the executive, judiciary and the politicians
5. Civil rights for all citizens
6. Rule of law and equality before law
7. Inter-party competition
8. Real representation of different interests
9. Free and responsible media
10. Personal freedom
11. Freedom of speech and writing
12. Freedom of religion and public worship
13. Freedom of association and assembly

Although democracy is based on majority rule, the protection of minority rights has always been regarded as an essential aspect of the democratic system. Also important are the equality before law, freedom of speech, press and assembly, and protection from arbitrary arrest in the political democracy.

There is a room for unlimited disagreement about the exact meaning of any and all of the above conditions that why democracy continues to be the focus of intense public and academic debate. There are many paradoxes of democracy which have engaged the attention of sociologists and political scientists. Political sociologists have explored the nature of the state as a sociological entity, political socialization, voting behaviour and political participation, the relationships between democracy and economic systems, and the manipulation of public opinion.

Types of Democracies

Democracies differ from society to society in their form and content. The main forms of democracy are as follows:

Participatory democracy (or direct democracy)

It is a form of democracy in which decisions are made communally by those affected by them. This was the original type of democracy practised in ancient Greece and India (Gram Panchayat) from where the idea of democracy originated. Participatory democracy is of limited importance in modern societies, where the mass of the population have political rights, and it would be impossible for everyone to participate actively in the making of decisions. Virtually, only a small minority actually participates in political process and political organizations on a local or national level.

Monarchical democracy

There are some modern states, such as Britain and Sweden, where traditional rulers—the king or the queen acts as constitutional monarchs—continue to head the elected government. Their power is severely restricted by the constitution, which vests authority in the elected representatives of the people. In most cases they are just symbols of national identity rather than personages having any direct power in political life. The vast majority of modern states are republican. In such states, there is no king or queen. Almost everyone, including constitutional monarchies, professes adherence to democracy.

Liberal (representative) democracy

Liberal democracy is a framework for the expression of diverse views and interests. It does not specify how we should behave apart from insisting that we should respect the views of others. As such, it is compatible with the pluralism of attitudes and ways of life. In practice, a liberal democracy is a representative multi-party democracy (such as in India), where citizens can vote for one of at least two parties. Liberal democracy is, in part, a theory about the relationship between the majority of the people and their leaders (the political elite). Liberal theorists state that democratic political elites are representative of the people and are ultimately accountable to them. In liberal democracies, voters can choose between two or more political parties and the mass adult population has the right to vote. It is a political system which is different from communism as found in the former Soviet Union (and which still exists in China). Communism was essentially a system of one-party rule. Since 1989, with the fall of the communistic regime, the processes of democratization have started across the world in all the countries which were ruled by the Soviet-style regimes. Liberal democracy involves several political parties and free and fair elections at regular intervals. Those who favour liberal democracy argue that parties and pressure groups should effectively represent people and influence government. They believe that the civil service is the 'servant' of government; the judiciary is regarded as independent of government and is not expected to concern itself with political matters.

Most Marxists may not agree with the model of liberal democracy described above as 'real' democracy. For them, it is merely 'bourgeois democracy', a smokescreen behind which the capitalist class pursues its own interests. Parliament and political government are not considered to be the major source of power. Capitalists make the decisions and control politicians. Marxists believe that in liberal capitalist democracies, the capitalists class rules, not the people. Many contemporary Marxists have different (modified) views about modern liberal democracies.

Problems of Democracy

Democracy has become a global force. While it has become widespread, but all is not going well with this political system. It has got into some difficulties almost everywhere. Democracy is in trouble even in the countries of its origin—Britain, the US and many European countries. Surveys show that increasing proportions of people are dissatisfied with this political system, or indifferent towards it. Political participation is decreasing day by day as is evident from the percentage of voters turnout at the hustings and the attendance in the parliament and assemblies during debates. Most of the people are unhappy because of the following reasons:

1. The government is unable to address many needs of its citizens.
2. Decisions affecting lives of the people are made by distant 'power brokers'—in Delhi or state headquarters—party officials, interest groups, bureaucratic officials, and the like.

3. People believe that government is unable to deal with important local issues as well, such as crimes, cleanliness, road repairs, unemployment, slums and encroachments.
4. Like all bureaucracies it created its own vested interests and tends to be slow-moving and at certain times, it becomes oppressive. Civil servants may give partial advice to ministers or take too long in producing it.
5. In India, especially, it has not produced the intended results because of many pitfalls (corruption, casteism. nepotism, communalism, regionalism, etc.).

For its failure, it is not the institution itself which is to be blamed; it is the way it has worked or the way its working has been distorted by those in power. It is because of the vested interests of a few people that the tangible gains could not go to the large masses of people. In spite of many problems and difficulties of liberal democracy, it is not only persisting in the countries, where this system was practised but is spreading to those countries also where other political system was operating. The freedom that exists in liberal societies, we cannot undervalue it. Within broadly defined limits, people can speak their minds and organize themselves for a cause. Private lives are largely left private by the state—in their own homes, at least, people can 'be themselves'. These freedoms might not seem so substantial or so precious if we did not experience the agony of totalitarianism practised in Germany and Soviet Union in the 1930s or Taliban's Afghanistan and Sadaam Hussain regime in Iraq. Perhaps the major argument in favour of liberal democracy is that there is every scope to bring improvement in this system. This is why Churchill once described liberal democracy as 'the least worst system'.

In spite of its many pitfalls and weaknesses, democratization is one of the major political forces in the world today. Like many aspects of contemporary societies, the realm of government and politics is undergoing major changes. In many parts of the world, pro-democracy movements have been successful in toppling authoritarian regimes. In the former Soviet Union and Eastern Europe, communism was overthrown by such movements. But democracy is still not a reality of China, though a movement in favour of democracy was launched as early as in 1989 and a demonstration was held in Tiananmen Square in Beijing. Democratic forms of government have also been established in recent years in much of Latin America and some countries in Africa and Asia such as Afghanistan, Iraq and some Arab countries.

Globalization and Democracy

Like all other social systems, the system of democracy has also not remained untouched by the recent phenomenon of globalization. In its train, it has brought many good as well as bad effects for democracy. When a question is asked, why are many unhappy with the very political system that seems to be sweeping all the world? The answers, curiously, are bound up with the factors that have helped spread democracy—the impact of capitalism, mass media and the globalizing of social life.

In this connection, Daniel Bell (1976) has stated that national government is too small to respond to the big question, such as the influence of global economic competition or the destruction of the world's environment … . Governments have little power, for instance, over the activities of giant business corporations, the main actors within the global economy … national governments are unable to control processes bound up with the world economy. Similarly, Anthony Giddens (2000) observed, 'governments have shrunk in relation to global issues; they have also become more remote from the lives of most citizens'.

Globalization is altering many other aspects of national politics too. David Held (1993), a foremost writer on the politics of globalization, analysed and promoted the possibilities of a new form of politics and democracy which transcends the nation-state. In his view, globalization is an opportunity as well as threat. He summarized the features of globalization as follows:

- Political, economic and social activity is rapidly becoming global in scope.
- States and societies are linked in ways that are greatly intensified, and this is facilitated by rapid communication.
- People, ideas and cultural products move around, merge and influence each other more rapidly than ever before.
- Military power and intelligence activity can operate on a truly global scale using high technology.
- Economic activity can create globally integrated production and marketing, extending global economic activity far beyond trade.
- Transnational political organizations such as United Nations, International Monetary Fund and World Bank go beyond the nation-state and its sovereignty.
- Globalization can generate forces of both fragmentation (as in the case of former USSR and Yugoslavia) and unification (such as European Union). These trends bring dangers and challenges of fragmented nationalism, localism and small-scale nationalism and dual dynamic of internationalism.
- With the end of cold war following the collapse of European communism (USSR), the world is no longer divided into two huge superpower blocs. The political map of Europe has been transformed after 1989. The state-socialist model is discredited in favour of capitalism, market economies and parliamentary democracies.

David Held has suggested that the above developments could provide a basis for a supernational state—a kind of *world government* to deal with the 'big' issues—which should have legislative and coercive powers. This *world parliament* would become an authoritative international centre for the consideration and examination of global issues, e.g., health and disease, ecological imbalance, environmental pollution, food supply and distribution. Thus, Held has a vision of a *cosmopolitan global democracy* to which the present world is heading.

State

According to the *Oxford Dictionary of Sociology* (1994), 'The state is a distinct set of institutions that has the authority to make rules which govern society.' These institutions, according to Miliband (1969), are the government, the administration (the civil service), the judiciary and parliamentary assemblies. State power lies in these institutions. Max Weber defined it as 'the social institution that holds a monopoly over the use of force'. It has a 'monopoly' of legitimate violence 'within a specific territory'. Hence, the state includes such institutions as the armed forces, civil service or bureaucracy, police, judiciary and local and national councils of elected representatives, such as parliament. Consequently, the state is not a unified entity. It is rather a set of institutions which describe the terrain and parameters for political conflicts between various interests over the use of resources and the direction of public policy. Sociologists have been particularly concerned with the state, but they have examined it in relation to society as a whole, rather than in isolation. Their main concern is the description analysis, and explanation of the state as an institution which claims a monopoly of the legitimate use of force within a given territory.

What are the state's interests or the boundaries of the state. It is very difficult to identify them clearly, since different parts of the state apparatus can have different interests and conflicting preferences. Because of this difficulty, there are frequently conflicts between elected politicians and non-elected civil servants or the judiciary over policy and resources. Moreover, its boundaries have not been clearly defined and are constantly changing. It is here useful to bear in mind Althusser's concept of state apparatuses. The capacity of the state to control the armed forces and police (repressive state apparatus) as well as the major means of communication, notably the media (the ideological state apparatus) is crucial to its power.

Defining state, Anthony Giddens (1997) writes: 'A state exists where there is a political apparatus of government (institutions like a parliament, civil services officials, etc.) ruling over a given territory, whose authority is backed by a legal system and by the capacity to use military force to implement its policies.' Dunleavy and O'Leary (1967) have suggested the following five characteristics of the modern state:

1. The state is a recognizably separate institution or set of institutions, so differentiated from the rest of its society as to create identifiable public and private spheres.

2. The state is sovereign, or the supreme power, within its territory, and by definition the ultimate authority for all law.
3. The state's sovereignty extends to all the individuals within a given territory, irrespective of formal positions held in the government or rule-making institutions.
4. The modern state's personnel are mostly recruited and trained for management in a bureaucratic manner.
5. The state has the capacity to extract monetary revenues (taxation) to finance its activities from its subject—population.

All modern societies are nation-states, usually having some form of congressional or parliamentary system. A nation-state is a nation governed by a state whose authority coincides with the boundaries of the nation. Their system of government lays claim to specific territories, possesses formalized codes of law, and is backed by the control of military force. Nation-states have come into existence generally after 19th century. The world today is largely organized into nation-states. According to Giddens (1997), their main characteristics, viz., sovereignty, citizenship and nationalism, are discussed as under:

Sovereignty

All nation-states are sovereign states. The notion of 'sovereignty' refers to the authority of a government over a clearly defined territory with clear cut borders, within which it is the supreme power.

Citizenship

In modern societies most people living within the borders of the political system are citizens, having common rights and duties and knowing themselves to be part of a nation. Almost everyone in the world today is a member of a definite political order.

Nationalism

Each community acquires a distinctive character through its association with nationalism. Nationalism can be defined as 'a set of symbols and beliefs providing the sense of being part of a single political community'. Thus, individuals feel a sense of pride and belonging in being Indian, British, American, Russian or French. It is the main expression of feelings of identity with a distinct sovereign community.

Nationalistic loyalties do not always fit with the physical boarders marking the territories of states in the world today. While the relation between the nation-state and nationalism is a complicated one, the two have come into being as part of the same process. Nationalism has become an increasingly powerful force in the world, serving as a basis not only of collective social identity but also for political mobilization and action, especially through the use of warfare.

The consequences of nationalism often breed extremism and feelings of ethnocentrism (a tendency to think and act blindly that our culture is superior to those of others) resulting into political conflicts. Extreme forms of nationalism have engulfed many nations into warfare.

Functions of the State

As with all social institutions, the state is organized around a set of social functions. It is an important agency of social control which performs this function through laws. The main functions are maintaining law, order and stability, resolving various kinds of disputes through the legal system, providing common defence, and looking out for the welfare of the population in ways that are beyond the means of the individual, such as implementing public health measures, providing mass education and underwriting expensive medical research. From a conflict perspective, the state operates in the interests of various dominant groups, such as economic classes and racial and ethnic groups. Lean Mayher (1971) stated the following basic functions of the state:

1. Limiting internal power struggles to maintain internal peace.
2. Bringing power to bear on other societies in defence of national interest or in expanding and building empire.
3. Controlling the members of society so as to bind them to the pursuit of collective goals.
4. Recognizing and implementing the interests and demands of various groups.

Analysis of State: Different Points of View

Sociological accounts of the state broadly fall into three categories:

1. Max Weber saw the state in capitalist and socialist societies as an independent force that has its own rules of action—the legal-national rules of bureaucracy—and dominates all social groups.
2. For Marxists, the role of modern states is determined by their location in capitalist societies. While the 'Instrumentalist' Marxism (Miliband, 1969) sees the state as simply an outpost of the dominant elite because its personnel are drawn from the capitalist class, the 'Structuralist' Marxism (Poulantzas, 1968) maintains that the state furthers the interests of

capital or the capitalist class even though it has relative autonomy. The state acts more or less at the behest of the capitalist class. Poulatzas, by contrast, argues that the question of who controls the state is irrelevant.

3. Pluralists follow a middle course regarding the state as a partly independent force which, via the workings of the democratic process, may still be influenced by the different interests that are represented politically They generally see the state as acting in the interest of groups in society. State actions are therefore reactions to group pressures.

Both the Marxist and pluralist approaches may be said to be society-centred, i.e., they view the state as reacting to the activities of groups within society.

State and Government

The 'state' is not the same as 'government' although the terms are often used interchangeably in common parlance. The state is a social institution, which means that it consists of a form or social blueprint for how various functions ought to be accomplished. The parliamentary system, for example, is one way of accomplishing various tasks of governance, such as enacting legislation. On the other hand, a government is a particular collection of people who at any given time occupy the positions of authority within a state. In this sense, governments regularly come and go, but the state endures and is slow and difficult to change. According to Giddens (1997), 'government' refers to the regular enactment of policies, decisions and matters of state on the part of the officials within a political apparatus.

State and Society

Society, as defined by MacIver (1937), is 'a web of social relationships and these relationships are hundreds or thousands of types. It includes every kind of willed relationship of man to man. State represents only one type of relationship to which we call "political relationship"'. Social scientists have long tried to explain the state in relation to society, to define it as the institutionalization of power. State is a political organization or an institution exists within the society. State is, thus, different from society both structurally and functionally. The main points of difference between the two can be exhibited as under:

1. State is a territorial organization, while a society does not have a definite territory. A society like the Theosophical Society may extend to the whole world. A state is purely a political apparatus (government) having power to rule within given boundaries and over those people within such boundaries.

2. Society embraces the whole of life of a man and it also brings men together. But a state is concerned only with political relationship—just one form of social relationships.
3. The state is not a universal institution. Some societies (e.g., African traditional societies) are stateless. The people lived in society much before the state emerged. In other words, society is prior to the state.
4. State is a structure not coeval and coexistent with society but built within it as a determinate order for the attainment of specific ends.
5. Society exercises authority largely through customs and persuasion. The state exercises authority through enacted laws and coercion.

The state is an agency of legitimate authority operating within established rules of the game accepted by the majority of citizens. It is an arena in which conflicts over economic and social interests are fought out. The conflict theorists view it as an arena of conflict marked by organized coercion. This fits the often expressed Marxian view that the state is simply an instrument of the ruling class.

Political Participation

Political participation is normally associated with the modern form of democracy. In this political system, participation by the individual in political activity is considered a virtue, a sign of political health and the best method of ensuring one's private interests. Participation gives an opportunity to express one's own point of view and secure the greatest good for the greatest number. It provides citizens a sense of dignity and value, alerts both the rulers and the ruled to their duties and responsibilities and facilitates broader political understanding. By involving people in the affairs of the state, participation promotes stability and order in the system. It not only stimulates political learning but also makes citizens responsible. It deepens the political awareness and increases the sense of political effectiveness.

Taking part in the political processes which lead to the selection of political leaders or determine or influence public policy is generally known as political participation. Despite the fact that elections are the major event in the political process, political participation cannot be limited to only electoral process, i.e., voting and campaigning. It is a term applied to various types of activities ranging from political orientations, attitude, knowledge, interest in politics, identification with a political unit (political party or its any wing) to taking active part in political action such as rally, demonstration, strike or campaigning for voting in elections. The most important political activities may be those carried out by parties or citizens between elections to influence government decisions about specific problems that concern them.

In brief, political participation refers to all those activities which influence the decision-making process. These activities may include voting, seeking information, discussing, attending public meetings, making financial contribution, communicating with representatives to become member in a political party, canvassing, speech writing, delivering speech, working in campaigns, competing for public and party offices, etc.

There is no consensus among scholars whether to include in its definition illegal as well as legal activity, unsuccessful and successful attempts of influence and involuntary as well as voluntary action. Huntington and Nelson (1976) have argued that voluntary (autonomous) and manipulated (mobilized) participation are not clearly distinguished categories. Myron Weiner (1962) restricts his definition to voluntary action—the activity which is designed by the actor himself to influence governmental decision-making. When we define political behaviour in such broad terms as any form of (individual or collective) involvement in the political process, or any activity which has political consequences in relation to government and policy, then naturally both legitimate forms of political participation (such as voting in elections, activism in interest groups, or social movements) and illegitimate political activities (including terrorism, revolutions and *coups d'etat*) come under its purview.

Factors Influencing Political Participation

Political participation is a complex phenomenon. It depends upon a variety of factors that influence it. These factors can be described as under:

Psychological or cognitive traits

Social psychologists have emphasized on psychological traits which stem from individual personality and cognitive structures. They include sense of efficacy, sense of civic responsibility, sociability, sense of alienation and authoritarianism. It is assumed that there is a relation between the cognitive status of low self-esteem and feeling of pessimism and alienation from society and political apathy. But this political apathy influences political participation, it is not much clear and certain.

Social environment

The social environment definitely has an impact on political participation. Social environment includes elements like education, occupation, income, age sex, race, caste, ethnicity, mobility and habitation. The more educated are better able to transmit their political interest and knowledge to their children and to the people of their neighbourhood. In this respect, educational institutions serve as the basic ground in the development of articulateness and skills of political participation through schools/college/university unions. One learns here to join in an organization, fulfil duties, participate in meetings, discuss social issues and organize to achieve group goals.

Political environment

To what extent an individual receives political stimuli to participate in political activities, depends on the political environment or the political setting in which he/she finds himself/herself. The right to participate is a defining feature of democratic political systems but is not fully exercised. Levels of political interest and apathy have often been taken as criteria of participation and non-participation, including party membership, expressed interest in politics and awareness of issues.

Political parties also have an important role to play in political participation. This role is partly expressive and partly instrumental. The party inspires in its members a feeling of belongingness. It acts as a powerful reference group in its own right. As a part of its instrumental functions, the party contacts and registers voters, selects party nominees, organizes campaign activities, mobilizes rallies to influence the electorate during elections to vote and at other occasions to favour their programmes. The campaign and rally have their effects on polarizing party attachments and reinforcing candidate preferences. A significant aspect of the relation of the individual to his/her political environment is his/her exposure to the influence of propaganda.

Level of modernization and urbanization

It has been argued that there is a positive correlation between these two processes and the political participation. Both the processes help in increasing the extent of political communication which leads to greater political awareness. Urbanization as the first stage of the modernization process tends to raise literacy; increased literacy tends to increase the media exposure; and increasing media exposure facilitates wider political participation. Economic modernization affects political participation through socio-economic status. High socio-economic status is conducive for an increase in the overall amount of political participation. Modernization not only tends to increase class-based participation but also decrease communal-based participation. A majority of lower-class persons generally vote for the left parties while the majority of the upper and middle class persons vote for the rightist parties.

Political socialization

Socialization is the mechanism by which people become aware about the issues and ideology and come to identify with a particular political party. It affects both the quality and amount of participation. The politically aware are usually better able to relate their social values to their political opinions, to achieve stable, internally consistent belief systems.

Modes of participation

There are varieties of ways in which people can participate in the political processes of a society. Some are directly associated with the electoral sub-system and some are with other political activities. Activities like voting, campaigning, etc., are some of the important modes of participation.

Voting

Voting is the most frequent citizen activity, especially in modern democracies. The scope and the outcome of voting is very broad affecting all the members of a society. Voting determines the leadership issues and policies of the party as well as the whole nation. The major criterion remains voting in elections which is consistently somewhat higher than the other measures.

Campaign activities

Participation in election campaign or other campaigns is another mode of political participation. Through this leaders can increase their influence over the citizens and the voter turnout. Campaign activity also produces collective outcomes.

Co-operative activity

People can also participate outside the electoral process— voting and election campaign. They can take part in groups or organizational activity to deal with social and political problems. In such activities they join hands with other people of the society to influence the actions of the government. The outcome of such a participation results in collective gain.

Non-Participation: Causes

The study of political behaviour also embraces the study of inactivity or non-participation. Research shows that apathy is extensive and politically concerned, public is everywhere in the minority. Why most of the people shun all forms of political participation or even if they do participate they involve themselves at the lowest level. The underlying important causes of non-participation are apathy, cynicism, feeling of alienation and anomic state of the society.

Apathy

There are some people who lack the necessary interest to participate in any political activity for this or that reason. This is the sign of apathy. It is a listless and indifferent behaviour which extends from inattentiveness to inactivity or withdrawal. Feeling of hopelessness induces apathy. Like many behaviour patterns, apathy is linked to a particular personality trait. People with apathetic attitudes towards life generally shun all types of political activities;

they even do not cast their vote in elections. Sometimes, general political environment is also responsible for making people apathetic towards political participation. It signifies the failure of the society to involve all members in their governance. It also marks the failure to inspire interest and loyalty in the people towards the political system. Electoral apathy is alleged to be affected by many factors such as frequency of elections, remoteness of polling booth, complexity of voting system, cumbersome registration procedures, etc. Apathetic people feel discouraged when they feel that they do not have any say in matters of decision-making. Apathy is a symptom as well as the cause of the weakness of the political system.

Cynicism

The attitude of cynicism develops because of the feeling that politics is a dirty game; that politicians are not to be trusted; that real power is enjoyed by unworthy people and that the individual is at the mercy of those people who can muster strength and successfully manipulate the things in their favour. People who held such types of attitude towards politics become cynical and feel that political participation in any form is a futile game. Cynic people become contemptuously distrustful of human nature. They also become skeptic about the actions and motives of others.

Alienation

Broadly, it denotes the estrangement of individuals from themselves and others. Robert Lane (1962) defined political alienation as 'a person's sense of estrangement from politics and government of his society … . It is a tendency to think of government and politics of the nation as run by others, for others according to an unfair set of rules.' He characterized those who are not active in politics as being 'politically divorced'. For such people, government is of very little use or of no consequences.

Anomie

It is a term coined by pioneer sociologist Emile Durkheim in his famous study of suicide. This is a social condition characterized by the breakdown of norms governing social behaviour. While the concept of alienation explains social action at the individual level, anomie is used to explain behaviour at the level of social structure. During anomic state of society (loss of cohesion and normlessness), people generally feel discouraged to participate in any political activity.

Voting Behaviour

Voting is the main form of political participation in liberal democratic societies. From a sociological perspective, the study of voting behaviour focuses primarily on explaining who votes and how they vote. The analysis of voting patterns invariably emphasizes on the determinants of why people vote as they do and how they arrive at the decisions they make. Early research pioneered by Paul F. Lazarsfeld and others (1967) concluded that voting depends primarily on socio-economic factors or people's location in social systems—their social class, occupation, gender, race, age, religion, ethnicity, family history of voting behaviour (political socialization) and membership in voluntary associations such as trade unions, recreational clubs, political parties and civic organizations. Political scientists have concentrated on the influence of political factors such as issues, political programmes, electoral campaigns, party loyalty (people's sense of identification with particular political parties) and voter's feelings about particular candidates, etc.

Various Approaches

A number of different (not mutually exclusive) approaches (models) have been used to explain voting behaviour. The major approaches may be distinguished as structural, ecological, social-psychological, rational-choice and radical.

1. Structural (or sociological) approaches concentrate on the relationship between individual and social structure, place the vote in a social context, and examine the effects of such variables as social class, language, nationalism, religion, and rural-urban contrasts on voting. This approach has placed much emphasis on the party identification and social class.
2. Ecological (or aggregate statistical) approaches relate voting patterns to the characteristic features of a geographical area (ward, constituency, state, etc.).
3. Social-psychological approaches relate voting decisions to the voter's psychological predispositions or attitudes, for example, his or her party identification, attitudes to candidates, and the like.
4. Rational-choice approaches argue that voting is governed less by group loyalties and class position than by individual's rational calculations of self-interest. These approaches attempt to explain voting behaviour as the outcome of a series of instrumental cost-benefit calculations by the individual.

   This model of voting behaviour sees the voter as a thinking individual who is able to take a view on political issues and votes accordingly. It rejects the notion that voting behaviour is largely determined by class affiliation or class socialization.
5. Radical approach regards class-based (structural) model as outdated and insufficient to explain contemporary developments and consider the rational-choice model as inadequate. This approach has suggested two main sources of influence which structure political alignments—(a) sectoral cleavages which separate people into groups with different

interests and priorities, e.g., public sector and private sector, and (b) dominant ideological messages which are conveyed mainly through the media and form 'political consciousness'.

Determinants of Voting Behaviour

Studies of voting behaviour have heavily used demographic variables, particularly income, occupation and education, for explaining both voting turnout and the direction of vote. These variables were related to frequency of participation and direction of vote and interest in politics, which, in its turn, had an impact on turnout. The idea of 'cross-pressure' is also applied to the analysis of voting behaviour.

Modern researches attach much importance to individual psychological processes like perception, emotion and motivation, and their relation to political action, as well as of institutional patterns, such as communication process, and their impact on elections. Renowned political scientist, Seymour Lipset (1960) has drawn certain conclusions of studies of many countries, such as Germany, Sweden, America, Norway, Finland and many others as under:

1. men vote more than women,
2. the better educated vote more than less educated,
3. urban residents vote more than the rural,
4. those between 35 and 55 vote more than the younger or older voters, and
5. members of organizations vote more than non-members.

In Britain, America and to some extent in other Western countries, class has constituted the single most important variable associated with the voting pattern. The pattern of voting behaviour found in these countries before the 1970s came to be known as *partisan alignment*. The idea of partisan alignment resumed that social class was the most important influence on voting behaviour and that the voters 'identified' with one party or the other. Recently, certain political and academic commentators took the view that the class politics of the 19th century and pre-Second World War capitalist societies was fast becoming an anachronism, that the death of class politics was imminent, and that the 'end of ideology' was just round the corner. The correlation between class and voting has become distinctly fuzzier today. Evidence in the last two decades have suggested that not only electoral political support has become less predictable and more volatile, but party loyalty has also become less stable and more blurred and problematic today.

Voting Behaviour in India

In India, studies on voting behaviour had been mainly undertaken under the auspices of Indian Council of Social Science Research (ICSSR). Nowadays, however, such studies are done by many governmental institutions (e.g.,

Institutes of Developmental Studies) and private agencies such as ORG, Chanakya, etc.

It is generally held that in national/state elections only nearly half of the electorate bother to vote. A large segment of voters do not vote. This fact is often noted and lamented. But there are social scientists like E.M. Lipset (1960) who argue that a low turnout of voters aids the democratic process. It indicates that there is a general argument on social matters and that people are confident that the outcome of an election will not disturb. A high turnout (as in the case of elections held after emergency), in contrast, is viewed as indicating a high level of conflict that threatens social stability and a possible breakdown of the democratic process.

But other social scientists view this differently. They see the alienated voters as apathetic who do not find elections a solution to the problems that most concern them. For them the present party system offers too little choice, too little change from the status quo. They feel that almost all parties are guided by their self-interests and not by the interests of common man. People, who are apathetic towards voting, feel they are without power. Directly or indirectly, this feeling is responsible for the low or decreased participation of the citizens in the elections.

The important determinants of voting are social class, occupation, race, ethnicity, age, gender etc. But, in India, generally, voters cast their vote on religion, caste or party lines. Party loyalty is based primarily on emotional basis. Most people are not well informed about political issues and do not choose a party on the basis of political opinions. Rather they support a party for traditional or emotional reasons—perhaps because their families have always supported that party—and they are then guided by the party's stand on the issues. In other words, voters are socialized by the political parties to view political issues in a certain way. Since independence, not only the level of political awareness is constantly rising among all segments of population, the level of identification with political parties or leaders is also increasing. The other factors that play an important part in deciding voting behaviour in India are community, religion and money.

Caste Politics: Voting and Political Pattern

Caste is one of the main determinants of voting behaviour in India. It has a decisive role in political matters, particularly voting. Voting provides an opportunity to castes to assert their influence. Just as in Britain, voting is class determinant, in United States, it is race determinant. Many scholars like D. Millar (1950), Key (1955), Colin Campbell (1960), Rajni Kothari (1970) and Norman Palmer (1976) and many others have written extensively on the relationship between caste and politics in India. Several empirical field studies of elections conducted by sociologists and political scientists have revealed that caste not only exerts influence during voting but also acts as an important factor. As early as in 1963, Christopher von Furer-Haimendorf (1982) observed, 'the very fact that a caste is capable of functioning as an effective pressure group, ... places it into a position of a political power, which cannot be ignored by the political parties depending for their mandate on the goodwill of the voters'. Politicians mobilize caste groupings and identities in order to organize their political power. They utilize caste identities and solidarities to cast votes on caste lines in every democratic institution from village panchayats to state assemblies and even parliament. Renowned sociologist, Andre Beteille once said that loyalties of caste are exploited in voting. Bhikhu Parekh, Professor at the London School of Economics (*India Today*, December 26, 2005) observed, 'it is hardly surprising that according to the 2004 national election survey, nearly 40 per cent of the people voted for their castes'. Long ago, Rudolph and Rudolph (1967) noted that democracy has entrusted caste an important political role in India.

Caste thus provides an extensive basis for the organization of democratic politics in India. It is the most convenient means of political mobilization. Elections are always fought utilizing the resources of caste loyalties.

1. The selection of candidates for a constituency is made on the basis of caste, who have a significant voice and can muster good number of votes in the constituency. Every party takes utmost care to see that its candidate in a particular constituency belongs to the caste which has a majority in the area.
2. People of a caste vote *en bloc* for a candidate of the same or different caste either in pursuance of the decision of Caste Panchayat or their leaders. They prefer a candidate of their own caste irrespective of the merits or demerits of the candidate.
3. When a single caste is not likely to be effective, alliances are made and that too on caste basis.
4. Even the office bearers of a political party are appointed on the basis of caste.

Commenting on the role of caste in democratic elections, S.C. Dube (1955) remarked, 'although nearly every political party in its platform slogans paid lip service to the ideal of a casteless and classless society, in actual selection of candidates due thought was given to the caste composition of the electoral districts'. What Dube said in 1955 still holds true today in 2013. These conditions are giving way to the process of partisan dealignment and class dealignment—a move away from consistent party identification.

Class Politics: Voting and Political Patterns

The distinctive feature of contemporary societies, including Indian society, it is argued, is that lines of social cleavage and conflicts persist, but they are no longer those of workplace and class. Social conflict has shifted away from workplace and class relations to civil society and non-economic, non-class forms of cleavage and identity. In case of India, it is mostly based on caste and religious lines. (Most of the elections from village panchayats to state assemblies and parliament are contested on caste and religious lines.) According to many theorists, there is a more fragmented character of modern societies with no single focus. New social movements, for example, reservation (for and against) movements, or feminist movements all reflect that their opposition is not towards capitalist society or capitalist social relations but they appeal on the basis of collective identity which transcends class and takes the form of gender identity, sexual identity, caste identity, membership of the planet (environmental movements), and the like. The concerns of feminist movements, for instance, are in principle addressed to all women, irrespective of class or country, on the basis that all women confront problems specific to them. Similarly, green movements, environmental pollution movements, peace movements and recently started health (yoga) movements are all explicitly concerned with human beings aiming at the forces of social transformation at the global level. Sociologists of all brands (perspectives) recognize today that the decline in the size of the industrial proletariat, after the fall of communist Russia, has waned the importance of class in organizing social movements.

The composition of these movements reflects clearly the fragmentation of class structure. These new social movements have attracted a broader cross-section of the population (like academics, social workers, students, retired and unemployed). In India, language and reservation movements, especially after the implementation of the Mandal Commission Report, *Chipko* movement, *Narmada Bachao Andolan* and the recent RTI and Lokpal Bill movements have taken place.

In the light of these facts, it is clearly tempting to say that 'class politics is dead' and to hail 'long live the politics of new social movements'. No doubt, new social movements have impacted significantly by challenging and extending the boundaries of conventional politics, but it would be premature to assume that class no longer plays (nor will pay) a part in shaping political identities and affiliations. Material inequality and disadvantage have become or are becoming more stark in many respects in both developed and developing countries, including India, in the past decade (especially after liberalization and globalization) as a result of government policies, so that class politics is unlikely to disappear completely so early. It remains to be seen whether or not the decline of class politics proves to be fatal. It is well to argue that we are moving into an era characterized by an absence of any dominant frameworks of political identity.

Power

The focal point of the study of political institutions is power and its uses. Although we think of the concept of power as being associated particularly with politics or so as to say political science, but it is, in fact, exists in all types of social relationships. For Foucault (1969), 'power relationships are present in all aspects of society. They go right down into the depths of society .... They are not localized in the relations between the state, and its citizens, or on the frontiers between classes'. All social actions involve power relationships whether it may be between employer and employee or between husband and wife (in patriarchal society). Thus, it is of fundamental importance for the sociology to study in its manifold ramifications. Sociologists are concerned with social interactions among individuals and groups and more specifically, how individuals and groups achieve their ends as against those of others. In their study they take note of power as an important element that influences social behaviour. Sociologists are today concerned to analyse the diverse nature of power and that complexities it creates in human relationships, especially between state and society.

In the very simple language, power is the ability to get one's way—even if it is based on bluff. It is the ability to exercise one's will over others or, in other words, power is the ability of individuals or groups to make their own interests or concerns count, even when others resist. It sometimes involves the direct use of force. Force is the actual or threatened use of coercion to impose one's will on others. When a father slaps the child to prohibit certain acts, he is applying force. Some scholars have defined it that it necessarily involves overcoming another's will. To summarize, it may be said that 'power is the ability of groups or individuals to assert themselves—sometimes, but not always—in opposition to the desires of others'. Many decisions are made without opposition because of the great power decision-makers wield.

According to Max Weber (1947), power is 'the probability that one actor within a social relationship will be in a position to carry out his own will despite resistance, regardless of the basis on which this probability rests'. He further writes, positions of power can 'emerge from social relations in drawing room as well as in the market, from the rostrum of lecture hall as well as the command post of a regiment, from an erotic or charitable relationship as well as from scholarly discussion or athletics'. It plays a part in family (husband and wife) and school (teacher and the taught) relationship also.

Thus, for Weber, power is the chance of a man or a number of men to realize their own will in a communal action even against the resistance of others who are participating in the action. Alvin Genldner (1970) noted that power is, among other things, the ability to enforce one's moral claims. The powerful can thus conventionalize their moral defaults. Celebrated sociologist Anthony Giddens (1997) sees, 'power as the ability to make a difference, to change things from what they would otherwise have been, as he puts it "transformative" capacity'. Power can be defined by saying that 'A exercises power over B when A affects B in a manner contrary to B's interests'. According to Steven Lukes (2005), power has three dimensions or faces: (1) decision-making, (2) non-decision-making, and (3) shaping desires.

For some social theorists, especially those linked to postmodernism, the very notion of large-scale macro structures of power has come under serious attack. For example, Foucault's conception of power demands that we should approach it in a micro way, seeing power in all social relationships, and working in specific ways in all kinds of particular institutional settings—whether the prison or the clinic. For Foucault, we must explore the intimate relationship between power and knowledge. Through his case studies of madness, medicine, prisons and sexuality, Foucault has highlighted the organization of knowledge and power. He argued that a new type of power, i.e., disciplinary power, has evolved during the 19th century. It is concerned with the regulation, surveillance and government. Disciplinary power is exercised in prison, schools and places of work. Disciplinary power operates at the expense of individual freedom and choice. In his opinion, notions like 'ruling class domination' simply obscure the micro-realities of power. Foucault's ideas fit very well with the shift towards diverse non-economic political struggles such as feminists demonstrations about 'control of bodies'. How far such conceptions of power/knowledge are useful as against the well-established approaches to power, such as Marxism, is a matter for debate among sociologists.

Types of Power

Max Weber (1958) believed that there are three (not one) independent and equally important orders of power as under:

Economic power

For Marx, economic power is the basis of all power, including political power. It is based upon an objective relationship to the modes of production, a group's condition in the labour market, and its chances. Economic power refers to the measurement of the ability to control events by virtue of material advantage.

Social power

It is based upon informal community opinion, family position, honour, prestige and patterns of consumption and lifestyles. Weber placed special emphasis on the importance of social power, which often takes priority over economic interests. Contemporary sociologists have also given importance to social status so much so that they sometimes seem to have underestimated the importance of political power.

Political power

It is based upon the relationships to the legal structure, party affiliation and extensive bureaucracy. Political power is institutionalized in the form of large-scale government bureaucracies. One of the persistent ideas has been that they are controlled by elites, that is, small, select, privileged groups. Political power concerns the activities of the states which is not confined to national boundaries. The networks of political power can stretch across countries and across the globe. Political power involves the power to tax and power to distribute resources to the citizens.

Besides, Weber's types of power, there are a few other types also which are as under:

Knowledge power

To Foucault (1969), power is intimately liked with knowledge. Power and knowledge produce one another. He saw knowledge as a means of 'keeping tabs' on people and controlling them.

Military power

It involves the use of physical coercion. Warfare has always played a major role in politics. Modern mass military systems developed into bureaucratic organizations and significantly changed the nature of organizing and fighting wars. According to Weber, few groups in society base their power purely on force or military might.

Ideological power

It involves power over ideas and beliefs, for example, are communism, fascism and some varieties of nationalism. These types of ideologies are frequently oppositional to dominant institutions and play an important role in the organization of devotees into sects and parties.

According to Michael Mann (1986), there are two types of power, viz., distributional and collective.

Distributional power

It is a power over others. It is the ability of individuals to get others to help them pursue their own goals. It is held by individuals.

Collective power

It is exercised by social groups. It may be exercised by one social group over another.

Sources of Power

There are three basic sources of power: force, influence and authority. These are explained below:

Force

As defined earlier, force is the actual (physical force) or threatened (latent force) use of coercion to impose one's will on others. When leaders imprison or even execute political dissidents, they thus apply force. Often, however, sheer force accomplishes little. Although people can be physically restrained, they cannot be made to perform complicated tasks by force alone.

Influence

It refers to the exercise of power through the process of persuasion. It is the ability to affect the decisions and actions of others. A citizen may change his or her position after listening a stirring speech at a rally by a political leader. This is an example of influence that how the efforts to persuade people can help in changing one's opinion.

Authority

It refers to power that has been institutionalized and is recognized by the people over whom it is exercised (Schaefer and Lamm, 1992). It is established to make decisions and order the actions of others. It is a form of legitimate power. Legitimacy means that those subject to a government's authority consent to it (Giddens, 1997). The people give to the ruler the authority to rule, and they obey willingly without the threat of force. We tend to obey the orders of police officer because we accept their right to have power over us in certain situations. Legitimate power is accepted as being rightfully exercised (for example, power of the king). Thus, sociologists distinguish power from authority. Authority is an agreed-upon legitimate relationship of domination and subjugation. For example, when a decision is made through legitimate, recognized channels of government, the carrying out of that decision falls within the realm of authority. In brief, power is decision-making and authority is the right to make decisions, that is, legitimate power.

Thus, there is a difference between authority and influence: (1) authority is an official right to make and enforce decisions, whereas influence is the ability to affect the actions of others apart from authority to do so; (2) authority stems from rank, whereas influence rests largely upon personal attributes; and (3) authority is based upon the status one holds, whereas influence is based upon the esteem one receives.

An admired institutional officer can have both authority and influence, whereas an unpopular officer has authority but little influence.

Types of Authority

Max Weber (1922) has identified three types of authority as described below:

Traditional Authority

It is the legitimate power conferred by custom, tradition or accepted practice. Traditional authority is 'hallowed with time', like that of a king, an established dynasty or a religious leader. It is based on an uncodified collective sense that it is proper and longstanding and should therefore be accepted as legitimate. In patriarchal societies, the authority of husbands over wives or of father over his children is obeyed because it is the accepted practice. Similarly, a king or queen is accepted as ruler of a nation simply by virtue of inheriting the crown. For the traditional leader, authority rests in custom or tradition (inherited positions), and not in personal characteristics.

Legal—Rational Authority

It is established in law or written regulations (formally enacted norms) that determine how the society will be governed. This is the form of authority found in workplaces, government, schools, colleges and most major social institutions. Leaders derive their legal authority from the written rules and regulations of political systems. It is this type of authority that characterizes modern bureaucratic organizations. Rational authority rests in the leader's legal right rather than in family or personal characteristics.

Charismatic Authority

Weber also observed that power can be legitimized by the charisma of an individual. Charisma is 'a certain quality of an individual personality by virtue of which he is set apart from ordinary man and treated as endowed with supernatural, superhuman, or at least specifically exceptional powers or qualities' (Weber, 1922). Charisma is, therefore, unusual spontaneous and creative of new movements and new structures. The term 'charismatic authority' refers to the power made legitimate by the exceptional personal characteristics of the leader, such as heroism, mysticism, revelations, or magic. Charisma allows a person to lead or inspire without relying on set rules or traditions. Charismatic authority is generated by the personality and the myths that surround the individual, like that of Jesus, Mahatma Gandhi, Martin Luther King, Hitler and Pandit Nehru. A charismatic leader attracts followers because they judge him or her to be particular wise or capable. It may be pertinent to mention that the charismatic authority is socially bestowed and may be withdrawn when the leader is no longer regarded as extraordinary.

Weber used traditional, legal—rational and charismatic authority as ideal types and as such are usually not found in their pure form in any given situation. In reality, particular leaders and political systems combine elements of two or more of these forms. To Weber's three major types of authority, some contemporary scholars have added a fourth type, *professional authority*

(authority based on expertise). The authority of physicians or atomic scientists, botanists, etc., is the example of this fourth type of authority.

Politics

Politics is the social process through which collective power is generated, organized, distributed and used in social systems. It is embedded within particular social structures and processes. It takes place in societies with distinct social and economic arrangements. The sociological analysis of politics concerns the study of political behaviour within a social context, exploring the relation of politics to the entire social structure in which it is embedded. Politics is about power and it occurs when there are differentials in power. Thus, any social relationship that involves power differentials is political. According to Anthony Giddens (1997), 'Politics concerns the means whereby power is used to affect the scope and content of government activities.' Power in society directly affects power in the state, but the impact of politics also changes the distribution of power in society. In most societies, politics is organized primarily around the institution of the state, although this is a relatively recent development. The sphere of the political may range well beyond that of state institutions. According to renowned political scientist Harold Lasswell (1936), politics may be defined as 'who gets, what, when and how'.

Although the concept of politics is most often associated with governing institutions at international, national, regional and community levels, sociologically it can be applied to virtually any social system in which power plays a significant role. We can, therefore, apply this concept about 'office' politics, university politics, the politics of family life and sexuality, or even the politics of art, music and films. In reality, the concept of politics draws attention to the fact that every social system has a power structure, not just those whose social functions are formally defined in terms of power. Since all areas of social life involve elements of power, politics cannot be seen as involving merely 'what politicians do'. Instead, any process involving the exercise of control, constraint and coercion in society is potentially political.

Sociologists, especially political sociologists, use the term 'politics' to refer to those processes that people use to resolve conflicts between private interest and common good that occur with the institutional framework of government. According to Max Weber, 'Politics means striving to influence the distribution of power, either among states or among groups within a state.' Though individual personalities are important in determining the course of political events, still sociologists studying politics have only passing interest in personalities. Their inquiries are much more likely to concentrate on the nature of political power, the major political and economic decisions are made (both within and outside of government bodies) and the differences that exist in the political socialization and ideologies of different social classes.

Power Structure

How society is governed? Where power resides? There can be many answers to these questions. There is always a divide between the rulers and the ruled or those with power and those without power even in normally democratic societies and institutions. In a totalitarian state, power may vest in the hands of one or a few persons, while in a democracy, it is assumed to be possessed by the people. The elite theory of power structure holds that every society is ruled by a minority group which has power or influence over others and is recognized as being in some way superior. This group of people occupies a position of privilege or dominance in the society. At the heart of this theory, there is clear presumption of the inadequacies of the average citizen. As a consequence, democratic systems must rely on the wisdom, loyalty and skill of their political leaders, not on the whole population. Wealth, family background (inheritance or heredity) and social connections help in many cases to win the label of the elite in general, and of the governing (political) elite in particular, for persons who otherwise held no claim upon it.

Who is Elite?

In every society, ancient or modern, tribal or rural, it is seen that there are a select few, however chosen, who always seem to rule over the many. These select few in the hands of which rests the power are known as elite. The word 'elite' was first used in the 17th century to refer to the superiority of a particular thing or object. Later on, it was started using for those people who have some distinct qualities by which they are differentiated from the general mass of people. These people form a minority group or category within a society, who may be socially acknowledged as superior in some sense and who influence or control some or all of the other segments of the society. It is a group of persons who in any society holds position of eminence. More specifically, it denotes such persons who are eminent in a particular field of activity. Thus, the people who have the highest indices in their branch of activity (painting, singing, sports, literature, politicking, etc.) are referred to as 'elites'. Recently, political scientist H.D. Lasswell (1952) has defined elites 'as those with greatest access to and control of values ... holders of high positions in a given society'. There are as many elites as there are values. For example:

(a) Political Elites (Elites of Power)
(b) Business Elites (Elites of Wealth)
(c) Social Elites (Elites of Respect)
(d) Intellectual Elites (Elites of Knowledge)
(e) Religious Elites (Elites of Faith)

Thus, elite is any socially visible small category of individuals who possess some valued characteristics, in, such as intellectual ability, high administrative position, military power, moral authority or charisma and who consequently have high prestige and widespread influence. Such individuals may and may not manifest some degree of group cohesion and may simply influence or be initiated by the ordinary people (non-elite). Their high position in the society enables them to transcend the ordinary environments of ordinary people and to make decisions having major consequences. Elites are also defined as those minorities which are set apart from the rest of the society by their pre-eminence in one or more spheres of distribution of various privileges and benefits. Parry Geraint (1969) defines elites as 'small minorities who appear to play an exceptionally influential part in political and social affairs'. Contrary to this view, T.B. Bottomore (1966) defined elites as 'functional', mainly occupational groups, which have high status in society. Vilfredo Pareto (1963) who popularized the concept of elite defines it as 'people in a society who possess in marked degree, qualities of intelligence, character, skill and capacity of whatever kind'. According to C.W. Mills (1956), 'Elite is composed of men who have the most of what there is to have money, power and prestige who are able to realize their will, even if others resist it.'

The distinguishing features of elites may be summarized as under:

1. A minority group or individuals, most influential and prestigious stratum in society.
2. Minority taking majority decisions. They are sometimes known as decision-makers of the society.
3. Outstanding performance in a particular field.
4. Shaping the values and attitudes of their followers.
5. Hold influence or/and power over non-elites.
6. Self-conscious, cohesive and exclusive nature of elite.

To conclude and answer the question, who is elite, we may state that an elite is any group or category of people in a social system that occupies a position of eminence, privilege or dominance by virtue of their superior qualities or specialized knowledge in any field of social activity.

In India, caste also plays an important role in the determination of elite status (especially political elite status), besides money, power, prestige, intelligence, education, etc. Many studies conducted by sociologists and political scientists revealed that higher caste has an extraordinary advantage over the middle and the lower castes but this situation is fast changing. The reservation policy enabled individuals from the lower castes (so-called untouchable castes) and OBCs to emerge as leaders.

Elite Theory of Power

Vilfredo Pareto (1848–1923) and Gaetano Mosca (1858–1941) are the two pioneer social scientists who propounded the elite theory of power. Pareto, who made popular the concept of elite (it is usually said that idea of elite was derived by Mosca), said, 'so let us make a class of people who have the highest indices in their branch of activity and to that class give the name of elite'. So we get two strata in a population: (a) a lower stratum—the non-elite (common men), and (b) an upper stratum—the elite.

Thus, elite is the highest stratum within a society. This stratum is composed of those persons who are recognized outstanding and are considered the leaders in a given field of competence. This class of elite (highest stratum) is further sub-divided into: (i) a governing elite; and (ii) a non-governing elite. The 'governing elite' comprises of individuals who directly play some considerable part in government. They wear labels appropriate to the particular political offices, namely, ministers, legislators, president, secretaries and so on. The 'non-governing elite' are those people not connected with the governmental activities.

Pareto takes existence of ruling class for granted and concentrated on the 'circulation of elite'. He was basically concerned with the consequences of 'open' and 'closed' elites. He argued that a closed aristocracy inevitably decays, producing cleavage and dissension within its own ranks. When it happens new elites emerge from other classes to give leadership to revolutionary change.

Gaetano Mosca, an Italian jurist and political theorist, expounded the familiar thesis that all human societies were always and everywhere ruled by a controlling social class and thus these are always divided between rulers and ruled. He contended that, whatever the form of government, power would be in the hands of a minority who formed the ruling class. Explaining the contentious historical division between the ruling class and the class that is ruled, Mosca explained the rule of minority over the majority by the fact that it is organized and is usually composed of superior individuals. The minority is organized for the very reason that it is a minority. Members of a ruling minority have some attributes, real or apparent, which are highly esteemed and are very influential in the society in which the minority lives. Mosca also introduced the concept of the *sub-elite*. This group is composed of civil servants, managers of industries, scientists and scholars and is also known as 'new middle class'.

Thus, there is a general agreement between Pareto and Mosca about the concept of elite as a minority which rules over the majority or the rest of the society. This class of people have the direct influence over the decision-making process by influencing the decision-makers. However, there is a difference between both the scholars regarding the nature of elites. Pareto stresses the universality of distinction between ruling elite and the masses. Mosca, on the other hand, distinguishes between masses and elite only with reference to the Marxian theory of economic classes; otherwise he says that the elite itself is influenced and restrained by the various social factors. Pareto has reserved his comments for the modern notions of democracy, while Mosca has recognized and to some extent appreciated the special characteristics of democratic elites.

Pareto differs from Mosca when he insists that the character of democratic elites is not qualitatively different in democracy. Mosca, on the other hand, lays emphasis on the pluralistic character of democratic elites and postulates a reciprocal relationship between the rulers and the ruled, instead of simple dominance by the rulers over the ruled. Mosca identifies the political class with men of property in general, and sometimes with intelligentsia, but most often with the political personnel in government. Not only this, as written earlier, Mosca introduced a concept of sub-elite in his theory, we do not find in Pareto's theory such distinction of elites.

Power (Political) Elite

Two more recent studies concerning elite power structure need explanation. In his pioneer work, *The Power Elite* (1956), American radical sociologist C.W. Mills identified three key institutions—the major corporations, the military and the government. Those who occupied the command posts in these institutions formed these ruling elites. Mills termed them as *power elite*. Mills argued that there are three types of elites: the political elite, military elite and the industrial elite. Together, these made up the power elite. 'The power elite is composed of men whose positions enable them to transcend the ordinary environments of ordinary men and women; they are in positions to make decisions having major consequences ... . They are in command of the major hierarchies and organizations of the modern society. They rule the big corporations. They run machinery of the state and claim its prerogatives. They direct the military establishments. They occupy the strategic command posts of the social structure in which are now centred the effective means of the power and the wealth and the celebrity which they enjoy.' Mills explained that elites rule in institutional rather than psychological terms. He rejected the view that they have superior qualities or psychological characteristics which distinguish them from the rest of the population. Instead, he argued that the structure of institutions was such that those at the top of the institutional hierarchy largely monopolized power.

Political elite come from a higher stratum that actually dominates and occupies all important posts of political command who influence major political decisions. In the words of Harold D. Lasswell, 'the political elite comprise the power-holders of a body politic' (Lasswell, Lerner and Rothwell, 1952). These power-holders include the leaders and the social formations also. This class of political elites performs all political functions, monopolizes power and enjoys all the advantages that political power brings. Elites believe that the power structure of any society is determined by the character and the abilities of its political leadership.

For 'political elite' different terminologies are used by different theorists. Mills has used the term 'power elite', Pareto has called them 'governing elite,' Marx referred to them as 'ruling class,' Riesman as 'veto group' and Floyd

Hunter as 'top leaders'. Sociologist Floyd Hunter in his book *Community Power Structure* (1953) described in detail an economic elite—mostly corporate executives and bankers—who by informal communication and because of a similar social point of view agree on the major decisions affecting the lives of all the citizens of the community. This is an elite which is not known to the community and does not usually hold official positions, and its decision-making activities are not publicly visible. Robert Michels (1949) interpreted elite structure of society as 'iron law of oligarchy' meaning the rule of the few over the many. He argued that social organization creates a set of conditions that makes oligarchy possible.

Ruling Elite and the Ruling Class

Ruling elites are sometimes distinguished from ruling classes in terms of the fluidity of their membership and the way outside pressures influence them. A ruling elite is sometimes simply that section of the dominant class with political power. Sociologist G. William Domhoff (1967), not completely agreeing with the power elite model of Mills, argued that the nation (US) is controlled by a social upper class 'that is a ruling class by virtue of its dominant role in the economy and government'. Unlike Mills, Domhoff was quite specific about who belongs to this social upper class. He contends that members of this class dominate powerful corporations, foundations, universities and the executive branch of government. Both theorists, in line with a Marxian approach, assume that the rich are interested only in what benefits them financially.

The difference between class and elite rests largely on the fact that classes are defined in terms of economic position and power, whereas elites may have a non-economic base.

Political Elite and Marx

Power elite model is, in many respects, similar to the work of Karl Marx.* But it differs from the Marxian concepts of dominant or ruling class and class struggle which are central to the Marxian ideas of fundamental changes in social structure. Marx argued that industrial societies were dominated by relatively small number of people who owned factories and controlled natural resources. In his view, government officials and military leaders were essentially servants of the capitalist class and followed their wishes. Therefore, any key decisions made by politicians inevitably reflected the interests of the dominant bourgeoisie. Marx, thus, believed that society is ruled by a small group of individuals who share a common set of political and economic interests.

* Basically Marxian approach is non-elitist and views relation between the elite (privileged class) and the non-elite (unprivileged class) as based on conflict.

The elitist theorists (Vilfredo Pareto, Gaetano Mosca, Max Weber, Robert Michels and others) believe that the power structure of any society depends on the abilities of its political leadership. It is political skill—or lack of it—which determines who will rule and who will be ruled. Marx, on the contrary, says that the political leaders from whatsoever class they may be drawn, will be representative of the dominant class. The elitist theorists were highly critical of the Marxian theory of social classes on two vital points. Firstly, they say that the Marxian conception of ruling classes is erroneous and demonstrates the continual circulation of elites which would prevent the formation of a stable or a close ruling class in modern industrial societies. Secondly, they disagreed with the Marxian prediction of future classless and egalitarian society. They viewed these ideas as impossible since, in every society, there will always be hierarchical division and the upper stratum of this division which is, and must be in minority, will actually rule.

Ruling elite maintains some level of exclusiveness and also remains accessible to the influence of the non-elite and recruits new personnel from it in order to retain its power position. In contrast, the Marxian analysis indicates continuing and increasing inaccessibility or polarization of the dominant and subordinate classes. Ruling elite theory places less emphasis than the Marxian class theory on economic power as the sole form of power and allows a variety of basis to the superiority of the ruling class. Yet, reminiscent of Marx, Mills argued that corporate rich were perhaps the most powerful element of the power elite.

Regarding the displacement of elite, Marxists provides an economic explanation for it. They are of the opinion that class change occurs as a consequence of major change in the economic system. This change is caused due to the introduction of new productive techniques to meet economic demands. With the change in the mode of production, the class which is associated with the new mode of production dislodges the class which is associated with the new outmoded productive forces from its position of predominance. Pareto's theory of circulation of elite to some extent resembles and modifies the Marxian view of materialistic interpretation of history. In his words, 'The history of man is the history of the continuous replacement of elites; as one ascends, another declines.'

Displacement of Elites

How elites are displaced? Analysing this question, Mosca, Pareto and the Marxists have given different answers. The Marxists have provided an economic explanation for this. They said that class change occurs as a consequence of major change in the economic system. This change is caused due to the introduction of new productive techniques to meet economic demands, which results into the change in the mode of production and its associated class system. The new mode of production dislodges the class which was associated with the outmoded productive forces from its position of predominance. This process brings changes in the structure of dominant power elite in a society.

Mosca, though to some extent followed the Marxian logic, but he was less deterministic in his approach. He relates changes in elite domination to the rise of new interests or social forces in a society. According to Mosca, the composition of the elite will reflect the balance of social forces in society. A ruling class has to take cognizance of the socio-economic changes; otherwise, it will be thrown out in no time. New intellectual discoveries and new ideological movements are bound to affect the composition of class and the dominance of elite in a society.

Altering the materialistic interpretation of history propounded by Marx, Pareto proposed the theory of 'circulation of elite'. According to him, it is not the economic power alone but the change in the religious and humanitarian sentiments that also help in the displacement of elites. Thus, there is a circulation between different categories of the governing elite and the rest of population.

Circulation of Elites

How elites maintain their positions? Answering to this question, Pareto argued that the ebb and flow of history could be explained by the circulation of elite. It implies that with every change in the society, new men of money or power replace old ones. This displacement takes place independently irrespective of its character and motivation. The concept of circulation of elite refers to the tendency for societies to be ruled by elites regardless of how democratic their political institutions might appear to be. While an election may bring with it the appearance of change, the interests of privileged (elite) groups are rarely if ever truly threatened by either party.

Opposition to the Marxists, who advocated the notion of equality, elitist theorists claimed that there would always be an elite inevitably. According to Pareto, two types of elites alternate in power: the 'lions' committed to specific beliefs and values, are succeeded by the 'foxes' who are most adaptive and flexible. When the elite is no longer open to talented men from below, the social order decays.

There are two broad sets of factors to explain the downfall and replacement of elites: (a) structural factors, and (b) socio-psychological factors. The dominant minority changes along with structural change in the society. The change in the attitudes or abilities of the elite may also lead to elite displacement or circulation of elites. In moving from one group to another, an individual generally brings with him/her certain attitudes, sentiments, values and inclinations that he/she has acquired in the group from which he/she comes.

Elite and Democracy

Historically, the elite theory has tended to be undemocratic. Of the two major early 20th century elite theorists, Pareto and Mosca, it was the latter who argued that the political elite could be generally representative of the people or 'masses'. The party system, free elections and pressure group activity were means to ensure representatives.

Is democracy 'real' only once every five years when people cast their vote? Robert Dahl (1982) believes that elections play an important part in controlling government and he also cites a second major means by which leaders are made answerable to the people. 'The election process is one of two fundamental methods of social control, which operating together, make governmental leaders so responsive to non-leaders that the distinction between democracy and dictatorship still makes sense. The other method of social control is continuous political competition among individuals, parties or both.'

Liberal elite theorists have stressed the necessity of leadership by political elite almost as much as its representative nature. In large societies only minority can be involved in leadership. The prime general function of leadership is to create social consensus and establish social order. Talcott Parsons (1951) argues that leaders use power for the general good or for collective goals. Defence of the country and maintenance of law and order are two examples of the necessary use of power for the general good. Marxists deny that in capitalist society it works for the common good. On the contrary, it merely misleads the working class.

Lord Hailsham, Britain's Lord Chancellor, speaking on the role of elites in democracy (Second Jawaharlal Nehru Memorial Lecture, 1971) said, 'It is a notable fact in history that democracies which have been most remarkable for success and survival have had in fact the most powerful elites.' Dilating upon the paradox, the necessity and the dilemma of an elite in democracy, he said that while those with elite behind them succeeded, democracies which have not had a powerful elite devoted in their loyalty to the regime have been among the most prone to succumb to dictatorship.

In every democracy, there is a danger of the dominance of mediocrity over merit. Rule by majority may degenerate into what Lord Hailsham called *philistinism,* the persecution of talented minorities and the pretence that goes with it that value judgements are simply expressions of subjective opinion incapable of measurement. When Coriolanus exclaimed that 'beast with many heads led me away,' he was tragically echoing the plight of every outstanding leader who is overthrown by the caprice of the majority. In the purely political field, the ups and downs of leaders are incidental to the electoral system, but the more serious problem for democracies is how to produce and protect an elite which provides genuine leadership to the people without constituting itself into a privileged class. It is obvious that even the avowedly socialist societies, with their loud accent on quality, have had to create their own privileged elites, whether they are described as party cadres or technocrats.

In democratic societies, the quest for merit is closely related to the principle of equality of opportunity. No democratic society can claim to be truly democratic until it has secured real equality of opportunity for every one of its citizens, regardless of class, caste and sex. But, by the same time, there must be no bar to the achievement of the highest positions by virtue of one's abilities and competence. Above all, there must be freedom for that inevitably small minority which in any society represents new ideas, new values and new adventures in thought and action. The creative thinkers and innovators are the real leaders of human progress in every field. If democracies neglect such people, they are plunging their future in peril. The crisis of democracy in many countries today, including India, is due to the absence of such leadership.

The question whether elites and democracy are incompatible is a very ticklish question and is difficult to answer in few words. Some scholars giving 'fatally superficial' answer said, 'everything depends on education'. But education does not solve all the problems and these will continue to exist at whatever level of literacy we choose to attain.

Political Elites in India

Up to the time of the introduction of the adult franchise in 1950 and for years later, the Indian political system was largely autonomous. During the struggle for freedom, the western-educated elite was dominant and it had no great difficulty in imposing its will on society because the Indian people were relatively passive. This remained true till Gandhi shook it a little. Characterizing the Indian elite, Yogendra Singh (2002) writes: 'Among the political elite, there existed a high degree of cultural and status homogeneity before independence. All of them came from upper castes and had an urban, middle-class background of English education. The top group was exposed to foreign culture and was educated there; hence their self-image in terms of expected roles was also that of generalist rather than a specialist. Following independence, this pattern of elite composition has considerably changed.' The momentum of the re-independence period, the strength of the Congress organization and the prestige of the governmental and party leadership enable these elite to dominate in the first two decades of independence, especially at the Centre. This elite was composed mostly by those who had a stable economic background, were highly educated, mostly belonged to upper castes, and were committed to societal interests.

The elite of this phase was not as highly politicized as we find today. They were mostly driven by nationalistic feelings having not much discriminatory attitude towards welfare work. But, as the people have become politicized through the spread of education, improved communication, economic progress and secularization, the long established dominance of the so-called political sufferers and selfless social workers was soon broken (in 1957 elections) and political power was snatched by the new breed of elites who were more or less vested interest oriented. These elites came from amongst land holders, traders, businessmen, professional persons, industrialists and social workers. Though these elites came to seek a greater role in policy formation, the older elites still remained influential. Both old and new elites changed their values to fit new emerging situations and to establish new relationships. For this new elite, politics was no more a means to serve the society but to serve themselves. Politics became a full-time profession for them. For some, it became a source not only to earn livelihood but to climb in the social ladder. They believed more in using the ties of kinship, caste and language to smoothen the way through the corridors of power.

Writing about the elite formation in India, Navlakha (1989) remarked that it is largely determined by the traditional social structure (particularly caste), religion, language, networks, income, occupational background, education, family background, etc. The findings of his study show that select social positions are usually taken by persons from select social strata. This select group controls the positions of prestige, power and responsibility. Jayaram (1990) noted that higher education is still under the grip of upper castes, hencc it is 'status stabilizer' rather than an invader on status rigidities.

Besides money, power, prestige and education, caste has become the most significant factor in the determination of elite status (especially political elite status) in the last few decades in India. Many studies conducted by sociologists and political scientists on political elite revealed that higher castes had an extraordinary advantage over the middle and the lower castes. Before independence, generally, the upper caste groups occupied the centre of the political stage. But, the situation is now fast changing. The reservation policy enabled individuals from the lower and middle castes, including scheduled castes, scheduled tribes and OBCs, to emerge as potent leaders. Since last few decades, caste has also been playing an important role in the selection of candidates for contesting elections from village panchayats to state assemblies and parliament. Due to the policy of reservation, many depressed and unprivileged castes, such as Mahars in Maharashtra, Jatavs in UP, and Yadavs in Bihar and UP, have not only climbed up in social hierarchy, but also assumed elite status. New elite structure has emerged in politics which is drawn from different castes. 'Entrenched' high castes are no more ruling the political scene. Thus, caste system which had only ritualistic function (including determining occupation and social status) assumes the new role of regulating political behaviour of the people.

Referring to trends of change in the political leadership (elite), Yogendra Singh (2002) pointed out: (i) there is increasing influence of rural-based political leaders; (ii) there is slight decrease in the influence of leaders drawn from various professions; (iii) there is significant increase in the number of persons belonging to the middle class; (iv) there is a greater articulation of regional and interest-oriented goals in political cultural ideologies; and (v) and there is slight breakdown in the exclusiveness of upper castes to the elite position. What was stated by Yogendra Singh about 25 years ago is true, with a slight change, even today.

Pluralist Model of Power Structure

Advocates of the elite model, such as Mills, Marx, Domhoff and other conflict theorists, see the nation as being ruled by a small group of individuals who share common political and economic interests. But several social scientists have questioned this model. They insist that power is more widely shared than the elite model indicates. In their view, a pluralist model, propounded by famous political scientists N. Polsby and Robert Dahl, more accurately describes the democratic political system. According to the pluralist model, 'many conflicting groups within the community have access to government officials and compete with one another in an effort to influence policy decisions' (Cummings and Wise, 1989). With reference to India, pluralists argue that the competition among various political parties, caste groups and other interest groups demonstrates the presence of multiple power centres in Indian politics. Nowadays government at the centre and in many states is formed by a coalition of several parties with different interests.

Robert Dahl, in his book, *Who Governs?* (1961) reported that while the number of people involved in any important decision was rather small, community power was nonetheless diffuse. Few political actors exercised decision-making power on all issues. Several other studies of local politics further document that monolithic power structures do not operate on the level of local government.

Like the elite model, the pluralist model has also been challenged on political and methodological grounds. The pluralist approach proceeds from the standpoint of actual decisions and initiations of policy within specific issue areas and has invariably failed to locate a ruling elite as Polsby says. But, the evidence indicates that centralized, fragmented, constrained, reversal and relatively uncoordinated decision-making is the rule. Domhoff (1967) re-examined the Dahl's study of decision-making and argued that Dahl and other pluralists had failed to trace how local elites prominent in decision-making were part of a larger national ruling class. Conflict theorists contend that these elites will not allow any outcome of the political process which threatens their dominance. Some theorists have also challenged this model on the ground that apparently pluralistic exercise in democracies may conceal the fact that some groups or interests actually dominate.

To conclude this discussion, we may emphasize one common point of the above two models that the power always remains unequally distributed in democratic political system. All citizens may be equal in theory, yet those high in the nation's power structure are 'more equal'.

Political Process and Political Parties

When people try to gain access to power and wield this for their own or group ends, they constitute the political process. The notion of a political process assumes that politics can be treated as an autonomous institutional sphere. But this view does not find much favour among contemporary sociologists. The study of this process focuses on the activities of political parties and interest groups, their internal organization, the nature of political decision-making, and the roles and background of politicians.

The sufficient diversity of interest, among those who compose a society, gives this interest an opportunity to combine. People will cluster into groupings which may be more or less formal or loosely organized. They do this in order to protect themselves in a better way and extend their influence to wider spheres. This organized group is known as *political party*. Political party is, thus, an organization of individuals whose goal is to maintain control of governmental power. Sociologically, this is an association of people who have like-minded ideas and ideologies in regard to the policies that a government should follow. Long back, the renowned political thinker Edmund Burke defined political party as 'a body of men united for promoting by their endeavours the national interest upon some particular principle in which they are united'. According to *Oxford Dictionary of Sociology* (1994), 'political parties are the organizational means by which candidates for office are recruited and ideologies are propagated.' These link the state to political forces in society, giving organized expression to interests and making them effective politically. Defining political parties, Anthony Giddens (1997) stated, 'a political party may be defined as an organization oriented towards achieving legitimate control of government through an electoral process'. In some situations, there may be political organizations which seek to achieve power but are denied the opportunity to do so through orthodox means. Political parties vary and can be distinguished by their structural forms, ideological orientations, leadership patterns, operational styles, programmes and strategies.

Since the state is the politically dominant and controlling force within a society, political struggles in a nation are struggles to influence the policies and decisions of the state. These struggles are generally organized by the kinds of groups known as 'political parties'—the most significant political groups. Max Weber said, parties 'live in a house of power' and 'are always structures struggling for domination' (cited in Girth and Mills, 1946). Political parties are not the only political groups that operate within the house of power. In most democratic countries there are many private and voluntary associations which influence political process. These include human rights groups, women's organizations, labour unions, environmental groups, chambers of commerce, manufacturers' associations, veterans' (senior citizens) associations and any other organized interest group in society. These are known as 'para-political groups'. These groups can and do operate in different ways, aiming their efforts at different targets.

Sociologists are concerned with political parties as social institutions/associations and relations between members, party leaders and the masses. Classical sociologist Max Weber contrasts a political party to class and status groups, arguing that the party does not represent class or status groups in society but is instead oriented towards achieving and holding power for its members.

Role (Functions) of Political Parties

In an age when large-scale organization is essential for successful social action, it is the organized group, and not the individual, that usually carries weight. Thus, in the political process of any political system, the party is an essential agency for social and political action. It is for the attainment of political power that parties strive. Political parties link the state to political forces in society, giving organized expression to interests and making them effective politically. This distinguishes political parties from other social groups in a political system. Underlying the main function of political parties, Joseph Schumpeter (1943) wrote, 'The first and foremost aim of each political party is to prevail over the others in order to get into power, or to stay in it.' In brief, the main functions of political parties are: (i) to assess the problems facing the country and suggest alternative suggestions, (ii) to educate the people in regard to these problems and stimulate them for political action (political socialization), (iii) to mobilize the people to participate in decision-making and party programmes, (iv) to critically evaluate the policies and programmes of other parties, (v) to mobilize the votes of non-members in elections, and (vi) to modify the goals, if necessary.

In the modern age, the political party is a key to political power in both the open (democratic) and closed (totalitarian) systems though their aims and character differ in both systems. In an open society, political parties compete for usurping political power as a game in which the rules are more or less commonly agreed upon. In the closed system, such competition for political power between parties normally is not allowed.

What is the role of political parties in the political process. There are two divergent views: (i) the liberal view, and (ii) the Marxist view.

The liberal view is that political parties, along with pressure groups and other interest groups, engage in competition for power as the representatives of different socio-economic groups in society. As a result of open competition, power in pluralist political systems is non-cumulative and shared. This view of the role of political parties in liberal democracies has been criticized severely.

It has been argued that certain groups dominate the political decision-making process, especially those who dominate in the economic realm.

While liberals emphasize the important role of political parties in representative democracies, neo-Marxists (like Adorno, Horkheimer, Marcuse) play down their significance. In their view, in capitalist societies, since the dominant economic power is also the ruling class, parliamentary politics is illusory, and simply an ideological strategy which diverts attention away from the real sources of political power. Many have argued that both Marxist and liberal views are unsophisticated. It is true that power may be concentrated, but it is possible for the ordinary people to influence political outcomes as we have seen in Bihar elections held in November 2005. In this respect, political parties are not inconsequential, but play an important role in the political process.

Types of Party Systems

Party systems take a variety of different forms, from the multi-party system at one extreme, to the one-party monopolistic system at the other. F. Von der Mehden (1952) considers political systems in terms of a continuum which include societies without parties, one-party non-competitive states, one-party semi-competitive systems, two-party democratic systems and multi-party democratic systems. In developing societies, David Apter (1965) has argued that the one-party system is crucial for the formation of national identity and rapid economic development, since a single political authority is more effective in the management of industrial development. In western capitalist societies a pluralistic competition between parties for political support is more pronounced. Whether a two-party system or a system involving more parties flourishes depends in large part on the nature of electoral procedures in a given country.

Systems with two dominating parties like that of Britain (Labour and Conservative) and United States (Democratic and Republican) tend to lead to a concentration on the 'middle ground', where most votes are to be found, and exclude more radical views. The parties in these countries usually cultivate a moderate image, and sometimes come to resemble one another so closely that the choice they offer is slight. Two-party system is compatible with liberal democracy. To organize the individuals in a democracy, political parties and other groups develop. Two parties tend to dominate the political system where elections are based on the principle of winner-takes-all. The candidate who gets the most votes wins the election, no matter what proportion of the overall votes he or she gets. Citizens are expected to participate on the political process by voting, debating issues, joining one of the two political parties or remaining independent.

Multi-party systems allow divergent interests and points of view to be expressed more directly, and provide scope for the representation of radical alternatives; on the other hand, no one party is likely to achieve an overall majority. This leads to coalitions which can suffer from an inability to make decisions because of major conflicts or rapid succession of elections and new governments, none able to stay in power for long. We have in India multi-party system and consequently coalition governments. A multi-party system is often thought to be a system which is compatible with the pluralistic features of capitalist society.

Parties in Western political systems tend to polarize between left-wing and right-wing ideologies. For example, the Labour Party in Britain seeks support mainly from the working class and certain sections of the middle class. The Conservative Party is traditionally the party of middle and upper classes. The Labour Party was regarded as socialist in the sense of seeking nationalization and in sharp contrast to clearly free enterprise policies of Conservative Party (Thatcher government of 1979). But this distinction of ideological positions is now no more applicable and both the parties actually behave rather similarly when in government. In India, we also find more or less the same position adopted by Congress and BJP in regard to economic matters.

Political Parties in India

In India, there are three main types of political parties: (a) parties which function on national basis (e.g., Congress(I), BJP, CPI, CPI(M), BSP); (b) parties which function in a few states (e.g., SP, Janata Dal); and (c) parties that function in one state (e.g., TDP, DMK, AIADMK, Akali Dal, Trinamool Congress, etc.). There are also some parties which have been recognized as political parties by Election Commission but do not hold power in any state.

In India, we do not have two-party system. At the time of independence there was only one majority party—Indian National Congress—and some small parties like CPI which had a limited hold in some states. To advance the personal ambitions of some leaders, these parties later on split to form new parties. Since 1980s, there are too many political parties in India. This situation forced for the coalition governments in the states as well as at the centre. Though there are multiplicity of political parties and coalition governments in many European countries, yet these do not make government in power ineffective and unstable as in India, e.g., Deve Gowda government (1996) and Gujaral government (1997). A unique feature of several political parties in India is that they mobilize caste support. Many studies relating to the role of caste in politics (Rajni Kothari, 1970; Andre Beteille, 1966; S. Verba, B. Ahmad and Anil Bhatt, 1971) showed that political parties mobilize castes for functioning and seek their support in winning elections. Yet another characteristic of Indian political parties is the disease of defection of elected members from one party to another. This has happened both at the centre and also in states.

It is worthy to note that there are parties which do not much differ in ideology and programmes and sometimes their manifestos are also more or less the same, except in wording, yet each party has its own flag, party office and shows allegiance to different personalities (leaders).

Political Socialization

Political parties stimulate large number of people for political action (strike, dharna, rally, demonstration, etc.) and political participation (voting, selection of leaders). They help in reinforcing the existing political attitudes and beliefs or inculcate new ones through the process of political socialization. It is 'the process of induction into a political system—by acquiring information on political symbols, institutions, and procedures, learning the role of a passive or active member of the polity and internalizing the value-system and ideology supporting the whole enterprise' (*Oxford Dictionary of Sociology*, 1994). In brief, political socialization is the process by which individuals acquire political culture, political attitudes and develop patterns of political behaviour. This involves not only learning the prevailing beliefs of a society but also accepting the surrounding political system.

Political socialization performed by political parties may be of two kinds:

(a) Reinforcement of existing political culture, i.e., the norms, values, symbols, attitudes, beliefs and rules that guide a political system, which are determined jointly by the history of the system and the experiences of its members.

(b) Initiation of significant change in existing political attitudes and beliefs—new patterns of political culture.

For political socialization, political parties sometimes organize formal training programme for their members. In such programmes, lectures by their seasoned leaders and renowned ideologues are delivered, necessary literature pertaining to their ideology is distributed and films relating to their ideology are shown.

It is generally seen that this process of political socialization starts from childhood quite unconsciously. Children often learn about political parties, especially about their symbol and slogans in the family. And, this process continues when children enter school. By the time children finish school and college education, they develop political attitudes that shapes their political behaviour in adult life. Later on, this process of learning continues through audio and visual mass media, which reinforces childhood socialization. Thus, family school and media play the role of principal institutions in one's political socialization.

Interest/Pressure Groups

Decision-making is the essence of political dynamics. Decisions involve compromises among conflicting interests of social groups and political parties. Decision-making is the resultant of the activity of organized groups and interplay between social configuration, ideology and government organs. Interest groups play an important role in decision-making—an indispensable part of the modern governmental process. It allows orderly expression of public opinion and increase political participation. The role played by pressure/interest groups has now been widely recognized by political scientists the world over. These groups often try to influence the legislature to promote, withdraw or repeal legislation.

Well-known political scientists Harold Lasswell and Abraham Kaplan (1950) remarked, 'A group is an organized aggregate and an interest group is an interest aggregate'. A group is recognized as some legitimate and established section of society. 'An interest group is a voluntary association of citizens who attempt to influence public policy' (Schaefer and Lamm, 1992). David Truman (1951) has described interest group as 'a shared attitude that makes certain claims upon or through institutions of government'. According to *The Blackwell Dictionary of Sociology* (1995), 'an interest (or pressure) group is an organization whose purpose is to influence the distribution and use of political power in a society'. Broadly speaking, an interest group is an association of people having mutual concern about a wide array of economic, social, cultural, political, religious or any other issues. Such associations may have specific and narrowly defined goals which may be moderate or local or national and international in scope. These groups are vital part of the political process. The political process is seen to result from a large number of competing interest groups.

Interest groups are occasionally referred to as pressure groups (often known as lobbies), implying that they attempt to force their will on a resistant public. When an interest group seeks governmental aid in achieving its own ends and succeeds in influencing governmental policy to its advantage, then it becomes a pressure group. Pressure groups are formally constituted organizations which are designed at least partly to bring pressure to bear on government, civil service and other political institutions to achieve ends that they favour. According to Harry Eckstein (1960), 'By pressure group, we mean any organized group which attempts to influence government decisions without seeking to exercise the formal powers of government.' These are the groups of persons, employers, or other organizations joining together to represent the interests of a particular sectional group vis-à-vis governments, the public at large or other interest groups (*The Concise Oxford Dictionary of Sociology*, 1994). Broadly speaking, pressure groups may be any group attempting to bring about any change in the working of any formal organization—state, government or any other social or economic organization. They are private association to influence mass public policy. When it makes through or upon any institutions of government, it becomes a political interest group.

Pressure groups, lobby groups and interest groups are distinct from clubs or social groups, in that their explicit purpose is to mobilize public opinion in support of their aims and to put pressure on decision-making bodies to agree to and support their demands—be they are for continuation of the existing state of affairs or for some change or innovation. Pressure groups are notorious for being anxious to strike but afraid to wound.

Types of Pressure/Interest Groups

A distinction is sometimes drawn between protective and promotional groups, the former defending a section of society, the latter promoting a cause. While the first category includes trade unions, professional associations, employer and trade associations, etc., the second category includes societies seeking to prevent cruelty to animals or to children, environmental groups, anti-abortion groups, groups arguing for or against censorship, and the campaign for nuclear disarmament. The distinction between the two types of interest groups is not watertight.

Pressure groups may be of different types. They may be temporary or permanent, large or small, powerful or weak. The pressure groups (interest groups also) formed on the basis of economic, professional, academic and ideological considerations have become a part of the democratic process. These groups often attempt to spur legislative and political actions that protect or advance the group's economic or other interests.

Professional and trade associations, groups representing industrial, commercial, religious, agricultural and other interests of the community, including activist groups like the ecology movement, are all examples of *interest groups*. Interest groups may represent one segment of the public (such as pensioners or students or women), or they may represent a value (for example, anti-abortion), at which point they shade into ideological or moral crusades.

From the conflict perspective, the limitation of interest groups is that they tend to represent mainly the wealthier or better-educated sections of the public, leaving the poor and minorities largely unrepresented.

There are literally thousands of interest groups everywhere, some of them are well organized and the others not. As stated above, these groups cover the interests of diverse segments of societies like business groups, farm organizations, religious organizations, etc. There is a marked difference between the political parties and interest/pressure groups so far their objectives and nature of functioning are concerned. They may co-exist with political parties or may develop into political parties by adopting a more open, less restricted platform. Many attempts have been made to classify these groups on different bases. There is an attempt to divide these groups into two categories: (a) situational, and (b) attitudinal. Situational groups are non-ideological, specific and utilitarian in character. These are concerned chiefly with the defence and improvement of the particular situation into which their members are put. On the other hand, attitudinal interest groups are primarily ideological, diffuse and somewhat utopian in their outlook. They are based on an idealistic view of social welfare.

Lasswell and Kaplan (1950) have categorized interest groups as follows: (1) special interest groups, (2) general interest groups, (3) expediency interest groups, and (4) principled interest groups. Gabriel Almond (1970) has categorized these groups in terms of structural forms as under:

1. Institutional interest groups (army and business associations).
2. Non-associational interest groups.
3. Associational interest groups.
4. Anomic interest groups (terrorist organization, criminal gang).

Interest/Pressure Groups in India

Pressure tactics and methods have become an integral part of the political process in India. The techniques of organized pressure, through mass campaigns, demonstrations, strikes, civil disobedience (*satyagraha*), *gheraos* and *bandhs*, have been frequently used by interest groups. Myron Weiner (1962) has rightly observed that the very frequency with which mass action has succeeded in vetoing government action, or in positively modifying public policy, has strengthened the public belief that such measures are both desirable and effective. Violence and anomic activities have become an instrument of interest articulation in the so-called developing nations, including India.

Like many Asian and African countries, India has a good number of interest groups, although they are not large in number and are different from those in western counties. In India, interest groups are organized mainly around traditional loyalties to caste, religion, community and also with regional, linguistic and ethnic loyalties. They are important forces in India. Weiner has termed them as 'community associations'. In his words, 'Indian social system has both hierarchical (caste and class) and horizontal (tribal, religious, linguistic) groups from which political expressions follow suit'. Of course, groups constituted on the basis of occupational and economic interests, such as trade unions, peasant organizations, teacher-student groups, women's associations, dalits (scheduled castes and tribes), organizations, businessmen(commercial) organizations, etc., have become very important in modern India. An interesting feature of interest groups in India is the 'caste lobby'. These lobbies try to influence the interests of particular castes and demand support for their members in the legislatures. Religion also plays an important role in furthering the interests of the followers of particular religion. There exists a bond of relationship between Indian legislators and religious leaders.

Interest groups of business class in India are extremely powerful. Business associations like Chamber of Commerce, All India Manufacturers Organization and many others developed after independence for the purpose of protecting and promoting their interests. Like these organizations, there have been some organizations, such as Kisan Sabha, to look after the interests of the peasants. Besides, different political parties have also established their own peasant organizations which are being used as political weapons. Similarly, political parties have also their own trade unions, student organizations and youth wings, which act as pressure groups in their respective fields. In India, such community associations are more effective and powerful than the economic and occupational organizations. By means of 'lobbying', behind-the-schemes bargaining, propaganda and information and electoral support, persuasion and threats of violence, these groups make tremendous pressure on the government political process. The overwhelming political clout of these powerful lobbies discourages participation by the individual citizen and raises serious questions.

Political Mobilization

'Mobilization' means the 'gearing up' of groups for collective action. Collective action can simply be defined as people acting together in pursuit of interests they share, for example, gathering to demonstrate in support of their cause. Mobilization helps a group to acquire sufficient resources (political support, supplies of material goods and weaponry) to make collective action possible. Neil Smelser (1962) in his *Theory of Collective Behaviour* and Charles Tilly in his *From Mobilization to Revolution* (1978) included mobilization as one important components of collective action. Collective behaviour begins when mobilization for action takes place. There are three main kinds of mobilization—vertical, horizontal and differential.

As elsewhere in the world at a comparable stage of political development, India has also been witnessing all the above cited three kinds of political mobilization. Traditional elite mobilize political support in local societies that are organized on the basis of rank, mutual dependence and the legitimacy of traditional authority. In rural India, which accounted for about 70 per cent of the population, traditional elite had consisted almost exclusively of the leaders of the dominant castes in 1970s (this situation has much changed today). The strategy of vertical mobilization remained viable for them until dependents, tenants and clients became sufficiently to be mobilized by ideological appeals to class or community (caste) interests and sentiments.

Horizontal mobilization, on the other hand, involves the marshalling of popular support by class or community leaders and their organizations. This challenges the 'vertical solidarities and structures of traditional societies' (Rudolph and Rudolph, 1967), irrespective of the nature of appeal. It is the character of horizontal mobilization that accounts for the difference between political modernization in India and the West. In India, political parties mobilize caste support. In this endeavour, caste associations enable their members to pursue the same goals of social mobility, political power and economic advantage as political parties, trade unions and other kinds of associations in the West pursue. While in our case, a central structure for this purpose has been a transformed version of caste, in Western countries class has played the dominant role in this type of mobilization.

Finally, differential mobilization is the handwork of political parties. Their appeal to stable but internally differentiated communities is based on ideology as well as sentiments and interests.

Globalization and Politics

While the term 'globalization' emerged in 1960s, as a tendency it existed in ancient and medieval times. Empires of great territorial reach have an ancient history in the world. Throughout history, trade, war and conquest have ensured that there has never been an isolated society. In its new or modern form it started in 16th century with the voyages of discovery. What is new is the range, scale and intensity of global links which shrinks space and time through the widespread network of modern speedy communication and transportation systems. Global networks have brought about the supersession of the nation-states resulting in the formation of a 'world society'. The world today is witnessing an intensification of circuits of economic, political, cultural and ecological interdependence.

Generally, the process of globalization is linked with economic transformation. But it cannot be tied with economic phenomenon. It is not only transforming economic life but it has also brought changes in non-economic life—in political sphere, in the family, in lifestyles and consumption patterns and even the very notions of individual identity. Thus, it may be defined as 'a social process in which the constraints of geography on social, political and cultural arrangements recede and slowly and gradually the political boundaries of nation-states become insignificant in a globalized world'.

Today, many of the economic, political, military and ideological powers that shape our lives work across nations—and increasingly they operate on a global scale. Multinational corporations and certain global and inter-governmental institutions developed a global power and presence. This has given rise to what Daniel Bell (1987) has observed, 'a crisis of the territorial nation-state'. He said that the nation-state is 'too small for the big problems of life, and too big for the small problems of life'. One of the main champions of globalization of politics, David Held (1993) has argued that nation-states have ceded some sovereignty to larger entities in order that a range of 'big' problems may be dealt with more effectively. Thus, WTO and IMF deal with trading and financial matters, NATO with military matters and in the case of Western countries, the European Union (EU) deals with a wide range of political, social and cultural issues. It is important to add that the United Nations is also a key global organization with a wide remit. Besides political matters, it is active in humanitarian, health (WHO) and education (UNESCO) fields, ecological issues, problem of terrorism, pollution and peace-keeping activities.

Chapter 11

Educational Institutions

KEY FEATURES

- What is Education?
- Aims of Education
- Education and Other Social Institutions
- Education: Different Viewpoints
- Functions (Objectives) of Education
- Education, Social Stratification and Inequality
- Meritocracy
- Education and Economy
- Education, Social Change and Modernization
- Education in India
- Women's Education in India
- National Policy on Education in India
- Right to Education
- Privatization of Education and Elite Reproduction
- Privatization of Education in India

Educational institutions are those which seek to socialize individuals in society or introduce them in formal ways into their social and cultural world. The main purpose of all educational institutions and practices is to make possible the acquisition of skills, the formation of habits, the learning of techniques, the comprehension of relationships, and other behaviour or characteristics of human beings. Education, whether formal or informal, is necessary for transmitting the accumulated cultural heritage from one generation to the next. Education, like all other institutions, helps a society to solve its problems. Education and society are closely related. Both affect each other. Societal values mould the education system and in turn new innovations in educations give direction to the society in future. It plays a central role in developing human resources and in migration and vertical mobility. The expansion of education also helps in reducing social inequality.

Basically, education is a pedagogical concept concerned with the techniques of the inculcation and management of knowledge. Sociologists study it as a branch of knowledge in the form of 'sociology of education' dealing chiefly with the organization of school system, functions of education, factors affecting social class and caste differences in attainment of education, social mobility and class, education and inequality etc. How education equalizes as well as enhances inequality and reinforces the capitalist system are the main topics of study in the modern sociology of education.

What is Education?

Education is a process of learning in which some people consciously and favourably teach while others adopt the social role of learner. In small pre-literate societies, such as hunting and gathering bands, informal education was widespread. Young child learned knowledge and skills, what they needed to know about the day-to-day life and trade of their parents informally by imitating the older members of society. In these societies, the training of new members about the adult roles was accomplished informally, but in more complex societies of industrial type required great and diverse formal systematic training for which societal educational institutions of modern types slowly developed, along with the specialized role of teacher. Education supplements what families can teach their children at home needed to function in the complex modern world. Education in its modern form involving the instructions of pupils within socially constructed school premises gradually began to emerge with the spread of printed material. Yet until about a century and a half ago, and even more recently, the children of the wealthy (kings, aristocrats, zamindars, etc.) were frequently educated by private tutors. Most of the population continued to have no schooling whatsoever until the first few decades of the 19th century when systems of primary schools began to be started in Europe and elsewhere.

Aims of Education

In simple terms, education is the skill of reading, writing and calculating. Education at primary level is the learning of the 'three Rs', i.e., reading, writing, and arithmetic, at secondary level of character building, at higher secondary level is understanding society, and at college/university level is skill training for the jobs. Schools do more than teaching 'three Rs'. They do attempt to control and regulate students' behaviour, reflecting the dominant social values of society. In modern society people not only have to be furnished with basic skills, such as reading, writing and calculating, but they must also have a general knowledge of their physical, social and economic environment.

The process of industrialization and expansion of cities served to increase demands for specialized schooling. People now work in many different occupations and work skills can no longer be passed on directly from parents to children. Formal education has become a necessary condition for obtaining modern jobs and is also one of the status indices to objectively assess the status mobility. Modern education widens people's mental horizons. When people can read, and learn things that can be done differently, they are presumably more ready to imagine the effects of change in their lives and to work for changes which they think will benefit them.

In a nutshell, the main aims of education are:

1. to gain knowledge;
2. to know the ways how to live life in a righteous way; and
3. to develop consciousness about his rights and duties towards society and fellow men.

Education and Other Social Institutions

Education is basically a social institution which has corresponding links with other social institutions—political, economic, family, and religious—of society. Not only this, education and other social institutions influence each other also. Educational institutions do not exist in a vacuum. No educational system can operate without being influenced by the norms and values of society. On the other hand, education is a powerful instrument which shapes the future destiny of society. Education, in its modern form, is the process of teaching and learning, usually at school, college or university premises. Educational sociologists looked at schools as agencies of cultural production and purveyors of a hidden curriculum. They have contended that a wide range of material, cultural and cognitive factors likely to depress intellectual development. Feminists sociologists have begun to investigate the role of school in reinforcing gender stereotypes among children. Gender differences have recently attracted the attention of sociologists. It was found that girls do better than boys until adolescence. The results of Secondary/Senior Secondary Board examinations reveal that girls get good grades at these examinations.

Education: Different Viewpoints

Education has become a vast and complex institution throughout the world. It prepares citizens for various roles demanded by other social institutions, such as the family, government and the economy. Both functionalists and conflict theorists view education differently. Functionalists stress the importance of education in transmitting culture, maintaining social control, promoting social and political integration and bringing about or stimulating social change and modernization. It also accelerates the process of human progress. This approach dominated the analysis of education in the early post-war decades. Since 1970s it has been severely criticized. Critics from the New Right movement have focused on the charge that schools and colleges fail to prepare people for jobs. Not only this, education divides the society into educated and uneducated, and this division has its own repercussion on society. It creates as well as reinforces existing social class inequality.

To conflict theorists, however, education is a means by which powerful groups prevent change. Schools stifle individualism and creativity in the name of maintaining order and, thus, the level of change promoted by education is relatively insignificant. They view education as an instrument of elite domination. They believe that educational system is used by the elite to maintain their social position. They teach children elite values and norms so that everyone believes that the position of elites and inequality both are justified. Elite children usually receive higher credentials and move into elite jobs, whereas those from the lower classes do lower jobs, thus preserving class-related inequalities. They also say that education functions not for the good of the society (masses) but for the good of elites (classes).

Reformers value education, of course, for its own sake—for the opportunity it provides for individuals to develop their abilities and aptitudes. Yet education has also consistently been seen as a means of equalization. How far this has happened? Many studies (e.g., Coleman's *Equality of Educational Opportunity*, 1966) have been done to answer this question. Its results are clear: 'education tends to express and reaffirm existing inequalities for more than it acts to change them' (cited in Giddens, 1997). Christopher Jencks' *Inequality*, published in 1972 reviewed some of the empirical evidence on education and inequality and concluded that educational reforms have only minor effects on existing inequalities.

Functions (Objectives) of Education

Education is more than a means to individual advancement; it is often seen as a solution to social problems, such as delinquency, poverty and unemployment, and as the key to a more civilized, more democratic and more prosperous society. Education, as an institution in various parts of the world, seeks to fulfil its functions of transmission of cultural heritage, social and political integration of society by moulding the individual to conform to norms, socialization and personal development in various ways that are socially acceptable and culturally defined. Broadly, education helps the students to achieve 'the ability to get along with others' and also 'learning to think for oneself'. In one of the documents of UNESCO (1973), it was declared that education is 'to know, to possess and to be'. How education functions to serve the individual and society?

What are the expectations of people about the educational system? We will discuss these questions in the following pages.

Education and Socialization

Human organism is not genetically programmed like all other organisms. Its specific behaviour is not provided by some set of inherited instincts. Instead, all human beings have to go through a complex learning process and this learning process is called *socialization*. This process encompasses both types of learning—informal and formal. Informal learning starts from childhood and ends with the life. It usually takes place as a part of everyday activity. Formal learning, on the other hand, is associated with the acquisition of specific skills, such as reading and writing, which usually are acquired in schools, colleges and other educational institutions.

Education has been accepted as one major agency of socialization and teachers and educational institutions as socializing agents. Pioneer sociologist Emile Durkheim wrote in his book, *Education and Sociology* (1922): 'Education consists of a methodical socialization of younger generation.' Structural-functionalists argue that it reinforces the socialization process that started with the family. There are scholars who regard socialization and education as synonymous. It helps children acquire complex skills and the knowledge necessary to function in the world through such courses as history, geography, social studies, and science subjects. In addition, students learn the values of the larger society. Most obviously, teachers tell their pupils formally what to do, how to eat, dress and speak, as well as what values they should hold. Students learn to tell time, be punctual, to co-operate with others, to achieve group goals, and to obey the rules necessary for a smooth-running organization. According to Yogendra Singh (2002), 'Education is that part of total socialization through which we learn those roles that are based on derived needs. Thus, we call it as a process of secondary socialization.' Both Durkheim and Marx emphasized that in order to survive, societies need to socialize their young to accept dominant norms and values and this function is performed by educational institutions. Durkheim particularly stressed on the role of ritual in forming patterns of behaviour and in reinforcing values. Thus, school assemblies might involve rituals in which national patriotism or a belief in a particular God or Goddess (for instance, Saraswati) is expressed and strengthened such as singing of national anthem, prayer and other national or religious songs.

Transmission of Culture

Besides providing fundamental information such as basic reading, writing and other skills needed to make one's way through a highly complicated world beset with many problems of life, education also transmits cultural heritage and society's values such as honesty, trust and concern for others. Much early schooling is concerned with transmitting norms regarding good citizenship—cleanliness, rules of the road, respect to elders, discipline, punctuality, etc., from one generation to the next. We learn respect for social control and reverence for established institutions, such as religion, family, government and economy. Through textbooks school children are taught to pay respect and bestow reverence to national leaders like Mahatma Gandhi, Jawaharlal Nehru, Swami Vivekananda, Bhagat Singh, etc.

While Durkheim emphasized that certain aspects of a common culture (for example, patriotism, respect for parliamentary democracy) are passed on to all members of a society through education, the contemporary French Marxist sociologist, Pierre Bourdieu analysed the role of the educational system in the reproduction of culture. He stressed that schools, in conjunction with other social institutions, help perpetuate social and economic inequalities across the generations. He argued that formal school curriculum is only one part of a general process of cultural reproduction, whereby schools influence the learning of values, attitudes and habits. Thus, 'hidden curriculum' plays a significant role in cultural reproduction.

Maintaining Social Control

In performing the manifest function of transmitting knowledge and preparing students for future career, educational institutions go far beyond these functions. They teach standards of proper conduct in public life (e.g., keep left on the road) which sometimes are quite different from the rules of behaviour in their families. Education prepares young people to lead orderly life as adult by introducing them to the norms, values and sanctions of the larger society. They learn general rules of society—punctuality, discipline and responsible work habits essential in their future career position—during schooling. Thus, schools serve as a transitional agent of social control.

Enhances Social Cohesion

Through standardized and uniform curriculum, education exposes all pupils—whether they are Hindu, Muslim, Christian or Sikh or belong to working class, middle class or upper class—central values of society and thus helps in building a cohesive society. Education, thus, serves the latent functions of promoting social, cultural and political integration by transmitting a diverse population composed of different racial, ethnic, caste and religious groups into a society whose members share, to some extent at least, a common identity and ensure fundamental agreement on basic human values.

Helps in Individual Development

Education fosters personal development and self-fulfilment. It encourages the individual to develop his/her mental, physical, emotional, and spiritual talent to the full. It also equips the individual with the knowledge, skills, construction of identities and official titles (e.g., Ph.D., M.D., M.S., I.A.S.) and training necessary for effective participation in labour force. It provides necessary knowledge and skills which enable an individual to operate ideally in the society and also contribute to its efficient functioning. It not only helps in broadening the mind for its occupational returns but it is liberating and fulfilling also.

Development of New Knowledge

The main function of educational institutions of higher learning is not only to develop new knowledge but also verify the existing knowledge to improve the quality of life in our society and thus aid in human progress. Numerous sociological studies have revealed that increased years of formal schooling are associated with openness of new ideas and more liberal social and political viewpoints. Sociologist Robin Williams (1955), for example, points out that better educated people tend to have greater access to factual information and diversity of opinion. According to Schaefer (1976), education can make one less likely to champion of outmoded beliefs and prejudices and more likely to promote and accept social change.

Bestowing Status

Functionalists and conflict theorists both believe that education performs the important function of bestowing status. Kingsley Davis and Wilbert Moore (1945), in their discussion of stratification, noted that society must distribute its members a variety of social positions. Education can contribute to this process by sorting people into appropriate levels and courses of study that will prepare them for appropriate positions within the workforce. Conflict sociologists view bestowing of status in a little bit different way. They stress that schools sort pupils according to social class background and thus help in perpetuating social inequalities in each new generation.

As an Agent of Change

Education can stimulate or bring about desired social change. Recently, the NCERT has proposed for the teaching of sex education at the school level in response to the soaring AIDS and abortion (female child feticide) cases. Affirmatives action (reservation) in education has been endorsed as a means countering caste and sex-based discriminations. Education also promotes social change by serving as a meeting ground where each community's distinctive beliefs and traditions can be shared.

Career Preparation (Placement)

Education develops the skills necessary to earn the living. Some schools and colleges offer students training in specific skills and courses. Educational institutions guide them into occupations most appropriate to their abilities and society's needs. This is why most of the people view education as a means for preparing future career. These people believe that the main purpose of education is to help the individual find a job, achieve a promotion or become a better citizen. The education system helps to develop the human resources of a modern industrial society. The fact that industrial societies have a plurality of occupations with varied levels of skill necessitates a sophisticated mechanism to select individuals according to their talents and train them for the job they can most effectively perform. Education helps in the selection of people in terms of their talents and abilities for appropriate roles (jobs) in adult life.

Today, a college degree or diploma has become virtually a minimum requirement for entry into the paid higher and lower (technical and non-technical) jobs in India and elsewhere. This change reflects the process of *credentialism*—a term used to describe the increase in the lowest level of education needed to enter a field. Credentialism is one symptom of the growing trend of professionalization of occupations. Max Weber anticipated such possibilities as far back as in 1916 (Girth and Mills, 1958).

This function of education has come under severe attack from several quarters. Critics have argued that whatever is taught in the schools—be it algebra or human biology—has little direct connection with the tasks that the pupils face when they enter employment. There are not enough jobs for the increasing educated persons. Moreover, education is not much rewarding to women and lower class people. In India and elsewhere, men earn more than women with the same level of education. But this situation is fast changing. The status of one's college also increases earnings.

Enhances Social Mobility

Education increases higher rate of social mobility and life chances in the society. Formal education allows a person to enter more prestigious occupations and gives greater opportunity for job mobility and advancement. By enhancing social mobility, it helps in pursuit of greater equality in society. Thus, it operates as a means of social engineering also, though this point is heavily contested in the work of American sociologist Christopher Jencks

(1972). Studies point out that illiteracy increases inequality and prevents occupational as well as social mobility.

Education, Social Stratification and Inequality

The development of education has always been closely linked to ideals of mass democracy. Reformers value education, of course, for its own sake for the opportunity it provides for individuals to develop their abilities and aptitudes. Yet education has also consistently been seen as a means of equalization. Universal education, it has been argued, will help reduce disparities of wealth and power by providing able young people with skills to enable them to find a valued place in society. How far education has been successful in achieving this goal? Sociological studies conducted to answer this critical question have openly argued that education tends to express and reaffirm existing inequalities far more than it acts to change them. The term 'inequality' here simply refers to the existence of socially created inequalities which is known as 'social inequality'. It is not biologically based.

Though it is a bare fact that all human beings are not born with equal physical and mental ability and proficiency, yet a society, if so wishes, can provide equal opportunities to all its members for achieving goals and aspirations of their life. Sociologists are not much concerned with inborn inequalities based on sex, age, bodily strength or quality of mind, but are concerned with inequalities in conditions of existence (Béteille, 1966). This inequality can be filled in to some extent through the efforts of a society by providing equality of opportunity to all.

How is education related to equality of opportunity? Equality of opportunity for achieving one's social standing is a recent idea, recognizing the importance of education in it. Achieving merit and ability is possible through education. Though education does not guarantee high status and positions to all people, yet it plays an important role in equalizing opportunities in three ways (Gore, 1994):

1. by making it possible for all those who have the desire to be educated and the ability to benefit by that facility;
2. by developing a content of education which will promote the development of a scientific and objective outlook; and
3. by creating a social environment of mutual tolerance based on religion, language, caste, class, etc., for providing equal opportunities of social mobility to all individuals in society, and for securing good education.

Do expansion of education (especially secondary and senior secondary education) help to iron out class differentials? As seen in general, it has benefited to some extent the depressed classes (SCs, STs and OBCs). They found a pattern of unequal access to the more prestigious schools. But class inequality grew more severe as pupils moved up the educational ladder. A boy or girl from upper class or higher middle class, compared with a working class (SC, ST), has more chance of entering school and university. Thus, the educational system helps perpetuate social and economic inequalities across generations. These class differentials can be reinforced by privatization of education, where money has a great role to play in perpetuating this disparity.

Of course, education is not the only channel to social mobility and class, cultural and family background, and parental and other support, etc., are also important variants but lack of education is bound to prove a great handicap in mobility. A study conducted under the aegis of ICSSR in 1974 indicated that illiteracy increases inequality and prevents occupational as well as social mobility. Many other studies conduced in this field also reiterate the idea that education works as a powerful instrument of equality and mobility.

Though education is an important means to upward mobility, it is not always open to all. In most countries, including India, students must pass qualifying examination(s) to gain admission in various courses, such as engineering, medical, architecture, MBA, etc. This system is known as *sponsored mobility*. Secondly, only those students can get as much education as they are willing and able to pay. The costs of remaining in school are enormous because students are dependent on their families longer and they lose additional years of income.

Education plays a very important role in maintaining the stratification system and justifying the unequal distribution of wealth. Like other social systems, schools reflect stratification and sometimes can be a cause of it. The schools that children attend can have an enormous influence on their life chances. Those who attend first-rate elementary (nursery or primary) and secondary schools usually are selected for professional courses (engineering, medical, etc.) and get high-paying jobs. Some scholars contend that schools (preparatory, nursery, primary) are biased in favour of high-middle and upper class students. It is seen that these schools are segregated by socio-economic class. Upper class children join the best private schools, while in government schools mostly pupils from lower status background are admitted.

While functionalists believe that education bestows status upon the recipients, conflict (Marxist) theorists argue that this bestowal of status causes differences in society. They stress that schools admit pupils according to social background, thus preserving class-related inequalities. According to this perspective, society is based on an unequal distribution of advantage and is characterized by a conflict of interests between the advantaged and the disadvantaged children from lower class and castes (SCs, STs and OBCs) who are much less likely to attend the private schools that give better chances for a good career. Although the educational system helps certain poor children (for example, children of SCs, STs and OBCs) to move into middle class professional positions, it denies the most disadvantaged children the same educational opportunities afforded to children of the affluent class. Thus, schools tend to preserve social class inequalities in each new generation. French sociologist Pierre Bourdieu (1993) named this process as 'cultural reproduction'. Through this concept of cultural reproduction, he established that schools reinforce variations in cultural values and outlooks picked up early in life; when children leave school, these have the effect of limiting the opportunities of some, while facilitating those of others. Paul Willis (1977) carried out a fieldwork study in a school in Birmingham (Britain) which reinforced this long established notion that working-class kids get only working-class jobs. Moreover, educational opportunities open to working-class students are limited than to the wards of service class (managerial and professional class). Education creates the conditions for the reproduction of inequality, that is, education helps to justify in people's minds a system of inequality and to reconcile them to their own position within it. How does schooling do this? As long as most people believe that education gives everyone a fair chance to prove their worth and as long as privilege and disadvantage are widely believed to stem from fair competition in the educational arena, then inequality may appear to be justified by different levels of educational attainment.

But, the above notion of Willis is not fully correct. There are many studies carried out in a number of countries which do not substantiate the findings of Will's study. These studies have demonstrated that social and family backgrounds are the major influences over school performances. Many studies have reaffirmed the findings that educational and occupational attainment is governed mainly by family backgrounds and this helps in perpetuating the existing inequalities.

Meritocracy

In a democratic system based on the allocation of position or occupation according to merit is seen as a ladder of opportunity to the children of weaker section to climb. Equal opportunities in education are believed as the key to a more open society. In this context, Michael Young coined the term 'meritocracy' (in his book, *The Rise of the Meritocracy*) 1961 to refer to a social system in which status is achieved through ability and effort (universal criteria of merit), rather than ascribed criteria of age, gender, caste, class, race, inherited wealth or other such particularistic or inherited advantages. In this system, people can move freely up or down the occupational hierarchy according to personal merit. The term 'meritocracy' implies that the meritorious deserve any privileges which they accrue. In a meritocracy, the educational system would ensure that individuals are allocated to a position befitting their ability and being born into a humble home would be no barrier to success. The goal of equality of opportunity through the educational system, with the most able rising to the upper echelons, leaving intellectual dullards to carry out humble manual work. Young attempted to force the extreme consequences of a society which fully implemented the goal of equality of opportunity through the educational system.

Education and Economy

There is a close relationship between education and economy. According to functionalists, it is the needs of economic system (industrialism) which shape the educational system. On the other hand, followers of conflict model, Bowles and Gintis (1976) and others argued that the education system reflects the organization of production in a capitalist society. There is a correspondence between the nature of work and the nature of schooling. Capitalist societies are characterized by persistent inequality and by relationship of subordination and domination between social classes. According to Bowles and Gintis, inequalities cannot be explained by reference to the distribution of intelligence; instead, these are the inevitable result of capitalist relations of production, in which the means of production are privately owned and all other people must compete in the market place to earn a living. Thus, class inequality is a necessary feature not of all societies, but of capitalist societies only. Education (schooling) plays an active part in reproducing inequality across generations. Sociologists Glenna Colclough and E.M. Beck (1986) pointed three factors that contribute to the role of education in maintaining social class differences:

1. public versus private schooling;
2. economic disparities between school and communities; and
3. tracking of students into curriculum groups.
   (Tracking here refers to the practice of placing students in specific curriculum groups on the basis test scores and other criteria). This type of classifying students into certain groups is not done in Indian schools.

The idea that education system reproduces class inequalities automatically is not shared by many scholars of conflict tradition. Whatsoever may be the relation between education and economy, it is well recognized that education plays a very important role in promoting economic growth and efficiency as we are witnessing here in India today. The expansion of education after the adoption of the policy of liberalization (privatization) in 1990s has boosted the Indian economy.

Education, Social Change and Modernization

Is there any relationship between education, modernization and social change? How education brings social change in society? What role education plays in the generation of the process of modernization? These are a few questions to be answered while analysing the relationships between education, social change and modernization.

Education is but one determinant factor in the processual dimension of social change. It is a bare fact that formal education is one of the main and important agents of socialization. School teaches not only reading, writing and other skills but how to think and behave in given ways also. They imbibe new values, attitudes, expectations and aspirations in them. Teachers as agents of change impart specific values, aspirations and attitudes to the children.

The school (college) with its graded curriculum provides the possible environment for learning certain attitudinal orientations for bringing changes in the social structure of society. The change is brought about by changing the content of education by making necessary changes in the curriculum. The forerunners of social reform in India, like Ram Mohan Roy, Ravindra Nath Tagore, Swami Vivekanand, Swami Dayanand Saraswati, Mahatma Gandhi and others, who were exposed to western education, emphasized values of egalitarianism, secularism, humanism, liberty, justice, brotherhood and gender equality. They worked for the removal of caste restrictions, untouchability and the *purdah* system. The new educational system played an important part in undermining ritual restrictions imposed by rules of purity and pollution: first, by promoting new ideas, beliefs and values; and second by its association with open and secular institutions in which interchange could no longer be regulated by ritual, rules and restrictions. In the colleges, the law courts, the hospitals, the banks and the offices, people have to operate according to procedures that made the old restrictions of purity and pollution appear anachronistic, cumbersome and obstructive.

Education is a potent force to affect social mobility in the society. It gives definite advantage to the educated person when he or she seeks the job in the employment market. Increased education leads to a better job, though this point is contested. It is said that family background, for example, is more closely related to further occupation and the level of education (Jencks, 1979). An increasing proportion of business executives come from families of high economic status (Keller, 1968). Similarly, it is often said that education is not as rewarding to women and the children of low castes, as it is to high caste men in India. These and many such generalizations do not hold good today in 2012 when much has changed in the contemporary world in the face of globalization and modernization. These facts might have been true in the last mid-century. Not only this, education represents an important way of effecting intergenerational mobility.

Achieving merit and ability is possible only through education. Though education alone does not guarantee high status and higher positions to all people, yet without education an individual is unlikely to achieve social mobility. M.S. Gore (1994) observed that acquiring technical expertise, occupying high administrative office and learning a new profession are some of the avenues for the achievement of monetary success and social esteem in society.

Education is related to equality of opportunity. While accepting this basic fact, as said above, that all human beings are not equal in ability, skill and proficiency, what Béteille (1977) has called inequalities in 'conditions of existence', yet providing equal opportunities to all people for achieving their goals and aspirations is necessary. This will not only enhance social mobility but also indirectly help in reducing poverty in society. The effort of a society, which seeks to equalize opportunity, may take many forms such as the provision of educational facilities, reservation of seats for the students of weaker sections (SCs, STs, OBCs and women) in the educational institutions, giving bank loans to the needy poor students on nominal rate of interest with liberal conditions of payment, and the like.

Modernization is the most overwhelming feature of the contemporary human society. It is a process of change in social, economic, educational and political systems drawn especially from the societies of Western Europe. It may be described as 'social change involving the elements of science and technology and their far-reaching effects on social values, social behaviour and practices'. It involves change based on rationality. It has varied facets and dimensions which cannot be encompassed in a few words. But here our purpose and understanding the process of modernization can be attributed to increasing levels of schooling and literacy, the development of mass media, increasing social and geographical mobility, the development of a very high level of technology, systems of transportation and communication, more and more urbanization, change from agricultural occupations, growth in per capita income, increasing division of labour and specialized roles, declining extended family and so on.

Education in India

If we look into the early history of Indian (Hindu) society, we find that in ancient India education was modelled on the *gurukula* system in which emphasis was placed on the direct relationship between the *guru* (teacher) and the *sisya* (pupil). This system of education laid emphasis on austere life and concentrated on the teaching of Vedic literature. It was mainly devoted to the teaching of theology, philosophy and philology. Education was all comprehensive spreading from philosophy and spirituality to the teaching of cannons of art of day-to-day life. Education was used to be given on the varna basis. The Sudras and women both were excluded from the right to education. Vocational trainings, if any, were used to be given by old members of the family and community.

In the medieval (Muslim) period, it was the 'madarsa' system which ruled the educational scene. The schools (*madarsas* and *pathsalas*) were conducted almost exclusively by *maulvis* for Muslim students and by Brahmin priests for Hindu students. There was really no change in the outlook of people towards education in this period also because the Muslims, like the Hindus, were traditional in their outlook and laid great emphasis on religions and philosophical education rather than secular education. Of course, one should not forget that secular education received an impetus even in Western Europe only after the 17th century, and more recently since the 19th century when the idea of scientific knowledge emerged.

In this period, religious leaders and priests were often the only available literate groups, using their knowledge to read and interpret sacred texts. For the vast majority of people, growing up meant learning by imitation the same social habits and work skills as their elders. As we know, children normally began assisting in domestic farm and craft activities at a very young age. Transmission of skill of the trade used to be handed down from generation to generation. Reading was not necessary or even useful in their lives. Education, in whatsoever form available, was limited to higher castes only. The untouchables were debarred and discouraged to receive education. There was no much specialization of professional roles as we find today.

The modern education system that we find in India today came with Britishers. They were accompanied by Christian missionaries who established schools to impart secular education to the Indian children but also to convert them to Christianity. Britishers had planned three stages of education in India: (1) primary, (2) secondary, and (3) higher education. The main aims in the starting of the schools for children as well as the institutions for higher learning in the 18th century were to propagate Christianity, to have competent scholars in the Muslim and Hindu law and to train the British civilians in Indian languages, law and history. The system of education that was established by Britishers had an objective to suit their own needs and further their interest of peaceful administration. They transformed the education into a commodity available to those who could afford to purchase it. These objectives were viewed to serve the purpose of colonial Britishers. This view has been sharply contested by many quarters. Those who disagreed with this said that it is altogether wrong to think that colonial education's sole goal was to produce clerks to serve the British administration as was widely believed. Its impact was much deeper. It had a penetrating effect and long-term consequences.

The colonial education was, in a way, also responsible for the germination and development of the nationalist movement in India. It is generally held that most of the social reformers of 19th century—Raja Ram Mohan Rai, Gokhle, Annie Besant, Lala Lajapat Rai, Tagore and later Gandhi and torch bearers of India's independent movement—were educated through English and were much influenced by the prevailing thought (liberty, social equality, nationality and political democracy) of the West. These people regarded education as a flame or light of knowledge which can dispel the darkness of ignorance.

In the 19th century, there were three kinds of schools. These included schools established by private efforts of the citizens (social reformers) or the Indian rulers to teach the students traditional learning either through Sanskrit *(pathsalas)* or through Persian and Arabic (*madarsas*) or through modern Indian languages. Secondly, there were missionary schools, run by Church or private citizens, which were established to teach English to the Indian children and also Christianity. Finally, there were government schools, run under the supervision of local government (Municipal Boards or District Board). These schools were established to impart secular education to the children from all classes and castes either through English or Indian languages. The process of industrialization and the expansion of cities served to increase demands for specialized schools and institutions of higher learning. Work skills of different occupations can no longer be passed on directly to children.

The colonial education system created hierarchy among Indians as educated elites and uneducated masses. The education was guided by the project of rationality and enlightenment which emerged in Europe in the 18th century. This was reflected in their educational project in India. The British policy makers who drafted the plan for the pedagogy, curriculum and the knowledge system almost ignored the erstwhile existing indigenous educational systems in India.

The important issues that emerged as a response to the colonial education and the struggle for freedom served three major quests as under:

The Search for Justice

This resulted in the demand or right to educational opportunity for the lower castes. Lester F. Ward, the first president of the American Sociological Society, said that 'the differences between at the top and at the bottom of the social ladder were not because of any differences in intellect but because of differences in the opportunity for education and knowledge'.

The Emergence of Movement for Self-identity

This movement was aimed at cultural revivalism which denounced the colonial education as an alien project. This view (nativistic) rejected everything that was foreign and not enshrined in the ancient heritage of society. In protest, a movement emerged to set a new agenda of education against the colonial education and fight its cultural imperialism. This cultural revivalism was a big success in the Hindi-speaking regions of the country.

Indigenization of Education

There were people, like Gandhi and Tagore, who gave a call for indigenization of education. It aimed at an alternative model of education and rejected modern learning of foreign origin. Gandhi not only severely criticized the

European model, but launched massive programme of socio-economic regeneration. In the quest for indigenization, Gandhi suggested a basic education model. The principal objective of this model was to make education more relevant to Indian conditions and impart to it a nationalist flavour. It was held that the national system of education should promote national consciousness in the youth and inculcate a deep love for the motherland and pride in cultural heritage.

To what extent we have made progress in the direction of indigenization of education? Free India experienced a phenomenal growth in education at all levels—primary, senior secondary, and college/university levels, but it cannot be contented that the quality of education has also increased simultaneously. The pattern of education, by and large, remained the same, i.e., colonial, leaving aside a few peripheral changes here and there. On the whole, the tendency was to maintain the status quo. Before liberalization (1990) most Indian education was public. They were funded by local (municipality), provincial or central government. The main weaknesses and deficiencies, as pointed out by various commissions and committees set up from time to time to review the educational system in India, may be described as under:

1. The present education system has failed to provide gainful employment to its beneficiaries. There is hardly any link between the education and the employment opportunities. In recent years, the state and the central governments have started giving attention to this complex problem. As a result syllabi of different courses are being modified to suit the requirements of various employment avenues. Many employment-oriented subjects are now being taught. The modern formal educational system that came with Britishers was minimally related to occupational training. Informal education given in the family was the only source of occupational training in traditional India.
2. There is great problem of drop-outs at the primary level. In spite of many educational programmes like recently launched 'Education to All', 'Rajiv Pathsala', 'Angan Badi', etc., we have not made much headway in education, especially in rural areas.
3. The present education system does not generate or fortify the type of knowledge that is relevant to the changed needs of Indian society. It even does not promote the development of scientific spirit and national outlook.
4. Today, the main aim of education is to get employment in government sector. India is a caste-ridden society with contempt for manual labour. There is a great eagerness on the part of the members of all castes, especially the higher castes, to seek a white-collar job through literary education and shun the traditional work of their family, if it entails manual labour. Even the children of agricultural castes after taking degree in agriculture prefer to become a clerk in a town than to return to

their village for tilling the fields, even if it is more gainful. After receiving education, they do not want to be identified as an agriculturist.

5. Modern education does not equip our youth with the necessary value framework needed to take the country to the highest level in every field. For the progress, the country needs committed youth who accord priority to the national interest than to the personal interest. This personal interest was the main cause for 'brain-drain' that started in the 1970s in India. Recently, it has reversed and there emerged as a new phenomenon called 'brain-gain' but that too not because of national interest but only for self-interest.

After independence planners and policy makers have given utmost importance to education. They have looked upon education as one of the principal instruments of development and modernization. The reflection of this idea we find in the following opt-quoted lines from the report of the Education Commission of 1964: 'The destiny of India is now being shaped in her classrooms … . In a world based on science and technology, it is education that determines the level of prosperity, welfare and security of the people.' In keeping with this faith, the Indian Constitution promises free and compulsory education to all children up to the age of fourteen.

The concept of 'universal education' developed recently is a new idea. It was only in the 20th century that most nation-states began to practise the concept of mass education in an earnest manner. Accordingly, every child has a right to an education is an idea accepted almost by all societies of the world. Today, the governments—central and states together—spend on an average Rs 4,000 per child per year on primary education and this amount seems to be quite sufficient to impart a decent education. Thus, money is not the problem, but given powerful teachers' unions, it is an impossible task. Lance Pritchett (1952) suggests that teachers should be made accountable locally to parents instead to bureaucrats at the state capital. But none of these will work unless we jettison our faith in what political scientist James Scott (1979) call 'bureaucratic high modernism' and recognize that government's job is to govern rather than to run everything, including schools.

In the budget proposals of 2007, the central government has made provision to hire two lakh teachers and to give one lakh merit-cum-means scholarships to school children from amongst the poor. The promised scholarship scheme will give parents the freedom to choose the school for their children. Merit testing of students will reflect on the school's quality, and the school will have an incentive to improve. Scholarships can thus empower and motivate students and incentivise teachers. The competition for scholarship money, it is hoped, would improve many government schools.

Progress has been dismal in education. We spend only 3.85 per cent of the GDP on education. Some 8 million children are still out of school, though gross enrolment ratio has improved but not enough. After independence, it was thought that nation's educational system needs an overall change in the light of the requirements and traditions of India. Many commissions and committees were constituted both at the central and state levels. But it is very pitiable to note that except a few outward changes here and there, the system exists as it is. Not much outstanding changes are visible as it was envisaged.

Women's Education in India

For more than 2,000 years, from about BC 300, there was practically no education for women in India. Only a few women of the upper castes and upper classes were given some education at home. But, even here, there was tremendous social resistance. Literacy of women at that time was looked upon as a disgrace. The notion of providing education to female children never entered into the minds of parents. A superstitious feeling was alleged to exist in the majority of the Hindu families that a girl taught to read and write will soon become a widow after marriage. According to the report of the National Committee on Women's Education (1959), 'It cannot be denied that the general picture of the education of women was the most unsatisfactory and women received practically no formal instruction whatever, except for the little domestic instruction that was available to the daughter of the upper class families.'

It was the American mission which first started a school for girls in Bombay (now Mumbai) in 1824. According to the figures available, by 1829 within five years as many as 400 girls were enrolled in this school. Then, in the first decade of the 19th century, with the efforts of the missionaries as well as the Indian voluntary organizations, some girls' primary schools, particularly in Bombay, Bengal and Madras states, started. The government also took the responsibility to promote primary education in general and that of the girls in particular. However, government efforts could not go a long way due to the Indian War of Independence of 1857. After the war municipal committees and other local bodies were encouraged to open primary schools. In the year 1870, training colleges for women were established for the first time and women were trained to become teachers in girls' schools. As a result of all these efforts, great progress was made in girl's education in the last quarter of the 19th century. However, in spite of these, there was a great gap between the education of men and women. It was estimated that for every 1,000 boys at schools, the number of girls was only 46. At the beginning of the 19th century there was hardly any literate woman in the country excepting a few in the aristocratic houses. It is astonishing that by the end of the century hundreds of thousands of girls were enrolled in the newly opened institutions all over the country.

Though girls and women have made much educational gains in recent years, but still have a long way to go before their historic educational disadvantage is eradicated. The education system of India, like many other social institutions, has long been discriminatory towards the women. In 1916 SNDT

Women University in Bombay became the first institution of higher learning to admit female students. It had a number of high schools and colleges affiliated to it. In the beginning, it was (and is still) believed that women should aspire to become good wives and mothers, not intellectuals, doctors, lawyers etc. Women used to wash men's clothing, cared for their rooms and served them meals. They were forbidden to speak in public (these practices are more or less still continuing).

The proportion of women students has increased steadily after independence and mostly in the last decade. The literacy rate of women has gone up from 8.86 per cent in 1951 to 29.75 per cent in 1981, 39.29 per cent in 1991 to 54.16 per cent in 2001. Enrolment of women in higher education has also grown since 1995. But these figures are not satisfactory when compared with the enrolment figures of boys. The main hindrance in the women education in India is rural residence, low caste, low economic standing combined with the traditional attitude towards women education as a whole. These factors tend to deny opportunities of education to a girl. While broadly speaking (and as shown above) education of female students has made strides and it is not surprising that today in many faculties and departments of universities and colleges, more girls than boys are seen.

National Policy on Education in India

Before 1976, education was the exclusive responsibility of the states. After the constitutional amendment of 1976, education became a new sharing of responsibility between the union and the states. To monitor the educational policies and programmes, the central government proposed a National Policy on Education (NPE) and the Programme of Action (PoA) in 1986 as updated in 1992. The main objectives of NPE was:

1. To bring radical change in education.
2. To improve quality of education at all levels.
3. To give more importance to science and technology.
4. To strengthen ethical values.
5. To develop feelings of common culture and citizenship.
6. To strengthen unity in society.

The main features of NPE and PoA were to bring about uniformity (10+2+3) in education, making adult education programmes a mass movement, providing universal access, retention and quality of elementary education, placing special emphasis on education of girls, establishment of pace setting schools like Navodaya Vidyalayas in each district, vocationalization of secondary education, synthesizing of knowledge and interdisciplinary research in higher education, starting more open universities in states, strengthening of the All India Council of Technical Education, encouraging sports, physical education, yoga and adoption of an effective evaluation method, etc. The PoA lays down a detailed strategy for the implementation of various policy parameters by the implementing agencies.

Right to Education

Article 21A of the Constitution says that the state shall provide free and compulsory education to all children of the age of six and fourteen in such manners the state may, by law, determine.

The Constitution (86th Amendment) Act, 2002 seeks to make free and compulsory education a fundamental right for all children in the age group of 6–14 years.

In pursuance of the Article 21A, referred above, Right to Education (RTE) Act was enacted in 2009. Accordingly, all children between 6–14 years of age have got the right to free and compulsory education. Till the end of primary education, no child will either be detained or be expelled on account of his/her bad performance. This Act will be applicable to all government schools. However, the fee-paying private schools continue to occupy a privileged place and play a key role in society. In some states, as is in Rajasthan, recently it has made obligatory for the private schools to enrol some number of children (in Rajasthan, it is 25%) of the depressed classes without taking any fees. This fees will, however, be reimbursed by the state governments.

Through this Act, parents and teachers both have been made responsible for the enrolment of children of the educational age. Parents have been made liable to send their children to school. It is the duty of teachers to enrol all children (6–14 years) of the adjoining area of the school. To attract children toward school, government has also started a scheme of 'mid-day meal'.

Privatization of Education and Elite Reproduction

Schools are most important vehicle in transmitting the dominant culture. Through schooling, each generation of young people is exposed to the existing norms, and value of culture. Besides transmitting fundamental values, schools are also most decisive in perpetuating social inequalities. The conflict perspective views education as an instrument of elite domination and elite reproduction. Schools convince subordinate and subaltern groups (SCs, STs, OBCs, ethnic minorities) of their inferiority, reinforce existing social class inequality and discourage alternative and more democratic visions of society. The inhibiting effects of education are particularly apparent in the nature and character of schools, and the existence of a dual system of private and public schools.

Some studies, have indicated that private schools have a major influence on academic development and overall character building of children. His results help us to understand just why schools tend to maintain inequalities and elite reproduction. The quality of teacher-pupil interaction, better teaching, an atmosphere of cooperation and healthy competition both and caring between teacher and students, and well-organized course preparation of private schools are the influential factors that determine the better performance of the students. These schools also provide superior learning environments in terms of school organization, material resources, buildings, furniture, and well-equipped laboratories with modern scientific instruments like TV, Internet, parks, etc. All these factors motivate students for good performance. Similarly, a study by sociologist James S. Coleman and his associates (1982) concluded that private schools provide better education than public schools. The study suggests that private schools have fewer absences, instances of cutting classes, and fights, along with more homework, smaller classes, and greater participation in games and sports. Not only this, the study pointed out that private school students do better than their counterparts in public schools on tests and measures of self-esteem. In line with Coleman's findings, a research conducted by Barbara Falsey and Barbara Heyns (1984) indicates that students who graduate from private schools are much more likely to enrol in college than public school graduates are. Educational achievements play a critical role in social mobility also. Students who have studied in public schools do not have positive experiences in schools that will assist them in later competition in job markets. There is a self-repeating cycle in which Children from relatively privileged homes attend a particular school, and perpetuate its qualities, good teachers are attracted and motivation is maintained. A school (public school) mainly attended by deprived children will have to work far harder to achieve similar results.

Such studies of public and private schools, though conducted outside India, but their conclusions are more or less true for Indian schools also. In brief, privatization of education has the following advantages:

1. Private schools give parents greater freedom of choice to get their children admitted.
2. Many of the private schools have centuries of old traditions (such as Mayo College, Ajmer) behind them and so they are a precious part of our national heritage and culture. They also often have excellent records of academic and sporting achievements.
3. These schools benefit from establishing social contacts which will help them in later life.
4. These schools have the freedom to use experimental methods of schooling.

How private schools contribute to elite reproduction? This is a very pertinent question as regards the perpetuation of inequality in the society. Though exact data about different elite professions is not available, but it is a fact that the very high representation of ex-so-called public (private) schools, such as Doon School, Mayo College, MGD, students in the so-called 'great' professions, in politics and in finance are dominating. Not only are the percentages high but as some estimates suggest, they have remained so over a long period of time. What seems to be happening today is that the better off middle class people are securing a route to the elite occupations via the private schools and other renowned institutions. This inequality does not exist only class-wise but it can be seen gender-wise also. Only recently women have become conscious about education, they have started occupying good positions in the so-called 'great' professions. But still their number is very meagre and the males are dominating the scene. Although private schools include students from all income levels, they have a greater proportion from higher social classes and castes than public (government) schools. Negative image of public education encourages not only more affluent parents but lower class people also prefer to send their children to private schools. This has accelerated the trend towards privatization of education.

Following the policy of privatization, universities and other educational institutions (from nursery to higher education) came under the pressure to obtain more their funding from big business houses in order to forge a closer relationship between business and education. Privatization of education is based on the criterion of success in getting employment. Schools and colleges are supposed to produce school-leavers and graduates with the type of skills that industry needs. They have to pursue the type of knowledge that business houses desire. In India, after the adoption of the policy of liberalization in 1990s, schools, colleges and universities, like hospitals have been enjoined to take the operation of the free market as their model. Local management of educational institutions, and provisions for parental choice, are intended to make schools/colleges operate more like businesses on the assumption that competition between educational institutions and the operation of a free market system within education would promote greater efficiency and wide choice for the consumer.

Mike O'Donnell (1997) suggested the following three ways in which private schools contribute to elite reproduction:

1. They offer academic advantage.
2. They provide suitable general socialization for elite participation.
3. They provide useful contacts.

Academic Advantage

In general, private schools offer better facilities and equipment and a better teacher-pupil ratio than state (public) schools. They do so because they can afford these advantages.

General Socialization: Character Formation

Traditionally tough academic and physical regimes of so-called public (private) schools generate qualities of leadership, self-discipline, confidence and punctuality among its inmates. These qualities play pivotal role in converting social/cultural capital into occupational and political power and position.

Contacts: The Old Boy Network

In addition to the character attributes inculcated by private schools, the more elite ones often provide a formidable network of contacts. Friendships and associations made at private schools may give a crucial career edge compared to those from state schools. Though this hypothesis is not always stand to be correct, it strongly suggests the dominance of ex-private school boys in elite areas of national life (industrial, financial and political areas). Discrimination in favour of a contact in, say, a job appointment may occur unconsciously. Over and above, private schools convince indirectly subordinate groups of their inferiority, reinforce existing social class inequality, and discourage alternative and more democratic visions of society.

Privatization of Education in India

Privatization of formal education in India is not new; it existed even before independence in the form of so-called public schools (like Doon School, Mayo College) and Christian missionary schools and colleges. They used to be run by their own Board of Management without much interference by the government. After independence, there was an expansion of education. Central and state governments both took initiatives to establish state-owned or government-aided schools. Teachers at all levels have their salaries determined according to national or state wage scales. After 1990s interlinked processes of globalization and liberalization have also tremendously affected the educational process in India. These have encouraged many forms of privatization and aided schools through processes like rise in private tuition, subcontracting the publication of textbooks to private agencies, selection and appointment of teachers by their own management boards on their own terms and conditions, etc. These processes have created new situations which in turn had brought both opportunities and challenges to educational institutions in India. The process of globalization has recently encouraged many foreign universities and educational institutions of repute (e.g., Oxford, Harvard) to start exploring the possibilities of establishing their branches in India.

Although the demand for schooling has increased among the people of all the strata of society, including the marginalized, over the years, standards of government schools have declined considerably. Despite an increase in enrolment, the content and quality and process of schooling and teaching practices are not only degrading but discriminatory also. There is an utter lack of infrastructural facilities in government schools, such as students' desks, tables, stools, carpets, teacher's chairs, black boards, drinking water, limited space with or without constructed class rooms, lack of play grounds and teaching materials, etc. All these shortcomings, along with the defective teaching system, have deleterious effects on the education of students. Moreover, the procedure of appointment of teachers in state schools is also very faulty. The truth is that politicians sell teaching jobs for a handsome price. Such teachers, who are appointed for life, are protected and believed that there is no need to teach. With such perverse incentives accountability disappears.

India spends a respectable 4 per cent of GDP on education and even in the recent budget proposals (2007), spending on education (and health and rural employment schemes) has increased 35 per cent. Sarva Shiksha Abhiyan to improve primary education is a success in numbers. An IIM study of 13 states has found that the out-of-school population in the 6–14 age groups fell from 28.5 per cent in 2001 to 6.94 per cent in 2005. The share of children from Dalit and tribal communities in primary education has also gone up. Gender disparities have also been reduced significantly. However, school dropout trends do not show a similar progressive decline. Out of 400 districts surveyed in the study, only 190 have experienced a decline in dropouts after primary school. However, these figures do not tell us the full story. The picture will be completed only if we also look at a World Bank study of teacher absenteeism. In some states it is as high as 50 per cent. The Kremer-Murlidharan survey shows that one out of four school teachers is absent in state primary schools, and of those present one out of two is not teaching. Thus, the heart of the problem is teacher's accountability. This problem becomes more heartbreaking when we look to the exalted status of the teacher as a *Guru* in Indian culture. There are over a million primary school teachers in India's state system, and going by these surveys, it means 6,70,000 teachers may not be doing their job. Not only this, Samuel Paul's study shows that the states with the highest level of privatization give the lowest rating to government schools. For example, only 1 per cent of the parents in Punjab are satisfied with teacher's behaviour in state schools. All these factors explain why more than 50 per cent of Indian children are dependent on private schools for education which is among the highest in the world.

According to Lant Pritchett, a Harvard economist, 93 per cent children in India are now in school. This figure is quite heartening. However, digging deeper into the SRI survey data, he finds that 53 per cent of all children in urban India are in private schools. In some states the ratio is much higher. In three of India's largest states, i.e., in urban Maharashtra 66.9 per cent, in Tamil Nadu 66.3 per cent and in Uttar Pradesh 65.1 per cent children are in private schools. It is estimated that urban India as a whole has the highest number of private educational institutions in the world. Children seek admission in private institutions due to the failure of state-run schools to provide quality education and many other reasons as stated above. Parents, even with meagre income (lower, middle income group), prefer to send their children to comparatively less expensive, private schools. These private schools are mushrooming rapidly in slums and villages all across the country. Even though these private schools pay a third of the salary or even less to their teachers than that the government school teachers get, they deliver better results. Hence, 53 per cent urban children and 18 per cent of rural children now attend private schools. This is very high by world standards. Even Chile, which privatized education in 1981, has achieved 46.5 per cent share of private enrolment after 25 years. Likewise, Holland, which has always believed in giving choice between private and public schools to its children as a matter of state policy, has only got a private school share of 68 per cent.

Over the years, the number of state schools has declined drastically. Field reports reveal that state schools in both rural and urban India now cater only to the most deprived sections of population. In many parts of rural India, it is now rare to find children of the professional class or the village elite attending a local government school. Such segregation of children along caste and class lines, even if not by design, is unwelcome and is a root cause of elite reproduction from the upper section of the society. Democratization of education does not mean a compromise in quality. Quality can be assured if infrastructure, including teachers and support staff, is in place. Not only this, monitoring systems have also to be tightened to ensure quality.

Education and schooling both are changing very fast and also substantially by the impact of information technology—computers, Internet and multimedia. Now-a-days, gradually, school is becoming less and less important, because pupils can learn through computers and Internet at home itself. This is creating an atmosphere of 'classroom without walls'. Sometime back, there was a good news that US children are taking coaching of Mathematics and English by Chennai (India)-based teachers on Internet. New technology will have radical implication for education. Scholars believe that they may reinforce educational inequalities. 'Information poverty' might become added to material deprivations.

In modern societies, virtually everyone can read and write. The printed word and electronic communication, combined with the formal teaching provided by schools and colleges, have become fundamental to modern way of living. Before independence, formal schooling was available only to the few who had the time and money available to pursue it.

Future of Education

Education in the modern form involves the instructions of pupils within specially designated educational institutions' premises. The expansion of education in the 20th century has been closely tied to perceived needs for a literate and disciplined workforce. With industrialization and the consequent expansion of cities, work became more specialized. The demand for specialized schools increased. People now work in many different occupations, and work skills can no longer be passed on directly from parents to children. In a modern society, people have to be equipped with basic skills in order to earn their living. And for this, they should not only know how to learn, but to master new, sometimes very technical forms of information. This is why education and schooling have changed very substantially by the impact of information technology—computers and multimedia. It may be that schools will become less important as a place of imparting instructions, because pupils can now learn through computers at the home itself. This is what is happening in advanced countries like America. It was reported in some newspapers that American students are taking coaching in Mathematics and English from Indian teachers on internet.

Chapter 12

Religious Institutions

KEY FEATURES

- Why Sociologists Study Religion?
- Religion Defined
- Dimensions of Religious Behaviour
- Religion as an Institution
- Functions of Religion
- Dysfunctions of Religion
- Current Trends in Religion: Secularization
- Classical and Modern Thinkers on Religion and Secularization
- Sources of Secularization
- Fundamentalism
- A New Religious Consciousness
- Religion and Science

From antiquity man has sought answers to questions concerning the mysteries of nature, such as why it rains, why volcanoes erupt, why accidents and incidents happen and questions about his own creation, his relationship to the supernatural, a satisfying philosophy of life, and life after death. In his quests, he has developed certain beliefs about the supernatural and also rituals and ceremonies for appeasement and propitiation of the supernatural. These rituals based on beliefs, convictions, and the ceremonies, and symbols accompanying prescribed roles and prescribed patterns of behaviour, together constitute religion. The religious beliefs, forms of worship, objects of worship, rituals, ceremonies of the people of the world are varied and most numerous, but most of them are basic in the profound influence that they exercise on the behaviour of individuals, groups and society as a whole in almost every aspect of life. It is found throughout the world because it offers answers to such ultimate questions as why we exist, why we succeed or fail and why we die.

People have believed in supernatural powers throughout history. Belief in supernatural powers or beings is, thus, the main basis of the phenomenon of religion. The most widespread manifestation of this belief we find in the form of rituals. Rituals are the observances, in a prescribed manner, of certain actions that help to establish liaison between the performer and the supernatural power. All religions—primitive or modern—have this base of belief and rituals.

Why Sociologists Study Religion?

As said above, religion is considered as a belief in some supernatural power. Sociologists are not interested in knowing what this supernatural power is or how it works? Sociologists regard religion as a non-rational knowledge or an explanatory system which 'believes in a unique truth and which believes itself to be in possession of it' (Gellner, 1992). Sociologists study religion as a system of ideas that have a great impact in directing human behaviour For a sociologist, religion is a non-rational, collective and symbolic action which acts as a response to the human need for meaning. Sociologists have no access to 'divinity revealed truth' but they themselves try to seek to reveal their own truth. Religious beliefs have social consequences and it is these sociology studies under the name 'sociology of religion'.

Religion Defined

How to define or even explain religion is a very difficult task as it is so diverse in historical development, so culturally varied, that all definitions developed so far often failed to encompass it adequately. In its simplest and purest form, religion is an emotional attitude towards the unknown and the uncontrolled. It is a universal phenomenon that exists in some or the other form everywhere but varies in character. At the one extreme, it is concerned exclusively with the demon world. At the other, it is social and personal and related with supernatural constructs—transmigration existence of God and soul, origin of universe, etc.

Pioneer sociologist Émile Durkheim (1916) defined it as '... a unified system of beliefs and practices relative to sacred things, uniting into a single moral community all those who adhere to those beliefs and practices'. Anything that people in a society consider to be sacred and celebrate in recognized rites becomes religion. Religion thus rests on beliefs, sacred things, prescribed rites and officially consecrated individuals—priest—to celebrate those rites. Durkheim believed that anything can be sacred. Sacredness is not a property that is inherent in an object. It exists in the mind of the beholder. Thus, a tree, an animal, a pebble or a piece of wood may be considered sacred. In Durkheim's view, the world is divided into two distant categories: (i) the sacred, supernatural, divine and spiritual, and (ii) the profane, natural, human and material. For early anthropologist E.B. Tylor, the belief in supernatural power is religion. Functionalists like Kingsley Davis (1949) believes that religion is an attempt to transcends the tedium of everyday life; that is, it involves a belief in and response to some kind of beyond'. It is any set of coherent answers to existential dilemmas (problems)—birth, sickness, ageing and death. It is human response to those things which concern us ultimately. It is a collective way of dealing with the unknown and unknowable aspects of human life—with the mysteries of life. It is also concerned with making of moral decisions. Thus, religion entails a system of beliefs, practices, rituals, a form of worship and symbols, obedience to divine commandments and a concern with transcendental realm that is beyond the rational and empirical. It can take many forms, such as bathing in the holy Ganges (Hindus), offering prayers in the temple, church or mosque or performing some sacrificial rituals, participating in Holy Communion (Christians), or performing the Mitzvah ceremony (Jews), etc.

Dimensions of Religious Behaviour

All religions have certain elements in common, yet they differ in expression and the manner. Most religions of the world have the following elements:

1. A set of beliefs and values regarding the ultimate power in the universe, life after death, in supreme beings, etc.
2. A set of ceremonial ways (rituals and behaviours) of expressing these beliefs.
3. Things considered sacred such as gods, spirits, special persons, or any object or thought defined as sacred.
4. A group of community of believers who make a religion or social existence as well as a personal experience.
5. A form of organization that reinforces the sacred, unites the community of believers and carries the rituals.

Each of the above elements will vary in form, in observance, in the response they evoke from individuals, and in influence according to the culture concerned—altogether, these prescribe specific lines of action, attitudes and values desirable under varying conditions according to which man is exacted to behave.

Religion developed slowly with the evolution of human society in its more primitive forms. In its evolutionary development, the earliest people are said to be pre-religious people—possessed no organization or special roles (no temple, church or priest or clergy), only a communal sharing in rituals and gave expression to religious symbols (Bellah, 1964). As religion and society evolved, a sense of sacredness takes concrete form in objects and images that become sacred, whether these are persons, animals or natural objects, human artifacts or symbolic expressions. The sacred also becomes conveyed and expressed for the living in ritual, where behaviour gives objective form to mood and feeling. A division among the sacred and the profane eventually marks off religious activity (Berger, 1967).

Religion as an Institution

In viewing religion as an institution, sociologists evaluate its impact on human societies. As an institution, religion has operated to standardize the religious emotions, beliefs and practices, and to spread and perpetuate them. It is a powerful instrument of social control and social integration. It is a strong bond of social unity through promoting a community of thought. It deals with divine sanctions as well as with present and future rewards and punishments. Through this, it exercises a profound influence on one's behaviour. In viewing religion as a social institution, sociologists have also evaluated its impact on individuals and society as a whole. As an institution, religion is characterized by its universality, its rituals, its sacredness and its persistence. Religion can be viewed from individual and societal points of view both. The functions of social cohesion and social control are oriented towards the larger society while providing emotional and social support and other psychological explanations are more oriented towards the individual.

Although religion, like all other institutions, has changed, it continues to be a potent force, rather with more vigour in our lives throughout the modern neo-liberal risky world. The assertion that 'God is dead' is not true for a large part of world's population. Despite the incredible growth in the importance of science and empiricism since 19th century, which has caused many people to regard religion as a superstition, an irrational belief and religiously and spirituality among people is increasing in some or the other way. At many times, religion persists in the face of scientific evidence. Even, the men who call themselves as scientists are not fully devoid of religious beliefs and they take part in many religious rituals in the home as well as at workplace. We often hear a doctor saying that he or she will do his/her best to save the life of the patient but it is ultimately He (God) who saves. This proves that religion has always been present and has also been a prominent institution.

In traditional societies the religious and non-religious spheres of life are not sharply differentiated. But, in modern industrial societies, religion and society are not the same. The emergence of different modes of life experience leads to different meanings about life, producing a religious differentiation. Religion may still provide cohesion, but now only for sub-groups of society.

Functions of Religion

Religion is a cultural universal because it fulfils several basic functions within human societies. It is a basic requirement of group life. In sociological terms, these include both manifest and latent functions. Among the manifest (open and stated) functions of religion are included defining the spiritual world and giving meaning to the divine. Religion provides an explanation for events that seem difficult to understand. By contrast, latent functions or religion are unintended, covert, or hidden. Functionalists suggest that religion is a requirement for society and individual both because it serves both manifest and latent functions. These functions are discussed below in brief:

Religion as an Integrative Force

Durkheim believed that the primary function of religion was to preserve and solidify society. It functions to reinforce the collective unity or social solidarity of a group. Sharing the same religion or religious interpretation of the meaning of life unites people in a cohesive and building moral order. The social cohesion is developed through rituals such as reciting prayer in the honour of God, institutions of worship (church, temple, mosque, etc.), performing *namaz,* and multitudes of observances and ceremonies practised by different groups. The unifying rituals of different faiths are also observed by individuals on the most significant occasions such as birth, marriage and death. This integrative function of religion was particularly apparent in traditional, pre-industrial societies.

Durkheim was particularly concerned with a perplexing question, 'How can human societies be held together when they are generally composed of individuals and social groups with diverse interests and aspirations'. In his view, religious bonds often transcend these personal and divisive forces. It gives people certain ultimate values and ends to hold in common.

Although the integrative impact of religion has been emphasized here, it should be noted that religion is not the only integrative force—the feelings of nationalism or patriotism may also serve the same end. In contemporary industrial societies, people are also bound together by patterns of consumption, ways of life, laws and other forces.

Creating a Moral Community

Religion provides a system of beliefs around which people may gather to belong to something greater than themselves in order to have their personal beliefs reinforced by the group and its rituals. Those who share a common ideology develop a collective identity and a sense of fellowship. Members of moral community also share a common life. This moral community gives rise to social community through the symbolism of the sacred that supports the more ordinary aspects of social life. Religion then legitimizes society. It provides sacred sanction for the social order and for its basic values and meanings.

Religion as Social Control

Frank E. Manuel (1959) had said that 'religion was a mechanism which inspired terror, but terror for the preservation of society'. While conservatives have valued religion for its protective function, radicals have also often recognized that religion can be a support of the established order, and have, consequently, been critical of religion. Friedrich Engels, a life-long close associate of Karl Marx, once noted that religion could make the masses 'submissive to the behests of the masters it had pleased God to place over them'. Durkheim also emphasized that besides acting as an integrating force, religion also reinforces social control in oppressive society.

Religious beliefs can influence the conduct of those who believe in them. It keeps people 'in line' through folkways and mores. It provides a foundation for mores of society. Religious sanctions are sought for certain desirable patterns of behaviour to persist in society in the forms of mores. Thus, many taboos in various cultures have religious sanctions, e.g., the taboo against eating of pork in Jewish and Muslims and cows meat in Hindus.

Provides Rites of Passage

Religion helps us in performing ceremonies and rituals related to rites of passage (birth, marriage, death and other momentous events) which give meaning and a social significance to our life.

Religion as Emotional Support

Religion is a sense of comfort and solace to the individuals during times of personal and social crises such as death of loved ones, serious injury, etc. This is especially true when something 'senseless' happens. It gives them emotional support and provides consolation, reconciliation and moral strength during trials and defeats, personal losses and unjust treatments. It provides a means whereby man can face the crises and vicissitudes of life with strength and fortitude. The concepts of karma and transmigration among Hindus and Jesus Christ as son of God and prayer among Christians seek to provide such fortitude and strength. Thomas O'Dea (1970) writes, 'Men need emotional support in the face of uncertainty, consolation when confronted with disappointments and anxiety.' It is often said that visiting places of worship and holy premises serves as outlets for releasing tension and stress.

Religion offers consolation to oppressed peoples also by giving them hope that they can achieve salvation and eternal happiness in the afterlife. Religion increases the 'God will provide' the attitude.

Religion Serves a Means to Provide Answers to Ultimate Questions

Why are we here on earth? Is there a supreme being? What happens after death? All religions have certain notions and beliefs that provide answers to the above questions. These beliefs are based on the faith that life has a purpose, and there is someone or something that controls the universe. It defines the spiritual world and gives meaning to the divine. Because of its beliefs concerning people's relationships to a beyond, religion provides an explanation for events that seem difficult to understand.

Religion as a Source of Identity

Religion gives individuals a sense of identity—a profound and positive self-identity. It enables them to cope effectively with the many doubts and indignation of everyday life. Religion may suggest people that they are not worthless or meaningless creatures and thus helps them alleviating the frustrating experiences of life which sometimes force a person to commit suicide. According to Thomas Luckman (1983), 'The prime function of religion is to give personal meaning to life'.

In industrial societies, religion helps to integrate newcomers by providing a source of identity. For example, Bangladeshi immigrants in India, after settling in their new social environment, came to be identified as Indian Muslims. In a rapidly changing world, religious faith often provides an important sense of belonging.

Legitimating Function of Religion

According to Max Weber (1930), religion may be used to explain, justify or rationalize the exercise of power. It reinforces the interests of those in power. Even in societies not as visibly ruled by religious dogma, religion legitimates the political sector. For example, India's traditional caste system defined the social structure of society. According to one theory, caste system is a creation of the priesthood (Brahmins)—the uppermost stratum of this system, but it also served the interests of political rulers by granting legitimacy to social inequality. Marx has acknowledged that religion plays an important role in legitimating the existing social structure. The values of religion reinforce other social institutions and the social order as a whole and as a consequence it perpetuates social inequality in society.

Psychologizing Religion

The notion of 'positive thinking' serves as an example of psychologizing religion. It provides peace of mind, promises prosperity and success in life, as well as effective and happy human relations. It is thus a source of security and confidence, and also of happiness and success in this world.

But at times religion can be debilitating and personally destructive. Persons convinced of their own essential wickedness can suffer extreme personal difficulties. As Kingsley Davis (1949) noted, 'Like other medicines, it (religion) can sometimes make worse the very thing it seeks to remedy. Innumerable are the psychoses and neuroses that have religious content'. But, in this role, religion is not always harmful. Many times, it serves as a liberating and integrating force for individuals. For instance, it helps in bringing change (sobriety) to seemingly hopeless alcoholics.

Religion Acts as Psychotherapy

In modern world, religion has also become a supporting psychology—a form of psychotherapy. Now, God is conceived of as a humane and considerate God. Such a hopeful perception helps the sufferer in alleviating his/her personal and social crisis. A new vocation of religious practitioner has recently come up in the mental health field as a helping professional. It already existed in village India and other places in the form of *shamans,* priests and magicians (*shamans* are treated as super-humans endowed with supernatural powers in some tribal societies).

Religion as an Agent of Social Change

While religion supports the status quo in its priestly function, it inspires great change in its prophetic function. It can enable individuals to transcend social forces; to act in ways other than those prescribed by the social order. Mahatma Gandhi, Jesus, Thomas More all died upholding spiritual beliefs that were not those of the social order in which they lived. Religion, in its prophetic function, provides individuals with an unshakable foundation of social criticism which later on becomes the basis for social change. Many religious groups of the world protested against Vietnam and Iraq wars and an age-old Buddha statue in Afghanistan.

Generally, religion is regarded as an impediment in the path of social change but many religious groups, by criticizing existing rules of social morality and social injustice, and community or government actions, help in bringing about social change. In this regard, Max Weber's pioneering work on the relationship between economy and the religion, *The Protestant Ethic and the Spirit of Capitalism* (1930) can be cited that how Protestant ethic had helped in the development of spirit of capitalism in certain European nations. Weber's major theoretical point to be noted here is that ideas can change history, and in so doing can contribute to changes in the material context of life.

Despite establishing relationship between religious ethic and economy, Weber argued that the effects of religion on society are unpredictable and varied. Sometimes it might have conservative effect, whereas in other cases it might contribute to social change. Thus, Buddhism militated against the development of capitalism in China, whereas in Northern Europe, Calvinism had the opposite effect.

Contrary to Weber, Marx has put forth a quite opposite thesis. He opined that religion impedes social change by encouraging oppressed people to focus on other worldly concerns rather than on their immediate poverty or exploitation. He said, 'Religion is the sigh of the oppressed creature, the feelings of heartless world … . It is the opiate of the people.' Whereas Marx had seen religion as a consequence of the economy, Weber believed that religion helped to shape a new economic system.

It should be noted that many religious leaders have acted in the forefront of many social and political movements. For example, Martin Luther King fought for civil rights of Blacks in America. Swami Dayanand worked aggressively for women education and widow remarriage in India.

Religion as an Agent of De-politicization

According to Bryan Wilson (1976), religion functions as an agent of de-politicization. Marxists suggest that by inducing a 'false consciousness' among the disadvantaged, religion lessens the possibility of collective political action. In simpler terms, religion keeps people away from seeing their lives and societal conditions in political terms.

Religion Controls Sexuality

According to B. Turner (1992), 'religion has the function of controlling the sexuality of the body, in order to secure the regular transmission of property via the family'. In feudalism, and now in capitalism, religious control of sexuality is an important vehicle for the production of legitimate offspring.

In the end, it may be said that in spite of being regarded as superstition, religion is persisting for such a long time as a social institution because of its varied functions cited above that it performs for the welfare of the individual and the society both. At many times, even the so-called educated people regard religious laws as superior to the man-made laws. In primitive and traditional societies and even some sections of modern societies, despite all-round attack over it, religion is a pervasive matter, and religious beliefs and rites play an important part in the activities of various kinds of groups—from family to occupational groups. Though inhabitants and citizens of a 'modern' society, many remain traditional in their religious and moral outlook. For some, this means that religious authority and principles override that of secular law.

Dysfunctions of Religion

In common parlance, the functions of religion are more highlighted. Its dysfunctions (negative functions), which may be covert, are not much talked about but in some instances religious loyalties are seen as dysfunctional; they contribute to tension and even conflict between groups or nations. Millions of European Jews were either exterminated or killed by Nazis during Second World War. Besides this, history is replete with the examples of wars which were fought on the issues of religion. Even in modern times, nations such as Lebanon (Muslims versus Christians), Israel (Palestinians/Hamas versus Jews), India (Hindus versus Muslims) and many others have been greatly affected by the religion.

Generally, it is held that religion makes a unique and indispensable contribution to social integration. This proposition is based on the studies of religion in non-literate societies. How far this proposition is true in complex and changing societies of today? What are the unintended consequences of religion? What are the functional alternatives to religion in meeting social needs—the need of social integration? It is difficult to defend the proposition that religion alone supported social integration or social control in modern societies like America or Britain or even in Indian society. It is often seen as a disintegrating force in some quarters. A small incident of the destruction of old structure of Babri mosque has deepened the gulf between Muslims and Hindus in India.

As noted earlier, Karl Marx described religion as an 'opiate' particularly harmful to oppressed people. In this view, religion often drugged the masses into submission by offering a consolidation for their harsh lives on earth: the hope of salvation in an ideal afterlife. From Marx's perspective, religion helps to perpetuate patterns of social inequality by reinforcing the notions of fatalism and rebirth. Religion deters individuals from overthrowing all those conditions in which man is abased, enslaved, abandoned, contemptible things. Marx argued that religions focus on otherworldly concerns, divert attention from earthly problems like unequal distribution of valued resources.

In the view of Marx and later conflict theorists, religion is not necessarily a beneficial or admirable force for social control. For instance, Hindu religion reinforces traditional patterns of behaviour that call for the subordination of the powerless. Subservient position of women in Hindu and many other religions is the outcome of this feeling.

Religion is a potent impediment to social change and progress. It supports the existing social order and encourages both the privileged and dispossessed to accept the status quo. The caste system and to some extent joint family system in Hindus are reinforced by the Hindu philosophy of religion. These two pillars of Hindu society have put many hindrances in the developmental process of the country.

Current Trends in Religion: Secularization

Any activity or belief which is not concerned with religion is, in brief, known as secular. For long time secular has meant 'worldly' contrasted to 'religious' or 'sacred'. The notion of sacred encompasses those elements beyond everyday life which inspire awe, respect and even fear. Fundamentally, 'secularization means the process by which sectors of society are removed from the domination of religious institutions and symbols' (Berger, 1967). The process indicates the decline in the religious permeation of other social institutions. It also refers to the process through which religion's influence on other institutions diminishes. It emphasizes that religion should be delimited to the private sphere of individual and family life. At the same time, other social institutions, such as economy, politics and education, maintain their set of norms independent of religious guidance. It may also thrive on personal level. According to Wilson (1976), 'Secularization is a process in which religious thinking, practice and institutions lose social significance.' Sometimes it is known as a movement away from the religious institutions.

Secularization may be said to consist fundamentally of two related transformations in human thinking. The first is the 'desacralization' of the attitude towards persons and things. Desacralization is a process in which no overarching religious symbolism for the integration of society and in which an understanding of human beings and their society is no longer stated primarily in religious terms. Secondly, it is a move from supernatural to rational explanation. There is the rationalization of thought—the withholding of emotional participation in thinking about the world. Rationalization implies both a cognitive attitude relatively free from emotion, and the use of logic rather than an emotional symbolism to organize thought. Secularization thesis places emphasis on a division to be made between the authority of church and the state which we find in western democracies. In Islam, however, such a distinction is not established.

Sometimes the process of secularization is interpreted as a loss of the power and effectiveness of religion. It tries to divest the world of much of the magic and miracles imbedded in religion. It reduces the sacraments in number and eliminates all the intermediaries between God and man—saints, sadhus, clergy men, miracles, and the sacraments through which grace could be dispensed. In the words of Peter Berger (1967) 'it (religion) divests itself as much as possible from the three most ancient and most powerful concomitants of the sacred—mystery, miracle and magic'.

Classical and Modern Thinkers on Religion and Secularization

Both Durkheim and Weber considered that secularization is a feature of modern life that the supernatural is little used to explain events and human behaviour. Religion is replaced by other ways of explaining reality and regulating social life. The medieval thinking and beliefs in mystery and miracle have receded to a great extent. 'Disenchantment', to use Weber's term for this, has set in. The triumph of science and reason has been at the cost of myth, fable and spiritual romantics. For Weber, secularization was an aspect of wider process of rationalization. He considered that the underlying principle behind modernization is rational, scientific thought—the use of the most effective means to achieve given ends. This rational thought has undermined religion and replaced it with various secular and largely materialistic explanations of our existence and relationship to nature. The works of four modern thinkers—Darwin, Freud, Marx and Nietzsche—have also helped to the replacement of religious explanations of human behaviour by scientific one and in generating the process of secularization. Marx saw religion as ideological mystification and Freud as projection of emotional need. Darwin is well-known for his 'origin of the species' without reference to God and Nietzsche became famous for his idea of 'the death of God'.

Sources of Secularization

Secularization is hardly a quite new or even a modern process. In Europe, secularization is held to be the consequence of the social changes brought about by industrial-urban society. Its origin in western world lies in the Christian religion. Max Weber credits Calvinism and the emergence of the Protestant ethic as being a major development in the rationalization of the world—and secularization is part and parcel of that rationalization. It can also be argued that the diversity of religious cults and practices in modern society demonstrates that religion has become a matter of personal choice rather than a dominant feature of public life. It is further suggested that there is a necessary connection between modernization and secularization. In the long run, the modernization of society does bring about modernization.

It is widely accepted by social scientists that the dominant trend in modern religion is secularization. There is fairly widespread agreement that there is a steady decline in formal religious observances. Nowadays fewer people are visiting temples or churches (places of worship) regularly, they are moving away from supernaturalism. It is a fact that though old type of religiosity (attending temples, churches regularly and the intensity of religious feelings) seems to be decreasing but its manifestation in other forms is heavily increasing. No person would claim that secularization has driven religiosity entirely from modern world. Rather, religion has remained more closely associated with the institution of family and is also not yet entirely divorced from education, economy and the state. We may find examples of ritualism in all the above-mentioned three spheres.

Furthermore, secularization has not affected modern society uniformly. It impacts more on men than on women, on young than on the aged, in the cities than in the villages, on those classes (or castes) directly linked to modern industrial production than on such more traditional occupations as artisans and small shopkeepers. Secularization has put much of social life under the domination of rational processes of science and under the control of bureaucratic and technological structures whose logic and legitimation is derived from science.

In the end, it may be said that religion has lost those basic functions that once defined it sociologically as an institution. Secularization, therefore, has been de-institutionalizing the religion. In such a world, the rational perspective of science becomes a major organizing belief for a secular and increasingly rationalized society.

It is a paradox that while on the one hand, with the advent of industrial-urban civilization, the idea of rationalization (secularization) is gaining ground in all spheres of life, on the other hand, what we observe is that fundamentalism is also increasing day by day in some way or the other in all religions. More and more religious activities (religious festivals, rites and rituals, ceremonies, rallies, etc.) are being performed with much pomp and show and with much attendance of the followers. In the last few decades many new places of worships (church, temples and mosques) have been constructed and many new religious organizations with great paraphernalia have cropped up. Religious texts are being reinterpreted and new rituals are being added or given new shape to suit their circumstances.

Fundamentalism

The term 'fundamentalism' refers to adherence to earlier accepted religious doctrines and is often accompanied by a literal application of historical beliefs and scriptures to today's world (Schaefer and Lamm, 1992). It is also defined as a movement or belief called for a return to the basic texts or 'fundamentals' of revealed religion. It encourages 'fixed identities' where 'slippages are suppressed' and 'sameness is prized'. It is commonly associated with the attempt to revive archaic modes of conduct and belief from the past. It is usually contrasted with modernism and liberalism in religion. It emphasizes the absolute truth of essential or 'fundamental' aspects of faith, especially those rooted in sacred texts such as the Christian Bible or the Islamic Koran or Vedas of Hindus. The term has been applied to Protestant trends within Christianity since the 1920s, recently in Hinduism after the demolition of Babri Masjid. These new trends in religion are sometimes termed as 'resurgent fundamentalism', meaning the revival of a conservative approach to religion.

Christian fundamentalism believes the Bible to be word of God, who is responsible for all creation. Although humanity has sinned and therefore fallen from grace, salvation from punishment has been made possibly by God's mercy in sending a saviour—Jesus Christ. Biblical religion introduced the conception of God as transcendent—as a 'Thou' utterly above the world—and of the world as 'desacralized', i.e., no longer a sacred entity to be responded to with emotional involvement. In Islam, however, it is believed that its holy texts are the Koran (the word of God as revealed to Prophet Muhammad by an angel) and the Hadith or sayings of the Prophet. It is the sacred duty of every believer to accept and practice the principles enshrined in the Koran and Hadith.

Fundamentalism is sociologically important not only because of its unique place among religions, but because it easily extends itself into political realm. There is an increasing entanglement of religion in politics around the globe. Despite its theological character, it is usually linked to projects of social reform and the acquisition of political power. In Middle East (Iran), Iraq, Afghanistan and more recently Egypt, Bangladesh, Indonesia, Pakistan, many countries of Europe and even the most modernized the United States of America and to some extent India, religious fundamentalism has affected the political process and has given rise to conservative political movements and blind faith in nationalism. Religious fundamentalists oppose secularization of society on one or the other basis. They sometimes even question about the removal of certain chapters from educational books. In recent years, there has been increasing efforts by fundamentalists and others to censor books used in school curricula. In Islam, fundamentalists issue *fatwa* against those who go against the principles of Islam(e.g., Ayatollha Khomeini of Iran issued one such *fatwa* against Salman Rushdie, the writer of *The Satanic Verses* in 1989.) There have been several deaths apparently related to the *fatwa* at many places. In Britain and in some European countries, male Sikhs had come into conflict for wearing turban in public. Recently, in France, girls were banned to wear *burka* in the school premises.

Fundamentalism is associated with a militant and sometimes violent attitude to enforcing 'moral purity' as defined by the fundamentalists. Frequently, fundamentalists seek to use the state to establish and enforce what they see as morality as we had seen in Taliban and Al Queda (fundamentalist organizations) controlled Afghanistan a few years back. Recently, some fundamentalist organizations banned yoga exercises in Far East countries like Indonesia. In Pakistan, its north-east part where a girl of sixteen years Malala was attacked by the fundamentalists for attending school (Swat) is under the full control of the fundamentalist organizations which compel the people to act according to Shariat law rather than the state laws.

It is very interesting and striking that fundamentalists are using latest modern communication technology—TV, radio, Internet, etc., to disseminate their ideas. While religious leaders directly attack many core values of the secular world, they are nevertheless willing to use its artifacts in their spiritual campaigns. Sociologist James Hunter (1983) argues that fundamentalists see 'technology as either neutral and thus not challenging to their faith or positive—as a gift of God to further his work on earth—and thus, an enhancement to faith'.

Why is religious fundamentalism on the rise all over the world, even in modern societies of Europe and America? Is religiosity (intensity of religious feelings) is increasing? So far as 'religiosity' is concerned, it is a qualitative factor which is difficult to measure accurately. Some studies have been made in western countries to assess church attendance which may provide some indication of religiosity. But this measurement cannot be regarded as a true measurement of religiosity because people go to church (or religious places) for many reasons—to worship, meet friends and relatives, participate in weddings, and sometimes even with an objective of thieving or pick-pocketing, and so on. Although a few people go regularly to church or temple or mosque, the vast majority believe in 'something' even if no more than a vague force behind the universe.

An important development in religious life has been the dramatic rise of religious programming (performance of many religious ceremonies, delivering religious discourse or sermons, prayers, chanting mantras, playing religious music, performing dance and drama on religious theme, etc.) in the electronic media. Organizing religious rallies and performing religious functions in public have increased tremendously. Religious personalities and groups have realized that the mass media represents an effective means of spreading religions values. Technological advances, such as TV, cable television and satellite transmission, have facilitated the rise of 'e-religion'. People who do not or cannot attend places of worship or listen discourses of religious personalities, regularly watch such programmes on TV and sometimes chant mantras and recite prayers with the preacher relayed on TV. Many people are seen kneeling to the images of God shown on TV. *Aastha* and *Samaskar* are the two most popular TV channels which relay such religious programmes regularly at appointed times. These channels are most popular among Hindus. Besides these, there are many other TV channels which relay religious programmes of different faiths. The audience for these religious programmes is increasing day by day. Besides elderly people, many adults have also included watching and listening to these programmes in their daily routine. Increasing this type of religions consciousness may be said to be the by-product of modern life which is full of stress and strains, pulls and pressures, great competitiveness and uncertainty. Modern religious activities and observances give some solace to the people torn by the exigencies of modern life. People visit temples for getting fast blessings like fast food. To use the phrase of Thorstein Veblen 'conspicuous consumption', we may call the modern religiousness as 'conspicuous religiosity'.

A New Religious Consciousness

There is thus an increasing influence of religion on contemporary life. People are turning to a variety of religions for answers to ultimate questions of existence or to seek help during the period of crises. In all major religions—Christian, Islam and Hinduism—a number of new sects and movements are emerging over the last few decades all over the world. Many of these are based on the personal religious experience of some man or woman (such as Brahmakumari, Gayatri); they are not rational, bureaucratic organizations. Such newly formed organizations also found in Christianity and Islam.

Why have these groups and movements arisen? A number of factors may be responsible for this. According to an early sociologist of religion, Emile Durkheim, as societies become more complex and diversified, so do the forms of religious beliefs and practices. Hans Mol (1976) suggested that the new religious consciousness is a sacred for identity and meaning. There are people who regard these movements as a reaction against the capitalistic and militaristic values that are emphasized by the contemporary modern society. Some scholars contend that the new religions have arisen in response to the environment of moral ambiguity. The decline of the established organizations such as Ram Krishna Mission or the Theosophical Society may also be responsible for this new phenomenon. In all probability, each of these factors along with some others may have an effect.

Almost in all the three world's major religions, the trend of resurgence and revivalism is going on. Many fundamentalist groups have recently appeared in a new garb. These groups share a conservative, 'back-to-basics' approach to religion and stress strict interpretation of holy books (Bible, Koran, etc.). This religious revival is called 'resurgent fundamentalism'—a term given by theologian Martin Marty. Revivalist groups place great emphasis on the adherence of the basic principles of religion enshrined in the holy texts and ask the believers to spread the faith among non-believers. Many such people not only hold the revivalist spirit but also infuse it in others through faith healing and many other persuasive techniques. At times, they resort to aggressive activities to spread their doctrine among others. This resurgence of fundamentalism has led to intense debate about secularization. We can agree to this view that liberalism in religion is increasing day by day but there are many other marks that reflect that human commitment to supernaturalism will remain. There are people who claim that they have no affiliation with any sect or religious organization, yet they accept whole range of supernaturalism—from astronomy to Zen. The findings of some studies carried out in the West and America reveal that a sizeable part of population has no commitment, although they are concerned with some religious belief.

The rebellious spirit towards established major religious may be said to be a source for the development of new religious consciousness among many youth. Renewed efforts are being made to restore the sacred in the lives of human beings which is being eroded by the process of secularization. For that reason, though in forms possibly strange and never before experienced, moves back to the centre of human experience. Since the 1960s, in the Western world, a renewed interest has emerged among American and British youth. The forms the new religious interest has taken are diverse and follow no single pattern. Hare Krishna and Zen Buddhism are examples of such new religious movements. Through these movements, people try to seek a radically new approach to spiritual meaning. In India, we can easily witness the increase of new religious consciousness during Navratra and Ganpati festivals when Goddess Durga and Lord Ganpati, respectively, are worshipped through community dances till late nights.

Religion and Science

Though this topic is not directly related to the subject 'religious institutions', but the students should have a bit idea of this because both are the ways of getting knowledge. Scientific knowledge is objective, based on logic and empirical facts whereas religious knowledge is subjective and is the outcome of beliefs and non-logical methods. Both are viewed as competing, and even in conflict, sometimes complementary to interpret the natural order of things and to explain and come to terms with events of our lives.

Both represent two opposite cultures. Two cultures here mean one of science and the other of humanism. C.P. Snow (1961) contended that scientists know little of the world of literary culture, and literary intellectuals do not have even a glimmer of understanding of the world of science. This situation splits scientists and humanists into two polar groups.

Scientists have an optimistic world-view about the society, and they believe that it is only science which can bridge the gap between the rich and the poor. It can rescue the world from the eternal problems like hunger, disease and squalor, etc. But humanists seem to be quite pessimist to the extent of despair. They saw the world becoming more and more rational—calculable, planned and unspontaneous, leaving no room for creativity, freedom and sensitivity. Many talented humanists have raged against this ever-increasing scientific and rational society. Such concerns were also echoed by classical thinkers like Max Weber in his writings. He expressed a despair about the future of humanity in a throughly rationalized world, yet see no reason to believe that the course of history could be altered.

These are the two radically opposed ways of viewing the world. There is no value preference about anything in the worldview of science. The humanist mind rejects this world-view and rebels against it.

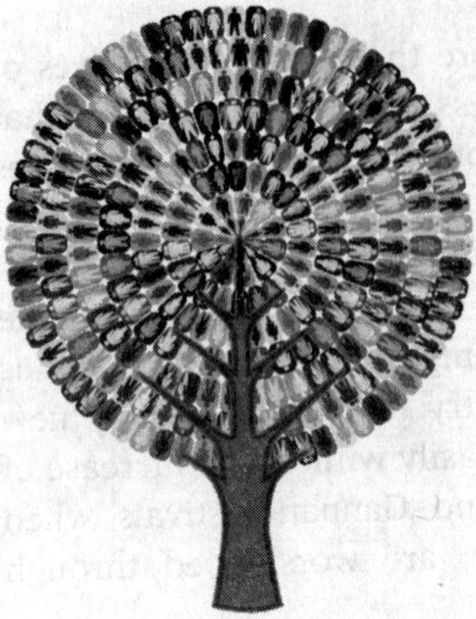

Chapter 13

Demography

KEY FEATURES

- Theories of Population
- Marx's Response to Malthus' Thesis
- Population Terminology
- Determinants of Mortality
- Determinants of Fertility
- Determinants of Migration
- World Population History
- World Population Explosion
- World Population Trends
- World Population, Inequality and Under-development
- Population as a Social Problem
- Population Problems in India
- Population Policy
- Population Policy in Different Countries
- Population Policy in India
- National Population Policy, 2000
- Family Planning and Family Welfare Programmes
- Family Planning in India
- Why Sociologists Study Population?

> 'Demography is destiny. The growth and composition of a country's population shapes a society's economy, culture and power as silently, but as powerfully, as the wind shapes the landscape.'
>
> —Suman Bery
>
> (*India Today*, February 20, 2006)

Most of us are aware that we live in the midst of what is commonly referred to as the 'population explosion'. How serious is this population explosion? What are its causes and consequences? In what ways does it involve us? This phenomenon of population constitutes the domain of a special science known as 'demography'. This term was probably first used by the Frenchman A. Guillard in his book, *Elements de Statistique Humaine* (1855). He defined it as 'the natural and social history of the human species, or in a narrower sense, the mathematical study of population, their general movements, and their physical, civil, intellectual and moral conditions'.

Etymologically, the word 'demography' is derived from the Greek term 'demos', which means people and 'graphy' means study or description. Combining the two terms, we can say that demography is the description or calculation of people. Today, the word is generally used to denote the study of phenomena connected with human populations such as births, marriages, deaths, migration and the factors that influence them. According to Hauser and Duncan (1959), 'Demography is the study of the size, territorial distribution and composition of population, changes therein, and the composition of such changes which may be identified as natality, mortality, territorial movements and social mobility (change of status)'. In simple terms, it is the study of the size, structure and development of human population.

The word 'demography' is often used to refer to the study of population statistics. It not only studies population statistics but also the causes and consequences of population changes, dependent on birth and death rates which are influenced by social factors like age at marriage, etc. These social factors form the subject matter of sociology. Demographers also study geographical variations and historical trends in their effort to develop population forecasts. Thus, demography is the scientific study of population in order to understand the social consequences of population.

Pointing out the importance of demography, Kingsley Davis (1949) said, 'demography' is the essential basis for understanding the human society. He has demarcated the following functions of demography:

(a) To know the population of a particular area;
(b) To ascertain as to which factors are influencing the population of that particular area;
(c) To explain the factors relating to changes in population; and
(d) To study the population trends on the basis of the above three factors.

Theories of Population

The theorizing about population (population size and change) have remained an important subject since time immemorial. Many of the ancient philosophers like Confucius (China), Kautilya (India), Ibn Khaldin (Arab), Plato (Greece) and modern thinkers like Adam Smith, David Richard and others, either directly or indirectly, have said somewhat significant on population issues. For instance, Kautilya, a contemporary of Plato, had written in his *Arthashastra* that 'a large population is a source of political, economic and military strength of a nation'. Similarly, the 14th century Arab historian, Ibn Khaldin maintained in his theory of 'rise and fall' that the growth of dense population is generally favourable to the maintenance and increase of imperial power. To the Jews, the injunction to Adam and Eve by the Almighty to 'be fruitful and multiply, and replenish the earth' has been a guiding principle for their attitude towards marriage and procreation. The Chinese philosopher, Confucius argued that a numerical balance be maintained between population and environment. Thus, he was not in favour of unchecked growth of population. He was the first who gave the concept of optimum population level. In ancient Greece, the earliest thinkers favoured the expansion of population, but Plato was a restrictionist who advocated as absolute limit of population.

One of the earliest demographers Edmond Halley (1656–1742) was the first scientist to use death statistics in different age groups to determine a person's likelihood of death as he or she passed through each age groups (*Population Today*, 1986). But, as a science, it emerged only in the last 250 years. The systematic compilation of data was first begun on a large scale in the 19th century Europe.

Malthus' Theory

Thomas Robert Malthus (1766–1834) was the key figure to analyse the population statistics. His formulation on population was a landmark in the history of population theories. He generalized the relationship between population factors and social change. In his *Essay on the Principle of Population* (1798) Malthus argued that because of the strong attraction of the two sexes, the population could increase by multiples, doubling every twenty-five years. He contended that the population would eventually grow so large that food production would be insufficient. Human capacity for reproduction exceeded the rate at which subsistence from the land can be increased. Malthus further wrote: 'Population when unchecked increases in a geometrical ratio. Subsistence increases only in an arithmetical ratio.'

Malthus contended that the world's population was growing more rapidly than the available food supply. He argued that the food supply increases in an arithmetic progression (1,2,3,4, and so on), whereas the population expands by a geometric progression (1,2,4,8, and so on). According to him, the population could increase by multiples, doubling every twenty-five years. He said the gap between the food supply and population will continue to grow over time. Even though food supply will increase, it would be insufficient to meet the needs of expanding population. Moreover, the famine and other natural calamities cause widespread sufferings and increase the death rate, which is nature's check against population.

In brief, Malthus theory states that:

1. Population is necessarily limited by the means of subsistence.
2. Population invariably increases where means of subsistence increased, unless prevented by some very powerful and obvious checks.

3. These checks, and the checks which repress the superior power of population and keep its effects on a level with the means of subsistence, are all resolvable into moral restraint, vice and misery.

Malthus based his above arguments on man's two basic characteristics essential to the maintenance of life: (i) the need for food, and (ii) the passion between sexes. It was the second which led people to marry at a relatively early age and would result in such a large number of births that the population would double itself in few years if unchecked by misery and vice.

Malthus referred to two classes of checks which kept population down:

1. *Positive means:* He spoke of famine (hunger), disease or war, pestilence and vicious customs about women.
2. *Negative means:* He explicitly demanded artificial means of birth control and suggested as an alternative that birth rate be decreased through *preventive measures* such as late marriage (postponing marriage until later age), moral restraint, and chastity (abstinence). He contended that without such restraints the world would face widespread hunger, poverty and misery.

The 'positive' and 'preventive' checks which occur in human population to prevent excessive growth relate to practices affecting mortality and fertility respectively. Malthus saw the tension between population and resources as a major cause of the misery of much of the humanity. He was not, however, in favour of contraceptive methods, since their use did not generate the same drive to work hard as would a postponement of marriage.

Malthus argued that the positive and preventive checks are inversely related to each other. In other words, where positive checks are very effective, the preventive checks are relatively less effective and vice versa. However, in all societies, some of these checks are in constant operation although in varying magnitude of effectiveness. Malthus believed that despite these checks, the inability of increased food supply to keep abreast of population increase always results in some kind of a situation of overpopulation.

Criticism

Malthus' views have been widely challenged on many grounds. The main criticisms about his theory are as under:

1. The validity of his two sets of ratios has been questioned by his critics. It is argued that population has rarely grown in geometrical proportion and means of production have rarely multiplied in arithmetic progression.
2. Malthus overemphasized the 'positive' checks and did not visualize the role of 'preventive' checks like contraceptives and family planning. Neo-Malthusists argued for the adoption of birth control within marriage. Human inventions in the fields of birth control, health and nutrition and agriculture have helped to a great extent to strike a balance between human reproduction and food supply.

3. Malthus was also severely criticized for ignoring the role of changing technology and the consequent transformation in socio-economic set-up of a society. He did not fully appreciate the extent to which improved agricultural technology and crop fertilization could sustain large population. Neo-Malthusians agree that there are absolute limits on food supply, energy and other resources. Furthermore, they suggest that the problem is intensified by the disproportionate consumption of such resources by so-called developed (industrialized) actions. This formulation has been challenged by other researchers.

   Yet none would deny that starvation is a very real fact even in 2012. According to International Food Policy Research Institute, out of 79 countries 65 come under the category of alarming level of hunger. Barundi, Ethiopia, Chad, Eritrea and Timor have been categorized as the five hungriest countries in the world. Around the world, we read many reports of starvation death and malnutrition. With such images in mind, a representative of the World Bank stated in 1981 that the 'ghost of Malthus is not buried yet'. Ironically gains in food supplies do not always lead to progress in the fight against starvation. It puts pressure on food prices that makes it more difficult for the poor to buy the food they need.
4. Both the positive checks of hunger and disease referred to by Malthus do not operate today, except the terrible disaster sometimes caused by *Tsunami, Katrina, Rita* and floods or rains in desert areas like Barmer and Jaisalmer in August 2006. But catastrophe of this nature in any part of the world is immediately rushed to the affected place from surplus areas all over the world. A marked decline in the death rate even in the developing countries is a significant factor in the context of the population spurt.
5. Moreover, natural calamites referred to above have occurred in under-populated areas also and thus there was no causal relationship between positive checks and overpopulation.
6. Malthus also failed to realize even the biological limitations that a population cannot grow beyond a certain limits.

Marx's Response to Malthus' Thesis

The debate about the Malthusian theory has continued down to the present. Economists such as J.S. Mill and J.M. Keynes supported his theory whereas others, especially, sociologists, have argued against it. According to them, the widespread poverty and misery of the working class people was, not due to an eternal law of nature as propounded by Malthus but to the misconceived organization of society. Karl Marx went one step further and argued that starvation was caused by the unequal distribution of the wealth and its accumulation by capitalists. It has nothing to do with the population. Population is dependent on economic and social organization. The problems of overpopulation and limits to resources, as enunciated by Malthus, are inherent and inevitable features associated with the capitalist system of production.

Marx's contention that food production could not increase rapidly was also debated when new technology began to give farmers much greater yields. French sociologist E. Dupreel (1977) argued that an increasing population would spur rapid innovation and development to solve problems, whereas a stable population would be complacent and less likely to progress.

During the depression of the 1930s, the debate changed somewhat because the birth rate fell sharply in industrial (western) nations. Some predicted that human species would die out. Schemes were proposed to encourage families to have more children by giving them allowances for each child born. The birth rate rose sharply after World War II, especially in the underdeveloped nations like India, Africa and Bangladesh. Birth control programmes were instituted to control the population so as to eliminate starvation.

Despite the criticisms, the Malthusian thesis gained widespread currency during his lifetime. His ideas had profound effects on public policies, on the classical and neo-classical economists, on demographers and evolutionary biologists led by Charles Darwin. His principle of population has been successful in highlighting the urgency to maintain a balanced relationship between population growth and means of subsistence. The critics of Malthus failed to realize that it was because of a large measure of truth in Malthusian principle of population that men today feel the need of resorting to contraception to keep their families within reasonable limits. Another main contribution of Malthus was to give a new line of thinking whereby the dynamics of population growth were viewed in the context of man's welfare.

Theory of Demographic Transition

Demographic transition is a term, first used by Warren S. Thompson (1929), and later on by Frank W. Notestein (1945), referring to a historical process of change which accounts the trends in births, deaths and population growth that occurred in today's industrialized societies, especially European societies. This process of demographic change began for the most part in the later 18th century. Demographic transition should not be regarded as a 'law of population growth', but as a generalized description of the evolutionary process. In simple terms, it is a theory which attempts to specify general laws by which human populations change in size and structure during industrialization. It is frequently accepted as a useful tool in describing the demographic history of a country.

The theory postulates a particular pattern of demographic change from a high fertility and high mortality to a low fertility and low mortality when a society progresses from a largely rural agrarian and illiterate society to a dominant urban, industrial, literate and modern society. It is typically viewed as a three-stage process: (i) that the decline in immortality comes before the decline in fertility, (ii) that the fertility eventually declines to match mortality, and (iii) that socio-economic transformation of a society takes place simultaneously with its demographic transformation.

The demographic transition theory is characterized by conspicuous transition stages. The transition from high birth and death rates to low rates can be divided into three stages (some scholars like Haggett, 1975 have divided into four or five stages):

- *Pre-transition stage:* High and fluctuating birth and death rates with little population growth.
- *Stage I:* High birth rates and declining death rates with rapid population growth.
- *Stage II:* Low birth and death rates with slow population growth.
- *Stage III:* Birth and death rates both decline appreciably leading to zero population growth.

The theory holds that pre-industrial societies were characterized by stable populations which had both a high death rate and birth rate. It postulates a little and slow population growth. The theory states that the high mortality rates characteristic of undeveloped areas will decline before fertility rates which are also high. In the first stage of transition, death rates (especially the infant deaths) begin to fall as a result of advances in public health and sanitation as well as improvements in nutrition and food supply. Since the birth rate continues to remain high relative to the declining death rate, there is a rapid 'transitional' growth as we find in India today. In the second stage, changes in social attitudes, the introduction of cheap forms of contraception and increases in life expectancy create social pressures for smaller families and for a reduction of fertility. The diffusion of knowledge and cheap medical technology has brought many non-industrial societies into this stage of the demographic transition, however, these societies have been unable to enter the third stage. The result has been very high rates of population growth in countries that are not experiencing corresponding economic growth.

In the last (third) stage of demographic transition birth and death rates decline appreciably which eventually becomes approximately equal, and in time it will result in zero population growth. Before this stage begins, there can be one more stage in which low birth and death rates lead to slow population growth. The populations of advanced, urban industrial societies, which have entered the last stage, are now stable with low birth and death rates. In some cases (e.g., Eastern and Central Europe) birth rates have fallen so slow that the rate of *natural increase* was actually zero or negative. In this stage, the technical know-how is abundant, the deliberate controls on family planning are common and the literacy and education levels are also very high.

The growth pattern of human populations is thus held to be S-shaped, involving a transition from one type of demographic stability with high death rates to another type of plateau with low death and birth rates.

Among the later demographers, Coale and Hoover further elaborated upon the role of development and modernization in the process of transition in demographic behaviour, maintained that a society characterized by peasant economy is marked with very high birth and death rates. Death rates are high because of lack of adequate nutritive food, primitive sanitary conditions and absence of any preventive and curative measures of control over diseases. A high birth rate, on the other hand, is a functional response to high death rates, particularly among infants and children.

In the present-day world, as would be true of any point in time, different countries of the world are at different stages of the demographic transition. In the opinion of Glenn Trewartha (1969), this is largely due to the dual nature of man. According to him, biologically, man is same everywhere and is engaged in the process of reproduction but culturally man differs from one part of the world to another. It is the cultural diversity of man that gives rise to varying fertility patterns in different areas resulting in different stages of demographic transition discussed above.

Criticism

Although the theory of demographic transition has been appreciated widely by the demographers, it has been criticized on many grounds also. There are even critics who have gone to the extent of saying that it cannot be called a theory. The main points of criticism are: Firstly, this theory is merely based upon the empirical observations or the experiences of Europe, America and Australia. Secondly, it is neither predictive nor its stages are segmental and inevitable. Thirdly, the role of man's technical innovations cannot be underrated, particularly in the field of medicine, which can arrest the rate of mortality. Fourthly, neither does it provide a fundamental explanation of the process of fertility decline, nor does it identify the crucial variables involved in it. Fifthly, it does not provide a time frame for a country to move from one stage to another. Finally, it does not hold good for the developing countries of the world, which have recently experienced unprecedented growth in population due to drastic decline in death rates.

In spite of these criticisms and shortcomings, the demographic transition theory does provide an effective portrayal of the world's demographic history at macro level of generalizations. As an empirical generalization developed on the basis of observing the demographic trend in the West, the transition process for any country can easily be understood.

Population Terminology

Demographers employ the distinctive terminology of their science in analysing and projecting population trends. By *population* we mean the numbers of people in a society. The *census* is the primary mechanism for collecting population information. A census is an enumeration or counting of a population in which people's sex, age and other informations are recorded. In India, a census is held every ten years. This periodic investigation is supplemented by vital statistics, i.e., the records of births and deaths, marriages, divorces, diseases, etc. In addition, the National Sample Survey (NSS), an organ of Census Department, provides up-to-date information on many topics of national interest.

Three variables can cause the size of the population in a given region to change: (1) births, (2) deaths, and (3) migration. Demographers measure these factors in terms of their rates.

1. *Birth Rate*: Birth rate (or more specifically the *crude* birth rate) is the number of live births per year per 1,000 population. It provides information on the actual reproductive patterns of a society.
2. *Death Rate:* It is the number of deaths per year per 1,000 population.
3. *Natural Increase:* Excess births over deaths per 1,000 of population. This does not include increase in population due to immigration.
4. *Fertility*: It is the amount of reproduction among women of child-bearing age; or, in other words, it is the number of live births per 1,000 women of childbearing age (15–49). The simplest measure, the crude birth rate, relates to the number of live births in a given year to the total population size in that year. Another measure is 'cohort rate' which is the number of live births for a group or cohort of women during their span of reproduction.
5. *Total Fertility Rate (TFR)*: TFR is the average number of child born alive to a woman, assuming that she conforms to current fertility rates.
6. *Mortality:* It denotes the amount of deaths. The infant mortality rate (IMR) is the annual rate of deaths of infants (0–12 months) per 1,000 live births. Mortality is measured in several different ways. The important measures are: (1) crude mortality rate, (2) age-specific mortality rates, and (3) life expectancy. The IMR also functions as a useful indicator of future population growth.
7. *Life Expectancy:* It refers to the average number of years a person can be expected to live under current mortality conditions. In other words, it is the average age at which people die. However, it is not the age at which most people die, e.g., in India, the figure is 69 years (2001), whereas in Japan and Britain, it is 80 and 77 years respectively. This is because more young children die in India and thus bring down the average expectancy.
8. *Fecundity:* The biological potential of individual woman for reproduction in a society is known as fecundity. This concept calls our attention to the powerful growth potential in human population. However, millions of couples around the world cannot conceive as many children as they would like to.

9. *Sub-fecundity:* It refers to a limited or diminished ability to reproduce. Sub-fecundity may affect the couple both singly and doubly either temporarily or chronically. Recent advances in reproduction technology offer hope for couples suffering from sub-fecundity. However, ethical concern has been raised about the impact of these technologies in light of many couples' desire for male versus female children. With such concerns, many feminists have raised their voices against using such devices. Not only this, it will affect the male-female ratio in the long run.
10. *Migration*: Migration constitutes a major component of population change from time immemorial. It includes both immigration—moving into the area, and emigration—movement out of an area. Migration is harder to measure than either births or deaths. Why do people move? Demographers speak in terms of push factors and pull factors. *Push factors* are those that push people away from their homes—economic deprivation, famines, wars, religious intolerance, lack of economic opportunity, political oppression, loss of job, marital and kinship ties or bad climate.

    Pull factors are those that make a new place seem more inviting—the chance to acquire land or jobs, the discovery of riches such as gold or oil, or the chance to live in a more desirable climate.
11. *Dependent Population:* It refers to non-productive members of the population. The dependency ratio is arrived at by dividing non-producers by producers.
12. *Rate of Population Change:* Birth rate and death rate are key determinants of population size. The difference between them shows the rate of 'natural population increase', or the rate of population growth. But, the rate of population change is also influenced by migration besides the birth and death rates. If the birth rate is high and the mortality rate is low, the population increases. If the mortality rate is high compared with the birth rate, the population will decline. Countries in which the population is very young, population is expected to grow rapidly. As against this, where there are older people, the people will grow slowly.

    The total growth rate is the difference between births and deaths, plus the difference between immigrants (those who enter the country to establish permanent residence) and emigrants (those who leave a country permanently per 1,000 population).
13. *Zero Population Growth:* It is the state of population when the number of births plus immigrants equals the deaths plus emigrants. Zero population growth is the goal of current world population policy, and can be achieved when parents have only two children, just enough to replace themselves. If this practice is followed, the population would remain the same generation after generation. The 2.1 ZPG is maintained in Japan and many European countries.

14. *Optimum Population*: The pressure of population on a region's resource base and the available technology determines whether the region is overpopulated or underpopulated. In other words, the extent to which resources are used and the way they are used determines an area to be underpopulated or overpopulated. A country is said to have an *optimum population* when the number of people is in balance with the available resources. The idea of optimum population is dynamic which changes with the change in conditions that determine the whole social pattern.

Determinants of Mortality

Mortality data are normally expressed in terms of the number of deaths per thousand individuals as specified by age, sex and social groups. It provides a measure of health risks, improvements in the quality of health care, and the comparative overall health of different groups in the population. Mortalities could be influenced by a number of social and cultural factors operating through the life cycle of human beings. It is shaped by nation's level of nutrition, provisions for sanitation, commitment to health care and health education. It is also dependent upon society's technological and medical knowledge and its willingness to use its resources to achieve the goals of good health and long life for its people. It reflects prenatal nutrition, delivery procedures and infant screening measures. Poverty and educational backwardness are most important factors that affect the high incidence of mortality.

There are several social factors which cause sickness and death. Sometimes in a society, aged and infirm may be left to their lot which may lead them to death. There are certain practices such as *sati* in India and female infanticide in many societies which actuate people to cause death. Likewise, practices of human sacrifice on ceremonial occasions or for magical rituals influence mortality to some extent in a society.

The infant mortality rate (IMR) provides a sensitive indicator of general social welfare in different societies and different regions within any one society. Differential mortality rates between social groups indicate inequalities in health care, wealth and working conditions. The IMR varies internationally mainly according to the quality of childcare and makes a critical contribution to the overall death rate. The countries with the lowest IMRs, such as Sweden, Switzerland and the Netherlands, have very little poverty and high educational standards.

Determinants of Fertility

Fertility is the actual level of childbearing of an individual woman in a population. It is different from fecundity. 'Fertility' refers to actual live births while 'fecundity' is the potential capacity of a woman for biological reproduction. The rate of fertility (the frequency at which births occur in a population) depends on biological and social factors. The most important biological factor is the number of women of childbearing age (15–49 years) in the population. Another biological factor is the general health of childbearing woman. Though fertility is basically a biological phenomenon, yet like other forms of human behaviour, it is also influenced by social and cultural factors. The greatest influence on a society's fertility rate, however, is the social attitudes towards reproduction. It is generally seen that every society puts limitations on its natural fertility. Procreation will not occur unless it is motivated.

The principal factors influencing fertility in a population may be grouped as under:

1. *Exposure to intercourse* such as age of first marriage, norms of premarital sexual behaviour and the value of chastity.
2. *Exposure of conception,* i.e., the availability of contraception, practices of contraception and ideals of family size or attitude towards family size, such as fatalistic attitude towards having children.
3. *Abortion and infanticide:* These are the factors that affect the actual birth and survival of the infant.
4. *Family structure* (joint or nuclear) has strong influence on fertility behaviour. Joint families in India have high fertility. Other aspects of the family such as patriliny or matriliny (dominance of husband or wife)) also affect the fertility behaviour.
5. *Cultural variables* that influence fertility are duration of married life caused by widowhood, separation or divorce, differential age at marriage, and roles and values of children. Religion also plays a significant role in regulating sexuality and fertility. Religious beliefs work as values which influence fertility.

Determinants of Migration

Along with births and deaths, migration is third important factor in population growth or decline. The term 'migration' refers to relatively permanent movement of individuals or groups with the purpose of changing their place of residence. It may be either external (between societies/countries) or internal (between regions). When people leave a country permanently, it is called *emigration*; when they enter, it is *immigration*.

As a social phenomenon, migration is fairly complex and results from a variety of factors. It is conventional to distinguish *push* from *pull* factors in the analysis of migration. We have discussed these factors earlier in this chapter. International immigration—changes of residence across national boundaries—has been a significant force in redistributing the world's populati n.

Immigration is a significant contributor to population growth as we see in the United States and Britain. Migratory movements within societies can vary in important wages. In modern societies, people move to places which offer greater economic opportunities and employment avenues, as we find in Bangalore, Pune, Mumbai, Hyderabad, Surat, etc.

According to UNO Report (June 2006) some 191 million people live outside their country of birth and migration is a major feature of international life. While most migrants move to wealthy nations (USA, Canada and the countries of Western Europe), 75 million people have moved to developing countries. Migration has several positive benefits for both the host nation and the country of origin. The speed of migration has recently declined due to the global factor of economic recession.

World Population History

It is held that in the initial phase of human history and pre-history, the human population grew at a snail's pace. The hazardous climatic conditions, the migratory character of early nomadic groups and the poor nourishment were all unfavourable for the growth of population. Until modern times, there were relatively few humans living on this planet. One estimate placed the world population of a million years ago at only 1,25,000 people. It has been estimated that the total population in 8000 BC was about 5 million people. Nowhere on the earth were population there. Until about 200 years ago, both birth and death rates were very high. As a result, the size of the world population remained stable. For every person who was born, someone died.

World Population Explosion

We hear of atom bomb explosion and hydrogen bomb explosion. We might be afraid of them but we do not seem to be scared of population explosion.

The population has exploded in last about 200 years and continues to accelerate rapidly. In 1850, the world's population was estimated to be 1 million. It doubled to 2 million by 1930. In 1975 it became 5 million and has reached 7 billion in 2011. Thus, it is clear that the world's population has greatly increased in the last few years.

The phenomenal growth of world population in recent years, particularly after Second World War (i.e., period after 1945), can be attributed to changing patterns of birth and deaths. It is a period in which the world population, including India, experienced unprecedented growth. In most parts of the world today, the birth rate has not declined dramatically, but the death rate has dropped sharply. For example, Japan's decadal population growth is as low as 1.1 per cent, China is growing at 5.4 per cent every 10 years, whereas

India is growing as a whopping 17.6 per cent. Pakistan's decadal growth rate is unbelievably 24.7 per cent. People who are born now live longer and add to numbers in the population. The most significant increase has been in the developing nations where some 75 per cent of the world's population is now concentrated. Although global population growth rates are gradually declining and many nations, especially in the developed world, have undergone demographic transition from state of growth to one population equilibrium. India also experienced an explosive growth of 127.4 per cent only between the period 1961–1999. It was estimated that in India population growth prior to 1921 was *sporadic*; between 1921 and 1951 it was *rapid*, and after 1951 it was called *explosive*.

Why has the death rate dropped? Death rates were high throughout most of human history because of poor nutrition and the prevalence of infectious diseases. People now are able to live longer because of advances in food production, better sanitation, nutrition and public health care. Modern science may have helped reduced the death rate from infectious diseases, such as plague, cholera, influenza, tuberculosis, pneumonia, measles, etc. These diseases were major causes of death. After the introduction of penicillin and other drugs, these diseases started declining steadily. Although, they may have helped in arresting the diseases, the reduction in infectious diseases was more a result of better nutrition, better sanitation, better housing and over and above better food supply.

World Population Trends

World's population is increasing at a rate of about 1.3 per cent, representing a doubling time of 54 years. We can expect the world's population of approximately 6 billion to become 12 billion by 2054 if the current rate of growth continues. Forecasts used to suggest that crises of global overpopulation would escalate beyond control early in 21st century. Reasons of this revolutionary rise of population are very many and can be summarized in the following points:

1. Decline in the death rate due to many factors explained in the previous section of this chapter. People today live longer as the malnutrition has been reduced, especially in so-called developed nations. The average life expectancy in such nations has increased from 40 to over 70 years. Currently, the major causes of deaths in these nations are heart disease, cancer, stroke and accidents. Malnutrition and starvation are still common among the world's poor.
2. 'Population always presses on the means of subsistence'—is factually untrue. Poverty is not the factor to lessen population growth. It is said that richer the nation, lower the population.

3. Higher birth rates, accompanied by large family tradition, especially in the underdeveloped nations, have helped in the increase of total population.
4. According to the former UN Secretary General Kofi Annan (June, 2006), some 191 million people now live outside their country of their birth and thus migration is a major feature of international life.

During the last five decades, the developed nations have passed through two different patterns of population growth: (1) the first marked by high fertility and rapid growth, and (2) the second marked by decline in fertility and little growth.

The State of World Population Report published by the United Nations (1982), indicated that a drop in the rate of population increase had at last occurred and the population will level off at about 10.54 billion in the year 2110. The report makes the following estimates of the world population at given times:

1950	1980	2000	2110
2.5 billion	4.4 billion	6 billion	10.5 billion

In poorer countries this reflects some success in the policy of governments and development agencies. In countries at an intermediate level of development, parents themselves often opt for smaller families, largely to secure higher living standards. For achieving this, they adopt the policy of having a car rather than a child. Threat of large family tended the individuals to postpone or avoid marriage and to limit reproduction within marriage by every means available. In brief, it was the clash between new opportunities and large families. The process of economic development itself provided the motives for curtailment of reproduction as British sociologist J.A. Banks has made clear in his book *Prosperity and Parenthood* (1954). The long run trend is one of low mortality, a relatively modest rate of production (nearing zero population growth) and slow population growth in the world population. If the above trends are proved correct, the world should be able to maintain its population adequately if resources are developed, distributed and used for this purpose.

World Population, Inequality and Underdevelopment

The relationship between the development of a society and its population size, composition and its growth rate in one of the most important issues often debated in academic circles. This debate has become more crucial in the wake of contemporary global issues: Why do some societies continue to languish in poverty, while others develop rapidly? Does the solution to stimulating development lie mainly in controlling population growth or elsewhere? Certain countries, like China and India, which were populous and already densely settled, took unprecedented increase in population as a constraint to socio-economic progress seriously. There was no time to wait for the demographic transition to lower fertility that accompanied prosperity; in the industrialized world this had taken at least a generation. There are three main approaches which have been adopted to solve the problem of population growth.

Liberal/Social Democratic View

This approach emphasizes on the reduction of population growth (plus aid) to create the conditions for development. It has been a widely held view of the western liberal/social democratic and even radical thinkers of 1960s that 'there is a population problem in the Third World countries'. These thinkers wanted to finance large-scale family planning projects and also favoured providing aid for developing infrastructural development such as roads, dams, factories, etc., in these countries. The view regards 'population control' as the key to development.

This view has been criticized severely by western and non-western scholars both on several grounds. In contrast the above view experts regard reduction in inequality within poorer societies as the key to reduction in population growth.

Radical/Marxist View

'Reduce inequality to reduce population growth' is the main plank of the followers of this view. Susan George and Fabrizio Sabelli (1994), for example, held that if the poor had more material and cultural resources, they would be less likely to have large families. This approach does not primarily argue that greater equality should be achieved through the distribution of aid. Aid can help deal with financial crises (as occurred in Ethiopia and Rwanda) but it can do relatively little to achieve greater economic production or more equal distribution of wealth within societies.

New Right/Laissez-faire View

There are scholars who say that population size is unimportant in development. P. Bauer argued that 'poverty in the Third World is not caused by population pressure' (*The Times*, 1995). In India also some writers held that there is no relationship between the population growth and the poverty. But this view cannot be accepted as proper on the ground of scientific facts.

Population as a Social Problem

It has long been a widely held view that there is a population problem in the Third World (including India) and that 'population control' is the key to development. In 1995, Robert McNamara, then President of the World Bank, observed, 'The greatest single obstacle to the economic and social advancement of the majority of peoples in the undeveloped world is rampant population growth ... . The threat of unmanageable population pressures is very much like the threat of nuclear war'. This view gave rise to a heated debate especially in the poorer nations. This view was later replaced by the view which is widely held outside the West that it is inequality—both global and within poorer societies—rather than population growth that explains underdevelopment. There is an 'overconsumption in the West'.

The population problems vary in space and time and also from region to region. It had soared in the poorer parts of the globe, especially Asia and Africa, with typical growth rates of over 2 per cent a year. The effect of this over time was startling. First, the population rapidly became younger, with up to half under the age of 15. Secondly, the rate of growth was exponential: 50 per cent more citizens in 16 years double the number in 25. World population had taken 120 years to grow from one to two billion people but just 35 years to reach three billion around 1960. The intervals to each successive billion would shorten dramatically.

When first observed, this unprecedented phenomenon provoked a Malthusian panic. How would a planet bursting at the seams manage to feed, shelter and provide for all these people? The spectacle arose of humankind reproducing itself at such a pace as to devour the world's supply of natural resources within a few generations. The growing pressure of population on resource base has created many socio-economic, cultural, political, ecological and environmental problems. Without a drastic curtailment in fertility, all prospects of development would lag further behind. No resource base could be expected to produce improvements in quality of life for populations that doubled themselves in less than a generation.

According to a recent U.N. Population Report, in 20th century, urban population has increased tremendously and is expected to be double in 2030 especially in Asia and Africa. In developing countries, the population in towns and cities shall be 81 per cent of their total population by 2030.

The Indian population is growing rapidly with the rate of 1.5 per cent per annum (2011) and the increasing numbers cannot be accomodated within the traditional economy of the rural areas. It is first time since 1921 when Indian urban population has gone up more than its rural population. This growth in urban population is due to migration from rural areas. The rate of migration to cities, even by Third World standards, is exceptionally high. Delhi, the capital has been the fastest growing of all, but Kolkata, Mumbai and Chennai have several million inhabitants. These cities are massively congested. In many areas large numbers of individuals wander the streets during the day and sleep on the streets at night. They have no homes of any kind. Other exists in shanty dwellings, set themselves around the edges of the city wherever there is little space. The shanty dwellers have virtually no possessions. Makeshift squatter housing surrounds the outer edges of the city. Squatter housing tends to spring up in any cleared or undeveloped area including in or around public parks and sometimes neighbourhoods which in the past have been affluent. In metropolitan cities, a sizeable number of the poor live in urban slums. These are overcrowed area of a city marked by poverty and poor living conditions. Besides acting as breeding ground for many types of crimes, slum living has a number of detrimental effects on health.

Population Problems in India

Most of the world population lives in the developing countries or poorer nations. China and India support over 21 per cent and about 16 per cent of the total world population respectively. Taking together the developing countries have over three-fourth of the total world population. India's growing population, as revealed by census of 2011, 121 crore, (an increase of more than 18 crore in the last decade) vitally concerns anyone interested in the solution of its various social problems. This huge population is not only unsustainable but also has an adverse impact on the environment. In addition to its size, the composition and distribution of the Indian population have an important influence on many of the policy issues. For example, the clustering of Indians in metropolitan areas, like Mumbai, Kolkata, Delhi, Chennai, Hyderabad and Bangalore, has intensified the housing problems. The steep rise in the proportion of citizens over 60 years of age has placed a severe strain on social services (especially medical facilities) available for the elderly people. According to UN estimates, in India, the size of elderly population (60+ population) in 1995 was 67.2 million which is estimated to be 324 million in 2050.

What have we achieved in the last 65 years (after independence) at the population front? Life expectancy at birth in India estimated to have gone up from 32 years in 1947 to 65 in 2010. The world population's life span has gained more than a decade since 1970—from 54.4 years in 1970 to 67.5 years in 2010 for an average man and from 61.2 years to 73.2 years for a woman. An average Chinese man, at 72.9 years, is living almost 10 years longer and a Chinese woman is living 11.5 years longer than their Indian counterparts which is 63.2 years for a man and 67.5 years for a woman. An average American is living nearly 13 years longer than an Indian. An average Indian man's life expectancy at birth has increased by nearly 15 years in the last 40 years, while an average Indian woman is living over 18 years longer than what she did four decades ago. Commenting over the India's life expectancy figures Professor Majid Ezzati of the University of Washington said, one of the main reasons behind India's impressive gain in life expectancy has been the reduction in rates of child mortality and also low mortality among young adults.

The death rate, which used to be around 45 per thousand, is down to just about 7.4 per thousand (2011). Hundreds of millions who have died in earlier times are alive. This happy outcome in the field of population is due to global medical advances. In the matter of birth rate we have been able to lower it down from 32.5 (1991) to 20.6 (2011) per thousand. But it is still very high in comparison to other advanced countries.

Some of the major population problems of India may be put briefly as under:

1. *Rapid Growth of Population:* We know that in spite of many attempts to check population growth, the birth rate is still high (annual exponential growth rate is 1.64 per cent as per 2011 census), but the death rate has been checked because of the development and extension of medical facilities. Family planning is not practised sincerely on a large scale, especially in rural areas. This situation has resulted into large proportion of youth (15–24 years, 2%) along with the aged (32% in 2011) who are dependent on relatively small workforce of the population. This large proportion of young population puts great pressure on the available medical, educational and other social amenities. It is estimated that due to the rapid population growth, 25 million people are homeless and 171 million people have no access to safe drinking water.
2. *Disproportionate Gender Composition:* According to Census 2011, national sex ratio (females per 1,000 males) is 940. Most countries in the world have more women than men. But India and some South Asian and East Asian countries differ. Female mortality is higher in these nations. This has resulted in there being more men than women in India and the sex ratio is lower than 1,000, except in two states—Kerala (1,084) and Puducherry (1,083). India is one of the few countries where the child sex ratio between age of 0–6 has been declining. The falling child sex ratio is the result of two main factors: (1) high female infant mortality (relative to male infant mortality), and (2) female foeticide. Both in turn reflect parental and social discrimination against girls and has been recognized essentially as an attitudinal problem. Experts cite societal pressure and dowry demands as the reasons for this menace rather than lack of education and awareness.
3. *Poor Standard of Living and Malnutrition:* Standard of living in a country is also affected by its population. In India, there is a great shortage of nourishment, especially that of balanced diet. The standard of living is low and housing conditions are often very poor which lead to health problems such as deficiency diseases. The ignorance of people, inadequate medical facilities, and lack of financial resources come in the way of improving the housing and health conditions.
4. *Unemployment:* The pressure of unwanted population growth increases the army of unemployed youths of employable age. Such desperate youths become a burden on the society. They may indulge in unlawful activities and cause harm to the law-abiding people. In India, a large

proportion of population is dependent on agriculture which is mostly done by traditional methods, obsolete equipments and inadequate financial resources. Consequently, the production per unit area is low. The secondary and tertiary sectors (industries and services respectively) are relatively less developed. Thus, there are very limited employment opportunities for both the unskilled and semi-skilled people. The agricultural sector does not provide employment to a large number of unskilled workers. The educated and skilled persons also have very limited opportunities of employment. Consequently, both the uneducated and educated, skilled and unskilled, workers migrate to urban areas in search of jobs. Thus, the towns and cities have become overcrowded, making living conditions poorer and resulting into socio-economic and environmental problems such as problems of crime and delinquency, prostitution, pollution, transportation, violence, etc.

Population Policy

A policy is a formalized set of procedures designed to guide behaviour. Its purpose is to maintain consistency in behaviour in order to achieve a specific goal. Population policy, for example, represents a strategy for achieving a particular pattern of population change. The strategy may consist of only one specific component—a single purpose goal—such as to lower the crude birth rate by ten points during a specific period, say five-year period or it may be multifaceted such as an attempt to 'rationalize' or 'modernize' reproductive behaviour.

In common parlance, the term 'population policy' refers to the legislative measures, administrative programmes and other government actions in a country intended to regulate its population size in order to attain social, political and economic goals. The United Nations have defined population policy as 'measures and programmes designed for the achievement of economic, social, demographic, and political and other collective goals through affecting critical demographic variables'.

According to UNEP (1973), population policy 'is an effort to affect the size, structure and distribution of characteristics of population'. It includes efforts to regulate economic and social conditions which are likely to have demographic consequences. The population policies of the different countries have been formulated to achieve different objectives. These may be classified in the following groups:

1. The antinatal policy which aims at discouraging the growth of population. This policy may be further grouped as under:
   (a) to reduce the population growth rate not necessarily to zero;
   (b) to achieve a negative rate of growth with a view to reduce the size of population; and

 (c) to stabilize the population by achieving a zero population growth rate.
2. Adopting the policy of population increase.
3. The distributional policy which deals with distributional imbalances of population. Such policies influence the demographic processes according to pre-set objective, for example, discouraging people to move from rural to urban or suburban areas. This is done by providing means of subsistence (employment) and basic facilities to the people in the rural area itself. Such policies aim at checking the unregulated movement of population and the increasing concentration of people in the urbanized areas.

There is a consensus among the scholars of demography that the only preventive way of achieving any of the above objectives would be to reduce the birth rate instead of permitting the death rate to increase. There is also a consensus that rapid growth of population in the developing countries need to be curbed and for this purpose containing the births is the best policy. It is needless to say that the desired national social, economic and political goals of a country can be achieved through any or more of the three components of population change, namely, fertility, mortality and migration. Through these components, not only the size and numbers but also the composition and regional distribution of population in a country can be regulated in a desired direction.

Population Policy in Different Countries

The size of population, its structure, composition and growth rate are closely influenced by the population policy of a country. Each country has its own population policy. These policies range from encouragement of high fertility to varying degrees of discouragement. Some of the developed countries (e.g., United States, Canada, Australia, Japan and Singapore) follow the policy of slow growth. This is known as policy of *pronatalism*. In these countries the populations are near the replacement level and birth and death rates are almost equal. Contrary to this, the population policies in some of the Afro-Asian and Latin American countries are to reduce the size of population, while in some European countries such as Germany, Russia and France, the governments are adopting the policies of population increase. These countries were experiencing an excess of death over births, which posed an imminent threat of population decline and as such they encourage growth in population.

As stated above, the developing countries, including India, are mostly following the policies to restrict the growth of population. During the last about five decades, numerous countries have adopted policies aimed at reducing population growth. The main aims of such policies are: (i) decreasing birth rate, (ii) decreasing mortality, (iii) limiting the number of children in the family to either three, two (as in India) or one (as in China), and (iv) checking concentration of population in urban areas.

In most of the developing and less developed countries, the governments have come out with a variety of policies focusing on mortality control, fertility control and individual well-being.

Some of the important measures taken by governments are:

1. Enacting laws like legalizing abortion.
2. Giving economic incentives (cash awards) for smaller families and disincentives to those producing more children above the norms prescribed by the government. This may be in the form of restricting employment in government services or to contest elections in democratic bodies like panchayats, etc.
3. The preferential treatment for small family members.
4. Financial rewards for sterilization.
5. Creating awareness among the masses regarding the adverse consequences of having more children.
6. Promoting voluntary family planning and birth control techniques through supplying necessary information and contraceptives.
7. 'Development is the best contraceptive,' an idea held to be true for some of the European countries where the trend is towards declining growth in population. It is argued by Susan George (1977) that if poor have more material and cultural resources, they would be less likely to have larger families.
8. Increase in age at marriage and restriction on pre-marital reproduction have also been suggested as a measure to bring down the birth rate. Raising the age at marriage will definitely help in reducing the size of the family.
9. Female education is regarded as the most important factor in reducing fertility rate. It has direct, indirect as well as joint effects. Directly it helps in changing attitudes towards a small family. Indirectly, it affects in following respects: (i) it delays entry into marriage, (ii) it increases awareness about family planning, (iii) it helps to accept birth control measures, (iv) it creates aspiration for a happy small family norm, (v) it reduces infant mortality, (vi) it creates an environment for social mobility, (vii) it enhances possibilities of outdoor female employment, and (viii) it increases rationality.
10. Last, but not the least, an important measure adopted by some countries is the 'Chinese model of coercion' in population control. In India, a tough sterilization policy was also adopted in 1976–77 during the Indira Gandhi regime but it was resisted by the masses. Some thinkers support the 'coercive model' as the only effective solution to check the formidable population growth. Other than sterilization, various other forms of coercion (such as heavy financial penalties for parents who have children above the prescribed norm) are used in different countries.

Population Policy in India

A growing concern regarding the adverse effects of population growth on development and prosperity has witnessed in the less developed parts of the world since the middle of the 20th century. After independence, Indian decision-makers also realized the importance and need of population control as early as in 1951–52, though before independence a sub-committee on population was also appointed by Indian National Congress in 1940 under the chairmanship of renowned social scientist Radha Kamal Mukerjee to suggest ways and means to arrest the galloping population. After 1921, the population of India began to increase by rapid strides. This committee laid emphasis on self-control, spreading knowledge of cheap and safe methods of birth control and establishing birth control clinics. It also recommended raising the marriageable age, discouraging polygamy and an eugenic programme of sterilization of persons suffering from transmissible disease. But, the Bhore Committee (1943) discarded the self-control approach and advocated 'deliberate limitation of family' approach as an effective way of birth control.

After independence, a population policy committee was created in 1952 which suggested for the appointment of a Family Planning Research and Programmes Committee in 1953. A Central Family Planning Board was created in 1956 which emphasized sterilization. Up till 1960s a rigid policy was not adopted to arrest the fast growth of population. The policy framed in 1951–52 was ad hoc in nature, flexible, and based on a trial and error approach. When the First Five-Year Plan was formulated, it was enumerated in the plan that the programme for family limitation and population control should (a) present an accurate picture of the factors contributing to the rapid increase of population; (b) discover suitable techniques of family planning and devise methods by which knowledge of these techniques could be widely disseminated; and (c) give advice on family planning as an integral part of the service of government hospitals and public agencies. Until the Fifth Plan, family planning programme concerned itself primarily with birth control but in this plan 'maternal and child health and nutrition services' were also included as an integral part of family planning programme. Despite all the Five-Year Plans (from First to Tenth) and policies, the population of India is growing at a faster pace and taking the shape of 'population explosion'.

The striking growth rate of population compelled the government to adopt a relatively more clear and less flexible policy of population which can stabilize the growth rate. In 1961–71, the population growth rate was 2.25 per cent which was highest in any decade after independence. At present (2001–2011), the population growth rate has declined to 1.50 per cent. In April 1976, the First National Population Policy was framed by the Union Ministry of Health and Family Planning which suggested a wide spectrum of programmes including raising the statutory age of marriage, introducing monetary incentives, paying special attention to improving female literacy, etc. Though this policy was endorsed by the parliament, it was planned at a time when the Emergency was clamped all over India. Sanjay Gandhi, the then President of Indian Youth Congress, took the programme of sterilization overzealously which made the masses hostile towards the government led by Indira Gandhi as well as the programme. One of the reasons for this was said to be the excesses committed in the programme. There was an overall resentment among the people (as a result of which the Congress was voted out of power in elections held in March 1977). This incident defeated the whole purpose of the family planning programme. The enthusiasm of the people about birth control was also to some extent slackened. The later governments became extremely cautious about the implementation of programmes of family planning. The term 'family planning' was replaced by 'family welfare'. While delivering a talk on 'Indian Population in the 1990s,' on February 8, 1991, the noted demographer Ashish Bose said that 'family planning programme has completely failed in the country and entirely a new approach is needed for its success'. The progress to arrest population growth has been extremely slow as is evident when we compare it with China. Through vigorous family planning programme since 1970 and a more rigid policy of having only one child per family in 1980, China has avoided the birth of more than 200 million children and brought the fertility rate down to 2.5 from 5.82 among eligible mothers. This is a classic example of the role of government policy in affecting birth rate.

To check the alarming population growth, an attempt has been made to rejuvenate the National Family Welfare Programme. The Ministry of Health and Family Welfare revised the strategy in the last decade of the 20th century seeking to broaden the area of family planning. It was emphasized that the population control programme would continue purely on voluntary basis as an integral part of a comprehensive policy package covering education, health, maternity and childcare, and women's rights and nutrition, including anti-poverty programme. It was made *people's programme* based on *welfare approach*. This revised strategy particularly focused on the provision of family planning strives at the doorsteps of the people. It is with this objective that the age of marriage is proposed to be raised for women from 18 to 20 years as envisaged in National Population Policy document, 2000, discussed later on. For raising the status of women, much emphasis on female education is also being given. Efforts are also being made to involve the voluntary organizations to promote family planning. As a part of family welfare and population control, the government has revised the PNDT Act in 2003, which was enacted in 1994. The main aim of the Act is to check female (embryo) infanticide.

The 1990s, however, witnessed a marked shift in the approach of family planning programme in the country. The early years of the decade had seen intensification of women's movement, both within and outside the country, in reaction to the overwhelming responsibilities imposed on women in family planning programme for achieving fertility reduction. The proponents of the movement were very critical of the approach and regarded the prevalent methods of birth control as an infringement on women's fundamental rights. It was against this background that an expert group under the chairmanship of Dr M.S. Swaminathan was appointed in August 1993 to prepare a draft on new population policy. The committee submitted its report in 1994. This draft could not take the shape of a fresh policy on population till 2000 due to some political happenings and change of governments. It was only in February 2000 that the Government of India announced its second population policy. The policy affirms the commitment of the government towards voluntary and informed choice and consent of the citizens.

National Population Policy, 2000

The National Population Policy (NPP) 2000 provides a policy framework of achieving goals and prioritizing strategies during the next decade to meet the reproductive and child health needs of the people of India along with the target to achieve the net replacement levels (Total Fertility Rate). It aims at stable population by 2045.

The following national socio-demographic goals were formulated to be achieved by 2010:

1. To address the unmet needs for basic reproduction (contraception), child health services, supplies and infrastructure (health personnel).
2. To make school education up to age 14 free and compulsory and reduce dropouts at primary and secondary school levels to below 20 per cent for both boys and girls.
3. To reduce infant mortality rate to below 30 per 1,000 live births.
4. To reduce maternal mortality rate to below 100 per 100,000 live births.
5. To achieve universal immunization of children against all vaccine preventable diseases.
6. To promote delayed marriages for girls, not earlier than age 18 and preferably after 20 years of age.
7. To achieve universal access to information/counselling, and services for fertility regulation and contraception with a wide basket of choices.
8. To achieve 80 per cent institutional deliveries and 100 per cent deliveries by trained persons.
9. To achieve 100 per cent registration of births, deaths, marriages and pregnancies.
10. To prevent and control communicable diseases, especially AIDS and sexually transmitted infections (STIs).
11. To promote vigorously the small family norm.

12. To integrate Indian Systems of Medicine (ISM) in the provision of reproductive and child health services, and in reaching out to households.

It is to be noted that like China, a coerced population control policy of one child only has not been accepted in India. It has been kept totally voluntary. For achieving the goals of family welfare programme, accredited social health activists have been appointed.

The policy document hoped that if NPP 2000 was fully implemented, India's population in 2010 would be 1,107 million. In other words, the absolute population would be lower by over 55 million if TFR is brought down to replacement level by 2010. The document stated a special strategic theme for underserved population—slum population, tribal communities, displaced migrant population and adolescents. Not only this, NPP 2000 had identified a separate strategic theme for the aged persons for their health care and support.

Ironically enough, the family planning (new welfare) programme failed to deliver desired results at least till recently. Much of the failure, as is generally suggested, can be attributed to a deep-rooted attitude of preference for a male child and also ignorance of the rural masses about the birth control techniques. Despite all efforts, there is little evidence of our capacity to arrest population explosion. An estimate suggests that about 8,000 persons are added to it everyday. According to the Human Development Report (2011), India ranks a low 134 position among 187 countries in terms of HDI. The HDI ranking is a combined measure of long and healthy life (expectation of life), education and standard of living.

Family Planning and Family Welfare Programmes

It has long been a widely held view in the West that there is population problem in the developing and underdeveloped countries including India. In the 1960s this view as often associated with liberal/social democratic and even radical thinkers who wanted to finance large-scale family planning projects in poorer countries. In addition, they often favoured providing aid for infrastructural or basic economic development, e.g., roads, dams, factories, etc. This view emphasizes that population control is a key to all-round development. Even, the World Bank has also endorsed it from time to time. In 1995, Robert McNamara, President of the World Bank said, 'The greatest single obstacle to economic and social development of majority of people in the undeveloped world is rampant population growth … . The threat of unmanageable population pressures is very much like the threat of nuclear war.'

During the last about five decades, numerous countries have adopted policies aimed at reducing population growth. Limiting fertility is the best way to slow down population growth in any population but it is also the most complex method. Most of the developing countries have applied the varying techniques for promoting family planning and birth control ranging from supplying contraceptives and information to much more direct involvement. It is widely believed that the rate of natural increase of population can be reduced if all the measures such as mortality control, fertility control and individual well-being are combined and used simultaneously.

The most common methods of family planning are sterilization, condom, loop, pill, withdrawal, rhythm, sheath and diaphragm. A good number of couples use more than one method, depending on circumstances, availability and mood of the moment. These days operations for family planning have become popular, especially among the middle class couples.

Family Planning in India

Till today, India is number two in the world in terms of population. As per our growth rate there is every possibility of its becoming the world number one within a few years. Crores of rupees are being spent from the national exchequers on various schemes of population control and family planning campaigns. All these years, one fundamental human right that we have successfully protected as a nation is the right to multiply ourselves. We have certainly proved to the world how fertile we are.

Family planning involves the provision of birth prevention, information, services and appliances. It also involves teaching women (sometimes men as well) about their body and how to prevent births, usually with contraceptives but sometime also with abortion or sterilization.

As written earlier, after independence, a Population Policy Committee was constituted in 1952 and a Central Family Planning Board was established in 1956 with a view to check the increasing population. During the 1960s, a more vigorous family planning programme was advocated for stabilizing the growth of population. Right from the very beginning, a voluntary family planning has been adopted in our country. The programme of family planning involved intensive education, provision of facilities and advice to the people in the far off areas through a network of family planning centres. The masses were educated about the merits of small family and the eligible couples were motivated to adopt the preventive methods of population growth. During the Fifth Five-Year Plan period (1974–79), a more rigid policy with an element of compulsion, monetary incentives, penalties and legalization of abortion was adopted. During 1975–77, when the emergency was in operation, a tough sterilization policy was adopted under the Prime Minister Indira Gandhi, which was opposed and resisted by the masses. Objections to the tough policy also became evident during the election held in 1977 after emergency wherein the Congress lost power at the centre. When in 1980, Indira Gandhi returned to power, she became extremely cautious in implementing the family planning programmes. Subsequently, Indian administration used less coercive methods of encouraging family planning. The new methods include placing health experts in all villages with more than 1,000 population, publicizing the merits of small families and offering financial rewards to parents who accept sterilization after having two children. The family planning organization attempts to provide a variety of contraceptives and other services to them. In its family planning awareness drive, the Government of India adopted the UNEP guideline of delaying the first child and spacing the subsequent births.

In 1977, 'family planning' was rechristened as 'family welfare'. Now, it embraces all aspects of family welfare, including improvement in women's educational level and their status in the society.

After 1980, the efforts of family planning (family welfare) of almost all governments in the states and at the centre have much slackened. In fact, for all practical purposes, the country is without an effective programme or target. Political parties cleverly skirt the subject, and election campaigns are conducted without a word about it. Now, it has become a tabooed subject. Because of this apathy towards the programme, the rate of population increase is still over 1.64 per cent. The total fertility rate (TFR) in India is as high as 2.58.

One of the biggest hurdles in population control is illiteracy and conservative mind-set. Condom still remains a taboo. A large section of the people of India are tradition-bound and religious in their attitudes who do not accept easily new ideas and modern outlook. Being religious, they generally do not observe family planning. Birth control is forbidden by some religious sects such as Catholic and Islam. In India, caste restrictions on occupation also help to slow down transformation of society and process of development. Thus, a positive and favourable attitude among the people towards birth control is essential for which, large-scale literacy is necessary.

Family planning programme in India has come to a standstill. It has taken a back seat today. In fact, the programme is moving backward as today we are producing 31 children every second. This stagnation is bound to wipe out all the efforts that have been made so far. Population control has been a hundred per cent centrally sponsored programme since its inception. Expenditure on the programme has been increasing over the years. From a budget of Rs 14 lakh during the First Plan period (1951–56), it increased to Rs 65 crore in the Eighth Plan period (1992–97) and to Rs 1,20,375 crore in the Eleventh Plan period (2007–2012). In spite of this increase in budget, family planning programme has not made any success but rather going backward.

When we compare our programme and the population growth with China, we are much disheartened to note that our programme is very slow, the fertility rate 2.58 is more or less standstill while China has brought the fertility rate down to 2.5 from 5.82 among eligible mothers. This success was achieved by China within the last decade by adopting the norm of one child per couple. They have reduced the family size from two children to one child only in 1980. Those who violated this norm were penalized. Penalties however vary with local conditions. Generally, they include ineligibility for better housing, reduced educational opportunities, fines, etc. The planned child was given special allowances till the age of 14 for education and upbringing and the couple was provided with land for building a house or for farm or machinery.

In China, free contraceptive and abortions are available in clinics throughout the country. A well-devoted organizational network exists for implementing the family planning programme. Women's contraceptive and fertility records are pasted at the local health centres. Friends and neighbours may strongly and repeatedly urge for the compliance of the one-child policy.

Social and institutional changes have speeded up the decline in fertility. Better health services and higher literacy of females have also helped in reducing fertility and consequently birth rate. Also, with the expanding role of woman from that of a traditional housewife to a working woman in a factory or an office, fertility rate declined. A major component of the programme in China is encouraging late marriage and late child birth. The marriage age is generally over 24 for women and 26 for men and pre-marital sexual relations are uncommon. Being a democratic country, India cannot adopt such a rigid and coercive policy. This policy is indirectly an encroachment over individual freedom. Very recently, population control policy and family planning (welfare) are being pursued with great zeal and vigour with the result that the birth rate has now been showing a steady decline.

Family Welfare: A Feminist View

Feminist analysis of inequality in general has also drawn attention on the construction and maintenance of female body. As a result of the feminist movement, started in 1960s women became more vocal in their dissatisfaction with the traditional health care system. Marked by the appearance of the book *Our Bodies Ourselves* (1969), in some developed countries like America and Britain, women's health movement emerged out of the realization that women are by far the most frequent users of health services for themselves, their children and other dependent family members. This movement took many forms, including organizations working for changes in the health care system, women's clinics, and birth and self-help groups. These health groups have expressed concern about the hazards of oral contraceptives and the intra-uterine device (IUD). This women's health movement has demanded increased entry of women into medical colleges and hospital administration positions. In India, this type of movement is yet to be emerged, though some problems have been raised by female medical students and some NGOs here and there.

Why Sociologists Study Population?

Many natural and social scientists are involved in the study of population-related issues from different viewpoints. Apparently, it appears that population is only a biological phenomenon, but this is not correct. Human population cannot exist without socio-cultural interaction. For a sociologist, social implications of population are equally important. Some elements greatly augment the population, while others greatly deplete it. In this connection, Kingsley Davis (1949) observed, 'Fertility, mortality, and migration are all to a great extent socially determined and socially determining. These are the inner or formal variables in the demographic system. Whereas the outer or ultimate variables are sociological and biological.'

Sociologists focus on the socio-cultural factors that influence population rates and trends. They study fertility, mortality and migration. These variables are profoundly affected by the norms, values, practices and social patterns of a society. The population affects our chances of finding a job and a spouse. If we have children, and if so how many, it may affect our standard of living, quality of life, education and what more is the chances of contesting election of Panch or Sarpanch for a Gram Panchayat.

For a sociologist, the following characteristics of population are important:

1. Size of population
2. Distribution of population
3. Other characteristics—relationship between population changes and economic, social and cultural variables like poverty, illiteracy, ill-health, family structure, etc.

The classical sociologist, Emile Durkheim has included the study of the size of population in his scheme of subject matter of sociology under the heading 'Social Morphology'. He placed emphasis on the study of density and volume of population both. Both affect the social structure of a society. While discussing the causes of division of labour in a society, Durkheim contended that the causes of division of labour should be discovered in the 'material and moral density' of society. By 'material density' he means simply 'population density', i.e., the number of people in a society and the amount of interaction that occurs among them. The growth of cities is a clear evidence of an increase in material density (population pressure). Increasing concentration of population brings with it an increasing intense interaction among people to which he calls 'moral density' (social volume). He said, societies become more voluminous as they advance. Increase in volume influences material density (number of social relationships) also which ultimately brings a change in the social structure.

Sociological studies of the institutions of marriage and the family and of the religious and moral values, associated with the universal human experiences of birth, illness and death, greatly illuminate the basic demographic processes. Beliefs and attitudes towards sex and procreation, marriage customs and the structure of the family, economic, political and military considerations play a large part in determining the frequency with which people have children. Levels of living, public health practices and methods of treating the ill are closely related to the incidence of morality. Ethnic and religious conflicts, territorial differences in economic opportunity, immigration laws and the uprooting of peoples by war and conquest are the principal determinants of migration (Wrong, 1961).

Chapter 14

Poverty

KEY FEATURES

- What is Poverty?
- What is Poverty Line?
- Measurement of Poverty
- Causes of Poverty
- Causes of Poverty in India
- Theories of Poverty
- Effects of Poverty
- Who is Poor?
- Why are the Poor Still Poor?
- Poverty and Inequality
- Poverty and Progress
- Alleviating Poverty
- Feminization of Poverty
- Globalization and Poverty
- Some Vital Facts about Poverty in India

Poverty is not a new phenomenon. The awareness about it is certainly a new phenomenon. It was only in 1889 when Charles Booth published a study about Londoners that the people came to know about the nature, form and extent of poverty in London and it was recognized as a social problem. It is an all-pervasive social problem found all over the world. Even the most wealthy nation—United States of America—is not free of this problem. Statistics reveal that in the US poverty has increased in recent years, but poverty, in the context of this country, usually means malnutrition and sub-standard housing, not starvation or total lack of shelter. The form and extent of poverty may differ but it is found in almost all developed, underdeveloped and undeveloped nations. It is the basic cause of many other social problems—illiteracy, crime, delinquency, suicide, etc. Not only that this problem is rampant widespread but the politics in all nations centres around it. In democracies like India, even elections are fought on this issue. In 1972, Indira Gandhi made *'Garibi Hatao'* as the main plank of her election campaign.

What is Poverty?

What is the definition of poverty? It is a very complex question because different scholars (sociologists, economists and even political scientists) have defined it in their own way. The question becomes all the more complicated when this phenomenon is linked with the price level which is ever changing. This is why sociologists and other social scientists found it difficult to develop a consensus definition of poverty. According to *Oxford Dictionary of Sociology* (1994), 'poverty is a state in which resources, usually material but sometimes cultural, are lacking'. It is generally determined by the standards that exist within a society. Its measurement differs from place to place and from time to time. This is why sociologists define it either in absolute or relative terms.

Absolute Poverty

Long back, Seebhom Rowntree, a pioneer of poverty studies, defined absolute poverty as the condition under which one cannot afford 'the minimum provision needed to maintain health and working efficiency'. He decided his 'poverty line' on the basis of nutrition a person gets from his/her diet. Families whose income fell below this poverty line were in absolute poverty. The definition of absolute poverty is based on a fixed level, usually known as 'poverty line'. It is the line below which poverty begins and above which it ends. According to *Oxford Dictionary of Sociology* (1994), 'Absolute poverty refers to a state in which individual lack the resources necessary for subsistence.' The notion of 'poverty line' describes poverty in subsistence terms. This is why absolute poverty is also known as 'subsistence poverty'. Charles Booth, another pioneer of poverty studies, was one of the first to try to establish a consistent standard of subsistence poverty. It refers to the lack of basic requirements to sustain a physically healthy existence (sufficient food and shelter to make possible the physically efficient functioning of the body). This notion of poverty is still used most frequently in the analysis of poverty worldwide. Mike O'Donnell (1997) defined it as 'absolute poverty is insufficiency in the basic necessities of existence ... . This usually means being without food, clothing and shelter'. It is a condition of actual physical want—state of starvation, malnutrition, disease and want of clothing, shelter and medical care. Though there are many flaws in defining poverty in terms of subsistence, yet a distinction is usually made between subsistence (absolute) and relative poverty.

The United Nations has defined absolute poverty as 'a condition characterized by severe deprivation of basic human needs, including food, safe drinking water, sanitation facilities, health, shelter, education and information'. It depends not only on income but also on an access to services. The UN definition of overall poverty includes ill-health, lack of access to education and other basic services, inadequate housing, unsafe environments, social discrimination and exclusion. The population below poverty line is unable to meet minimum human needs. This requires 'minimum' income to buy necessities of life and this varies from society to society and time to time. Then, there is a question—what is the standard poverty line below which absolute poverty exists? This is again a problematic question because poverty line and its criteria of determination differ from place to place and time to time. The poverty line in USA in 1980 was 8,414 dollars, while in India it was per capita monthly expenditure of Rs 107 for the rural and Rs 122 for urban areas in 1990. According to a recent (March 2012) estimate of Planning Commission, a person earning Rs 28.65 in cities and Rs 22.42 in rural areas is considered as poor. From this standard, a large section of India's population is also stricken by absolute poverty.

The World Bank has defined absolute poverty as 'the amount of spending needed to ensure a person a minimum daily diet of 2,150 calories. The poverty line corresponds to an annual income per person of about 275 to 370 dollar'. Using such guidelines, the World Bank estimated in 1990 that at least 1.1 billion people in developing (Third World) countries—or about one-third of the population of these nations—are extremely poor. In India, poverty line is drawn on the basis of per capita (adult) daily intake of 2,400 calories for the rural and 2,100 calories for the urban.

Relative Poverty

In view of the problems of measurement of the notions of physical and/or cultural needs, many scholars have abandoned the concept of absolute poverty and in its place they have developed the idea of relative standards, i.e., standards which are relative to the particular place and time. For scholars advocating relative poverty, it is a concept that generally refers to the phenomenon of relative deprivation. According to *Oxford Dictionary of Sociology* (1994), 'Relative poverty refers to individual's or group's lack of resources when compared with that of other members of the society—in other words, their relative standard of living.' The concept of relative poverty is used to measure the degree of poverty. Accordingly, people are poor because they are deprived of the opportunities, comforts and self-respeet regarded as normal in the community to which they belong.

Peter Townsend (1979) has argued that those who have 'resources so seriously below those commanded by the average individual or family that they are, in effect, excluded from ordinary living patterns, customs and activities' are relatively poor. Thus, for him, relative poverty applies on those people who cannot afford the amenities and activities that are customary.

Some scholars consider that relative poverty exists in the absence of a minimum standard of living on socially or culturally established criteria and not the criteria of survival or subsistence as contended in the definitions of absolute poverty. Since relative poverty is a matter of differences with regard to material resources, it is judged on the basis of a floating standard of deprivation of the disadvantaged people at the bottom. It involves the comparison between the living conditions of some groups and those enjoyed by the majority of a population. Thus, the difference between absolute and relative definitions of poverty is the absolute level of deprivation (subsistence level) and culturally defined standard of living. Most of our country's current social progress is viewed in relative terms. Our commonly used measure of relative poverty is the nation's poverty line.

To sum up, it can be said that poverty signifies economic and social conditions wherein a section of society is unable to fulfil even its basic necessities of life, i.e., sufficient food, clothing and shelter needed for physical existence. It also includes deprivation of opportunities to health, education, employment etc.

What is Poverty Line?

It is a measure of (relative) poverty used by the government as a definition of poverty. It sets the boundary, and consequently the numbers of the poor. It serves as an official definition of poverty. This is why it differs from place to place. Every government fixes its own poverty line. This definition determines which individuals and families will be eligible for certain government benefits. Generally, poverty line is determined by the prevailing standards of what is needed for health, efficiency, nurturing of children, social participation and maintenance of self-respect. It usually involves a judgement of basic physiological needs (for survival, safety and security).

Sociologist Greg Duncan's book *Years of Poverty and Years of Plenty* (1987) is an oft-quoted study which reveals that the 'poor' are not a static class. Instead, the composition of the poor continually changes, with some families moving above the poverty level after a few years while others step below the level. In India, to emancipate the downtrodden people, it is not the class but the caste which has been made the basis for giving benefits.

Measurement of Poverty

Broadly, the poverty of a given society is expressed in terms of national income, minimum per capita income, expenditure, amount of resources and nutritional level (per capita daily intake of calories) and health care. In America, a measure of poverty takes into account the size of the family, the number of children and whether the family lives on a farm. The income level considered impoverished varies with these factors. Scholars said that minimum food intake (in terms of calories) alone is an incomplete measure of poverty. Human dignity requires more than physiological needs—food, shelter, clothing, medicines. The social needs and the need of self-improvement, such as education, should also be included in the measure of poverty. The differences in measures of poverty have always created a row among the scholars and different institutions about the estimates of poverty—the number of persons below the poverty line. Generally, poverty line is drawn on the basis of barest minimum desirable nutritional standard of calorie intake and on its basis minimum income required is calculated taking account the 'price level' at that time.

Causes of Poverty

There are many causes of poverty. Different scholars have placed emphasis on different causes. For an easy understanding, all these causes may be grouped into two main divisions: (1) individual causes (causes pertaining to the individual himself/herself), and (2) societal causes or social structural view of poverty.

Individual Inadequacy

This ideology ascribes poverty to be the result of an individual's working abilities or lack of motivation. This view finds the causes of poverty within the individual and contends that it is the fault of the individual poor because he/she is lazy, dull, and inefficient or lacks initiative. Liberal reformists believe that poverty is frequently the result of the situation an individual experiences. Thus, illness, unemployment, low pay and loss of income in old age can be immediate causes of poverty, yet these are rarely the 'fault' of the people concerned. According to this ideology, success and failure in life depends upon individual's inherent qualities and as such poverty is a personal matter. The 19th and early 20th century writers on poverty and other social problems commonly attributed their causes to individual pathology—weakness of either a physical, mental or moral kind. Belief in self-help and the idea of 'survival of the fittest' (Spencer) supported this view on general ground that the deserving should succeed and the weak and worthless fail. So, if anybody fails in his/her life or caught in the grip of poverty, nobody is to be blamed but herself/himself—his or her laziness, dullness, bad habits (such as alcoholism, gambling) and other vices are responsible for his/her poverty. The 19th century thinker, Max Weber had also attributed the development of capitalism to hard work, honesty, punctuality, discipline, etc.—the core of ethics of Protestantism.

Individualistic explanations of social problems (including poverty) flourished again in the 1970s and 1980s in western world, including United States of America. After the adoption of the policy of liberalization in 1990s,

India also vigorously campaigned for the philosophies of individual enterprise and reward and cut back on many welfare programmes. It is argued that those who say that poverty in capitalist society is largely social structured in nature, such comments misleadingly individualize poverty and inequality. In their view, welfare dependents are more likely to be the victims rather than the villains of capitalism.

Societal Causes (Social Structural View)

Protagonists of this view link poverty to social structure—social institutions, belief system, economy, large family structures (joint family), education, and social practices, such as child marriages, dowry system, death feasts, ritualism, etc. This view emphasizes that the cause of poverty does not lie in the individual but in the social structure itself. Radical structuralists and Marxists believe that it is the capitalist system which produces fundamental social problems including poverty.

Causes of Poverty in India

The causes of poverty in India are mainly high population growth, slow job growth, slow economic growth, chronic unemployment, natural calamities, unequal distribution of wealth and rampant corruption.

The ever-increasing population is the main cause of many ills of Indian society. Religious attitude, child marriages, preference for male child, joint family system, illiteracy and to some extent the agricultural economy are the main causes of population increase. The growth of population has a direct effect on the standards of living of the people.

There is a relationship between poverty and age structure of the society. The older we are, the more difficult it is to obtain employment. Older people, particularly those over 60 years of age, are often without adequate savings and have to depend on their children for economic support.

Poverty is also related with the size of family. Many large families (having more children) than small ones are poor. This is even truer if the head of the family is a female. The larger the family, the lower the per capita income and the standard of living. Everywhere we see poverty and large families going hand in hand. Those least fit to carry on the race are increasing most rapidly.

The educational level of the people also contributes to poverty. Functionally illiterates who have meagre education and lack job skills do not find employment and thus they are forced to remain poor. It is sometimes said that poor are poor because they are uneducated. Poverty is also one of the main determinants of health. The greatest impediment to better health is the lack of adequate income. If people can get employment and good incomes, they would secure better health for themselves.

In India, besides general demographic factors (age structure, family size, educational level etc.), the factors of casteism, communalism, fatalism, regionalism, discrimination, prejudices also affect poverty indirectly by impending the employment opportunities. People still stick to their traditional occupations, even if it is not gainful and do not want to leave their place of origin. The feeling of casteism and communalism also sometimes put hindrance in providing jobs to the members of other castes and religion. Recently, the sentiments of regionalism have driven people from Assam, and other North-East provinces and Maharashtra due to upsurge of regional agitations. Not only these factors, Indian people are prone to spend large amount of money on (unproductive) social ceremonies like marriage (dowry, pomp and show), death feast, religious rituals, etc., even at the cost of incurring heavy debt, which ultimately leads them towards the evil of poverty.

It is argued that belief in the Hindu concept of rebirth and other worldliness is an important contributing factor of poverty in India. According to this philosophy, suffering of all kind including poverty flows from deeds of the past life and is the God's justice. It is only means of salvation. Amelioration of suffering is tantamount to interference with the spiritual system. Therefore, the wholesale acceptance of poverty and misery by masses; the parading of poverty and its elevation to virtue. A Hindu attaches more importance to the world to come than to this world. He believes the poverty of this life is a boon in disguise to accomplish and accumulate good deeds for the other world. However, this explanation of the cause of poverty is weakening with the spread of education.

Theories of Poverty

There are many theories of causation of poverty. The main among them are: (1) The Culture of Poverty Thesis, (2) The Cycle of Deprivation Thesis, (3) The Dependency Culture Thesis, and (4) The Capitalist Economic System Thesis.

The Culture of Poverty Thesis

'Culture of poverty'—a most popular concept—was developed by Oscar Lewis (1961) in his study of poor people of Mexico. He used this concept to explain the phenomenon of poverty. Accordingly, poverty is generated and regenerated by the cultural attitudes and lifestyles of the poor, which are the product of sub-culture of poverty. Why the sub-culture of poverty has the effect of keeping the poor in poverty, he argued that the poor develop a sense of fatalism, a feeling that one's destiny cannot be altered. This fatalistic attitude creates a sense of resignation and distinctive patterns of behaviour and belief among poor and this is perpetuated by childhood socialization.

Thus, culture of poverty (fatalistic attitude, particularly lifestyle) is transmitted over generations. This sub-culture of poverty is marked by violence, deviance and illicit conduct. Besides, there is a strong inclination to live for the present and unwillingness to plan for the future. Then, there is a feeling of worthlessness and isolation from the rest of the society; and a lack of interest in joining political parties, trade unions or pressure groups which campaign for social change (eradication of poverty).

Many sociologists have not accepted Lewis' above thesis. All those who are poor cannot be forced into single cultural model. The pejorative implications of the concept, 'that the poor are to blame for their own plight and the parents raise the children to be socially deprived, in turn, have been contested by many scholars'. Sociologist Hyman Rodman, for example, has argued that poor people have no choice to adapt to the unrewarding conditions of poverty and much of their behaviour can be accounted for in this way. The poor have behaved as they have, not from a radically divergent cultural perspective, but out of force of circumstances and lack of alternatives. In that sense, much of their behaviour is adaptive to the circumstances of poverty, deprivation and powerlessness. The culture of poverty thesis is rejected by the view that emphasizes the importance of 'life-cycle of family'. This view stresses that many of the poor are not so very poor different from the majority of population.

The Cycle of Deprivation Thesis

Keith Joseph's concept of 'cycle of deprivation' has some similarity to the Lewis concepts of 'culture of poverty' and 'class culture', but it lays greater stress on the effect of material factors, such as poor housing and low income, in undermining prospects for self-improvement from generation to generation. Among the cultural factors, he particularly emphasizes the inadequacy of parental upbringing and home background.

The Dependency Culture Thesis

The notion of 'dependency culture' is essentially a version of the culture of poverty thesis. According to Charles Murry (1989), there are broadly two types of poverty—that of the 'deserving' and 'undeserving' poor. It is the latter who have created for themselves a 'culture of dependency' and have been able to do this by living off welfare. He argues that many poor find it preferable to be 'on welfare' (i.e., in poverty) than to work. Such people take advantage of what he calls 'the generous' (welfare) revolution. It is often observed that many beggars do not want to leave begging even if they are offered lucrative work. For such people, begging is an easy job than earning money through working somewhere.

The Capitalist Economic System Thesis

Scholars of leftist leanings argue that the real cause of poverty is to be found in the way that our society is organized. Marxists claim that poverty is an inevitable feature of the capitalist economic system. A laissez-faire policy (liberalization) or the free market economy allows capitalists who own means of production and businesses to make huge profits while paying low wages to their workers. Sometimes, their workers are bonded labourers who live just on hand-to-mouth existence. The Marxists have not only rejected the culture of poverty theory but also blamed the capitalist system for the inequality and poverty in society.

Effects of Poverty

Poverty unquestionably has a marked influence on people's lives. Max Weber saw class as closely related to people's life chances—that is, their opportunities to provide themselves with material goods, positive living conditions, and favourable life chances. Life chances are reflected in such measures as housing, education and health. Occupying a higher position in a society improve one's life chances and bring greater access to social rewards. By contrast, people in the lower social classes are forced to denote a larger proportion of their limited resources to the necessities of life. It is estimated the working class and other poor people spend 80 per cent of their income on food which they often buy on credit from nearby grocer's shop who charges exorbitant rates. They have to pay a higher interest rate for credit.

The affluent and powerful not only have more material possessions than others, they also benefit in many non-material ways. Children from higher income families are much more likely to attend school and college than are children in poor families. The children of the working class either do not go to school or even if they manage to join some school, they generally drop out at primary level or at the most secondary level. They often live in such neighbourhoods with poor government schools, at which they may not even learn, read and write. They quit as soon as they are old enough. It seems education is a life chance very closely associated with family income.

As is true of educational opportunities, a person is also affected in important ways by his or her class position. The chances of a child's dying during the first year of his or her life are approximately 80 per cent higher in poor families than in a middle class family. This higher infant mortality rate results in part from the inadequate nutrition received by low-income or no-income expectant mothers. Even when they survive infancy, the poor are more likely than the affluent to suffer from serious chronic illnesses like malaria, TB, etc. Besides high rate of infant mortality, the poor also suffer from major health problems. These include nutritional problems because they cannot afford vegetables, meat and fruits. Whenever they fall ill, they do not get proper medical care. They cannot afford to visit private doctors and clinics. In poor neighbourhoods (e.g., slums) either there are no government clinics and hospitals or if luckily these exist, they are likely to be overcrowded, understaffed and poorly equipped. Doctors who work in such hospitals and clinics are either not available or they do not pay much attention to the patients. This is a common feature of government hospitals in India.

Most rural poor people live in dilapidated huts thatched with cow dung, sand and grass. In urban areas, working class poor live in rented one-room tenements located mostly in slum areas. Sometimes two families share the same tenement which may be very overcrowded and lack privacy. The poorest people do not even have homes or tenements. They live on the streets. They are homeless people.

Like housing, education and health, crime can be particularly devastating when it affects the poor. Whether innocent or guilty, such a person may sit in jail or judicial custody for months because of his/her inability to arrange money for bail. If assured of a crime, a person with low income and status is likely to be not represented or if represented, by an inexperienced public defender (lawyer). Being unrepresented and powerless, they are always the targets of attacks and hostility by the powerful and the police.

Poor people also suffer from social discrimination and condemnation. They are looked as inherently inferior, stupid, lethargic, unreliable and lacking the qualities of moral responsibility and individual initiative. Because of this attitude towards poor, they are harassed, humiliated and discriminated against at every level. They receive little or no attention in offices they visit.

Who is Poor?

E.M. Foster says, 'We are not concerned with the very poor. They are unthinkable, and only to be approached by the statistician or the poet.' Generally, or in common parlance, a 'poor' is that person who does not have sufficient amount of money to purchase food to keep him and the members of his family alive and the necessary clothing and a shelter in the form of a house. These are the persons who do not have a proper diet, no shelter or have depleted shelter, live in insanitary conditions, and have a lower life expectancy than the majority of population. Their house is often overcrowded. Many of them sleep on streets, subways, footpaths, doorways or park benches under the open sky. In extreme winter, they sometimes freeze to death in certain areas. In rural areas, they live in mud thatched small huts and in urban areas in ghettos (slums), devoid of all basic utilities—water, latrines, bathrooms, electricity, etc. Thus, such persons must be defined as poor, no matter whether society recognizes their poverty or not.

Most poor people are either engaged in low-paying jobs or are without jobs. Some are too ill or disabled to work and others are living alone (aged, widowed), who cannot earn enough to support themselves and their children, if any. The poor cannot get loans for self-employment. They cannot seek employment where work is available. They also pay more for most of what they buy. Most of their incomes, if any, are spent on food. Moreover, the commodities they purchase from nearby grocery shop are often of low quality, adulterated and stale devoid of any nutritive value. The situation becomes more grim when the earning member of a poor family loses his/her job even for a short period or dies. The poor have no assets to protect them from the collapse of their precarious financial situation. They thus have hand-to-mouth existence at such times.

The nature of poverty has undergone considerable change over the years. Who the poor are today is quite different from those called poor in an earlier period. In the 19th century and even more than half of the 20th century, people living in villages (in India about 70 per cent of the population lives in villages) depended directly or indirectly mostly on agriculture (as landless labour or small farmers) for their livelihood, having a very small mud thatched hut, were regarded as poor. According to UNDP report (1996), 39 per cent of the rural population was living below the poverty line or earning less than Rs 2,444 per person per year. This figure might have changed a bit due to the implementation of many rural development and *Garibi Hatao* (poverty eradication) programmes but still most of the village India is suffering the consequences of poverty.

The change in technology has changed the face of poverty. There is a great exodus of population from villages to urban areas in search of jobs. The use of electricity, tractors, and many machines in agricultural pursuits, along with the improved hybrid seeds and method of cultivation, have forced many people to leave villages. This change in technology has made many people poor while a meagre (i.e., big farmers and zamindars) affluent. Technology often displaces workers by abolishing their jobs, while creating other, better paying ones for people more technically trained. This happens to both rural and urban workers. Thus, loss of job by technological change is but one factor—a very important factor—in accounting for the poor. The use of computers in banks, railways, colleges and schools and in many government and private sector organizations has not only thrown many persons out of job and but also lessened the opportunities for jobs. People who do not have technical education today have less and less opportunities in the job market.

Why are the Poor Still Poor?

In spite of the government welfare measures and so many schemes and programmes of poverty alleviation (about one lakh crore of rupees yearly are being spent on different programmes), in conjunction with government policies for uplifting the conditions of poverty-stricken people (people below 'poverty line') set by the government, why are the poor still poor? Why the picture of rural India has not much changed even after 65 years of our independence? Based on CIA World Factbook, about 30 per cent (2010) poor people of the world live in India. Many answers have been given to this question.

Besides the theoretical explanations discussed earlier, the practical reasons that are keeping the poor still poor in spite of so many programmes of alleviating poverty are the followings:

(a) Rampant corruption at every stage and in every scheme of development has affected the poor in many ways. Corruption and inefficiency mean that little of the allotted money reaches the poor. Our late Prime Minister Rajiv Gandhi once remarked that out of every one rupee, it is only 15 paise that reaches to the needy poor.

(b) Utter indifference and apathy of the officials towards poor people.

(c) Partiality in all schemes of development, such as in selecting BPL families, allotting water and electric connections.

(d) Lack of initiative in the leaders as well as at every level of administration.

(e) Most of the programmes are based on ideologies rather than the ground realities and requirements of the poor people.

(f) Uncertainty of developmental schemes because of the uncertainty of the government. With the change of the government, priorities also undergo changes.

(g) Lack of co-ordination between different developmental schemes related to poverty alleviation.

(h) Growing population which makes all our efforts of removing poverty futile.

In the end, it may be stated that planning by itself is not enough. What matters most is sincere and honest efforts along with commitment on the part of the implementing agencies and authorities in making the anti-poverty drive a success. Last but not the least, unless India's population growth is checked, rather frozen, no scheme of development can make headway in the achievement of its objectives and for this, it is necessary to build a political consensus on population control and put a stern check on the immigration of people from the neighbouring countries. After every five years, the old government goes and the new one comes with some new schemes (sometimes just change in the name of the scheme) and slogans like *'Garibi Hatao,'* but nothing changes substantially except some figures relating to the number of poor and rich people or GDP, etc.

Poverty and Inequality

According to the Marxist view, the major cause of poverty is inequality or uneven distribution of wealth and income—a main consequence of capitalism. Weber also recognized the inequality of capitalist society; he did not attribute it essentially to capitalism. Rather, he thought that large, rational organizations or bureaucracies, including the capitalist corporations, are responsible. These are necessarily hierarchical and unequal. He anticipated that socialist societies developed large-scale bureaucracies; they would be characterized by inequality.

There is a considerable controversy about poverty and its relationship within inequality. From one point of view, any society with inequality is bound to have poverty. In other words, poverty is more likely to occur in a society which accepts inequality. Sociologists who adopt a relative definition of poverty accept that for the eradication of poverty, it is necessary to first abolish all inequality in income.

There are scholars who do not find any relationship between poverty and inequality. A wealthy businessman and a well-paid government official (IAS or RAS) or teacher are materially unequal but the teacher or official are not poor. Thus, poverty and inequality are not the same. Social inequality means that certain individuals or groups have more material or cultural resources than others, whereas poverty implies some insufficiency in the material or cultural resources of an individual or group (O'Donnell, 1997).

Poverty is an absolute concept, while inequality is a relative one. It is possible for poverty or head count ratios to decline (so that every one is better off), while inequality simultaneously increases, because income growth for richer segments is relatively more. But if inequality increases, it causes resentment because of the perception that deprived class, castes, women, ethnic or religious groups or geographical regions are not gaining enough from the trickle-down benefits of growth.

National Sample Survey Organization's (NSSO) data between 1993 and 2005 shows that while poverty figures are down, in absolute terms poverty is still rampant. One of every four Indians lives below the tide of poverty at less than a dollar (about Rs 50) a day. The income levels of the poor may be rising but they do not come even to the rate at which the rich are getting richer. The

20 per cent of salary earners in India earn 50 per cent of the country's total salary income while the bottom 20 per cent earn less than 5 per cent (*India Today*, September 24, 2007). This gap shows that how inequality is increasing in spite of the poverty figures are down.

As regards the expenditure, the bottom 20 per cent in rural India in 1993–94, enjoyed 9.61 per cent of the total expenditure and in 2004–05 this declined further to 9.40 per cent. Conversely, the share of the top 20 per cent of rural India in total expenditure was 38.59 per cent in 1993–94 which increased to 40.23 per cent in 2004–05. In rural India, the expenditure of the relatively rich increased more than that of the relatively poor. The detailed figures show that shares declined for all except the top 20 per cent. That is the reason inequality has increased. The urban Indian picture is no different (Debroy and Bhandari, 2007).

Poverty and Progress

It is alleged that poverty is associated with progress. With material progress, poverty grows more serious. As we move from rich to richer regions in the so-called developed nations, the poverty goes worse. Although discovery has followed discovery and invention has followed invention, neither has lessened the numbers of poor, nor the toil of the masses who most need respite. Following this line of argument, Henry George (1839–1897), a great champion of socialism, associated poverty with land situation. He said as 'land increases in value, poverty increases'. Land is more valuable in Mumbai than in Jaipur or Ajmer and there is more squalor and misery in Mumbai than in Jaipur or Ajmer. When increasing people live in limited area under a system of private property in land, rents are raised and land values go up. The cost of living mounts, wages are kept to a minimum, overcongestion of population and development of slums ensues, and again rents and land values are increased. To some extent above the assertion of George seems to be true. The poverty that we see today in urban areas is mostly the result of industrialization and its concomitant process of urbanization—development of centres of trade, commerce and education.

Alleviating Poverty

For tackling the problem of poverty and unemployment, the first requirement is to put a stern check on the rate of growth of population along with the illegal influx of population from the neighbouring countries. Explosion of population indirectly has put a great strain on India's economy and, in turn, hit all programmes of alleviating poverty. The increased population devours all the resources and benefits of economic and social developments. To solve the poverty problems, some measures as discussed below are suggested.

India is said to be an agricultural economy though it is now no more fully true, yet about 70 per cent of India's population still live in rural areas. The major portion of this population is poor. It requires rapid land reforms meaning a ceiling on landholdings and distribution of excess land among the landless. The holding must at least be of a size that a family cultivating it to normal standards is able to maintain itself on the yield. Even today, the large majority of holdings in the country are below such a size, which is largely the cause of the poverty and underemployment in rural areas. Any realistic land policy will help in achieving the twin objectives of alleviating poverty by creating employment and increase in production.

Providing the basic amenities in rural areas such as roads, drinking water, schools, medical help, credit supply (banks) and marketing facilities and so on is must. All these will create employment opportunities in rural areas and shall help in reducing poverty. There will be an indirect benefit also. It will decrease the drift of people from rural to urban areas.

After independence governments (central and state both) have launched many schemes and programmes for the overall development of the country. The important measures adopted for the removal of poverty are as under:

- *Five-Year Plans:* The First Five-Year Plan was launched in April 1951. Since then eleven plans have been formulated and implemented. The central objective of all the plans was to raise the living standards of people and to open out to them opportunities for a richer and more varied life. The social objectives are to reduce inequalities of income and wealth on the one hand and the welfare of the community on the other.
- *Policy of Nationalization:* To achieve the 'socialistic pattern of society', one of the objectives of economic policy, the government adopted the policy of nationalization. As a result, many banks were nationalized in 1969. Following this policy, the coal mines were also nationalized in 1972. Later on, this policy was adopted in many other fields also.
- *20-Point Programme:* In consonance with her slogan of *Garibi Hatao* (1971), Indira Gandhi, the then Prime Minister, launched 20-point programme of development.
- *Integrated Rural Development Programme (IRDP):* It was a programme of poverty alleviation launched in March 1976. Its main objective was to enable selected families to cross the poverty line.
- *Antyodaya Yojana:* This programme was initially launched by the then Government of Rajasthan on 2nd October 1977 and later on the governments of Uttar Pradesh and Himachal Pradesh also followed this model of development in 1980. The main plank of this programme is to develop

the poorest of the poor. *Antyodaya* means development (*udaya*) of the people who is at the bottom level (*ant*) of the ladder.

- *Training Rural Youth for Self-Employment (TRYSEM):* It is a scheme started in August 1979 to provide technical skills to the rural youth living below poverty line, in the age group of 18–25, to enable them to seek employment in fields of agriculture, industry, services and business activities.
- *National Rural Employment Programme (NREP):* This programme was launched in April 1977 to create additional employment opportunities in rural areas. This programme has now been merged into Jawahar Rozgar Yojana.
- *Rural Landless Employment Guarantee Programme(RLEGP):* This scheme was aimed to provide supplemental employment to the poor on public works. This programme too has now been merged along with NREP into the JRY.
- *Jawahar Rozgar Yojana (JRY):* This programme was launched in April 1980. This is an amalgamation of two previous employment schemes—NREP and RLEGP. According to this programme, at least one member of each poor family would be provided with employment for 50 to 100 days in a year at a workplace near to his/her residence. About 30 per cent of the jobs under this scheme are reserved for women.
- *Mahatma Gandhi National Rural Employment Guarantee Scheme (MNREGS):* This scheme was started in February 2006. It was first applied only in 100 most backward districts on an experimental basis. Later on, in September 2007, it was extended to whole of India. The main objective of this scheme is to provide wage employment to rural people. The present UPA government has proposed many changes in this scheme. Unfortunately, like all other government schemes, it is also found to be full of corruption and weaknesses as revealed by the report of Comptroller and Auditor General of India.
- Recently, the UPA government is trying to enact a Food Security Act, as a major step in alleviating poverty.

Feminization of Poverty

The gap between women and men in the cycle of poverty is a phenomenon commonly referred to as 'the feminization of poverty'. This term is used by social scientists to refer to the increasing proportion of the female poor in a country. Women are increasingly dominating the ranks of impoverished. Worldwide, women on an average are only slightly over 50 per cent of male earnings. Women experience unequal treatment almost in all fields. They are often denied inheritance rights. Though women are not segregated from men, they are the victims of prejudice and discrimination in the labour force, in family matters, in the legal system (inheritance laws), and in other areas. Their labour goes unrewarded and unrecognized (domestic labour is unpaid and their paid work is poorly rewarded). They are the first to be dismissed from paid work in any economic crisis. They are the first to die of hunger or poverty. In India, they are the last to eat (as per custom) and that too if something remains after eating by the males of the family. Their health care and nutritional needs are not given priority. They lack sufficient access to education (in India, they had been denied education till some decades ago) and support services. Their participation in decision-making at home and in the community is minimal. They have the lowest degree of personal autonomy. They are not allowed to have any rights regarding property. They are obliged to be isolated or veiled for religious reasons or to expose their bodies for commercial profit.

The life chances of women belonging especially to low income groups are very pitiable. They have to earn their livelihood, tender their children along with doing all domestic work. In many such families the menfolk do not work at all and depend on the earnings of female members. Moreover, the menfolk often beat and harass their wives for satisfying their sexual and material needs. The burden of supporting a family is very difficult for women who have not adequate source of income. Children whose mothers live in poverty run an increased risk of birth defects and malnutrition. They are deprived of education and even if they somehow get admitted in schools, they fare poorly in elementary (government) schools and drop out of secondary schools or even earlier than children from other types of families. Low income women suffer higher level of stress than other women and are much likely to receive adequate medical care. Like western countries, households headed by divorced or never-married women are not much common in India but by widowed women in low income groups are much in numbers. Though the exact figure of female-headed households is not available, but it is estimated about half of Indian women in poverty are in 'transition' coping with an economic crisis caused by the departure, disability, or death of a husband. The other half tends to be economically dependent either on the relatives (members of the joint family or her own parents or other nearest kith and kin), leaving nearby, or on the welfare system of the state (schemes like BPL, old age pension, etc.).

It must be emphasized that poor women share many social characteristics with poor men—low educational attainment, lack of skilled or unskilled jobs, and residence in economically deteriorating areas, named as slums. They experience more sexual harassment, victimization and abuse at the workplace. Such women are at a clear disadvantage in the labour market too in terms of both horizontal and vertical social mobility.

Globalization and Poverty

Globalization has evoked very different reactions in different fields across the world. It has yielded mixed results in India and other nations. It has affected almost all aspects of one's life—social, economic, political, educational, familial, religious, communal and health care, and even day-to-day life. So far as the poverty is concerned, globalization is generally seen in negative terms—a great source of increasing inequality in the society. From the international magazine *Fortune*, we learn how many Indians have been included in the list of very wealthy (super rich) persons. The small minority owns most of the wealth in India. While there is a multitude of poor, there are very few people who are rich. This exposes the process of concentration of wealth in the hands of tiny minority and resulting into the increasing inequality in India. After liberalization, along with globalization, the disparities between the poor and the rich are more and more increasing. According to one estimate, every fifth young Indian is without job (unemployed) and every fourth farmer is a destitute. Not only this, a new phenomenon of suicide by farmers, which was never heard before, has taken roots in Indian soil.

But there is also a bright side of globalization. It has for the first time in history made poverty an advantage (Swaminathan, *Times of India*). It obliges companies to search the globe for the ways to cut costs. The lower the wages in any country, the more competitive production there is, other things being equal. Once it does so, poverty becomes advantage and global jobs and production shift to it. China and India and many other Asian countries have long provided it. China is leading in manufacturing while India in services. What we are witnessing a boom, especially in IT (BPO) sector, in India is the result of this globalization. More and more jobs are being created to meet the demands of America and other western countries.

Some Vital Facts About Poverty in India

Poverty is the greatest socio-economic problem of India, yet there is a great contradiction about its estimate between the national and international agencies. This problem becomes all the more complicated and confusing when every day a new definition of poverty is proposed. To identify who is poor, sometimes the criterion of expenditure and at other time the income of a person is adopted.

- According to NSSO, the people living below poverty line (BPL) is:

1977–78	51.3 per cent
1993–94	36.0 per cent
2004–05	27.5 per cent (28.3% in rural areas and 25.7% in urban areas)
2010	37.2 per cent (UNDP)

- According to the latest Planning Commission data a person is considered living under BPL who earns less than Rs 28.65 per day in urban areas and Rs 22.42 in rural areas. It is estimated that the urban poor are some 80 million in comparision to the rural poor, who are some 120 million.
- According to an Economic Survey of Government of India (2007), about 86.2 crore of people spend less than Rs 20 per day. In rural areas, their population is 71.9 per cent and 32.3 per cent in urban areas. In rural areas, a person spends Rs 356.30 per month and in urban areas this is Rs 538.60 per month. In this expenditure food, fuel, light, rent, tax, clothes, education, medical care and all items of permanent utility are included. About 72 per cent of population still lives in villages.
- According to UNDP (2010), 37.2 per cent people in India still live below poverty line.
- In the last one decade more than one lakh farmers have committed suicide.
- According to the following three world institutions, the average income of a person in India per day is:

($1 = ₹ 56)

United Nations	*World Bank*	*Asian Development Bank*
1 dollar	1.25 dollar	1.35 dollar

An average expenditure per man is Rs 625 per month in rural areas while in urban areas, it is just double, i.e., Rs 1,171 per month. Kerala leads in expenditure per man. In villages 19 per cent of the villagers still live in huts, however 50 per cent of the people now live in their own *pucca* house.

- According to International Food Policy Research Institute's World Poverty (Hunger) Index, 2007 in a list of 118 countries, India ranks at 94th, Pakistan at 88th and China 47th.
- In Human Development Index Report (2011), India ranks at 134th position among 187 countries.
- On the basis of GDP, India ranks at 9th position in a list of rich countries of the world according to United Nations (2010) data.
- The number of millionaires in India is more than China.
- According to *Forbes* magazine, 2010, number of billionaires is 57 in India.
- India has per capita income of Rs 54,835 per annum in 2010–11.

According to a pilot survey of BPL people, conducted by Planning Commission (2011), based on the representative sample of 166 villages across 22 states, SCs and STs constitute half of the total "poor, deprived housholds". In other words, it is merely 25 per cent of the "non-poor households". The parameters used to identify the poor were ranging from huts, *kaccha* housing to illiteracy to homelessness, destitution and landlessness. Vivek Kumar, a sociologist, commented that the findings proved that caste and class identities in the country overlapped. He said, "economic deprivation depends on social identity" (SCs and STs form about 22 per cent of the population which is half of the rural people). The above results concurred Y.B. Damle's conclusions who said that social identity has an impact on the economic performance of people.

There is no reason to believe that the things will change radically in near future. Economic growth by itself largely benefits the middle classes, and arouses resentment among the rest. We need to rethink and find ways of creating an egalitarian society. Social equality generates mutual respect, trust and shared identity which moderates conflicts.

Chapter 15

Social Problems, Social Welfare and Social Security

KEY FEATURES

- What is a Social Problem?
- Elements of Social Problem
- Sources of Social Problems
- Types of Social Problems
- Social Welfare and Social Security
- Social Security in India

The explanation of social order and cohesion in society has been a central concern of sociology since the times of founder sociologist Emile Durkheim. Such issues have been discussed that how society works, how order and cohesion are maintained, how these are disturbed and what are the consequences of this disturbance. Whenever social order is disturbed because of some or the other reasons (mostly by social changes), the condition of social disorganization becomes apparent that gives rise to many kinds of social problems. No society is perfectly integrated. This is why, in almost all societies, past or present, we find varied social problems that have been the cause of the concern to the people of that society.

The origin of sociology is rooted in the study of social problems that developed as a result of industrial revolution and the consequent upheavals in 19th century. This revolution gave rise to many problems, such as urban slums, poverty, crime and prostitution on a large scale. This prompted many social scientists to study these problems scientifically and suggest solutions. It was felt that to solve social problems effectively, a considerable reliable knowledge about the functioning of the society is needed. This practical interest in social problems led thinkers like Auguste Comte, Emile Durkheim and Max Weber to establish a new branch of knowledge labelled as sociology.

A perfectly integrated society should have no social problems. But such society is rare. A changing society inevitably develops problems. Either conditions themselves change or become unacceptable to most of the people of a society. What has been acceptable behaviour becomes old fashioned (such as large family system), suspected, superstitious and barbaric (such as the custom of *sati*), or the society's changing values define an old condition as no longer tolerable such as child labour, low status of women, lack of education, poverty, low wages in the factories, etc.

What is a Social Problem?

Let us first define a problem? A problem is a condition of discontentment resented by someone. But when it is resented by many people, it becomes a social problem. For a problem to be social, it must involve a large number of people, sometimes groups and institutions, who consider a particular condition as undesirable and intolerable and want to correct through collective action. Thus, not all problems are social, unless the discontented persons come in contact, and vocalize their discontentment and associate to do something for its solution. A problem becomes social when it is communicated to others and the activity of one person leads to similar activity of other persons. Thus, a social problem is different from an individual problem. Individual problem is one which is felt by only one person or a small group of people. It does not affect the public at large. Its resolutions lie within the power and immediate milieu of the individual or group. A public issue however requires a collective approach for its solutions. No one individual or a few individuals are responsible for the appearance of a socially problematic situation and the control of this situation is also beyond the ability of one person or a few persons.

"Social problem is a generic term applied to a range of conditions and aberrant bahaviours which are manifestations of social disorganization. It is a condition which most people in a society consider undesirable and want to correct by changing through some means of social engineering or social planning" (Oxford Dictionary of Sociology, 1994).

The concept of social problem was first developed by sociologists. Fuller and Myers in 1941. They defined it as 'those conditions or situations which members of the society regard as a threat to their values'. Elucidating their ideas, they said at other place that it is 'a condition which is defined by a considerable number of persons as a deviation from some social norms which they cherish'. Reinhardt defined it as 'a situation confronting a group or a section of society which inflicts injurious consequences that can be handled only collectively.' Raab and Selznick (1959) hold that a social problem is 'a problem of human relationship which seriously threatens society or impedes the important aspirations of many people'. Merton and Nisbet (1961) have defined it as 'a way of behaviour that is regarded by a substantial part of a social order as being in violation of one or more generally accepted or approved norms'. Walsh and Furfey have defined a social problem as a 'deviation from the social ideal remediable by group effort'. Horton and Leslie (1970) wrote that a social problem is 'a condition which many people consider undesirable and want to correct. It is a condition affecting a significant number of people in ways considered undesirable, about which it is felt that something can be done through collective measures'.

Thus, in social problems two things must be present: (1) an objective condition, like crime, poverty, communal tensions and so forth, the presence and magnitude of which can be observed, verified and measured by impartial social observers; and (2) a subjective definition by some members of the society that the objective condition is a 'problem' and must be acted upon. Here is where values come into play. People start perceiving that some values are being threatened.

Elements of a Social Problem

Though the above cited definitions differ in ways these are explained, but the following important characteristics may be discerned from them:

1. A condition or situation resented as objectionable by a significant number of people.
2. It is considered as undesirable because of its injurious consequences.
3. All social problems want correction through collective action. They warrant change in conditions via some means of social engineering.
4. All aberrant behaviours or deviations from accepted norms are termed as social problems such as crime, juvenile delinquency, prostitution, rape, drug addiction, domestic violence, ethnic or communal tension.
5. Social problems are not static but change with the change in time and space. Changes in law and mores change the concept of social problem.

Recognizing an undesirable condition and defining it as a social problem are two different things. There can be disagreement if some people believe some condition or situation as undesirable but also think it unavoidable because it is a part of the human condition or the price we pay for 'progress' as we see in the case of environment imbalance caused by cutting of trees for constructing roads, dislodging people for constructing dams and canals, air and noise pollution due to increasing motor vehicles, rising rate of accidental deaths involving automobiles, etc. The steadily rising rate of accidental deaths involving automobiles is long considered to be unavoidable but after effective criticism by many people, automobile safety became a social problem. In the initial stages of industrialization, development of slums and ghettos was also regarded as unavoidable and not a social problem. People may not define a condition as a problem because it is desirable and natural, and not a threat to their values. Casteist/gender discrimination was not a problem for those who believe the castes/sexes to be naturally unequal. They would deny that differential treatment is 'discrimination' (for them, integration is a threat to their values, and thus a social problem). In reality, it requires a belief in equality in order to define discrimination as a problem. There are people who still do not believe that poverty is a social problem. They regard it as unavoidable fate of the masses. Poor people are to blame for their own condition of poverty. Such people define poverty as the personal failure of those who are poor, not a consequence of the arrangement of social structure.

But such old notions have changed in the modern societies and people started believing that something could be done about such condition and society (government) should take step to do something.

Sources of Social Problems

A perfectly integrated society has no social problem. But no society is perfect, and cannot be perfect, so utopian expectations are unwarranted. The existence of social problems indicates some unsatisfactory and value-threatening aspects of an otherwise satisfactory society. The sources of social problems are so many and may be grouped as under:

1. Social problems occur because modern society is so complex, and so intricate in its internal organization that an inconsistent and loosely meshed social structure cannot help but generate strains and social tensions. Most social problems are intricate and interwoven, like housing, poverty, unemployment, and inequality.

2. If modern society is highly productive and highly rewarding in status and material goods for so many, it still has a dark side to it. There are costs and casualties to any social system. It is often said that progress has its own price. Many developmental schemes have brought different types of problems for the people, e.g., construction of dams on the rivers has displaced many persons from their villages. Similarly, construction of roads has forced cutting of trees which in turn has led to environmental degradation. Roads construction has also displaced many persons.

3. Social change continually alters social structure and therefore disrupts established relations among social groups (such as relationship between Gujjars and Meenas in Rajasthan), redefines social roles (such as between working husband and wife), and renders some beliefs and behaviour patterns outmoded or dysfunctional.

Types of Social Problems

Sociologists distinguish between two types of social problems. First, problems of social organization which are created by the way the community or the society is organized. Community or society produces situations that some members of the society refuse to accept as right or necessary or even inevitable. These are, for instance, communalism, casteism, regionalism, poverty, gender discrimination, population, environmental imbalance (different kinds of pollution, health hazards, etc.). Second, problems of deviance having to do with the adjustment of people to conventional ways of living. These include, for example, delinquency, drug addiction, alcoholism, mental illness, various forms of sexual behaviour (rape, incest, sodomy), bigamy, prostitution, vandalism and host of other behaviours, most of which are forbidden by law.

Scientific Remedies for Social Problems

Durkheim's analysis of social problems and solutions can be presented in the following form:

Problems in modernity	*Causes*	*Solutions*
Anomie: lack of moral regulations, limitless ambitions, sense of worthlessness, lack of meaning in life	(a) Rapid social change (b) Decline of moral authority (e.g., religion) (c) Increased complexity in social roles and rules (d) Fragmentation of work	A new non-religious civic moral order. This is to be promoted through state, laws and education. Moral unity to be based on a sense of mutual social interdependence.
Lack of social integration, excessive individualism, class conflict	(a) Unfettered market system (b) Unregulated competition (c) Unequal opportunity for natural talents	Regulation of markets and working conditions, equal opportunity, abolish inheritance, fair inequality of reward.

Adopted from Tony Bilton and others, *Introductory Sociology*, 1996.

The Role of Sociologists

The social sciences, e.g., sociology, like all social sciences, have dual role. They serve to help the people to solve their problems and at the same time to explore and understand the world around them. They seek to understand the fundamental mechanism of social reality but their desire to understand is always motivated by the wish to control. The main aim of sociologist (pure/applied) is to improve social life, to bring welfare in society through scientific investigation, and to manage change in society. In this role, though he/she is specialist of scientific knowledge about the society, he/she tries to direct the change to establish harmonious relations in society.

As a pure scientist, the role of a sociologist is limited to the study of social problems—their causes and effects—and to suggest measures to solve them effectively. In this role, he/she is required to be just analyst of the problems. At the most he/she can devise ways and means to correct them, though this is also the task of a social worker—a different discipline from sociology. But, in no case he/she should involve himself/herself in the action programme to solve the social problem. It is advised that he/she should not assume the role of an activist.

Nowadays, there is a serious debate about the role of sociologists in solving social problems. There are sociologists like Alain Touraine (1988) who developed a radical new approach known as *actionalism*. He claimed that sociologist is an agent of change, not a neutral observer. He/she has a stake in the conflicts of his/her society. As such, he/she should play the role of a 'sociological interventionist' in which he/she should study social change movements by participating in them directly. Long back, founder sociologist Durkheim also wished to apply sociological knowledge to social intervention in order to create social harmony and regain balance in society disturbed by social change.

Social Welfare and Social Security

Social welfare is a very old concept. Its origin is in the spontaneous and neighbourly assistance extended to persons in distress. People used to help others in times of calamity and need—financial and physical. In this sense, it is as old a concept as the community life itself. Early social welfare philosophy was mainly dominated by religious and moralistic motives rather than the selfless desire to assist them materially. It was closely related with the religious ideas of philanthropy and alms giving. People used to carry welfare activities for the poor, downtrodden and infirm as charitable activities. And, this idea is still continuing. Charity gets over into the mores and it used to have powerful religious sanction. Most of these activities are performed individually or in the form of a trust. But, in recent decades, social welfare has taken an institutional character as has been defined by Kuid and Koller (1975): 'social welfare is an institution which covers a wide range of functions such as charity, family planning, social security, community centres and unemployment compensation.'

As a contemporary concept, 'social welfare' arose with the phenomenon of industrialism in the 19th century which brought in its train many social problems such as poverty, unemployment, squalor, prostitution, slums and many diseases. Before industrialization either these problems were non-existent or their amount was not so large that they could attract the attention of the people. Generally, such problems were used to be solved individually and through trial-and-error method as at that time modern scientific methods did not come into existence. After the development of science and technology, it was felt that the problems caused by industrialization may be solved with the use of scientific methods and thus the concept of social welfare came into existence.

In sociology, the concept of 'social welfare' came through the ideas of Auguste Comte, the founder of sociology. He argued that sociology should contribute to the welfare of the humanity by using science to understand and control human behaviour. He said, 'a true science of humanity must find out both the laws of order and progress'. Comte believed that sociology was the means by which a more just rational social order can be established and society can be reconstructed. In this connection, it will not be out of place to mention that the early sociologist W.G. Sumner and many others were against all state-directed welfare schemes. Sumner said, 'Society needs first of all to be free from meddlers—that is to be alone.' Similarly, Spencer (1886) advocated laissez-faire policy (no interference policy). He believed that an unfit has no right for support. They have to leave the planet.

The term 'social security' is used generally to refer to protective measures to assist people and households facing severe shortages in income and basic survival needs due to different work, health or family related risks such as unemployment, old age and illness.

It is also an important instrument for the well-being of workers (of organized and unorganized sectors both) and their family members as well as too young and old people who are unable to earn their living to sustain their life for a variety of reasons. The protection and assistance traditionally afforded by kin and community to the young, elders and other disabled members of the family is now dwindling after industrialisation due to the breakdown of joint family. The Beveridge Plan may be said as the first planned effort, directed to integrate social welfare and security programmes. Its attack on five giants, namely, want, disease, ignorance, squalor and idleness, was the beginning of the modern social security programmes. A comprehensive social security programme, launched to provide a national minimum standard of living for every citizen, is thus understood as a distinguishing feature of a welfare state. A welfare state is responsibile for providing the means whereby all its members can reach minimum standard of health, economic security and civilized living and can share according to their capacity in the social and cultural heritage. On the other hand, social welfare programmes seek to supplement the statutory social security programmes and meet the particular individual needs which do not fit into the common pattern. It was said that welfare without security or vice versa is not possible.

Social welfare and social security are thus intimately linked up but they are pursuing different ends. Social security refers to a state of mind as well as an objective fact. It is mainly directed towards providing income security as a preliminary to a state of social and psychological well-being. Social welfare, on the other hand, is broadly understood as the end product of possession of goods, positions in life and supply of services to help a person live in wholesome contentment and communication with others in the group. Narrowly speaking, social welfare refers to a set of institutional or personal services provided either by the state or voluntary organizations to prevent serious incident or to reform or rehabilitate the victims of disabilities, or disorganization or delinquencies or destitution and so on.

Social Security in India

In India, the modern social security measures were planned and implemented after independence. They were too meagre and limited to the organized sector workers only, which constituted about 8 per cent of the total workforce, despite a majority of the workforce (about 93% in 2004–05) comes in the unorganized sector (self-employed or casual workers). Importantly, the need to ensure social security for all, especially those in the unorganized sector, is an overarching concern recognized in the Eleventh Five-Year Plan (2007–12). The Constitution of India provides strength and spirit to the social security for organized and unorganized workers through its Directive Principles of the State Policy. Social security legislations came into existence as a part of industrial policy after large-scale industrialization. Some social security benefits in the form of Acts for the organized workers working in the big industrial units (factories, mills, etc.) were also enacted during the British period. But major social legislations were passed only after independence. The important social legislations and social security measures relating to industrial workers may be cited as under:

1. The Workmen's Compensation Act, 1923
2. Provident Funds and Miscellaneous Provisions Act, 1952
3. The Employees State Insurance (ESI) Act, 1948
4. The Maturity Benefit Act, 1961 (amended in 1976)
5. The Payment of Gratuity Act, 1972
6. Universal Contributory Health Insurance Act, 2004
7. The Aam Admi Bima Yojana, 2008
8. The National Health Insurance Scheme, 2007
9. The Indira Gandhi National Old Age Pension Scheme

To mention a few, followings are the ameliorative programmes and schemes for the tribals, rural and urban poor:

1. Five-Year Plans and Community Development Projects (CDPs)
2. Food for Work and Antyodaya Yojana, 1977
3. Integrated Rural Development Programme (IRDP), 1976
4. National Rural Employment Programme (NREP), 1977
5. Jawahar Rojgar Yojana (JRY), 1980
6. Mahatma Gandhi National Rural Employment Guarantee Scheme (MNREGS), 2006

7. Integrated Tribal Development Plan
8. Swarna Jayanti Gram Swrozgar Yojana, 1999
9. Swarna Jayanti Shahri Swarozgar Yojana
10. Sarva Shiksha Abhiyan, 2001
11. Indira Awas Yojana
12. Rajiv Awas Yojana, 2009
13. Pradhan Mantri Gram Sadak Yojana
14. Bharat Nirman, 2005
15. Jnanani Suraksha Yojana, 2011
16. Pradhan Mantri Swastha Surksha Yojana
17. Total Sanitation Programme or Nirmal Bharat Abhiyan, 2012

Thus, while a large proportion of the organized sector workers have been be benefiting from legally mandated and budget-provided social security benefits since independence, but most of the workers in the unorganized sector have been left out (only less than 10% of the total unorganized were benefited). According to the World Labour Report, 2000, the public sector expenditure on social security in India was as meagre as 1.8 per cent of the GDP, whereas it was 4.7 per cent in Sri Lanka and 3.6 per cent in China. The eligibility criterion is also too tight as the exclude many a vulnerable persons. The below poverty line (BPL) criterion is a minimalist and inappropriate approach to extend social security to the unorganized workers. About 55 per cent of the population though not comes in the category of the poor in India but is vulnerable. Not only this, most of the unorganized workers suffer from the lack of awareness about social security and social welfare measures.

It has been argued that globalization has adversely affected social welfare programmes of the state. The state often promotes rather than accepts globalization. This is why, it is bound to impact on the policy regime and welfare character of the state.

Social welfare and social security are intimately linked up but they are pursuing different ends. Social security refers to a state of mind as well as an objective fact. It is mainly directed towards providing income security as a preliminary to a state of social and psychological well-being. Social welfare, on the other hand, is broadly understood as 'the end product of possession of goods, positions in life and supply of services to help him to live in wholesome contentment and communication with others in the group'. Narrowly speaking, social welfare refers to a set of institutional or personal services provided either by the state or voluntary organizations to prevent the incidence or to reform or rehabilitate the victims of disabilities, or disorganization or delinquencies or destitution and so on.

Chapter 16

Social Exclusion and Minorities in India

KEY FEATURES

- Definition
- Mechanisms of Social Exclusion
- Impact of Social Exclusion
- Social Exclusion in India
- Social Exclusion and Caste
- Social Exclusion and Women
- Social Exclusion and Ethnic Groups (Minority Groups)
- What is Meant by 'Majority' and 'Minority'?
- Minorities in India
- What is a Minority Group?
- Characteristics of Minority Groups
- Majority-Minority Group Relations
- Problems of Minorities
- Improving the Minority-Majority Relations
- Minorities and Development
- Sachar Committee and Muslims in India

In almost all human societies, exclusion in some or the other form exists. Certain groups or individuals are excluded from the mainstream society. They are deprived of some opportunities which are needed for the full blossom of human life. While, the way in which individuals or groups are excluded is context-specific, certain social differences continue to serve as grounds for exclusion. These differences include belonging to a particular ethnic, religious, caste, gender or age group; or living in a particular geographic area; or having certain physical or mental disabilities. Various forms of social differences overlap and intersect in complex ways over time. Some of the most common categories of excluded groups will be described later in this chapter.

Definition

Social exclusion has been interpreted differently in different contexts at different times. It is a multidimensional term. This is why it is a bit difficult to define it in a precise manner. The term was initially coined in France in 1974 where it was defined as a rupture of social bonds. Later on it became the central theme of social policy in many European countries. As a broader framework of social policy, it was suggested that social exclusion is the process that excludes individuals, groups and aggregates from full participation in the society in which they live. This term was used to denote various categories of people, identified as mentally and physically ill or handicapped, suicidal people, aged invalids, abused children, substance abusers, delinquents, single parents, marginal asocial persons and other social misfits (Silver, 1994). Because of stigmatized and narrow view, this notion of social exclusion was later on abandoned and was used for neo-poverty—the poverty that culminated due to technological change and economic restructuring. In this sense, the concept of social exclusion was broadened to refer an overall process of social disintegration meaning rupture of the relationship between the individual and society.

Nowadays, the term 'social exclusion' is used for the population which is excluded in community life. Such populations are discriminated in providing basic services, amenities and equal opportunities necessary for their development. Not only this, they are deprived of social life. Thus, social exclusion is a process of limiting social relations and the denial of providing equal and living opportunities imposed by certain groups of society upon others which leads to the inability of an individual to participate actively in the basic political, economic and social functioning of the society. It involves both the act of restricting access to resources and the consequences that follow. In brief, social exclusion refers to the process through which groups are, wholly or partially, excluded from full participation in the society in which they live. These main processes include discrimination, deprivation, isolation, shame, etc.

In Indian context, the main bases of social exclusion are religion, ethnicity, gender and caste. Social exclusion, which is based on discrimination, may be active or passive. In active exclusion, its agents (government or private agencies) refuse to lure or accept the participation of the members of the group excluded despite their equal formal qualifications. Generally, such agents favour those who are equally or less qualified. In passive exclusion, discriminated group is prevented indirectly through discouragement and intimidation and thus lowering their self-confidence. This results in their poor performance, directly through routes that limit access to income or education. Passive exclusion is caused through unintended attempts and circumstances or through inability of some persons to relate to other persons. As said above, exclusion may be direct or indirect. In direct exclusion, fair norms of exclusion are violated which sometimes is termed as unfavourable exclusion while in indirect exclusion, fair norms of inclusion are violated and is also termed as unfavourable inclusion.

Exclusion is both a process and product. It involves mainly four components: (1) the excluded, (2) the agents whose actions result in the exclusion, (3) the institutions from which they are excluded, and (4) the process through which it occurs. Power holds the key in the process of exclusion and those with power are implicated and those without it are affected. In course of exclusion power asymmetries are observed resulting in the exclusion of certain groups and individuals.

Mechanisms of Social Exclusion

Christine Bradley (1994) pointed out following five main mechanisms through which social exclusion is practised:

1. *Geographical segregation*: It is generally observed that the so-called untouchables (dalits) and even minorities are residentially segregated from the mainstream society. They are made to live and construct their residential places and dwellings outside the villages or at the periphery of village or town. Most of the tribals live in hills and forests and are excluded from the mainstream population.
2. *Intimidation*: To exclude, intimidation in any form is used as the main arm. Verbal abuse, sarcastic remarks, threat of harm are the main means of intimidation. It can be observed at every level in a society. Intimidation is a major form of control used by men over other men and women.
3. *Physical violence*: When threat of harm does not work, actual (physical) violence is used. It can be committed by the state, community, group or individuals. Violence against women in the household and against poor people and ethnic and religious minorities is reported to be practised all over the world. Domestic violence is rooted in the norms of gender inequality and patriarchy.
4. *Barriers to entry*: At many places and in many spheres, people excluded are debarred from entry. Barriers to entry involving the state are mostly related to documentation requirements. Other than documents, transition costs is another way to put hurdle in the entry of the excluded. Transition costs are the costs that are involved in acquiring a good service above and beyond its actual price.
5. *Corruption*: Corruption is the main cause of many social evils in India and elsewhere. It prevails all over the world. The people who are excluded from obtaining goods and services do not have the required necessary amount to pay for securing jobs, health care and other public services. It causes insecurity among the excluded. Corruption denies access to resources, opportunities and information.

Impact of Social Exclusion

Social exclusion results in the following main consequences:

1. It leads to various kinds of deprivations—economic, educational, cultural and social.
2. It leads to the impoverishment of human life and develops a poorer sense of well-being.
3. It leads to inequality, poverty, unemployment and involuntary migration.
4. It leads to social stigmatization and marginalization.
5. It develops fear complex among the excluded.
6. It puts various restrictions on the excluded about their free and full participation in the economic, cultural and political activities.
7. On the whole, it puts an intense negative impact on the quality of life.

Social Exclusion in India

Exclusion as a social phenomenon is expressed in different forms all over the world. It is not altogether a new phenomenon in India. It was practised from time immemorial here. In Indian context, exclusion revolves around institutions that discriminate, isolate, shame and subordinate groups on the basis of caste, religion and gender (Thorat and Newman, 2007). It is observed in certain groups like the dalits, backward classes, religious minorities along with women and aged people. These groups are systematically excluded from getting accruing advantages of development and institutional inequality. They are wholly or partially restricted from full participation in the economic, political, educational and social institutions that define social membership. In India, the most rigorous form of exclusion is practised by the institution of caste, followed by income, gender, religion, ethnicity and territory. The contours of the exclusion perpetuated by these variables constantly change with the context and actors. So is the intensity of the discrimination.

Social Exclusion and Caste

In India, social exclusion is mainly based on paternity and caste. Paternity breeds gender inequality and social exclusion of weaker sections. It is closely associated with the discriminatory practices and inequality embedded in the institution of caste. Inequality is the organizing principle of the caste-based hierarchy, which spews discrimination and has kept numerous groups outside the gamut of Hindu social life. The rigid barriers of caste not only practise the most pungent form of exclusion but also regulate economic and social life. The salient features of social exclusion on the basis of caste are social stratification, social inequality, hierarchy and hegemony. The caste system's fundamental characteristics of fixed civil, cultural and economic rights for each caste, with restrictions for change, imply 'forced exclusion of one caste' from the rights of other castes, or from undertaking the occupations of other castes (Ambedkar, 1917). Caste-based discrimination and exclusion occur mainly in the following spheres:

1. Untouchables or so-called dalits faced discrimination in the use of public services such as public roads, gardens, temples, schools, health and other public services.
2. In the political sphere, these people were excluded from decision-making process.
3. They faced physical (residential) segregation or general societal exclusion. They were boycotted.
4. In economic spheres exclusion is practised in various ways. It operates through market and non-market transitions and exchange.

Firstly, it is practised through the denial of access to hiring for jobs, in sale or purchase of leasing of land, in the factor inputs, and in commodities and consumer goods. Secondly, as noted economist Amartya Sen has said, discrimination can occur through unfavourable inclusion, i.e., through differential treatment in terms and conditions of contract. As a result, discriminated groups can get lower prices for the goods that they sell and could pay higher prices for the goods that they buy as compared with the market price or the price paid by other groups. Thirdly, discrimination can occur in terms of access to social needs supplied by the government or public institutions or by private institutions in education, housing, health (hospitals, etc.) and many other spheres. Fourthly, a group (particularly the untouchables) may face discrimination from participation in certain categories of jobs (such as the sweeper is being excluded from inside household jobs) because of notions of purity and pollution attached with occupations and engagements. Lastly, social exclusion leads to economic poverty and a poorer sense of well-being.

According to a recent UN report (2012) of a group of independent experts, more than 260 million people across the world are still victims of human rights abuses due to caste-based discrimination. The report says Caste-based discrimination remains widespread and deeply rooted, its victims face structural discrimination, marginalization and systematic exclusion and the level of impunity is very high. This form (caste-based) of discrimination entails gross and wide-ranging human rights abuses, including brutal forms of violence. This group experiences social and economic exclusion, segregation in housing, limited access to basic services, including water and samitation and emplyment, and work in conditions similar to slavery.

Historically, the class system classified people by their occupation and status. Each caste had a specific place in the hierarchy of social status. However, since the 19th century, the link between caste and occupation has become less rigid as it became easier for people to change occupation. This change was brought about by many factors like education, science and technology and economic boom since the early 1990s (i.e., after adoption of the policy of liberalization).

To solve the problem of caste-based discrimination, two years age, Nepal adopted the caste-based discrimination and untouchability bill, a landmark law that protects the rights of dalits (weaker sections of the society). Recently, the British government enacted the Equality Act that would cover caste-based discrimination also to protect dalits in diaspora communities.

Social Exclusion and Women

As said above, social exclusion is also based on gender. Women are considered as subordinates to men in almost all traditional societies even today. Even in the so-called modern western societies women are treated as subordinates to some extent. They are ostracized by individuals and discriminated against by the state and other institutions. Almost all household functions, including rearing and caring of children, are still performed by women, including working women. Their husbands rarely perform any household functions. In many parts of India, widows are considered as an excluded group. They are ill-treated by the members of the family and the society at large. They are excluded from attending certain social ceremonies and rituals performed at both family and community levels. Socially, they are often neglected and considered a burden on the family.

Dalit women and girls are particularly vulnerable and face multiple forms of discrimination and violence, including sexual abuse. Children are also at high risk of being sold and sexually exploited.

Social Exclusion and Ethnic Groups (Minority Groups)

Social exclusion due to ethnic differences is a common feature in many societies, including India. In an ethnic group membership is based on national origin, religion, language or region. An ethnic group shares a common culture and a way of life which is known as ethnicity. Ethnicity is often a major source of social cohesion and conflict. Nationalism, for example, often has a strong ethnic base as does the oppression of minorities. The existence of a minority in a society implies the existence of a dominant (majority) group with higher social status and greater privileges. Minority status, therefore, carries with it the idea of social exclusion from full participation in the life of the society. As a result of social exclusion, a minority (ethnic) group may feel disgust, frustration and estrangement. Majority group members often enforce a very rigid code of interaction with minority group members (for detailed discussion, also see section on minority-majority group relations).

What is Meant by 'Majority' and 'Minority'?

In common parlance, we use the terms 'majority' and 'minority' to indicate numerical strength, i.e., minority represents the lesser number than to majority. Thus, we generally assume a majority group has larger number of people than a minority group. There are many minorities in statistical sense, such as homosexuals, handicapped, the aged poor, tax payers, TV viewers, etc. These are numerical minorities. However, these numerical minorities are not considered to be minorities in the sociological sense. In fact, the number of people in a group does not necessarily determine its status as a social minority (or dominant group). Sociologists do not use these terms in the sense of numbers because it may be irrelevant to majority or minority status in a society. Numerical superiority, although it is influential, does not necessarily confer a group majority status. Sociologically, there are additional considerations about such groups. When sociologists define a minority group, they are primarily concerned with economic, political and social power or powerlessness along with the discrimination and deprivity of the people of a group. Therefore, the term 'minority' does not necessarily involve relatively small number of people. A group can be a minority group even if it is numerically greater than others in the same society. In colonial countries, the white rulers are usually fewer in number than the native coloured people. For example, in South Africa, white comprise less than one-fifth of the total population but they are in a position of dominance. Minority designates a status and not a quantity. Sociologically, a minority group is not primarily defined by its numbers.

A minority is a category of people singled out for unequal and inferior treatment simply because they are identified as belonging to that category. Minorities are usually defined in terms of ascribed status characteristics such as race, gender, and ethnic or religious background, as well as acquired statuses such as sexual orientations. Unlike numerical minorities, social minorities may be in the numerical majority as are blacks in South Africa and females in virtually every society in the world. In sociology, members of a minority group are regarded as disadvantaged as compared with the majority population and have a sense of group solidarity or of belonging together. In India, Muslims are considered to be the largest minority group constituting about 13.4 per cent (2001) of the total population, followed by Christians (2.3%), Sikhs (1.9%), Buddhists (0.8%) and Parsis (0.007%).

Minorities in India

What is meant by the word 'minority' in the Indian context? There is no agreed definition of the phenomenon of minority as discussed earlier. The Census of India listed seven religious categories—Hindus, Muslims, Christians, Sikhs,

Jains, Buddhists and others. This categorization is based on their numerical strength and not on any sociological definition. Officially, five religious groups—Muslims, Christians, Buddhists, Sikhs and Zoroastrians— have termed as minorities in India. They constituted about 18.4 per cent of the population in 2001. Hindus are a 'majority' in India from the point of their numbers. They constituted 82.6 per cent (2001) of the total population and all other categories have been termed as minority communities. In India, the major criterion that has been used to distinguish minority groups is religion and cultural patterns. Accordingly, Muslims are the largest community in India. The aged and disabled have also been given minority status. In the most other societies, especially the USA, physical differences, national origin and distinctive cultural patterns have been used to distinguish ethnic groups. According to Milton H. Gordon (1940), an ethnic group is 'any group which is defined or set off by race, religion or national origin or some combination of these categories'. Some authors like F. Giddings (1955) have preferred to focus on 'sense of peoplehood' or 'consciousness of kind' as the important defining characteristic of ethnicity. Ethnicity may encompass both biological and cultural characteristics.

What is a Minority Group?

Since the 1930s, the term 'minority group' has been applied to social groups that are opposed or stigmatized on the basis of racial, ethnic, biological or other characteristics. In this regard, Louis Wirth (1969) provided a very useful definition. He said, 'We may define a group of people who because of their physical or cultural characteristics are singled out from others in the society in which they live for differential and unequal treatment and who, therefore, regard themselves as objects of collective discrimination'. However, seen in these terms, a minority group could in fact constitute a numerical majority in any society, for example, Blacks in South Africa. It might be more useful, therefore, to distinguish between groups which are actually a minority in numbers and those which are marginal in terms of their access to power.

Anthony Giddens (1997) observed, 'A minority group is a group of people in a given society who, because of their physical or cultural characteristics, find themselves in situations of inequality within that society'. According to Schaefer and Lamm (1992), 'A minority group is a subordinate group whose members have significantly less control or power over their lives than the members of a dominant or majority group have over theirs'. Generally, the groups formed on the basis of religion are termed as minorities as we find in India. But, the main criterion for minority status is any group which is suffering from discriminatory treatment. On this basis, other than racial and ethnic groups, women, elderly, physically handicapped are also termed as minorities as they are also victims of prejudice and discrimination.

Characteristics of Minority Groups

Sociologists have identified the following basic properties of a minority group:

1. *Physical and cultural traits*: Members of a minority group share some physical and cultural characteristics that distinguish them from the dominant (majority) group. Each society has its arbitrary standards for determining which characteristics are most important in defining dominant and minority group.

   Physical characteristics such as skin colour are commonly called racial. Cultural (ethnic) distinctions are rarely neutral and commonly associated with antagonism between groups.
2. *Unequal treatment*: Members of a minority group experience unequal treatment. They are usually physically and socially isolated from the dominant (majority) community. For example, the management of a community hostel or an apartment complex (or building) may refuse to rent members of a minority community. For example, in India, it is often accused that the members of minority groups (Muslims or Christians) are refused accommodation—renting or selling flats in the buildings managed or owned by the members of dominant group. Not only this, in villages and small towns, it is seen that the members of minority groups are forced to live in separate geographical localities. Physical segregation ultimately leads to social segregation.
3. *Ascribed status*: Membership in a dominant (or minority) group is not voluntary. People are born into the group. Thus, race, gender, ethnicity and religion are considered ascribed statuses.
4. *Solidarity*: Minority group members have a strong sense of group solidarity. This sense of solidarity is the outcome of prejudice and discrimination experienced by the minority group members. It is based on 'in-group consciousness' which in turn gives rise to the feeling of 'us' versus 'them' or 'i' versus 'they'. It heightens feelings of common loyalty and interests. W.G. Sumner, in his book *Folkways* (1906), noted that individuals make distinctions between members of their own group called 'in-group' and everyone else 'out-group'.
5. *In-group marriage*: Members of a minority group generally marry within their own group in order to keep alive their cultural distinctiveness and to maintain group solidarity. Parsis, in India, and members of other minority groups (Muslims or Christians) seldom marry in other groups.
6. *Subordination*: The minority is subordinate to the dominant (majority) in the distribution of power and privileges in a society. This is the key characteristic of a minority group. The members of minority groups have relatively low power, prestige and economic position in a society's system of social stratification. Not only this, they have to observe the norms, values, cultural patterns and laws of the majority (dominant) group.

Majority-Minority Group Relations

Man is not always a logical animal. He is logical only on those subjects on which he wishes to be, and not always then. His all behaviours are not only governed by logic or rationality but at times by emotions (reverence), traditions and evaluations. Minority-majority relations are to a great extent result of emotions which may be termed as prejudices. Prejudices refer to opinions or attitudes held by members of one group towards another. These are mostly based on hearsay rather than direct evidence. Prejudices operate mainly through the use of stereotypical thinking which means thinking in terms of fixed and inflexible categories. People vent their antagonism against 'scapegoats', and blame for things that are not their fault. This stereotypical thinking leads to discrimination which refers to actual behaviour towards the other group. It is through the process of discrimination that a minority group comes into existence. The very act of discrimination—in jobs, housing, income, social services, property purchase, renting flats or houses, education—is a social process by which racial or ethnic groups are converted into a minority group. This process is deeply rooted in certain basic assumptions and practices of the society.

For understanding minority-majority relations at the theoretical level, the following concepts should be taken into account which play an important role in the solutions of the minority problem in any society:

1. *Ethnocentrism*: It is a term coined by sociologist W.G. Sumner (1906) to describe prejudicial attitude between in-groups and out-groups by which we assume that our attitudes, beliefs, customs and behaviour, in brief, culture and way of life, unquestionably and uncritically are superior and more correct to those of others. It develops a feeling of suspicion about outsiders and also a tendency to evaluate the culture of others in terms of one's own culture—judging other cultures inferior to our own culture. Outsiders are thought of as aliens, barbarians or morally and mentally inferior. Virtually, all cultures have been ethnocentric to some degree.

Most groups in any society tend to be ethnocentric. Many religious groups believe they have the 'truth' and only their ways (rites and rituals) are the assured path to reach the 'truth'. As one manifestation of ethnocentrism, we believe that people who walk around half-naked are shameless. Such beliefs sometimes become the root cause of minority-majority problems in a society.

2. *Social group closure*: Ethnocentrism and group closure frequently go together. 'Closure' refers to the process whereby groups maintain boundaries separating themselves from others. For maintaining boundaries generally following devices are used:

(a) Limiting or prohibiting intermarriages between groups.
(b) Restricting social contact and economic relations like trading.
(c) Creating physical or geographical boundaries in the form of separate housing colonies for different groups. In India, so-called untouchables

were secluded from the upper caste groups. They were forced to live at the periphery of the villages or towns.

(d) Maintaining exclusive control over the valued resources by the dominant group or preventing access to the minority groups.

(e) Sometimes the devise of usurpation is also used for maintaining boundaries. Usurpation refers to the attempts of the less privileged to acquire resources previously monopolized by others.

Above both concepts—ethnocentrism and social group closure—help us to understand both the dramatic and the more incidious differences that separate communities of people from one another. These coincides with resource allocation, instituting inequalities in the distribution of wealth and material goods.

Problems of Minorities

Worldwide, minorities suffer from the following three main problems:

1. *Problem of identity*: Because of the differences in socio-cultural practices, history and backgrounds, minorities have to grapple with the issue of identity everywhere which give rise to the problem of adjustment with the majority community.
2. *Problem of security*: Different identity and their small number relative to the rest of the society develops feeling of insecurity about their life, assets and well-being. This sense of insecurity may get accentuated at times when relations between the majority and the minority communities in a society are strained or not much cordial.
3. *Problem relating to equity*: The minority community in a society may remain deprived of the benefit of opportunities of development as a result of discrimination. Because of the difference in identity, the minority community develops the perception of the sense of inequity.

So far as the problems of Muslims are concerned, which is the largest minority community in India, they fall into three categories:

(a) Problems that are common to all poor people.

(b) Problems that are common to all minorities.

(c) Problems that are specific to Muslims only.

Here, we will deal especially the third category which is specific to Muslims only.

Religion is a complex phenomenon in India. Though India is declared a 'secular' state, yet the problem of secularism looms large here. Conversion to Islam and Christianity has been a much controversial issue over the last couple of decades. Reasons for this are varied—ranging from poverty to perceived discrimination resulting in alienation of Muslims and Christians in India. The

Government of India has constituted a committee on 9th March 2005 under the chairmanship of justice Rajendra Sacchar to enquire and analyse the problems faced especially by Muslims in India. The main recommendations of this committee have been discussed at the end of this chapter. The Indian socio-economic fabric is very complex because it is much affected by caste, religion and all the more regional/linguistic differentials. At the same time, the Indian economic, social and political institutions which are persisting since centuries have a historical basis also. These factors have given a unique character to Indian society. It has become a conglomeration of various layers and segments divided and sub-divided.

Improving the Minority-Majority Relations

Wherever different ethnic groups came in contact, there seems to be a tendency for one of them to establish dominance over the others. It is usually seen that members of a dominant group practise violence against a minority and exploit it. Prejudices and conflicts against minority groups are common everywhere. This takes shape of rivalry between in-group and out-group. Differences in culture patterns cause mutual antagonism. The major culture pattern in India has always been based on Hindu religion. Most traditional people of this dominant group, especially people of older generations, manifest various prejudices against Muslims—the main minority group. Their huge numbers significantly affect inter-communal relations. They are regarded as 'outsiders' by the Hindus, the dominant group. Can prejudices be changed? Most old people with prejudices against minority group (Muslims) cannot be changed. The main possibility is change of attitudes with new generation. Many prejudices can be decreased, however, by removing economic sources of rivalry and friction and by education of children from the early childhood in certain ways of believing. But deep-rooted prejudices cannot be altered suddenly.

A slight change in attitude can be affected through association and mixing of people of majority and minority groups. Most people of the majority group not like to live in the vicinity of minority groups but ordinarily they never come in contact with them except in office dealings and business transactions. They know almost nothing of the home life, religious values, customs and beliefs of the other peoples except by hearsay and fictionalized accounts. How many Hindus, for example, ever discuss their community problems with Muslims or Christians or take lunch or dinner in their homes.

For improving the minority-majority relations, the following models have been suggested:

1. *Amalgamation*: The process by which a majority group and a minority group combine through intermarriage to form a new group. This can be expressed as A+B+C = D. Here, A, B, C represent different groups present

in a society and D signifies the end-result. This process is not possible everywhere, especially where minority-majority relations are strained.

2. *Assimilation*: A term used to describe the process by which an outsider, immigrant, or subordinate group becomes indistinguishably integrated into the dominant (host) society. Assimilation implies that the subordinate group actually comes to accept and internalize the values and culture of the dominant group. Here in the context of minority-majority relations, assimilation means that the minority group persons are required to forsake their own cultural tradition in order to become fully absorbed into the majority culture. It simply means abandoning original customs and practices by the minority people and moulding their behaviour to the values and norms of the majority by adopting the attitudes and language of the dominant group.

3. *Accommodation*: The process of assimilation as described above is generally not accepted by the people of the subordinate group because it strikes at the very roots of a person's identity. In place of it, another sociological process known as accommodation, comes into effect. Accommodation simply means adjustment—developing temporary working agreements with the people of dominant group. It requires maintaining equilibrium between the people of two groups. In this process, the people of minority group simply try to work with the institutions and culture of the majority group without surrendering one's own ethnic identity. It is a low-key approach somewhat akin to what Goffman describes as 'playing it cool'. But it does not appeal to the new generation because of their frustrated aspiration experienced by many.

4. *Melting pot*: It is the merging together of different cultures and outlooks of different groups in a society. It does not require dissolving of the traditions of any group (minority) in favour of the dominant (majority) group. In this process of 'melting pot', all become blended to form new, evolving cultural patterns. Many believe this to be the most desirable outcome of ethnic diversity. This model is an expression of American cultural development.

5. *Segregation*: It refers to the physical separation of two groups of people in terms of residence, work place and social functions. Generally, it is imposed by a dominant group on a minority group. Total minority separation is virtually impossible in highly inter-connected modern societies. Inter-group contact inevitably occurs even in the most segregated societies.

In many African countries, such as South Africa, segregation restricted the movement in Blacks and other non-whites under the policy of apartheid (1948–1991) in certain areas. Certain Islamic states enforce the segregation of men and women in public places and in private homes.

6. *Resistance*: It occurs when the majority and minority fail to accommodate each other. At many times it is seen that minority group tries to resist the majority or dominant culture and its institutions. Resistance can occur at the level of culture or lifestyle as well as through political action.

7. *Cultural or ethnic pluralism*: It is considered to be the most appropriate model or method to foster the development of a genuinely plural (multicultural) society in the present-day world fragmented by many conflicts and competition. In this model, the equal validity of numerous different cultures is recognized. In a pluralistic society, a subordinate group will not have to forsake its lifestyles and traditions. People of different cultures live side by side adhering to their own values, retain their own customs and identity but also fully participate in the mainstream society's economic, political and social life.

Pluralism is based on mutual respect between various groups in a society for one another's cultures. It allows minority group to express its own culture. Newman (1973) described the following three processes algebraically as under:

Amalgamation: A + B + C = D

Assimilation: A + B + C = A

Pluralism: A + B + C = A + B + C

Pluralism allows all groups to co-exist in the same society. Indian society needs this model to be adopted not only as an ideal but also in a reality. It is said that Switzerland is the only country in the world which exemplifies a modern pluralistic society in the real sense of the term.

Minorities and Development

The United Nations, declaration on the rights of persons belonging to national, ethnic, religious and linguistic minorities lays down that the promotion and protection of the people of such minorities is the responsibility of the state in which they live. This will contribute to the lessening of tensions among groups and individuals and ultimately help in promoting the political peace and social stability of the states. All developed and developing countries of the world have put lot of emphasis on the interests of the minorities. Meeting their aspirations and ensuring their human rights and acknowledging the dignity and equality of the individuals have become an acid test for them. Their role in the overall development of the state has also been recognized by almost all modern states. Institutions like National Human Rights Commission (NHRC), National Commission for Minorities (NCM) and many NGOs are there to look into the complaints made by the minorities with respect to the state action.

The Indian Constitution, which is wedded with the aims of equality, paternity, liberty and justice, is committed to provide all safeguards and security to the minorities living in India. Emphasizing equality, the Indian Constitution lays down in its part III on 'Fundamental Rights' that the state shall not discriminate against any citizen on the ground of caste, religion, creed and gender. To ensure that no discrimination will be practised in any form, the Indian State was declared as 'secular', which meant that: (a) each citizen would be guaranteed full freedom to practise and preach his religion, (b) state will have no religion, and (c) all citizens, irrespective of their religious faith, will be equal. Thus, minorities in India enjoy all rights as the people of majority in India. Not only this, the Constitution also prescribes certain protective and safeguards measures for their development in all spheres of life.

Despite consistent and gigantic efforts by the government as well as the civil society and NGOs, these marginalized and excluded groups have not made much headway as was expected. They continue to experience exclusion at various levels and in different ways. It is not much uncommon to see that the SC people (so-called dalits) are still treated as untouchables in villages in India. In urban areas, however, we do see some change in respect of untouchability but that too is more peripheral than real. How many people of upper castes visit the residences of their dalit colleagues? Reservation policies have undoubtedly brought some changes in the lives of the oppressed sections (SCs and STs) of the society but that too is very meagre to mention. Reviewing the effectiveness of policies and programmes related to these vulnerable sections, it has been seen that not much desirable outcome yet could be achieved.

Throughout the recorded history, we find numerous social movements, especially led by lower castes, e.g., Bhakti movements started by Ravidas and Kabir, that called for equality through spiritual awakening. Later on, during the colonial era, the reform movements were initiated by Hindu religious and social reformers like Dayanand Saraswati, the founder of the Arya Samaj, and non-Brahmin movements such as the Satyashodhak Samaj in Maharashtra and Tamil Nadu, the Adi-Dharma Movement in Bengal and UP, and finally the nationalist movement, which were aimed at ending caste-based discrimination and untouchability and integrating the vulnerable sections into the mainstream of Hindu society.

After independence, the philosophy of inclusion and egalitarianism was clearly articulated in the Constitution of India, which is the most important document that seeks to uplift the marginalized sections of the society. As stated earlier, the Constitution provides equality to all citizens irrespective of caste, creed, religion and gender. It also directs the state to take various steps to remove the different forms of discrimination and inequality and thereby helps to eradicate social exclusion. Untouchability, the main feature of caste system, has been prohibited by the Constitution of India. It has been made an offence by the Act of 1955. Following directive principles enshrined in the Constitution, the Government of India as well as the state governments introduced a number of policies and programmes (described elsewhere in this book) to empower and alleviate the weaker sections, viz., the dalits (SCs), backward classes (OBCs) and tribal people (STs), women and religious minorities. In 2005, the government had appointed a committee (Sachar

Committee), as mentioned above, to investigate about the problems of Muslims – the biggest minority in India – and suggest measures to improve their conditions.

Sachar Committee and Muslims in India

The main aim of constituting the Sachar Committee was to investigate how far different socio-religious categories in India could reap the benefits of development programmes started after independence. The focus of the committee was Muslims in India because they constitute the largest minority community. According to 2001 census, their population was 13.4 per cent of the total population. The relevant statistics of 2011 is not available. It is widespread perception that this community is much lagging behind in comparison to the majority community—the Hindus—on human development indicators such as literacy, education and health. Since independence no systematic effort was made to evaluate the conditions of minorities in the country. A wide variety of policy initiatives and programmes have been launched by successive governments to promote the economic, social and educational development of the minority communities in India. They have made some visible progress but the perception remains that they are lagging behind in many fields with majority community. The main terms of reference of the committee are: to gather relevant information about social, economic and educational status of Muslims in India at the state, regional and district level regarding following questions:

(a) How they live?
(b) What is the geographical pattern of their economic activities?
(c) What are their asset basis and income level?
(d) What is the level of their socio-economic development?
(e) What is their relative share in public sector employment?
(f) What is the pattern of variation?
(g) What is the proportion of OBCs from the Muslim community in the total OBC population in various states?
(h) Does the Muslim community have adequate access to education and health services and bank credit programmes?

The committee strongly suggested that to deal with the problem of their (Muslims) relative deprivation an attention is to be given on their inclusive development and mainstreaming while respecting diversity. The need for equity and inclusion in a pluralistic society can never be overemphasized. In a nutshell, committee recommended the following measures to uplift the conditions of Muslims in India:

1. To evaluate, assess and monitoring the development schemes which were started for the minorities, besides creation of a National Data Bank.

2. Enhancing the legal basis for providing equal opportunities.
3. Constitution of Equal Opportunity Commission (EOC) to look into the grievances of the deprived groups.
4. Enhancing their participation in governance at all levels—national, state and at the grassroots—panchayats, Zilla Parishads in rural areas and municipalities and corporations in urban areas and para-governmental institutions like cooperative societies, etc.
5. A mechanism is to be evolved to give them adequate representation at various levels of polity and governance.
6. To enhance diversity in living, educational and work spaces, the state should encourage the development of mixed localities and across neighbourhoods.
7. To develop interaction and understanding between different communities, creation of public spaces such as public parks, libraries, etc., was also suggested.
8. Sensitization of public functionaries which implement development programmes with a focus on health personnel, teachers, police and other security personnel.
9. Enhancing access to credit and government programmes.
10. To encourage the members of this community for forming self-help groups.
11. Training programmes should be organized to improve skills of artisans in traditional occupations.
12. Primary education up to 14 years should be made compulsory.
13. To improve educational conditions, religion-based old curriculum of *madarsas* is needed to be revised and linked with mainstream education curriculum.
14. To impart technical education, training programmes should be organized for non-matriculates.
15. Change in the value system was also suggested.
16. Recruitment procedure in government and semi-government departments should be so evolved that it may be transparent and develop confidence in the candidates of minority communities.
17. To develop a sense of confidence and involvement in them, and increase their employment share where there is great deal of public dealing.
18. To enhance the efficacy of infrastructure provisions such as primary education and health services, be the members of minority committee should be encouraged for the setting up of their own civil society organizations (NGOs).

The report emphasizes that the situation of Indian Muslims is very depressing as compared to most other socio-religious categories and problem is more acute for girls/women particularly in the field of education. Education deprivation may be considered the main cause of their depressing state. A large segment of Muslim community is engaged in self-employment activities. The policy intervention needs to help such workers. Skill upgradation, education and credit availability referred earlier will have an important role in enhancing employment opportunities. Provision of social security to self-employed home-based workers (informal sector workers) is also needed.

The above recommendations of the committee have provided an overview of the perceptions of people on aspects such as infrastructure, security, education and employment. It was recognized that the three most important issues that the Muslim community is facing are identity, security and equity and all the three are interrelated. The committee has addressed most of the problems related to the above issues. It has made comprehensive recommendations for bringing some revolutionary changes that will help for setting the community on the road to progress. The issues relating to disparities across socio-religious communities are of utmost importance to our nation and if the suggestions contained in this report are implemented with all the thoroughness, the committee's efforts deserve to be commended and rewarded.

To make above measures more efficacious and successful the community's active participation in all development plans is needed. In this endeavour partnership between government, private agencies (NGOs) and community may prove to be quite successful. In the end, it may be said that mere material change in their conditions without change in their mentality will not set good and amicable relations between majority and minority communities in India and which is the utmost and urgent need of the time. The above measures would provide a broad thrust to diversity, equity, inclusiveness and their true empowerment.

Chapter 17

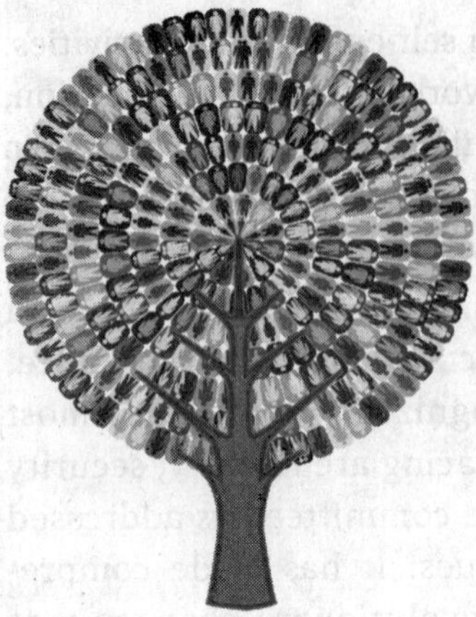

Environment and Ecological Crisis

KEY FEATURES

- Ecology and Ecological Crisis
- Major Environmental Problems
- Natural Hazards and their Impact on Environment
- Human Population and the Environment
- Increasing Consumption and the Environment
- Religion and Ecological Crisis
- Religions of India and Environment
- Environmental Planning
- Environmental Movements
- Indian Scenario

> 'We are indeed travellers bound to the earth's crust ... Yet we collectively behave as if we were not aware of the problems inherent in the limitations of the spaceship Earth.'
>
> — Rene Dubos (French-born American scientist)

Environment is the source of life. It not only directs but also determines the existence, growth and development of human beings and all their activities. The quality of our social life depends mostly on the quality of the natural environment. Primitive man was solely dependent for its existence (food, water and shelter, etc.) on the environment around him. From geographical point of view, environment includes the entire range of external influences—both physical and biological—that affects the life and death of an organism. It is the force of nature in the form of physical, climatic and biotic factors. This spatial aspect of the environment is studied in details by geographers. Sociologists are not directly concerned with the spatial aspect of the environment. But they do study environment (natural) to the extent that it affects the individual's activities and society. Sociologists use the term 'environment' in a wider perspective to include social, cultural, economical and historical and geographical environment.

Society is but one component of human life and is never independent of environment; instead, there is a complex interactive process among organization (society), population, technology and environment. A society is the organization of a population but the size and characteristics of any population depend upon the sustaining environment. Society is playing a vital role in spoiling, denegrating and degeneration of environment. As such, it has become an important social problem to be studied by sociologists. Human actions have a direct impact on the ecosystem. These actions have brought immense changes in our planet earth that have resulted into many environmental problems. It is the impact of human beings on nature in the form of technology and industry that has created so many consequences which are social.

Technology is the crucial factor in the interaction of people with environment. It changes the terms and conditions of the interaction; it provides more sustenance and permits population to grow. The power of modern technology is immense and its indiscriminate use has altered the environment in ways unimagined only a few decades ago. It extends the human capacity to modify environment but its indiscriminate use is the root of an ecological crisis. Modern society itself is now utterly dependent on technical intervention and technological harnessing of the forces of nature. If this goes wrong in a serious way (as we are witnessing today), then, the consequences are likely to be correspondingly very serious. According to Milbrath (1989), 'the technology that enabled the unprecedented economic growth of the 20th century has had a dramatic effect on our natural resources'. It has resulted into the following environmental problems:

1. A rapid growth of world population.
2. The depletion of natural resources such as (a) shrinking of forests and wetlands, (b) erosion of soil and coral reefs, (c) depletion of underground water and severe shortage of fresh drinking water, (d) vanishing of plants, and (e) salinization in some countries of Asia, Africa, Latin America and Middle East.
3. The depletion of living organism—loss of biodiversity, the rapidly extinction of many animal species, collapsing of fisheries, etc.
4. The rising pollution of air and water.
5. Rising of temperature (global warming and its disastrous effects).
6. The thinning of the ozone layer.
7. Poisoning of rivers, seas and underground resources.

Until recently we exploited and changed the environment (and still changing and exploiting) without concern for the future, but extensive pollution and the destruction and depletion of natural resources will mean the destruction of ourselves, or destruction of society. Even though science and technology have radically altered the terms of adaptation to the nature, we still need to adapt to the environment. Human society is embedded in an environment. We must not forget that the human being is first and foremost an animal, sharing living space with other animal species in an environment on which they are mutually dependent. If we do not give attention to our environment, we are putting our own existence in grave peril. Not only this, we are spoiling the fate of our future generations also. People now have started realizing that the civilization that they have built for the last thousands of years may not survive more if some drastic steps are not taken immediately to save our environment from degradation. Fresh air, clean drinking water, natural gas, petroleum and the earth's topsoil are all finite resources that will exhaust if we continue to exploit them at the present rate in the name of the development. As we deplete precious natural resources and degrade the environment, we also destroy its ability to rejuvenate itself.

Ecology and Ecological Crisis

Otis Dudley Duncan (1964) writes: 'Taking more from environment and reacting back upon the environment in more drastic and varied ways, industrial man has carried the process of "living into" the environment beyond any precedent.' The world is facing a great environmental crisis today and, therefore, social catastrophe. If in the near future unless mankind radically modifies its behaviour, certain practices and perspectives towards environment, among other things, there is every likelihood about the doom of modern civilization. Gradually, public is becoming aware of this crisis and as a result, many governments and national and international organizations have started working on this in order to save the planet in time.

To preserve and improve environment is the basic need for the existence of mankind and the approach which is used to study environment is termed as 'ecology'. It is a term taken from biology that studies the mutual interrelationship between living organisms and their environment. It holds that not only does the environment influence the life of organisms but organisms too modify their environment. In biology the term 'ecology' is used to mean the study of the adaptation of plant and animal organisms to environment. Ecological approach has had considerable influence well beyond the biological sciences.

In sociology, ecological approach (perspective) was used by some sociologists of Chicago between 1920 and 1940. This approach was later known as Chicago School of Sociology. The main figures of this school were Robert Park, Ernest Burgess and Louis Wirth. They developed this approach in the study of some societal problems especially in urban context.

Recently, in the context of environmental problems, a new term has developed—environmental ecology. Industrialization and its concomitant process—urbanization—have done irreparable damage to our environment. If economic growth is the goal of human progress and if it still continues without paying any serious attention to the protection of environment, then our existence may be in peril. Environmental problems as discussed in earlier section of this chapter have become much serious in many countries of the world. Indiscriminate economic growth or development of the developed nations has endangered the life as a whole on this earth. As travellers on 'spaceship earth', no matter where we live, we are all menaced by corrosion of the environment. The German sociologist Ulrich Beck (1992) has spoken of this situation as producing a global 'risk society'. He has raised the question of environment and development in the context of postmodernity to which he named 'late modernity'. He argues that the unintended and often negative consequences of modern development (such as dam and road construction, use of pesticides in agriculture and industrial development) are the destruction of the environment and parts of the eco-system (i.e., the system of planetary interdependence). We live now in such a global society where we face to our security, including ecological risks or crises, which previous generations did not experience. The risks associated with global warming are one example.

If humanity is to survive then we must keep the ecosystem in equilibrium and for this we shall have to implement effective policies to control the growth of population, material production and the indiscriminate use of natural resources. Unlimited growth is neither desirable nor sustainable. To save this planet from total destruction, the 2009 State of the Future report warned the nations that unlimited and indiscriminate exploitation of the resources will invite their own extinction and in this developed nations are more responsible than the poor undeveloped or developing nations. Western model of development is forcing the planet towards its own destruction. About 70 per cent of the CFC emission is done by the developed nations which is the main cause of environmental degradation and global warming. Recently, the Centre for Global Development Institute predicted that due to global warming the average temperature has already reached to its highest level in many countries and because of this by the year 2080 the agricultural productivity of these countries will decrease to 10 to 25 per cent and even more. Not only this, downward trend of average rainfall at certain places, problem of storms like Alneno, acid rain and .nelting of glaciers are also the results of the phenomenon of global warming.

Major Environmental Problems

Now, we will discuss some of the most crucial environmental problems in detail:

Ozone Depletion, Greenhouse Effect and Global Warming

All the three physical phenomena are related to one another to a great extent. To understand their effect on environment, we must first of all know what their meaning, interrelationship and working is.

Ozone is a form of oxygen, which is away from the earth's surface at a height of about 20 to 30 km in the atmosphere. It is scattered in the stratosphere in the form of a layer about three millimetre thick. This layer works as a shield to protect the earth against the ultraviolet radiation that comes from the sun. Near the earth's surface, ozone is an increasingly troublesome pollutant but it is also as important to life as oxygen itself. If this layer disappears or thins, all terrestrial life will be annihilated. The thinning and depletion of the ozone layer has generated global concern during the last few years. This is due to several chemical pollutants discharged by industries and produced through other chemical reactions. The main cause of the ozone depletion is generally attributed to the chlorofluoro carbons (CFCs) which is mostly produced by highly industrialized developed countries. CFCs is a source of energy which is needed most in the modern life. It is found in many household implements and products. When it is released into the air, it accumulates in the upper atmosphere which destroys the ozone layer. The depletion of ozone layer is linked to both 'greenhouse effect' and the phenomenon of 'global warming'.

The phenomenon commonly known as 'greenhouse effect' occurs due to the emission of certain gaseous pollutants (methane, CFCs, water vapour and carbon dioxide are known as greenhouse gases) in the air which after the heating of the atmosphere causes the average global temperature to rise. This is known as 'global warming'. In fact, the build up of carbon dioxide in the earth's atmosphere functions like the glass of a greenhouse. It allows the sun's rays to pass through, but acts as a barrier to prevent them from passing back. The effect is to heat up the earth. Global warming is sometimes termed the 'greenhouse effect' for this reason. Carbon dioxide emissions which cause global warming are mostly from automobiles. The gases used in the aerosols and refrigerators produce particles that react with the ozone layer in such a way as to weaken it. It is thought that these chemicals have produced detectable holes in the ozone layer at both poles and thinning it elsewhere. These holes have become a serious cause of concern for the environmental scientists of the whole world.

The increase in ozone layer depletion will invite the lethal ultraviolet rays from the sun which will increase cancer (especially skin cancer), eye damage (increase in cataracts of the eyes), injure plants and animals and marine life. It will also help in the re-emergence of diseases such as cholera and viral fevers. (Recently spread bird flu and swine flu may be transformed form of the old viral fevers). Not only this, it may even reduce our immunity to many diseases. Where population concentration is more, such as in big cities, the effects of ozone depletion will be more disastrous on human health, crops and ecosystem. It has its effect on the earth's climate by adding to the greenhouse effect which ultimately results in global warming. The consequences of global warming are likely to be very devastating and disturbing. Among other things, sea levels will rise as a result of melting of glaciers at the poles and the oceans will warm and expand. Cities that lie near the coasts or in low-lying areas will be flooded and become inhabitable. Large tracts of fertile land will become desert.

Looking at the above cited consequences of depletion of ozone layer and global warming, it has been increasingly realized that human existence is in peril unless something is done to check the depletion of ozone layer and global warming. It has become a major concern of the world today. It is not a local, regional or national problem but a global problem and requires solution at the global level itself. It is only through the combined efforts of the people of this planet that we can, if not fully solve, at least, minimize these environmental problems. The scientific and technological progress in many ways has improved the quality of human life but at the same time it is also responsible for the depletion of resources, excessive use of fossil fuels, deforestation and desertification, loss of fertility of soil, changes in atmospheric conditions resulting into serious problems like greenhouse effect depletion of ozone layer and global warming.

It is said that atmospheric carbon dioxide has risen since 1950 which has to some extent responsible for the alteration in the earth's climates. The concern about ozone layer protection began in the late 1970s and early 1980s. In 1978, the United States banned the principal CFCs for most uses and in 1980 many European countries placed a limit on the production of CFCs. They have cut their use by 30 per cent. In 1975, the UNEP has also expressed concern about the depletion of ozone layer—a biggest environmental problem, and also developed a plan of action on the ozone layer. As CFCs are mostly used by developed (industrialized) nations, it is their primary duty to check the ozone depletion. Industrialized countries represent about 20 per cent of the humanity but they utilize over 80 per cent of the world energy.

Desertification

There is no environmental problem in the world that affects people, especially poor people, as extensively as land degradation or desertification. UNCOD defines desertification as 'the diminution or destructing of the biological potential of land, which can ultimately led to the desert-like conditions'. The causes of desertification are numerous. However, the important ones include climate change, overgrazing, deforestation and expansion of agriculture. About 35 per cent of the earth's area (about 6.1 billion hectares) and 900 million people are affected by the problem of desertification. Desertification leads to loss of vegetation which forces men to migrate for their livelihood while the women are left behind to struggle on.

Deforestation

Deforestation is one of the important issues of environmental change and degradation of soil. About 30 per cent of earth's surface is covered by forests. South America, especially Brazil, West Central Africa and South-East Asia, are home to regions of dense forests. The human pressure on forests has significantly increased in recent decades. The need for agricultural land, increased demand for fuel and commercial wood, more and more dam construction, large-scale ranching and mining along with growing industrialization and urbanization have ruthlessly exploited the forests and have in turn created chaotic conditions and severe environmental imbalances. The main cause of deforestation is commercial exploitation of forests. Besides this, as a part of developmental drive, large dams are constructed across many rivers thereby destroying forests.

The forests play a pivotal role in balancing the ecosystem or, in other words, in maintaining the oxygen and carbon balance of the earth. Forests have a multiple ecological role to play which affects all types of life in a variety of ways. They thwart the dangers of cloud drifting, soil erosion, floods, wind erosion and groundwater evaporation. They also protect a wide variety of flora and fauna, provide recreation and can effectively control air pollution. Deforestation destroys symbiotic relationship between ecological infrastructure and animal and human species also.

There has been a growing concern among professional foresters along with social workers about the rate of deforestation everywhere. FAO, UNDP, World Bank and other government and non-governmental organizations (NGOs) have expressed their opinion about deforestation and suggested plans to protect and renewal of forests. In India, the *Chipko Andolan* and *Narmada Bachao Andolan* are the two popular movements which have developed consciousness among the people to raise voice against the ruthless destruction of forests.

Loss of Biodiversity

Today, the extinction of several species or loss of biodiversity is a much debated issue among the environmentalists at international level. Many species are disappearing rapidly. According to an estimate, 20 to 75 species are becoming extinct each day because of deforestation. This loss of biodiversity is mainly due to the degeneration of life support system. It provides the basis for life on earth. Biodiversity means the variety of life on earth. The diversity is a condition for long-term sustainability of the environment. The maintenance of its integrity is, therefore, recognized as being indispensable to sustain human life. Biological diversity encompasses all species of plants, animals and micro-organisms and the ecosystem and ecological processes of which they are a part.

The increasing interest in biodiversity is a result of concern regarding species extinction, depletion of genetic diversity and disruption to the atmosphere, water supplies, fisheries and forests. Some bird species such as vultures and kites became almost extinct. Many species of animals and plants are disappearing rapidly because of their high consumption or destruction. All the species are the integral part of ecosystem and extinctions of some species threatens the balance of ecosystem, and also diminishes the well-being of the remaining species, including human beings. Our earth's biodiversity provides varied sources of food and medicinal plants.

The main causes identified for the loss of biological diversity are: (i) habitat loss, fragmentation and modification; (ii) overexploitation of resources; and (iii) chemical fertilizers, pesticides and oil pollution.

Disposal of Wastes

The high energy consumption and high population densities of the urban societies give rise to large quantities of waste water and sewage as well as household rubbish. Industrialization and urbanization are the main causes of domestic, industrial and nuclear wastes. The contaminated water supplies cause many diseases of epidemic nature. The industrial waste consists of chemicals, detergents, metals and synthetic compounds besides the solid waste and garbage. Thousands of tonnes of mercury, nitrogen, phosphorus, cadmium, lead, zinc and other waste is dumped every day in the river and sea waters. The increased nuclear fuel is becoming as one of the sources of non-conventional energy. The nuclear waste contains radioactive isotopes which generate large quantities of heat. The domestic, industrial and nuclear wastes are serious health hazards and may endanger the biosphere as well. Industrial waste, pesticides and herbicides enter the waterways through dumping as well as runoff from farms and homes. Many rivers of India including the long seashore are the victims of this disposal of waste. Because of dumping of heavy waste, it is now very difficult to get a cup of totally uncontaminated water from the so-called sacred rivers like Ganga and Yamuna. Inadequate system of solid waste disposal causes adverse impact on health, infant mortality and the birth rate.

Pollution

The dictionary definition of pollution is to make air, water, soil, etc. dangerously dirty and not suitable for people to use. The main forms of pollution are air, water, soil, noise, thermal and radioactive waves. It is a man-made problem mainly caused by human waste material, release of poisonous gases and other chemical pollutants from the industry, agricultural pollutants like pesticides, and chemical fertilizers, pollutants by automobiles and dumping of chemical and nuclear wastes, etc. It has led to a worldwide environmental crisis. In many ways, it has changed both the individual and social ways of life.

Air Pollution

The main sources of air pollution in India and elsewhere are mineral dust and gases, automobiles, thermal power plants and industries. Any contamination in the air may not only cause many diseases and loss of vision but can also disturb the whole atmospheric system. Air pollution can also cause acid rain which damages soil, vegetation and aquatic life of the region.

The heavy use of automobiles causes pollution and smog from automobile emissions. This has become a serious problem in almost all the countries—developed and developing. The bad urban air burns the eyes, damages lung tissues and increases the levels of lead and other poisons in the human body and agricultural products. It is not known how many deaths occur nationally because of air pollution. Air pollution caused massive smog in London in 1952 killing some 4,000 people.

Water Pollution

Contamination of water from any external source that makes it harmful to life is known as water pollution. With the fast industrial development and modern civilization, the problem of water pollution is increasing day by day. The major sources of water pollution are domestic effluents, agricultural effluents, sewage disposal, industrial wastes, radioactive wastes and oil leakages, etc. All the Indian rivers, including the holy river Ganga, have become highly polluted today. Even, the Ganga Action Plan to control its water from pollution has not been proved successful. The impact of water pollution is widespread. It causes many severe water-borne diseases, such as diarrhea, trachoma, intestinal norms, hepatitis, jaundice, etc. According to WHO, 21 per cent of all communicable diseases in India are water-born diseases. Oil is the major pollutant of the sea water. Huge tankers routinely dump oil into the sea. This act of dumping poisons smothers or coats sea plants and animals and kills them.

Noise Pollution

All sounds are not noise. Noise is any sound that is unwanted and goes beyond its certain limit, i.e., above 80 decibels Harsh sounds of lightening and thunder, noise produced by machines, automobiles, railways, aeroplanes and the blaring sound of loudspeakers and some musical instruments come under the category of noise pollution. More and more noise is the creation of modern civilization and has now become a major environmental pollutant, specially in urban areas. The most notable effect of noise pollution is on hearing. It may cause total loss of hearing that may result in the reduction of worker's efficiency. At the higher levels, it may lead to physical and psychological damage. There is evidence that noise is one of the major causes of stress and anxiety. It also causes headaches and irritability. It may also affect blood pressure and heart beat.

Air, water and noise pollutions are very common which are creating havoc for all types of life. They have disastrous transnational consequences.

Natural Hazards and their Impact on Environment

In every part of the world, several natural phenomena such as volcanic eruptions, earthquakes, cyclones, storms, tornadoes, landslides, floods, droughts, famines and melting of glaciers have had their impact on environment. These natural phenomena are unpredictable and have uncontrollable character. Such phenomena are generally termed as disasters and catastrophes caused by forces extraneous to man. These are prevalent throughout the world. Often their impact is adverse not only on human beings but also on environment. These natural hazards cause damage to all types of life—human, animal and marine life, vegetation and also pollute the air and water.

The scientific interest in environmental hazards is of fairly recent origin. As a result, hazard-related research became established in a wide variety of academic disciplines ranging from geology to sociology. It is now recognized that proper planning in advance about the hazard-prone areas can save much loss of life and property damage.

Human Population and the Environment

The interaction between population and environment is very complex and dynamic. The environment not only directs but also determines the growth of population, its distribution and functional structure. Human population not only uses the environment as habitat but through its multifarious activities also changes certain natural processes in the ecosystem, thus becomes a cause of the ecological crises. The situation becomes all the more alarming due to the population pressure and overexploitation of environment. Because of human activities, environment is constantly changing that leads to problems like soil erosion, devastating floods, acute droughts, desertification, deforestation, unforeseen climatic changes, etc. Human activities create chain of reactions in the ecosystem. The rapid growth of population leads to chronic problems like growth of slums, malnutrition, unemployment, disease and, of course, degradation of environment. There was complete coordination and co-existence between man and nature but with the rapid growth of population this balance has not only been disturbed but has also become a threat to the ecosystem.

When we talk about the relationship between population and environment in context of India, it is extremely clear that the rapidly increasing population has done a great harm to the environment. India's population has very rapidly grown since 1921 and that too especially after independence. India's total population in 2001 was about 102.8 crore, which has now increased to about 121.2 crore in 2011. This growth of population has created several environmental problems referred to above. These problems in turn have given rise to many social, economic and health problems such as migration from rural to urban areas, growth of slums in metropolitan cities, air, noise and water pollution, problem of disposal of solid waste and waste water, problem of safe drinking water, malnutrition, adverse effects on human health and quality of life, etc.

Increasing Consumption and the Environment

The world today seems to be heading towards a consumption revolution. Since the 1950s, the rate at which we consume energy, vegetables, meat, copper, steel and timber has more than doubled, car ownership has quadrupleted, while plastic use has quintuipleted and air travel has multiplied by a staggering about forty times. In general, today, people are much more consumption-oriented and wealthier than 50 or even 20 years ago. They buy and consume more. This is why scholars have called modern society as 'consumer society'. The demand for the sources of energy and raw materials is increasing day by day from the modern industries for making the life more and more comfortable and happy. But the world's supply of energy sources and raw materials is limited. It is estimated that at the current rate of consumption, the known oil sources of the world will be completely consumed by the year 2050. These resources will run out if global consumption is not checked and controlled. Consumption is putting extra pressure on agricultural land and fisheries also.

The unintended consequences of this consumption revolution are very serious. To take a very small example, the British consume about 7 crore chickens per annum. These chickens are only produced and consumed to an acceptable level of safety by the use of some antibiotics in their feed. But suppose chickens widely develop immunity to antibiotics and develop some disease like 'bird flue' (2007) or 'mad cow disease' (1996), what would be the result? Such consumption is not without risk. This is why the sociologist of risk, Ulrich Beck calls this condition as the 'acceptable' risks of late modernity. The growth in world tourism has also enhanced the surge in consumption. Rapid use of non-renewable or limited resources puts the whole ecosystem at risk.

Religion and Ecological Crisis

Almost in all primitive religions, the nature and its products have been given proper respect in some way or the other. It has been seen that there were ways through which nature was protected. There were many ancient civilizations in which nature was even worshipped. In Greek writings, there is a reference of *Ge* or *Gaia* as the Goddess of the Earth—the founder figure of natural replenishment. In Vedic (Hindu) religion also, earth was regarded as goddess with other elements (air, water, fire) of nature.

The ecological crises, like growth of population, depletion of natural resources, depletion of living organism and the consequent disturbance between food chains system and pollution and poison, have its roots in the religious perspective. According to historian Lynn White, Jr (1967), it is Western Christianity which is responsible for destroying the ecological balance and endangering the lives of human beings. White called Western Christianity the most anthropocentric (human-centred) religion the world has ever seen. He wrote, 'Christianity, in absolute contrast to ancient paganism and Asia's religions (except perhaps Zoroastrianism), not only established a dualism of man and nature but also insisted that it is God's will that man exploits nature for his proper ends.' Quite opposite to the ancient paganism, Christianity viewed man as apart from and destined to be the master of the natural world. This spirit had scientific roots. Look at the statement of Francis Bacon, 'Our main object is to make nature serve the business and conveniences of man.' Similarly, Descartes exclaimed, 'To render ourselves the masters and possesses of nature.' Thus, science reflects values that promote destruction rather than protection of nature. This is particularly the case when science is linked to technology and practical goals. The natural world becomes a thing apart and hostile, and humans feel they must conquer it. It was superb technology which enabled the small nations of Europe to conquer, loot and colonize much of the rest of the world (White, 1967). Christianity destroyed the pagan religions which used to pay respect to the spirits residing in natural objects and developed in people an indifference to feelings in nature. White wrote, 'The whole concept of sacred grove is alien to Christianity and to the ethos of the West. For nearly two million Christian missionaries have been chopping down sacred groves which are idolatrous because they assume spirit in nature' (ibid.).

Religions of India and Environment

When we look at the religions of India (Hinduism, Buddhism, Jainism and Sikhism), we find a different story to tell. Man-nature relationships have differently been conceived in religions of India. Right from ancient times, in India, much importance has been given to nature or environment. This we come across in ancient Indian writings, where nature has been considered as the controller of all human activities including economic development. India is a country where all the components of environment have been considered as life support systems right from ancient times and their protection has also been accorded paramount importance. These components are air, water, land, vegetation, soil, rivers, mountains, trees and animals, etc., and these have been considered sacred in one form or the other. They are worshipped in the name of some God or Goddesses such as air as *Vayu Devata*, water as *Varun*, and the like. Many trees and plants such as *Pipal* tree or Banyan tree and animals like serpent as *Nagdevata* are worshipped. The Hindu religion enshrined a respect for nature, environmental harmony and conservation. Many verses in the *Rigveda* and *Atharvaveda* have been devoted to please *Surya Devata* (Sun), *Vayu Devta* (God of Air), *Agni Devata* (God of Fire), *Varuna Devata* (God of Water), *Prithvi Mata* (Mother Earth) and *Vanya Devi* (Goddess of Forests), etc. Being considered as gods and goddesses, it is the sacred duty of every person to protect all these objects as a part of their religious activity. It was because of this reason that there was no problem of environmental degradation or specie extinction in ancient India. Not only this, the limited population and the simple pattern of life enjoined by religious faith also posed no problem to environment.

Indigenous people live in harmony with nature combining reverence for nature with sustainable management of resources. Because of their deep-rooted cultural ties with nature, indigenous people use land and its resources with utmost care and frugality without disturbing the eco-balance. These people, while dealing with nature, are generally driven by the feelings of empathy, respect and reverence towards it. Only one example will testify the gratitudinal attitude of people of India towards nature. About three centuries back the Vishnois of Khejarilli village (near Jodhpur) in Rajasthan protested against the royal forces of the state for the felling of green trees by them. It is said that a woman named Amrita Bai with her four family members and other 363 persons scarified their lives to save trees of the village, popularly known as 'Green Khejaris' (Shiva and Bandopadhyaya, 1985). This tree 'Khejari' is still preserved and protected not only by the Vishnoi community but other communities of this region also. Not only the tree 'Khejari' is protected but particular specie of deer is also protected in this region. Cutting of trees, harming animals, polluting air, water and land in any way are regarded as sin in Hindu religion.

Environmental Planning

The concern over the environment planning has grown the world over since the seventies. The world community's resolution to protect and enhance the environmental quality found expression in the first Conference on Human Environment in 1972 organized by the United Nations at Stockholm. While several measures have been taken for environmental protection both before and after the conference, the need for a specific legislation to protect the environment was emphasized highly. In this conference, it was declared that man has the fundamental right to freedom of equality and adequate conditions of life in an environment of a quality that permits a life of dignity and well-being. It was suggested in the conference that all governments must evolve necessary laws to protect and improve the flora and fauna, non-renewable resources, wildlife and human health.

Several strategies, policies and concepts have been developed by ecologists and planners to deal with environment resource management, such as the 'zero growth' strategy of Daly (1977), 'organic agriculture for self-sustaining societies' of Naess (1977), and use of environment-friendly techniques and products approach. In this connection, some books worth mentioning are: *US Global* 2000, *Report* (1980), *Resourceful Earth* (Simon and Kohn, 1984), *The Global Possible* (Repetto, 1985) and *Our Common Future* (WCED, 1987). These and many other books have generated a serious debate highlighting the consequences of overexploitation of resources and neglect of common interest. As a result of this, the United Nations Environment Programme (UNEP) was created.

From educating people about the conservation of environment to enactment of laws about environmental protection, efforts are being made for the proper management of environment in such a way that air, water, noise pollution, disposal of hazardous and toxic wastes, radiation hazard and loss of biodiversity can be controlled. This is done at the government level and by private agencies (NGOs). Not only this, many educational institutions have started courses in environmental management and are imparting degrees and diplomas. Many research institutes and action groups are doing research in this field and also mobilizing public opinion on environmental issues. The programmes of environmental awareness have also been taken up by different organs of print and visual media. The UNEP has also launched several programmes of environmental protection.

Environmental Movements

With the increase in ecological crisis, there has been a corresponding increase in the awareness and concern about it all over the world. This has, in turn, led to widespread protest movements by aggrieved communities and concerned citizens. Bhopal gas tragedy in 1984, nuclear disaster at Chernobyl (Russia) in 1986, Alaskan oil spill from Exxon Valdez tanker in 1989, and the Gulf War in the early 1990s are some examples of hazardous and undesirable happenings that led to ecological crisis in the human history.

Late 20th century (near about the early 1970s) concern about the impact of human activities on the environment has resulted in new social, political and ecological movement and the growing salience of so-called 'green issue'. It has given rise to a steady growth of environmental-ecological movement all over the world, including India. These movements have been put under the category of 'new social movements' because they were not class-based and do not raise any economic issue like earlier agrarian or industrial movements. Such movements were a resurgence of an interest of the people in their natural environment. In the early decades of the last century, a conservation movement grew up to conserve such rapidly depleting natural resources as forests. More recently efforts to protect various birds and animals in danger of extinction by human predators led to the enactment of concerned laws in many countries. These deve.opments have boosted the formation of many environmental protection and preservation organizations, such as 'Green Network' or the 'Greenpeace' or 'Friends of the Earth' (1969) throughout the world, including India.

Guha and Gadgil (1989) defined the environmental movements as 'organized social activity consciously directed towards promoting sustainable use of natural resources halting environmental degradation or bringing about environmental restoration'. In the West environmental movements focus on consumption, productive use of natural resources and conservation or protection of natural resources. In India, such movements are based on the use of, as well as control over, natural resources.

As stated earlier, the first conference on human environment initiated by UNO was held at Stockholm in 1972. It paved the way for the studies on the condition of the environment and its effects on human beings. It expressed serious concern to protect and improve the environment for present and the future generations. As a result of this conference environmental movements under different names such as 'Green Politics', 'Eco-greens' or 'Green Movement' (Germany and North America) developed in the 1980s. First scientific warning of serious depletion of protective ozone layer in upper atmosphere by CFCs was raised during the Stockholm Conference (1972). The 1989 European elections (1989) put green issues firmly on political agenda as Green parties across Europe gave top priority to this in their election campaign. In 1992, the United Nations Earth Summit was held in Rio de Janeiro to discuss the issues of environmental crisis faced by almost all developed and developing nations. In this conference, about 1,000 NGOs and about 50,000 individuals participated from all over the world. The issues of climate change and loss of biodiversity dominated the conference. A list of 27 principles was framed to preserve and improve the environment. The various programmes of UNO, specially the UNEP, have emphasized the need for sustainable development. It is agreed upon that environment and development are for the people and not people for environment and development. A parallel informal group assembled at Flamingo Park and formed a global forum on environment under the presidentship of Morris Strong in 1972.

Environmental Movements in India

The model of development established since independence has fundamentally altered the use of and access to natural resources. The studies on social movements in India revealed that the developmental paradigm followed by the Indian state after independence caused environmental degradation and gave rise to protests by some environmentally conscious social workers like H.N. Bahuguna, Arundhati Roy and others. As a result, some movements like *Chipko Andolan, Narmada Bachao Andolan, Clean Ganga Andolan* and many others started. These movements rose because the development process in India has threatened the survival of poor and powerless. Most of the environmental movements in India were centred around the issue of their livelihood which is connected with natural resources. They were the expression of protests against the destruction of the two vital economies of natural resources and survival from the anarchy of development based on market economy.

Indian Scenario

Since Vedic times, the main motto of Indian culture was to 'live in harmony with nature'. It was well recognized by ancient sages that to save oneself from destruction and damage, it is necessary to accord proper regard to the elements of nature. This is why all the great teachers and originators of religions (like Mahavir and Buddha) have emphasized in their teachings on the need of co-existence with nature. This philosophy of co-existence with nature is well-reflected in Articles 48A and 51A(g) of the Constitution of India adopted after independence. While Article 48A is a pointer to the state to protect and improve the environment, Article 51A (g) confers a fundamental duty on the citizens of India to protect and improve the environment and have compassion for living creatures. The language used in these articles clearly indicates that the principles of tolerance, non-violence, equity, compassion and reference have been given legal recognition. The use of the term 'protect and improve, implies the improvement of the natural environment as well as quality of life. Further, protection of the environment implicitly directs us not to cut trees, harm any animal, and to keep the water of rivers, lakes, etc., clean and wholesome. The phrase 'to have compassion for living creatures' used in Article 51A(g) impliedly recognizes the principle that all creatures are made equal and that animal killing should be prohibited as per the principle of non-violence. According to the moral code of conduct, killing of animals and birds is regarded a sin of highest order.

Abiding by this philosophy of ancient times, the Indian Parliament passed two statutes, viz., the Wild Life (Protection) Act, 1972 and the Cruelty Against Certain Animals Act, 1962. The object behind these statutes is not to harm and attack mute birds and animals. Wildlife is the guardian and protector of our forests. Decay of wildlife implies decay of forests and vice versa. Both are interdependent and complementary to each other. It would not be out of place to mention here that Indian judiciary has also accepted the Indian social and moral ethics related to environment and this is reflected in many of their judgments concerning environmental issues.

Besides the constitutional provisions regarding environmental protection, many legislations have also been enacted before and after independence. The environmental laws were passed as a human right or fundamental right to have a clean and pollution-free environment. It has been recognized that pollution-free environment is the basic need for the survival of humanity and it cannot be ensured without ecological balance. Any attempt to defile the natural environment would amount to violation of human right to clean environment. The inspiration to amend Constitution and enact environment protection and conservation legislations came from the Stockholm Conference (1972) referred to above.

The modern phenomena of environmental degradation and pollution started growing in India in the 20th century with the growth of population, increasing industrialization, urbanization, materialistic philosophy of life (consumer culture) along with the growth of other economic activities. To put a check on environmental degradation and to contain the problems of air, water, land and radiation pollution, and also to maintain eco-balance, many laws have been passed, of which the important ones are as follows:

1. The Wildlife (Protection) Act, 1972
2. The Water (Prevention and Control of Pollution) Act, 1974
3. The Forest (Conservation) Act, 1080
4. The Air (Prevention and Control of Pollution) Act, 1981
5. The Environment (Protection) Act, 1986

The Environment (Protection) Act, 1986 is a special law that extends to the whole nation. It gives wide powers to the government to contain all kinds of pollution and to maintain eco-balance. The Act consists of 26 sections which provide various rules to put a check on pollution. Some important rules are as under:

1. Hazardous Wastes (Management and Handling) Rules 1989
2. Recycled Plastics Manufacture and Usages Rules, 1999
3. Noise Pollution (Regulation and Control) Rules 2000

For protection and conservation of environment, there exist sufficient laws. What is needed is their proper monitoring and implementation that will ensure the healthy life of the people in India. In this respect, there is immediate need for sustainable development—a development which is not harmful to environment. The eco-friendly development can solve the problem of environmental degradation. This development emphasizes on improving the quality of human life while living within the carrying capacity of supporting system. It is a development without compromising the ability of future generations to meet their own needs.

Tackling all problems related to ecological crisis referred to above is not very easy. Conservation, recycling and production of eco-friendly products can help in diminishing pollution, the creation of waste and the depletion of resources but cannot be eliminated totally. The amount of waste produced each day in the modern societies is staggering. Most of these wastes is thrown away haphazardly. This is why some people have named the modern societies as 'throw-away societies'. When environmental analysts speak of waste materials, they mean not only goods that are thrown away, but also gaseous wastes pumped into the atmosphere. Examples are carbon dioxide (CO_2) released into the atmosphere by the burning of fuels like oil and coal in automobiles and power station, and gases released into the air by the use of aerosol cans, material for insulation and air-conditioning units. Carbon dioxide is the main factor for the generation of the process of global warming.

Some 'Green' authors argue that people in rich countries must react against consumerism and materialism and resort to more simple ways of life if global disaster is to be avoided. We see clearly that modern industry, technology and science are by no means wholly beneficial in their consequences as regarded a few decades ago. Our world is much more popular and wealthy than ever before, yet it hovers close to economic and ecological disaster. In this respect, sociology offers a profound consciousness about human social institutions and this will help us to maintain a realistic and hopeful outlook about the future. Concern about the environment is a social issue, not just an issue of economic growth and development.

Sociology and Environmental Crisis

Sociology of today reflects many new issues and concerns of the so-called postmodern or late modern period. We do not find any reference of these issues in the textbooks of sociology published before 1970s. Like terriorism, environmental (eco) crisis has become one of the key issues of this period. We are alive because our environment (natural) is alive, though it is now fragmented in many ways by the forces of modernity and development. Recent developmental initiatives, which are the culmination of modern way of living, have endangered, especially the life and livelihood of the people so affected but the whole world in general. This is why, ecological concerns and issues have found prominent place in the syllabi of sociology at the degree and post-degree level courses. Not only this, it has become one of the main topics of research for the sociologists of today.

Some sociologists regard this new phenomenon of environmental crisis as the byproduct of modernity and development. Increasing use of technology and the consequent industrialization and urbanization has resulted into this problem of ecological crisis. Modern society is utterly dependent on technical intervention and technological harnessing of the forcess of nature. This intervention has badly affected the environment. Deforestation, desertification, shortage of rains and many other problems, discussed above, are the result of over-exploitation of nature and blind and excessive use of technology. Throughout the world, in the name of development, tropical forests are being destroyed and animals dependent on these forests are disappearing. This has caused not only the loss of biodiversity but the very existence of life itself of every kind is now engulfed in danger. Technological advance often has destructive consequences; fertilizers, for example, increased agricultural products but polluted river, DDT and many other chemicals as pesticides saved crops but destroyed wildlife and birds. These chemicals have affected the lives of human beings also.

Destructive consequences of modernity (technology and science) have given rise to the great awareness towards preservation of life and so as to environment. This awarness was named in a way post or late modernity. Postmodernity simply means what comes after modernity. It is often said that what was created by modernity, is being rejected or condemned by postmodernity. It looks with skepticism all the vague notions of progress and development. It is the radical criticism of modernity. Postmodernists tend to argue that the people no longer believe in the inevitability of progress and the power of science to solve all problems, the possibility of running societies in a rational way. People are becoming more and more pessimistic about their future due to the gradual ecological degradition and uneven development. Many postmodernist theorists believe that the modern approach to environmental crisis has become outdated.

Sociology of postmodernity in deeply concerned with the environment and humans' relationship with it. Ullrich Beck (1992), the sociologist of risk, arguing the characteristics of late modernity, has expressed concern about the unintended and often negative consequences of modernity, especially modern uneven development. He referred above all the human destruction of the environment and part of the ecosystem. The varied environmental movements may be cited as examples of the emergence of a greater sense of responsibility of the people towards nature/environment. People are now becoming more and more conscious about their duty towards nature. All these reflect the ethos of postmodernity.

Bibliography

Abel, T., 'Sociology: Its Nature and Scope', *Social Forces*, 11, 1932.

Abercrombie, N., Hill, S. and Turner, B.S., *The Penguin Dictionary of Sociology*, 3rd Edition, London: Penguin, 1994.

Abraham, M. Francis, *Modern Sociological Theory: An Introduction*, New Delhi: Oxford University Press, 1982.

Abraham, M. Francis, *Perspectives on Modernization: Toward a General Theory of Third World Development*, Washington, DC: University Press of America, 1980.

Abraham, M. Francis, *Sociological Thought*, Delhi: Macmillan India Limited, 1985.

Abraham, M. Francis, *The Agony of India*, Madras: East West Books, 1998.

Adorno, T.W. et al., *The Authoritarian Personality*, New York: Harper, 1950.

Ahuja, Ram, *Indian Social System*, Jaipur: Rawat Publications, 1993.

Albert K. Cohen, *Delinquent Boys: The Culture of the Gang*, Glencoe: The Free Press, 1955.

Alexander, J.C. (ed.), *Theoretical Logic in Sociology*, Vol. 1, Berkeley: University of California Press, 1982.

Almond, Gabriel A., *Political Development: Essays in Heuristic Theory*. Boston: Little Brown and Company, 1970.

Almond, Gabriel and James Coleman (eds), *The Politics of Developing Areas*, Princeton, NJ: Princeton University Press, 1960.

Altekar, A.S., *The Position of Women in Hindu Civilization*, Benaras: Motilal Benarasidas Publications, 1962.

Althusser, L., *For Marx*, London: Verso, 1969.

Ambedkar, B.R., 'Caste in India: Their Mechanism, Genesis and Development', *Indian Antiquary Journal*, 1917.

Ames, Michael, 'Ideological and Social Change in Ceylon', *Human Organization*, 22, 1963.

Anderson A. and Sabatelli, R., *Family Interaction: A Multigenerational Developmental Perspective*, Boston: Allyn and Bacon, 1999.

Anderson, W.A. and Parker, F.B., *Society: Its Organization and Operation*, New Jersey: Van Nostrand Company, 1964.

Apter, David E. (ed.), *Ideology and Discontent*. New York: The Free Press of Glencoe, 1965.

Aron, R., *German Sociology*, London: Heinemann, 1957.

Aron, R., *Main Currents in Sociological Thought*, Garden City, NY: Doubleday, 1970.

Aron, R., *The Industrial Society*, New York: Simon & Schuster, 1968.

Asch, Solomon E., *Social Psychology*, New York: Prentice Hall, 1952.

Babbie, Earl R., *The Practice of Social Research*, Belmont, California: Wadsworth, 1983.

Bagchi, Jasodhra (ed.), *The Changing Status of Women in West Bengal, 1970-2000*, New Delhi: Sage, 2005.

Bailey, F.G., *Tribe, Caste and Nation*, Manchester: Manchester University Press, 1963.

Bales, Kevin, *Disposable People: New Slavery in the Global Economy*, Berkeley: University of California Press, 1999.

Balsara, F.N., *Sociology*, Bombay: Lakhani Book Depot, 1956.

Bandura, A., *Social Learning Theory*, Englewood Cliffs, NJ: Prentice Hall, 1977.

Banks, J.A., *Prosperity and Parenthood*, London: Routledge and Kegan Paul, 1954.

Baudrillard, J., *Simulations*, New York: Semiotext(e), 1983.

Beattie, J., *Other Cultures*, London: Cohen & West, 1964.

Beck, U., *Risk Society: Towards a New Modernity*, London: Sage, 1992.

Becker, H., *Systematic Sociology*, New York: John Wiley & Sons, 1932.

Bell, D., *The Coming of Post-Industrial Society*, New York: Collier, 1976.

Bell, D., *The End of Ideology*, New York: Free Press, 1960.

Bellah, R.N., 'The New Consciousness and the Crisis in Modernity', in Charles Clock and Robert Bellah (eds.), *The New Religious Consciousness*, Berkeley: University of California Press, 1976.

Bellah, R.N., *Beyond Belief: Essays on Religion in a Post-Traditional World*, New York: Harper & Row, 1970.

Bellah, Robert, 'Religious Evolution', *American Sociological Review*, 29, 1964.

Bendix, R. and Lipsit, S.M. (eds.), *Class, Status and Power*, London: Routledge, 1967.

Bendix, R., 'Max Weber', in David Sills (ed.), *The International Encyclopedia of the Social Sciences*, New York: Collier Macmillan Company, 1968.

Bendix, R., *Max Weber: An Intellectual Portrait*, London: Methuen University Press, 1966.

Bendix, Richard and Lipset, Seymour Martin, *Class, Status and Power: Social Stratification in Comparative Perspective*, New York: Free Press, 1966.

Berger, P.L., *Pyramids of Sacrifice*, New York: Penguin, 1974.

Berger, P.L. and Berger, B., *Sociology: A Biographical Approach*, New York: Penguin, 1976.

Berger, P.L. and Luckmann, Thomas, *The Social Construction of Reality*, Garden City, NY: Doubleday, 1966.

Berger, Peter, 'Protestantism and the Quest of Certainty', *The Christian Century*, 26 August 1998.

Berger, Peter, Berger, Brigitte and Kellner, Hansfried, *The Homeless Mind: Modernization and Consciousness*, Harmondsworth: Penguin Books, 1979.

Berger, Peter, *Invitation to Sociology: A Humanistic Perspective*, New York: Doubleday, 1963.

Berger, Peter, *Peter Berger and the Study of Religion*, New York: Routledge, 2002.

Berger, Peter, *The Sacred Canopy: Elements of a Sociological Theory of Religion*, New York: Doubleday, 1967.

Berghe, P. van den, 'Dialectic and Functionalism', *ASR*, 1963.

Bernard, Jessie, *The Female World*, New York: Free Press, 1981.

Béteille, André and Madan, T.N., *Encounter and Experience: Personal Accounts of Fieldwork*, Delhi: Vikas, 1975.

Béteille, André, 'The Paradox of Democracy', *Times of India*, 2008.

Béteille, André, *Class, Caste and Power*, Bombay: Oxford University Press, 1966.

Béteille, André, *Inequality Among Men*, Oxford: Basil Blackwell, 1977.

Béteille, André, *Sociology: Approach and Method*, Delhi: Oxford University Press, 2002.

Bierstedt, Robert, *Power and Progress: Essays on Sociological Theory*, New York: McGraw-Hill, 1974.

Biesanz, F. and Biesanz, M., *Modern Society: An Introduction to Social Science*, Englewood Cliffs, NJ: Prentice Hall, 1964.

Blau, P.M., *The Dynamics of Bureaucracy*, Chicago: University of Chicago Press, 1963.

Blood, Robert O. Jr. and Wolfe, Donald M., *Husbands & Wives: The Dynamics of Married Living*, New York: The Free Press, 1965.

Blumer, Herbert George, 'Collective Behavior', in Robert E. Park (ed.), *Principles of Sociology*, New York: Barnes & Noble, 1939.

Blumer, Herbert, *Symbolic Interactionism: Perspective and Method*, Englewood Cliffs, NJ: Prentice Hall, 1969.

Bogardus, E.S., *Sociology*, New York: The Macmillan Co., 1954.

Bottomore, T.B. and Nisbet, R. (eds.), *A History of Sociological Analysis*, New York: Basic Books, 1978.

Bottomore, T.B., *Classes in Modern Society*, London: George Allen & Unwin, 1965.

Bottomore, T.B., *Dictionary of Marxist Thought*, Oxford: Blackwell, 1983.

Bottomore, T.B., *Elites and Society*, Harmondsworth: Penguin, 1966.

Bottomore, T.B., *Marxist Sociology*, London: Macmillan, 1975.

Bottomore, T.B., *Sociology: A Guide to Problems and Literature*, London: George Allen & Unwin, 1962.

Bourdieu, Pierre and Passeron, Jean-Claude, *Reproduction in Education, Society and Culture* by Richard Nice (trs.), London: Sage, 1990.

Bourdieu, Pierre, *Homo Academicus* by Peter Collier (trs.), Stanford: Stanford University Press, 1988.

Bourdieu, Pierre, *Outline of a Theory of Practice*, Cambridge: Cambridge University Press, 1997.

Bourdieu, Pierre, *The Field of Cultural Production*, New York: Columbia University Press, 1993.

Bowles, Samuel and Gintis, Herbert, *Schooling in Capitalist America,* New York: Basic Books, 1976.

Breese, Gerald, *Urbanization in Newly Developing Countries*, Englewood Cliffs, NJ: Prentice Hall, 1966.

Broom, L. and Selznick, P., *Sociology: A Text with Adopted Readings*, New York: Harper & Row, 1957.

Brown, Lester R., *State of the World, 1996: A Worldwatch Institute Report*, New York: W.W. Norton, 2005.

Brundland, Harlem, *Our Common Future Report,* World Commission on Environment and Development, 1987.

Bukatko, Danuta and Daehler, Marvin W., *Child Development*, Boston: Houghton Mifflin Company, 2004.

Burgess, E. and Locke, H.J., *The Family,* New York: American Book Company, 1953.

Burgess, Ernest W., Locke, Harvey J. and Thomas, Mary M., *The Family: From Institution to Companionship*, 3rd ed., New York: American Book Co., 1963.

Cancian, Francesca M., 'Varieties of Functional Analysis', in David Sills (ed.), *International Encyclopedia of the Social Sciences*, Vol. 6, New York: Macmillan Company, 1968.

Canetti, Elias, *Crowds and Power*, New York: Seabury Press, 1979.

Carr, E.H., *What is History?* Harmondsworth: Penguin, 1961.

Carr, L.J., *Analytical Sociology*, New York: Harper & Row, 1955.

Castells, Manuel, *End of Millennium*, Malden, MA: Blackwell, 1998.

Charon, J.M., *The Meaning of Sociology*, Englewood Cliffs, NJ: Prentice Hall, 1980.

Chester, Robert, 'The Rise of the Neo-Conventional Family', *New Society*, pp. 185–88, 9 May 1985.

Chinoy, E., *Society: An Introduction to Sociology*, New York: Random House, 1961.

Chinoy, E., *Sociological Perspective*, New York: Random House, 1954.

Cloward, Richard and Ohlin, Lloyd, *Delinquency and Opportunity*, Glencoe: The Free Press, 1960.

Cohen, P.S., *Modern Social Theory*, London: Heinemann, 1968.

Coleman, James S., *Equality of Educational Opportunity*, Washington: US Department of Health, Education, and Welfare, Office of Education, 1966.

Coleman, James, Hoffer, Thomas and Kilgore, Sally, *Sociology of Education*, Chicago: The University of Chicago Press, 1982.

Coleman, John A., 'Civil Religion', *Sociological Analysis*, 31(2): 1970.

Collins, R., 'An Asian Route to Capitalism: Religious Economy and the Origins of Self-transforming Growth in Japan', *American Sociological Review*, 62 (December), 1997.

Collins, R., *Theoretical Sociology*, New York: Harcourt Brace Jovanovich, 1977.

Coltrane, Scott and Collins, Randall, *Sociology of Marriage and the Family: Gender, Love and Property*, Belmont, CA: Wadsworth, 2001.

Coltrane, Scott, *Families and Society*, Belmont, CA: Wadsworth, 2004.

Comte, A., 'The Course of Positive Philosophy', *Edinburgh Review*, 67, 1838.

Connor, S., *Postmodernist Culture*, Oxford: Blackwell, 1989.

Cooley, C.H., *Human Nature and Social Order*, New York: Schocken Press, 1964.

Cooley, C.H., *Social Organization*, New York: Schocken Press, 1962.

Coser, A. Lewis, *Masters of Sociological Thought*, New York: Harcourt Brace Jovanovich, 1971.

Coser, A. Lewis, *The Functions of Social Conflict*, New York: Free Press, 1956.

Cox, Harvey, *The Secular City*, New York: Macmillan, 1966.

Cuber, J.F., *Sociology: A Synopsis of Principles*, 2nd Edition, New York: Appleton-Century-Crofts, 1951.

Cuber, J.F., *Sociology: A Synopsis of Principles*, 6th Edition, New York: Appleton-Century-Crofts, 1968.

Cuff, E.L. and Payne, G.L.F. (eds.), *Perspectives in Sociology*, London: George Allen & Unwin, 1979.

Cumming, Flaine and Henry, William E., *Growing Old: The Process of Disengagement*, New York: Basic Books, 1961.

Cummings, Milton C. and David Wise, *Democracy Under Pressure*, Sixth Edition, New York: Harcourt Brace. 1989.

Dahl, Robert, *Dilemmas of Pluralist Democracy*, New Haven: Yale University Press, 1982.

Dahl, Robert, *Who Governs?* New Haven, CT: Yale University Press, 1961.

Dahrendorf, Ralf, 'Toward a Theory of Social Conflict', in Amitai Etzioni and Eva Etzioni-Halevy (eds.), *Social Change*, New York: Basic Books, 1973.

Dahrendorf, Ralf, *Class and Class Conflict in Industrial Society*, Stanford: Stanford University Press, 1959.

Daly, H.E., *Steady-state Economics*, San Francisco, CA: W.H. Freeman, 1977.

Darwin, Charles, *On the Origin of Species*, London: John Murray, 1859.

Darwin, Charles, *The Descent of Man*, Princeton, NJ: Princeton University Press, 1871.

David, Held (ed.), *Prospects for Democracy: North, South, East, West*, Stanford: Stanford University Press, 1993.

Davies, James C., 'Toward a Theory of Revloution', *American Sociological Review*, 27 (February), 1992.

Davis, K., 'The Theory of Change and Response in Modern Demographic History', *Population Index*, 1963.

Davis, K., *Human Society*, New York: Macmillan, 1949.

Davis, Kingsley and Moore, Wilbert E., 'Some Principles of Stratification', *American Sociological Review*, 10, 1945.

Davis, Kingsley, *The Population of India and Pakistan*, Princeton, NJ: Princeton University Press, 1951.

Dawson, C.A. and Gettys, W.E., *An Introduction to Sociology*, New York: The Ronald Press, 1948.

Debroy, Bibek and Bhandari, Laveesh, *Economic Freedom for States of India*, Delhi: Excel Books, 2007.

Desai, A.R. (ed.), *Essays on Modernization of Underdeveloped Societies*, Atlantic Highlands: Humanities Press, 1976.

Desai, I.P., 'The Joint Family in India: An Appraisal', *Sociological Bulletin*, Vol. V, No. 2, September 1956.

Desai, Mihir, 'A Justification for Reservations and Affirmative Action for Backward Castes in India', *South Asia Bulletin*, 11 (1 & 2): 1991.

Desai, Neera, *Women in Modern India*, Bombay: Vora Publishers, 1957.

Deshpande, Satish, *Contempo. ıry India: A Sociological View*, Delhi: Viking, 2002.

Dewey, John, *Democracy and Łducation*, New York: Macmillan, 1916.

Dillon, Michele, *Handbook of Sociology of Religion*, Cambridge, UK: Cambridge University Press, 2003.

Domhoff, G. William. *Who Rules America? Power, Politics and Social Change*, Englewood Cliffs, N.J.: Prentice-Hall, 1967.

Douglas, J.D. (ed.), *Introduction to Sociology*, New York: Free Press, 1973.

Dube, S.C., *Indian Village*, London: Routledge & Kegan Paul, 1955.

Dube, S.C., *Modernization and Development*, New Delhi: Vistaar Publications, 1988.

Dumont, Louis, *Homo Hierarchicus: The Caste System and Its Implications*, Chicago: University of Chicago Press, 1970.

Duncan, Greg, *Years of Poverty and Years of Plenty*, New York: Russell Sage Foundation, 1987.

Duncan, Otis Dudley, 'Social Organization and the Ecosystem', in Robert E.L. Faris (ed.), *Handbook of Modern Sociology*, Chicago, Illinois: Rand McNally, 1964.

Dunleavy, P. and O' Leary, B., *Theories of the State*, London: Murray, 1967.

Dupreel, E.G., *The Evolution of Population Theory*, Overbeek, J., (ed.), Westport, Connecticut: Greenwood Press, 1977.

Durkheim, Émile, *Education and Sociology*, Glencoe, Ill.: The Free Press, 1922.

Durkheim, Émile, *Rules of Sociological Method*, New York: Free Press, 1958.

Durkheim, Émile, *Suicide*, New York: Free Press, 1951.

Durkheim, Émile, *The Division of Labour in Society*, New York: Free Press, 1965.

Durkheim, Émile, *The Elementary Forms of Religious Life*, New York: Free Press, 1965.

Dutt, R.C., *A History of Civilization in Ancient India*, London: Macmillan, 1893.

Eckstein, Harry, *Pressure Group Politics, the Case of the British Medical Association*, Stanford: Stanford University Press, 1960.

Eichler, Margrit, *Family Shifts: Families, Policies and Gender Equality*, Toronto: Oxford University Press, 1997.

Eisenstadt, S.N., *Modernization: Protest and Change*, Englewood Cliffs, NJ: Prentice Hall, 1966.

Eisenstadt, S.N., *Tradition, Change and Modernity*, New York: John Wiley, 1973.

Ekeh, P.P., *Social Exchange Theory*, Cambridge: Harvard University Press, 1974.

Elias, N., *What is Sociology?* New York: Columbia University Press, 1970.

Elliott, M.A. and Merrill, F.E., *Social Disorganization*, New York: Harper and Brothers, 1961.

Engels, Friedrich, *The Origin of Family*, Chicago: C.H. Kerr, 1902.

Erikson, E., *Childhood and Society*, New York: W.W. Norton, 1963.

Eshleman, J.R. and Cashion, B.G., *Sociology: An Introduction*, Boston: Little, Brown & Company, 1983.

Eshleman, J.R., Cashion, B.G. and Basirico, L.A., *Sociology: An Introduction*, New York: Holt, Rinehart & Winston, Inc., 1988.

Etzioni, A. and Etzioni, E., *Social Change: Sources, Patterns and Consequences*, New York: Basic Books, 1964.

Eubank, E.E., *Concepts of Sociology*, Lexington, MA: D.C. Heath, 1932.

Fairbanks, A., *Introduction to Sociology*, New York: Scribner's, 1964.

Fairchild, H.P. (ed.), *Dictionary of Sociology*, New York: The Philosophical Library, 1944.

Fairchild, S.M., *Mysteries of Civilization: Or How I Earned My Homestead and Lost It?* Minneapolis: The Author, 1908.

Faris, R.E.L. (ed.), *Handbook of Modern Sociology*, Chicago: Rand McNally, 1964.

Feagin, Joe R. and Feagin, Clairece B., *Racial and Ethnic Relations*, Upper Saddle River, NJ: Prentice Hall, 2003.

Featherstone, Mike (ed.), *Global Culture: Nationalism, Globalization and Modernity*, London: Sage, 1990.

Featherstone, Mike, *Consumer Culture and Postmodernism*, London: Sage, 1991.

Ferrell, Ronald A. and Swigert, Victoria L., *Deviance and Social Control*, Glenview, Illinois: Scott, Foresman, 1982.

Fichter, J.H., *Sociology*, Chicago: University of Chicago Press, 1964.

Fletcher, R., *The Making of Sociology (Vols. 2)*, New York: Scribner's, 1971.

Foucault, Michel, *The Archaeology of Knowledge,* London: Tavistock, 1969.

Fox, R., *Kinship and Marriage*, Cambridge: Cambridge University Press, 1996.

Freedman, Ronald et al. (eds.), *Principles of Sociology*, New York: Henry Holt, 1952.

Freire, Paulo, *Pedagogy of the Oppressed*, New York: Seabury, 1970.

Freud, Sigmund, *Standard Edition of the Complete Psychological Works of Sigmund Freud*, London: Hogarth Press, 1920, 1923, 1930.

Freund, J., *The Sociology of Max Weber*, New York: Pantheon Books, 1968.

Friedman, Betty, *The Feminine Mystique*, New York: W.W. Norton, 1963.

Friedman, Bruce D., *The Research Tool Kit*, Pacific Grove: Brooks/Cole Publishing Company, 1998.

Friedmann, J., *Regional Development Policy: A Case Study of Venezuela*, Cambridge: MIT Press, 1966.

Friedrichs, R.W., *A Sociology of Sociology*, New York: Free Press, 1970.

Fromm, Eric, *Marx's Concept of Man*, New York: Frederick Ungar, 1961.

Fulcher, James and Scott, John, *Sociology*, Oxford: Oxford University Press, 2003.

Fuller, C. and Myers, R.R., 'The Natural History of a Social Problem', *American Sociological Review*, 6, 320–329, 1941.

Furer-Haimendorf, Christopher von, *Tribes of India: The Struggle for Survival*, Berkeley, CA: University of California Press, 1982.

Garey, Anita Ilta, *Weaving Work and Motherhood*, Philadelphia: Temple University Press, 1999.

Geertz, Clifford, *Peddlers and Princes*, Chicago: University of Chicago Press, 1963.

Geertz, Clifford, *The Interpretation of Cultures: Selected Essays*, New York: Basic Books, 1973.

George, Susan and Sabelli, Fabrizio, *Faith and Credit: The World Bank's Secular Empire*, Boulder: Westview Press, 1994.

George, Susan, *How the Other Half Dies: The Real Reasons for World Hunger*, Totowa, N.J.: Allanheld, Osmun, 1977.

Geraint, Parry, *Political Elites Political Elites*, New York: Praeger Publishers, Inc., 1969.

Gerth, H.H. and C. Mills, Wright, *From Max Weber*, New York: Oxford University Press, 1946.

Ghurye, G.S., *Caste and Class in India*, Bombay: Popular Book Depot, 1950.

Ghurye, G.S., *Gods and Men,* Bombay: Popular Prakashan, 1962.

Gibbon, Edward, *The Decline and Fall of the Roman Empire*, New York: Peter Fenelon Collier, 1914.

Giddens, A. (ed.), *Emile Durkheim*, Chicago: University of Chicago Press, 1978.

Giddens, A. (ed.), *Positivism and Sociology*, London: Heinemann, 1974.

Giddens, A., *Central Problems in Social Theory*, London: Macmillan, 1979.

Giddens, A., *Modernity and Self-Identity*, Cambridge: Polity, 1993.

Giddens, A., *New Rules of Sociological Method*, London: Hutchinson, 1976.

Giddens, A., *Politics and Sociology in the Thought of Max Weber*, London: Macmillan, 1972.

Giddens, A., *Sociology*, Cambridge: Polity, 1997, 2000.

Giddens, A., *The Constitution of Society*, Cambridge: Polity, 1984.

Giddings, F.H., *Inductive Sociology*, New York: The Macmillan Co., 1901.

Giddings, F.H., *Principles of Sociology*, New York: Macmillan, 1896.

Gillin, J.L. and Gillin, J.P., *An Introduction to Sociology*, New York: Macmillan, 1947.

Gillin, J.L. and Gillin, J.P., *Cultural Sociology*, New York: Macmillan, 1948.

Ginsberg, M., *Essays in Sociology and Social Philosophy*, London: Heinemann, 1956.

Ginsberg, M., *Reason and Unreason in Society*, New York: Longman, 1947.

Ginsberg, M., *Sociology*, London: Oxford University Press, 1934.

Gisbert, P., *Fundamentals of Sociology*, Bombay: Orient Longmans, 1957.

Goffman, E., *Encounters*, Indianapolis, IN: Bobbs-Merrill, 1961.

Goffman, E., *Presentation of Self in Everyday Life*, New York: Doubleday Anchor, 1959.

Goldthrope, J.E., *An Introduction to Sociology*, Cambridge: Cambridge University Press, 1969.

Goldthrope, J.E., *Social Mobility and Class Structure in Britain*, Oxford: Clarendon Press, 1980.

Goode, William J., 'The Theoretical Importance of Love', *American Sociological Review*, Vol. 24, pp. 38–47, February 1959.

Goode, William, *World Revolution and Family Patterns*, London: Free Press of Glencoe, 1963.

Gore, M.S., *Indian Education: Structure and Process*, Jaipur: Rawat Publications, 1994.

Gould, J. and Kolb, W.L., *Dictionary of Social Sciences*, London: Tavistock, 1964.

Gouldner, A.W. and Gouldner, H.P., *Modern Sociology: An Introduction to the Study of Human Interaction*, London: Harcourt, Brace & World, 1963.

Gouldner, A.W., *The Coming Crisis of Western Sociology*, New York: Basic Books, 1970.

Government of India, *India 2003*, New Delhi: Publications Division, 2003.

Green, A.W., *Sociology: An Analysis of Life in Modern Society*, New York: McGraw-Hill, 1956.

Green, B.S.R. and Jones, E.A., *An Introduction to Sociology*, Oxford: Pergamon, 1966.

Grusky, D.V., *Social Stratification: Class, Race and Gender*, Boulder, Colorado: Westview Press, 1994.

Guha, R. and Gadgil, M., 'State Forestry and Social Conflict in British India: A Study in the Ecological Bases of Agrarian Protest', CES Technical Report, No. 51, 1989.

Guha, Ramachandra, *Environmentalism: A Global History*, Delhi: Oxford University Press, 2000.

Guillard, A., *Elements de Statistique Humaine*, Paris: Guillaumin, 1855.

Gupta, Dipankar, *Social Stratification*, New Delhi: Oxford University Press, 1993.

Gupta, Dipankar, *The Caged Phoenix: Can India Fly?* New Delhi: Penguin Books, 2009.

Gurvich, G. and Moore, W.E., *Twentieth Century Sociology*, New York: The Philosophical Library, 1945.

Gusfield, Joseph R., 'Tradition and Modernity: Misplaced Polarities in the Study of Social Change', *American Journal of Sociology*, 72(4): 1967.

Habermas, J., *The Theory of Communicative Action*, London: Beacon Press, 1981.

Habermas, J., *Towards a Rational Society*, Boston: Beacon Press, 1970.

Haggett, Peter, *Geography: A Modern Synthesis*, New York: Harper and Row, 1975.

Hallen, G.C., 'The Future of the Family', *Social Science*, 42(3): 1967.

Halsey, A.H., Floud, J.E. and Anderson, C.A. (eds.), *Education, Economy and Society: A Reader in the Sociology of Education*, New York: Free Press, 1961.

Hamilton, Malcolm, *The Sociology of Religion: Theoretical and Comparative Perspectives*, New York: Routledge, 2001.

Hankins, F.H., *An Introduction to the Study of Society*, New York: Macmillan, 1928.

Haralambos, M. and Holborn, M. *Sociology*, London: HaperCollins, 2000.

Hargrove, Barbara W., *Reformation of the Holy*, Philadelphia: F.A. Davis, 1971.

Harris, Marvin, 'The Cultural Ecology of India's Sacred Cattle', *Current Anthropology*, 7, 1966.

Harris, Marvin, *Culture, People and Nature*, New York: Crowell, 1975.

Harvey, D., *The Condition of Postmodernity*, Oxford: Blackwell, 1990.

Hatt, P.K. and Goode, William J., *Methods in Social Research*, New York: McGraw-Hill Book Co., 1952.

Hauser, P.M. and Duncan, O.D., *The Study of Population*, New York: Plenum Press, 1959.

Hauser, Philip and Schnore, Leo (eds.), *The Study of Urbanization*, New York: John Wiley & Sons, 1965.

Hauser, Philip, 'The Social, Economic and Technological Problems of Rapid Urbanization', in Bert Hoselitz and Wilbert Moore (eds.), *Industrialization and Society*, Paris: UNESCO-Mouton, 1970.

Henslin, James M., *Sociology: A Down to Earth Approach*, Boston: Allyn & Bacon, 1997.

Hertzler, J.O., *Social Institutions,* Lincoln: University of Nebraska Press, 1946.

Higgins, Benjamin, 'Urbanization, Industrialization and Economic Development', in Glenn Beyer (ed.), *The Urban Explosion in Latin America*, Ithaca: Cornell University Press, 1967.

Hiller, E.T., *Principles of Sociology*, New York: Harper & Brothers, 1933.

Hobhouse, L.T., *Morals in Evolution*, New York: Henry Holt, 1907.

Hobhouse, L.T., *Social Development*, London: Allen & Unwin, 1924.

Homans, G., 'Bringing Men Back', *American Sociological Review*, 29(5): 1964.

Homans, G.C., *Social Behaviour: Its Elementary Forms*, London: Routledge & Kegan Paul, 1961.

Homans, G.C., *The Human Group*, New York: Harcourt, Brace, 1950.

Horton, P.B. and Hunt, C.L., *Sociology*, New York: McGraw-Hill Co., 1964.

Horton, Paul and Leslie, Gerald, *The Sociology of Social Problems*, New York: Appleton-Century-Crofts, 1970.

Hunt, E.F., *Social Science: An Introduction to the Study of Society*, New York: Macmillan, 1955.

Hunter James, *American Evangelicalism*, New Brunswick, N.J.: Rutgers, 1983.

Hunter, Floyd, *Community Power Structure,* Chapel Hill: University of North Carolina Press, 1953.

Huntington, Samuel P. and Nelson, Joan M., *No Easy Choice: Political Participation in Developing Countries*, Cambridge, MA: Harvard University Press, 1976.

Hutton, J.H., *Caste in India: Its Nature, Functions and Origins*, New York: Oxford University Press, 1963.

Illich, Ivan, *Deschooling Society*, New York: Harper & Row, 1971.

Inkeles, A., *What is Sociology? An Introduction to the Discipline and Profession*, Englewood Cliffs, NJ: Prentice Hall, 1964.

Jain, Devaki (ed.), *Indian Women*, New Delhi: Publications Division, 1975.

Jameson, F., *Postmodernism*, New York: Verso, 1991.

Jayaram, N., *Sociology of Education in India*, Jaipur: Rawat Publications, 1990.

Jencks, Christopher et al., *Inequality,* New York: Basic Books, 1972.

Johnson, A.G., *The Blackwell Dictionary of Sociology*, Cambridge, MA: Blackwell, 1995.

Johnson, Doyle P., *Sociological Theory*, New York: John Wiley & Sons, 1981.

Johnson, H.M., *Sociology: A Systematic Introduction*, New York: Harcourt Brace & Co., 1960.

Jones, M.E., *Basic Sociological Principles*, New York: Ginn & Col, 1949.

Kakar, Sudhir and Kakar, Katharina, *The Indians: Portrait of a People*, Delhi: Penguin-Viking, 2007.

Kapadia, K.M., *Marriage and Family in India*, New Delhi: Oxford University Press, 1966.

Kaplan, Abraham, *The Conduct of Inquiry*, San Francisco: Chandler Publishing Company, 1964.

Kapp, K.W., *The Social Costs of Business Enterprise*, 2nd edition, New York: Asia Pub. House, 1963.

Karve, Irawati, *Hindu Society: An Interpretation*, Poona: Deccan College, 1961.

Kaviraj, Sudipta, 'The Modern State in India', in Sudipta Kaviraj and Martin Doornbos (eds.), *Transforming India*, New Delhi: Sage, 2000.

Koeing, S. et al. (eds.), *Sociology*, New York: Prentice Hall, 1953.

Kothari, Rajni, *Caste in Indian Politics*, Delhi: Orient Longman, 1970.

Kroeber, A.L., *The Nature of Culture*, Chicago: University of Chicago Press, 1952.

Kuhn, T.S., *The Structure of Scientific Revolutions*, Chicago: University of Chicago Press, 1996.

Lal, A.K. and Ahmad, S. Sami, *Social Change in Post-Independence India*, Jaipur and New Delhi: Rawat Publications, 2001.

Lal, Vinay, *Empire of Knowledge,* London: Pluto Press, 2005.

Landis, P.H., *Introductory Sociology*, New York: Ronald Press Company, 1958.

Lane, Robert E., *Political Ideology,* New York: Free Press, 1962.

Lang, K. and Lang, G., *Collective Dynamics*, New York: Thomas Y. Crowell, 1961.

Lang, K. and Lang, G., *International Encyclopedia of Social Sciences,* Vol. 2, New York: MacMillan, 1968.

Lapiere, R.J., *Sociology*, New York: McGraw-Hill, 1946.

Lappe, Frances Moore, Collins, Joseph and Rosset, Peter, *World Hunger: Twelve Myths*, New York: Grove Press, 1998.

Lasswell, H.D., Lerner, D. and Rothwell, C.E., *The Comparative Study of Elites,* Stanford, California: Stanford University Press, 1952.

Lasswell, Harold Dwight, *Politics: Who Gets What, When, How*, New York: McGraw-Hill Book Company, 1936.

Lauer, Robert H., *Perspectives on Social Change*, Boston: Allyn & Bacon, 1991.

Lazarsfeld, Paul Felix et al., *The Uses of Sociology*, New York: Basic Books, 1967.

Le Bon, Gustave, *The Crowd*, London: Ernest Benn, 1952. Originally published in 1896.

Leach, Edmund, *A Runaway World*, London: BBC Publications, 1967.

Lefebvre, H., *The Sociology of Marx*, New York: Random House, 1968.

Lemert, Edwin, *Human Deviance, Social Problems and Social Control*, Englewood Cliffs, NJ: Prentice Hall, 1972.

Lenski, Gerhard and Lenski, Jean, *Human Societies*, New York: McGraw-Hill, 1982.

Lenski, Gerhard, *Power and Privilege: A Theory of Social Stratification*, New York: McGraw-Hill, 1996.

Lerner, Daniel, 'Modernization: Social Aspects', in N. Smelser and P. Battes (eds.), *International Encyclopedia of Social and Behavioural Sciences*, New York: Macmillan Company, 1968.

Levi-Strauss, C., *The Elementary Structure of Kinship*, Paris: PUF, 1949.

Levy, M.J., *The Structure of Society*, Princeton: Princeton University Press, 1952.

Lewis, Oscar, *The Children of Sanchez*, New York: Random House, 1961.

Lifton, Robert Jay, *Destroying the World to Save It*, New York: Henry Holt & Company, 2000.

Lindsey, L. Linda and Beach, Stephen, *Sociology*, Upper Saddle River, NJ: Pearson Education, Inc., 2004.

Linton, R., *The Study of Man: An Introduction*, New York: Appleton- Century, 1936.

Lipset, S.M. and Smelser, N., *Sociology: The Progress of a Decade*, Englewood Cliffs, NJ: Prentice Hall, 1961.

Lipset, S.M., *Political Man*, New York: Doubleday, 1960.

Lofland, John and Lofland, Lyn H., *Analyzing Social Settings*, New York: Wadsworth Publishing Company, 1995.

Lofland, John, 'Collective Behaviour: The Elementary Forms', in N. Rosenberg and R.H. Turner (eds.), *Social Psychology: Sociological Perspectives*, New York: Basic Books, 1981.

Loomis, C.F., *Fundamental Concepts of Sociology*, New York: American Book Company, 1940.

Lowie, R.H., *Social Organization*, London: Routledge and Kegan Paul, 1950.

Lukes, S., *Emile Durkheim: His Life and Work*, New York: Harper & Row, 1972.

Lukes, S., *Power: A Radical View*, 2nd Edition, Basingstoke: Palgrave Macmillan, 2005.

Lumley, F.E., *Principles of Sociology*, New York: McGraw-Hill, 1928.

Lummis, C. Douglas, 'Equality', in Wolfgang Sachs (ed.), *The Development Dictionary*, Atlantic Highlands: Zed, 1992.

Lundberg, G.A., *Foundations of Sociology*, New York: Macmillan, 1956.

Lundberg, G.A., Schrag, C.C. and Larsen, O.N., *Sociology*, New York: Harper, 1958.

Lyotard, J.F., *The Postmodern Condition*, Minneapolis: University of Minnesota Press, 1984.

Macionis, John J., *Sociology*, Englewood Cliffs, NJ: Prentice Hall, 1995.

MacIver, R.M. and Page, C.H. *Society: An Introductory Analysis*, London: Macmillan, 1962.

MacIver, R.M., *Society: A Textbook of Sociology*, New York: Rinehart & Company, 1937.

Madan, T.N. (ed.), *India's Religions: Perspectives from Sociology and History*, New Delhi: Oxford University Press, 2004.

Madan, T.N., *Modern Myths, Locked Minds: Secularism and Fundamentalism in India*, New Delhi: Oxford University Press, 1997.

Madan, T.N., *Religion in India*, New Delhi: Oxford University Press, 1991.

Madan, T.N., *Social and Economic Change*, Bombay: Allied Publishers, 1970.

Madge, J., *Tools of Social Science*, Garden City, NY: Anchor Books, 1965.

Malinowski, Bronislaw, *Argonauts of Western Pacific*, London: Routledge & Kegan Paul, 1922.

Malinowski, Bronislaw, *The Foundations of Faith and Morals*, New York: Folcroft, 1936.

Malthus, Robert, *An Essay on the Principle of Population*, Oxford: Oxford University Press, 1798.

Mann, Michael, 1986, *Sources of Social Power*, Vol I., Cambridge: Cambridge University Press, 1986.

Mannheim, K., *Essays on the Sociology of Culture*, London: Routledge & Kegan Paul, 1956.

Mannheim, K., *Essays on the Sociology of Knowledge*, London: Routledge & Kegan Paul, 1952.

Mannheim, K., *Systematic Sociology*, London: Routledge & Kegan Paul, 1959.

Marcuse, H., *One-Dimensional Man*, Boston, MA: Beacon Press, 1964.

Marshall, G. (ed.), *The Concise Oxford Dictionary of Sociology*, Oxford: Oxford University Press, 1994.

Marshall, T.H., *Social Policy in the Twentieth Century*, London: Hutchinson, 1967.

Marshall, T.H., *Sociology at the Crossroads*, London: Heinemann, 1963.

Martindale, D. and Monachesi, E.D., *Elements of Sociology*, New York: Thomas Y. Crowell Company, 1956.

Marx, K. and Engels, F., *The Communist Manifesto*, London: Penguin, 1848.

Marx, K., *Capital, 3 Vols.*, Moscow: Progress Publishers, 1867, 1885, 1893.

Marx, K., *Selected Writings in Sociology and Social Philosophy*, London: McGraw-Hill, 1964.

Mauss, Armand L., *Social Problems of Social Movements*, Philadelphia: Lippincott, 1975.

Mauss, Marcel, *The Gift*, London: Cohen & West, 1925, 1954.

Mayer, Kurt B., *Class and Society*, New York: Random House, 1955.

Mazumdar, H.T., *The Grammar of Sociology*, Bombay: Asia Publishing House, 1966.

McClelland, David, *The Achieving Society,* New York: Van Nostrand, 1961.

McKee, James B., *Introduction to Sociology*, New York: Holt, 1969.

McMichael, Philip, *Development and Social Change: A Global Perspective*, Thousand Oaks, California: Pine Forge Press, 2000.

McPhail, Clark, and Miller, David L., 'The Assembling Process: A Theoretical and Empirical Examination', *American Sociological Review*, 38: 721–735, 1973.

Mead, George Herbert, *Mind, Self and Society*, Chicago: University of Chicago Press, 1934.

Mead, Margaret, *Sex and Temperament in Three Primitive Societies*, New York: William Morrow, 1963.

Meadows, P. and Mizruchi, E. (eds.), *Urbanism, Urbanization and Change: Comparative Perspectives, Reading*, MA: Addison-Wesley, 1969.

Merrill, F.E. and Eldrege, H.W., *Culture and Society: An Introduction to Sociology*, Englewood Cliffs, NJ: Prentice Hall, 1965.

Merton, R.K. and Nisbet, R. (eds.), *Contemporary Social Problems*, New York: Harcourt, Brace & World, 1961.

Merton, Robert K., *Social Theory and Social Structure*, Glencoe: Free Press, 1957.

Meyer, David S., Whittier, Nancy and Robnett, Belinda (eds.), *Social Movements: Identity, Culture and the State*, New York: Oxford University Press, 2002.

Michels, Robert, *Political Parties,* Glencoe, Ill.: The Free Press, 1949.

Mihanovich, Clement S., *Glossary of Sociological Terms*, Milwaukee: Bruce Publishing Co., 1957.

Milbrath, Lester W., *Envisioning a Sustainable Society: Learning Our Way Out*, Albany: State University of New York Press, 1989.

Miliband, Ralph, *The State in Capitalist Society*. New York: Basic Books, 1969.

Mills, C. Wright, *The Power Elite*, New York: Oxford University Press, 1956.

Milton, Kay, *Environmentalism and Cultural Theory: Exploring the Role of Anthropology in Environmental Discourse*, New York: Routledge, 1996.

Mitchell, D., *Dictionary of Sociology*, Chicago: Aldine, 1968.

Mol, Hans, *Identity and the Sacred: A Sketch for a New Social-Scientific Theory of Religion*, New York: The Free Press, 1976.

Moore, Wilbert, *Industrialization and Labor, Ithaca:* Cornell University Press, 1951.

Moore, Wilbert, *Social Change*, Englewood Cliffs, NJ: Prentice Hall, 1963.

Moore, Wilbert, *The Impact of Industry*, Englewood Cliffs, NJ: Prentice Hall, 1965.

Mullins, Nicholas C., *Theories and Theory Groups in Contemporary American Sociology*, New York: Harper & Row, 1973.

Murdock, George P., *Culture and Society: Twenty-Four Essays*, Pittsburg: University of Pittsburg Press, 1965.

Murry, R.W., *Introductory Sociology*, New York: FS Crofts Co., 1946.

Myrdal, Gunnar, *The Challenge of World Poverty*, New York: Random House, 1970.

Navlakha, Suren, *Elite and Social Change: A Study of Elite Formation in India*, New Delhi: Sage Publications, 1989.

Nehru, Jawaharlal, *The Discovery of India*, Calcutta: The Signet Press, 1946.

Nisbet, R.A., *The Social Bond: An Introduction to the Study of Society*, New York: Alfred A. Knopf, 1970.

Nisbet, R.A., *The Social Impact of Revolution*, Washington, DC: American Enterprise Institute of Public Policy Research, 1974.

Nisbet, R.A., *The Sociological Tradition*, London: Heinemann, 1967.

Nisbet, R.A., *The Sociology of Emile Durkheim*, New York: Oxford University Press, 1974.

Nurkse, R., *Patterns of Trade and Development*. Oxford: Blackwell, 1962.

O'Dea, T.F., *Sociology and the Study of Religion*, New York: Basic Books, 1970.

O'Donnell, M., *Introduction to Sociology*, Walton, UK: Nelson, 1997.

Odum, H.W., *Understanding Society: The Principles of Dynamic Sociology*, New York: Macmillan, 1947.

Ogburn, W.F. and Nimkoff, M.F., *A Handbook of Sociology*, Boston: Houghton Mifflin Company, 1958.

Ogburn, W.F. and Nimkoff, M.F., *A Handbook of Sociology*, London: Routledge & Kegan Paul, 1964.

Ogburn, William F., 'How Technology Changes Society', *The Annals of the American Academy of Political and Social Science*, Philadelphia, 1947.

Ogburn, William F., *On Culture and Social Change*, Chicago: University of Chicago Press, Phoenix Books, 1964.

Ogburn, William F., *Social Change*, New York: Huebsch, 1922.

Omvedt, G., *Dalit Visions: The Anti-caste Movement and the Construction of the Indian Identity*, Hyderabad: Orient Longman, 1995.

Pannikkar, K.M., *Caste and Democracy*, London: Hogarth Press, 1933.

Pareto, V., *The Mind and Society*, New York: Dover, 1963.

Park, Robert Ezra and Burgess, Ernest W., *Human Ecology*, Chicago: University of Chicago Press, 1921.

Park, Robert Ezra and Burgess, Ernest W., *Introduction to the Science of Sociology*, Chicago: University of Chicago Press, 1921.

Park, Robert Ezra and Burgess, Ernest W., *The City*, Chicago: University of Chicago Press, 1967.

Parsons, T. & R. F. Bales (eds.), *Family, Socialization and Interaction Process,* Glencoe: The Free Press, 1955.

Parsons, T. and Shils, Edward (eds.), *Toward a General Theory of Action*, Cambridge: Harvard University Press, 1951.

Parsons, T. and Smelser, N., *Economy and Society*, New York: Free Press, 1956.

Parsons, T., *Essays in Sociological Theory*, New York: Free Press, 1954.

Parsons, T., *Social System,* Glencoe, Ill.: The Free Press, 1951.

Parsons, T., *The Structure of Social Action*, New York: Free Press, 1937.

Phillips, Derek L., *Abandoning Method*, San Francisco: Jossey-Bass, 1973.

Phillips, Derek L., *Knowledge from What?* Chicago: Rand McNally, 1971.

Piaget, J., *The Child's Conception of the World*, London: Routledge & Kegan Paul, 1929.

Piaget, J., *The Construction of Reality of the Child*, New York: Basic Books, 1954.

Pocock, D.F., *Understanding Social Anthropology*, London: Athlone Press, 1998.

Population Reference Bureau, World Population Data Sheet 2005, Washington, DC, www.prb.org.

Poulantzas, N., *Political Power and Social Classes*, London: NLB, 1968.

Presthus, Robert V., *Men at the Top: A Study in Community Power*, New York: Oxford University Press, 1964.

Queen, Stuart A. and Habenstein, Robert, *The Family in Various Cultures*, Philadelphia: J.B. Lippincott Co., 1972.

Quinn, J.A., *Sociology: A Systematic Analysis*, Philadelphia: J.B. Lippincott, 1963.

Raab, Earl and Selznick, Jaeger, *Major Social Problems*, Evanston, Ill.: Row, Peterson, 1959.

Radcliffe-Brown, A.R., *Methods in Social Anthropology*, Delhi: Asia Publishing, 1958.

Radcliffe-Brown, A.R., *Structure and Function in Primitive Society*, New York: Free Press, 1952.

Rao, K. Raghavendra, 'Caste, Secularism and Democracy in India', *International Journal of Comparative Sociology*, 7: 1996.

Rao, M.S.A., *Urban Sociology*, New Delhi: Orient Longman, 1991.

Reuter, E.B. and Hart, C.W., *Introduction to Sociology*, New York: McGraw-Hill, 1933.

Reuter, E.B., *Handbook of Sociology*, New York: Dryden Press, 1941.

Rex, J., *Discovering Sociology*, London: Routledge & Kegan Paul, 1973.

Rex, J., *Key Problems of Sociological Theory*, London: Routledge & Kegan Paul, 1961.

Riley, Matilda White and Riley, Hohn W., 'Connections: Kin and Cohort', in Vern Bengston and Andrew Achenbaum (eds.), *The Changing Contract Across Generations*, New York: Aldine de Gruyter, 1993.

Ritzer, George, *Sociological Theory*, New York: McGraw-Hill, 1996.

Robertson, Ian, *Sociology*, New York: Worth Publishers, 1977.

Robertson, R. and Lechner, F., 'Modernization, Globalization and the Problem of Culture in World-System Theory', *Theory, Culture and Society*, 2(3): 1985.

Rogers, Everett, *Modernization Among Peasants*, New York: Holt, Rinehart & Winston, 1969.

Rose, A.M., *Sociology: The Study of Human Relations*, New York: Alfred A. Knopf, 1957.

Rose, Peter I. (ed.), *Socialization and the Life Cycle*, New York: St Martin's Press, 1979.

Rosenfeld, Eva, 'Social Stratification in a 'Classless' Society', *American Sociological Review*, 1974.

Ross, Aileen D., *The Hindu Family in its Urban Setting*, Bombay: Oxford University Press, 1961.

Ross, E.A., *Social Control*, New York: Macmillan, 1901.

Ross, E.J., *Basic Sociology*, Milwaukee: Bruce, 1953.

Rossi, Alice S. and Rossi, Peter H., *Of Human Bonding: Parent-Child Relations Across the Life Course*, New York: Aldine de Gruyter, 1990.

Rothman, Robert A., *Inequality and Stratification: Class, Color and Gender*, Upper Saddle River, NJ: Prentice Hall, 2001.

Roucek, J.S. (ed.), *Social Control*, New York: D. Van Nostrand Company, 1947.

Rubin, Lillian, *Families on the Fault Line*, New York: Harper, 1994.

Rudolph, L. and Rudolph, S., *The Modernity of Tradition*, Chicago: University of Chicago Press, 1967.

Rushdie, Salman, *The Satanic Verses*, London: Fourth Estate, 1989.

Sachs, Wolfgang (ed.), *The Development Dictionary*, London: Zed Books, 1992.

Sagarin, E. (ed.), *Sociology: The Basic Concepts*, New York: Holt, Rinehart & Winston, 1978.

Samuelsson, Kurt, *Religion and Economic Action*, New York: Basic Books Inc., 1961.

Sapir, Edward, *Culture, Language and Personality*, Berkeley: University of California Press, 1961.

Schaefer, Richard T. and Lamm, Robert P., *Sociology*, New York: McGraw-Hill, 1992.

Schroyer, Trent, 'A Reconceptualization of Critical Theory', in Alan Wells (ed.), *Contemporary Sociological Theories*, Santa Monica: Goodyear Publishing Company, 1978.

Schumpeter, Joseph, *Capitalism, Socialism and Democracy*, London: George Allen & Unwin, 1943.

Schutz, A. and Luckmann, T., *The Structure of the Life-World*, London: Heinemann, 1074.

Schutz, A., *The Phenomenology of the Social World*, London: Heinemann, 1972.

Shah, A.M., 'Basic Terms and Concepts in the Study of Family in India', in *Family in India: Critical Essays*, New Delhi: Orient Longman, 1998.

Shah, A.M., *Family in India*, New Delhi: Orient Longman, 1998.

Shah, Ghanshyam (ed.), *Dalit Identity and Politics*, New Delhi: Sage, 2001.

Shah, Ghanshyam, *Social Movements in India: A Review of Literature*, New Delhi: Sage, 1990.

Sharma, K.L., *The Changing Rural Stratification*, New Delhi: Orient Longman, 1974.

Sherif, Muzafer and Sherif, Carolyn W., *Social Psychology*, New York: Harper & Row, 1969.

Sherif, Muzafer, 'An Experimental Approach to the Study of Attitudes', *Sociometry*, 1, 1938.

Shills, E.A. and Finch, H.A., *Max Weber on the Methodology of the Social Sciences*, New York: Free Press, 1949.

Shiva, V. and Bandyopadhyay, J., *Ecological Audit of Eucalyptus Cultivation*, Dehradun: English Book Depot, 1985.

Silver, H., 'Social Exclusion and Social Solidarity: Three Paradigms', International. Labour Review, 19, 2, 133–63, 1994.

Simmel, Georg, 'The Metropolis and Mental Life', in Richard Sennet (ed.), *Classic Essays on the Culture of Cities*, New York: Appleton-Century-Crofts, 1969.

Simmel, Georg, *Conflict and the Web of Group Affiliations*, trans. and ed. by Kurt Wolff, Glencoe: Free Press, 1955.

Singer, Milton, *When a Great Tradition Modernizes*, New York: Praeger Publication, 1972.

Singh, Yogendra, *Culture Change in India: Identity and Globalization*, Jaipur and New Delhi: Rawat Publications, 2002.

Small, A.W., *General Sociology*, Chicago: University of Chicago Press, 1905.

Smelser, N.J. (ed.), *Sociology: An Introduction*, New York: Wiley, 1970.

Smelser, N.J., *The Theory of Collective Behaviour*, New York: Free Press, 1962.

Smith, David A. and Borocz, Jozsef (eds.), *A New World Order*, Westport: Praeger, 1995.

Smith, R.W. and Preston, F.W., *Sociology: An Introduction*, New York: St. Martin's Press, 1977.

Sorokin, P.A., *Contemporary Sociological Theories*, New York: Harper & Brothers, 1928.

Sorokin, P.A., *Social and Cultural Dynamic*, Boston: Porter Sargent Publisher, 1937.

Sorokin, P.A., *Social and Cultural Dynamics*, New York: American Book Company, 1941.

Sorokin, P.A., *Social Mobility*, New York: Harper, 1927.

Sorokin, P.A., *Sociological Theories of Today*, New York: Harper & Row, 1966.

Southerland, Robert L., Woodward, Julian L. and Maxwell, Milton A., *Introductory Sociology*, Chicago: J.B. Lippincott Co., 1952.

Spencer, H., *Principles of Sociology*, London: Williams & Norgate, 1886.

Spengler, Oswald, *The Decline of the West*, New York: Alfred A. Knopf, 1926.

Sperling, Gene B., 'Towards Universal Education', *Foreign Affairs*, September/October, 2001.

Srinivas, M., Shah, A.M. and Ramaswamy, E.A., *Fieldworker and the Field*, New Delhi: Oxford University Press, 1996.

Srinivas, M.N., *Caste in Modern India and Other Essays*, New York: Asia Publishing House, 1962.

Srinivas, M.N., *India: Social Structure*, New Delhi: Publications Division, 1969.

Srinivas, M.N., *Social Change in Modern India*, Berkeley: University of California Press, 1966.

Srivastava, Vinay Kumar (ed.), *Methodology and Fieldwork*, New Delhi: Oxford University Press, 2004.

Stark, R. and Bainbridge, W.S., 'Of Churches, Sects and Cults: Preliminary Concepts for a Theory of Religious Movements', *Journal of the Scientific Study of Religion*, 18(2): 1979.

Stewart, E.W. and Glynn, A.G., *Introduction to Sociology*, New York: McGraw-Hill, 1971.

Sumner, Colin, *The Sociology of Deviance: An Obituary*, Buckingham: Open. University Press, 1994.

Sumner, W.G., *Folkways*, Boston, MA: Ginn, 1906.

Sutherland, E.H. and Cressey, D.R., *Criminology*, Philadelphia: Lippincott, 1978.

Sutherland, E.H., *Principles of Criminology*, Philadelphia: Lippincott, 1939.

Sutherland, R.L., Woodward, J.L. and Maxwell, M.A., *Introductory Sociology*, Chicago: J.B. Lippincott, 1961.

Theodorson, George A. and Theodorson, Achillees G., *A Modern Dictionary of Sociology*, New York: Thomas Y. Crowell Company, 1969.

Thio, Alex, *Sociology: An Introduction*, New York: Harper & Row, 1986.

Thomas, W.I. and Znaniecki, F., *The Polish Peasant in Europe and America*, ed. by Eli Zaretsky, New York: Social Science Research Council, 1939.

Thorat, Sukhadeo and Newman, Katherine, 'Caste and Economic Discrimination: Causes, Consequences and Remedies', *Economic and Political Weekly*, October 2007.

Thrasher, Frederic, *The Gang*, Chicago: The University of Chicago Press, 1927.

Tilly, Charles, *From Mobilization to Revolution*, Massachusetts: Addison-Wesley Pub. Co., 1978.

Timasheff, N.S., *Sociological Theory*, New York: Random House, 1967.

Tischler, Henry, *Introduction to Sociology*, Philadelphia: The Harcourt Press, 2002.

Toffler, Alvin, *The Third Wave*, New York: Bantam Books, 1980.

Tonnies, F., *Community and Association*, East Lansing: Michigan State University Press, 1957.

Tonnies, F., *Gemeinschaft and Gesellschaft*, New York: Atheneum, 1887.

Touraine, Alan, *The Postindustrial Society*, New York: Random House, 1971.

Touraine, Alan, *The Return of the Actor: Social Theory in Postindustrial Society*, trans. M. Godzich, Minneapolis: University of Minnesota Press, 1988.

Townsend, Peter, *Poverty in the United Kingdom: A Survey of Household Resources and Standards of Living*, Harmondsworth: Penguin Books, 1979.

Toynbee, Arnold J., *A Study of History*, London: Oxford University Press, 1956.

Trewartha, Glenn T., *A Geography of Population: World Patterns*, New York: Wiley, 1969.

Truman, David, *The Governmental Process: Political Interests and Public Opinion*. New York: Knopf, 1951.

Tuchman, Gaye, *Hearth and Home: Images of Women in India*, New York: Oxford University Press, 1978.

Tumin, M., 'Some Principles of Stratification: A Critical Analysis', *American Sociological Review*, 1953.

Tumin, M., *Social Stratification*, Englewood Cliffs, NJ: Prentice Hall, 1967.

Turner, J., 'Introduction', *Societal Stratification: A Theoretical Analysis*, New York: Columbia University Press, 1984.

Turner, J., *The Structure of Sociological Theory*, Homewood: Dorsey Press, 1974.

Turner, R. and Killian, L.M., *Collective Behaviour*, Englewood Cliffs, NJ: Prentice Hall, 1972.

Uberoi, Patricia, *Family, Kinship and Marriage in India*, New Delhi: Oxford University Press, 1997.

United Nations, Millennium Development Goals Indicators Database, August, 2005.

United Nations, *World Population Report*, 1982.

Vanfossen, Beth E., *The Structure of Social Inequality*, Boston: Little, Brown & Company, 1979.

Veblen, T., *The Theory of the Leisure Class*, New York: New American Library, 1953.

Verba, Sidney, B. Ahmad and Anil Bhatt. Caste, Race, and Politics (Berkeley: Sage Publications, 1971).

Wallace, W.L., *Sociological Theory: An Introduction*, Chicago: Aldine, 1969.

Wallerstein, I., *The Modern World-System*, New York: Academic Press, 1974.

Ward, Lester F., *Dynamic Sociology*, New York: Appleton, 1902.

Ward, Lester F., *Pure Sociology*, New York: A.M. Kelley, 1970.

Watson, John B., 'Class, Status and Party', in H. Gerth and C.W. Mills (eds.), *Essays in Sociology*, New York: Oxford University Press, 1958.

Watson, John B., *Behaviourism*, New York: Norton, 1930.

Weber, M., *Economy and Society*, New York: Oxford University Press, 1968.

Weber, M., *The Methodology of the Social Sciences*, New York: Free Press, 1949.

Weber, M., *The Protestant Ethic and the Spirit of Capitalism*, London: Allen & Unwin, 1930.

Weber, M., *The Religion of India*, Glencoe: Free Press, 1959.

Weber, M., *Theory of Social and Economic Organization*, New York: Free Press, 1947.

Weber, M., *Wirtschaft and Gesellschaft*, Tubingen: Mohr, 1922.

Weber, Marrianne, *Max Weber: A Biography*, New York: John Wiley & Sons, 1975.

Weignberg, M. and Shabat, D.E., *Society and Man*, Englewood Cliffs, NJ: Prentice Hall, 1956.

Weiner, Myron, *Politics of Scarcity: Public Pressure and Political Response in India*, Chicago, University of Chicago Press, 1962.

Westermarck, Edward, *The History of Human Marriage*. New York: Macmillan, 1891.

White, Leslie, *The Science of Culture*, New York: Farrar Straus, 1949.

White, Lynn Jr, 'The Historical Roots of Our Ecological Crisis,' *Science*, 155 (3767): 10 March 1967, pp. 1203–07.

Whorf, B., *Language, Thought and Reality*, Cambridge: MIT Press, 1956.

Wickman, Peter M., 'Deviance', in *Encyclopedic Dictionary of Sociology*, 4th ed., edited by Dushkin Publishing Group, pp. 85–87, Guilford, CT: Dushkin, 1991.

Williams, Robin M. Jr. and Margaret, W. Ryan (ed.), *Schools in Transition: Community Experiences in Desegregation*, Chapel Hill: The University of North Carolina Press, 1954.

Willis, Paul E., *Learning to Labour: How Working Class Kids Get Working Class Jobs*, Aldershot: Gower, 1977.

Wilson, B., *Contemporary Transformations of Religion*, Oxford: Clarendon Press, 1976.

Wirth, Louis, 'Urbanism as a Way of Life', in Richard Sennet (ed.), *Classic Essays on the Culture of Cities*, New York: Appleton-Century-Crofts, 1969.

Woods, S.F.J., *Introductory Sociology*, New York: J.B. Lippincott & Co., 1956.

World Development Indicators, 2003. COMPLETE ?

Worsley, P. (ed.), *Modern Sociology: Introductory Readings*, Harmondsworth: Penguin Books, 1970.

Wright, F.J., *Elements of Sociology*, London: University of London Press, 1965.

Wrong, D.H., *Population and Society,* New York: Random House, 1961.

Xaxa, V., 'Transformation of Tribes in India', *Economic and Political Weekly*, 1999.

Yinger, J. Milton, *Countercultures: The Promise and Peril of a World Turned Upside Down*, New York: Free Press, 1982.

Yinger, J. Milton, *Sociology Looks at Religion*, London: Macmillan, 1961.

Young, K. and Mack, R.W., *Sociology and Social Life*, New York: American Books, 1959.

Young, K., *An Introduction to Sociology*, New York: Macmillan, 1942.

Young, Michael, *The Rise of the Meritocracy*, Baltimore: Penguin Books, 1961.

Index